Scottish Education and Society since 1945

Scottish Education and Society since 1945

Democracy and Intellect

Lindsay Paterson

EDINBURGH
University Press

Edinburgh University Press is one of the leading university presses in the UK. We publish academic books and journals in our selected subject areas across the humanities and social sciences, combining cutting-edge scholarship with high editorial and production values to produce academic works of lasting importance. For more information visit our website: edinburghuniversitypress.com

© Lindsay Paterson, 2023, 2024

Edinburgh University Press Ltd
13 Infirmary Street,
Edinburgh, EH1 1LT

Typeset in 11/13 Ehrhardt MT Std by
Manila Typesetting Company

A CIP record for this book is available from the British Library

ISBN 978 1 4744 9841 8 (hardback)
ISBN 978 1 4744 9842 5 (paperback)
ISBN 978 1 4744 9843 2 (webready PDF)
ISBN 978 1 4744 9844 9 (epub)

The right of Lindsay Paterson to be identified as author of this work has been asserted in accordance with the Copyright, Designs and Patents Act 1988 and the Copyright and Related Rights Regulations 2003 (SI No. 2498).

Contents

List of Figures — vi

List of Tables — ix

Preface — xii

Acknowledgements — xv

1. Scottish Education since the Middle of the Twentieth Century — 1
2. Sources of Evidence: Scotland's Unique Social Surveys — 15
3. The Impact of Policy and Social Change on Schools — 37
4. School Curriculum: Liberal Education for Everyone? — 61
5. Student Choice and Respect — 87
6. Young People and the Labour Market — 103
7. Schools and Higher Education — 127
8. Higher Education and Breadth of Study at School — 147
9. Social Mobility and Lifelong Learning — 169
10. Education, Social Attitudes and Scottish Governance — 197
11. Conclusions — 227

Further Information — 237

References — 239

Index — 255

Figures

3.1 Percentage sitting at least one mid-secondary course, by sex and social class, 1952–2016 — 41
3.2 Percentage passing at least one mid-secondary course, by sex and social class, 1952–98 — 42
3.3 Percentage sitting at least one Higher, by sex and social class, 1952–2016 — 43
3.4 Percentage passing at least one Higher, by sex and social class, 1952–98 — 44
3.5 Percentage passing at least one Higher, by sex, social class and intelligence at age c. 11, 1952–86 — 45
3.6 Percentage passing at least one mid-secondary course, by sex, stage of school's becoming comprehensive, and social class, 1952–98 — 50
3.7 Father's social class by school origin, 1952, 1978 and 1998 — 51
3.8 Percentage passing at least one Higher, by sex, social class and selected school origins, 1952–98 — 54
4.1 Percentage attaining breadth at mid-secondary, by sex and social class, 1952–98 — 71
4.2 Percentage attaining breadth at Higher, by sex and social class, 1952–98 — 73
4.3 Percentage attaining breadth at mid-secondary, by sex, social class and selected school origins, 1952–98 — 78
4.4 Percentage attempting breadth at mid-secondary (excluding Foundation-level Standard Grade), by sex and social class, 1952–2016 — 80

4.5	Percentage attempting breadth at Higher, by sex and social class, 1952–2016	82
4.6	Scottish results in science from the PISA study, by sex and social status, 2006–18	84
6.1	Percentage in post-school education, by social class, sex and school attainment, 1952–98	112
6.2	Percentage employed with any training, by social class, sex and school attainment, 1952–98, among people who were not in post-school education	113
6.3	Percentage in post-school education, by social class, sex, attainment, and whether took a low-level course at school, 1976–98	119
6.4	Percentage employed with long training, by social class, sex and school origins, 1952–98, among people who were not in post-school education	121
7.1	Social class of school-leaver entrants to sectors of higher education, 1952, 1962, 1978 and 1998	135
7.2	Percentage of all school leavers entering old universities, by attainment, sex and social class, 1952–98	136
7.3	Percentage entering non-degree higher education among all school leavers who did not enter degree-level higher education, by attainment, sex and social class, 1952–98	137
7.4	Percentage entering old universities at mean attainment, by social class, sex and school origin, 1962–98	142
9.1	Percentage having attained full secondary education or better before age c. 30, by sex, class, survey year and nation of birth within Britain, people born 1946–c.1984	178
9.2	Education score (common metric) at age c. 30, by sex, class, survey year and nation of birth within Britain, people born 1946–c.1984	179
9.3	Education score (nationally specific metrics) at age c. 30, by sex, class, survey year and nation of birth within Britain, people born 1946–c.1984	180
9.4	Percentage having attained full secondary education or better before age c. 30, by sex, survey year and class: people born in Scotland, 1936–c.1984	182
9.5	Percentage having entered class I, II before age c. 30, by sex, class, survey year and nation of birth within Britain: people who attained full secondary education or better, born 1946–c.1984	184
9.6	Percentage having entered class I, II before age c. 30, by sex, class, survey year and nation of birth within Britain: people at upper quartile of common metric of relative attainment, born 1946–c.1984	186

9.7	Percentage upwardly mobile between various ages (23 to 54), by sex, previous social class, and whether upgraded education: people with average intelligence at age c. 11, born in 1958 in Scotland	190
9.8	Percentage upwardly mobile between various ages (26 to 42), by sex, previous social class, and whether upgraded education: people with average intelligence at age c. 11, born in 1970 in Scotland	191
10.1	Percentage generally trusting of other people, by survey year (2000–15), sex and education: birth cohorts 1927–36, 1957–66 and 1977–86	206
10.2	Position on liberal-conservative scale, by survey year (2000–16), sex and education: birth cohorts 1927–36, 1957–66 and 1977–86	210
10.3	Percentage believing that Scottish Parliament gives Scotland a stronger voice in the UK, by survey year (2000–16), sex and education: birth cohorts 1927–36, 1957–66 and 1977–86	213
10.4	Percentage supporting independence, by survey year (1979–2016), sex and education	215
10.5	Percentage supporting independence, by survey year (1979–2016), sex, and education: birth cohorts 1927–36, 1957–66 and 1977–86	216

Tables

2.1 Distribution of ages at which parents left full-time education, 1952–2016 — 24
2.2 Distribution of Registrar General social class of father, 1952–2016 — 25
2.3 School sectors, defined by origin — 30
2.4 Combinations of parental education and father's social class for percentages estimated from statistical models: students at all levels of attainment, and social classes I, III and V — 33
2.5 Combinations of parental education and father's social class for percentages estimated from statistical models: grouped social classes, for all students and for students who passed at least one Higher — 34
3.1 School progression and attainment, 1952–2016 — 39
3.2 Percentage passing at least one Ordinary Grade, by sex, social class and stage of becoming comprehensive, 1976 and 1980 — 47
3.3 Percentage passing at least one Ordinary Grade, by sex, social class and stage of becoming comprehensive, 1976 and 1984 — 48
3.4 Percentage passing at least one Higher Grade, by sex, social class and school origin, 1976 and 1998 — 53
3.5 School progression and attainment, by school denomination, 1952–98 — 57
4.1 Aspects of passes in the mid-secondary curriculum, 1952–2002 — 68
4.2 Aspects of passes in Higher curriculum, 1952–2002 — 69
4.3 Percentage attaining breadth at mid-secondary level, by social class, sex, and stage at which school made the transition to Standard Grade — 76
4.4 Aspects of sitting Higher curriculum, 1952–2016 — 81

4.5	Scottish results in the PISA studies, 2006–18	83
5.1	Engagement with school, 1974–2016	92
5.2	School environment, 1974–2016	93
5.3	Preparation for life after leaving school, 1974–98	95
5.4	Engagement with school, by social class and sex, 1980–98	97
5.5	Comparison of education authority and independent schools, by attainment, 1980s and 1990s	100
6.1	Destinations around a year after leaving school, by sex, 1952–98	111
6.2	Percentage in post-school education, by social class, sex and attainment: difference associated with mid-secondary curricular breadth, 1976–98	116
6.3	Percentage employed with any training, by social class, sex and school attainment, among people who were not in post-school education: difference associated with mid-secondary curricular breadth, 1976–98	117
7.1	Percentage entering sectors of higher education, 1952–98	134
7.2	Percentage entering sectors of higher education, among people who had passed at least one Higher, 1962–98	139
7.3	Percentage entering sectors of higher education, by sex and whether school was education authority or independent, 1960–2 to 1996–8: Class I, II	141
7.4	Percentage entering sectors of higher education, by sex and school origin, 1960–2 to 1996–8: Class I, II	143
8.1	Aspects of attempted senior-secondary curriculum, among people who sat at least four Highers, 1952–2016	153
8.2	Aspects of successful completion of senior-secondary curriculum, among people who passed at least four Highers, 1952–2002	155
8.3	Percentage entering old universities, by social class and sex: difference associated with school curricular breadth	156
8.4	Percentage entering old universities, by school origin, whether followed broad curriculum at school, and sex, 1962 and 1990s: Class I, II	159
8.5	Percentage entering old universities, by school origin, whether followed broad curriculum at school, and sex, 1962 and 1990s: Class IV, V, unclassified	160
8.6	Percentage entering professional employment among graduates who entered employment directly, by sex, school attainment, broad university faculty, and whether followed a broad school curriculum, 1960–2002	164
9.1	Highest educational attainment before age c. 30, by survey year and nation of birth within Britain, people born 1936–c.1984	174

9.2	Social class of upbringing, by survey year and nation of birth within Britain, people born 1936–c.1984	177
9.3	Social class of destination at age c. 30, by survey year and nation of birth within Britain, people born 1936–c.1984	183
9.4	Percentage upgrading their formal qualifications at various ages (23 to 54), by sex and nation of birth within Britain: people born in 1958	188
9.5	Percentage upgrading their formal qualifications at various ages (26 to 42), by sex and nation of birth within Britain: people born in 1970	188
10.1	Scale of civic participation (2009–16), by sex, education and birth cohorts from pre-1926 to early 1990s	207
10.2	Liberal-conservative scale (2000–16), by sex, education and birth cohorts from pre-1926 to early 1990s	209
10.3	Percentage supporting independence, by vote in EU referendum, views about effectiveness of Scottish Parliament, and education: 2016 only	221

Preface

In 1932 and again in 1971 two remarkable social surveys were led by two redoubtable Scottish academics. These decisions left a legacy that has made this book possible.

The first was Professor Godfrey Thomson. He had become Professor of Education at Edinburgh University in 1925, a post that also involved being director of the teacher training centre at Moray House in the city. Working with the recently established Scottish Council for Research in Education and with colleagues at the university, he led the first-ever testing of the intelligence of an entire nation's children, the Scottish Mental Survey of 11-year-olds in 1932. That survey was pioneering, and led to fundamental developments in the science of mental testing (Deary, Whalley and Starr, 2009). Its most immediate practical legacy was in a second survey, of all 11-year-olds in 1947. A representative sub-sample was then interviewed every year until 1963. That longitudinal study was the first full-scale sociological investigation of Scotland's children as they grew into adulthood. It is the starting point for everything that follows here.

The second pioneer was Professor Andrew McPherson. In the early 1970s, he was a lecturer in sociology at Edinburgh University, and founded the Centre for Educational Sociology there in 1972. This was in the midst of two very large reforms in British education. One was the introduction of comprehensive secondary schooling – replacing the selective system in which children were allocated to academic or vocational courses according to tests of intelligence taken at ages 11–12. Although many of these tests were the outcomes of Thomson's work, he had believed that comprehensive schooling was the most effective way of educating a whole community, the only form of schooling that was consistent with democracy. He had believed also that testing was a way of matching pupils to courses that would suit them. But the ways in which the tests had been used to send children to different kinds of school was increasingly found in the 1950s to be unfair. McPherson saw that the resulting revolution could be studied by the same kinds of social surveys as Thomson had pioneered. These could also then provide insights into the other main reform that was in full flow in the early 1970s, the first expansion of UK higher education, following the Robbins Report (Committee on Higher Education, 1963). So McPherson had the foresight to plan and manage in 1971 a survey of school leavers that in due course ran almost every second year from then until 2003. Along with Thomson's 1947 survey and a one-off survey of school leavers undertaken in 1963, the series founded by McPherson provides the core of this book's analysis.

These surveys were internationally unique. There is no parallel anywhere in the world for their detail and longevity. The young people who took part – some 120,000 in total, spread over 50 years – and the people who managed them left an archive of evidence during a period of profound social change and of varied attempts by policy makers to respond to it. Reflecting on the series in 1987, McPherson and his colleagues proposed that its rationale lay in 'the public practice of scepticism' (Burnhill et al., 1987). Under the leadership of McPherson and Professor David Raffe, who joined the Centre in 1975 and became its co-director in 1987, the surveys were the focus of Scotland's most internationally distinguished contributions to educational research in the second half of the twentieth century. This book aims to build upon that rich legacy, drawing also on the Scottish parts of other social surveys.

All these surveys also provide the most sustained test available anywhere in the world of the compatibility of the two words in this book's sub-title: democracy and intellect. The tension between them was analysed controversially by the most influential book on Scottish education in this whole period, George Davie's *The Democratic Intellect* of 1961. Davie claimed that the dominant Scottish educational tradition embodied that tension between the two terms, and he was pessimistic that the intellectualism could be sustained in an era of widening participation. Our surveys allow an empirical assessment of that pessimism.

The historical scene is set in Chapter 1. Chapter 2 describes the data sources in more detail. It explains the range of other surveys that are used, including a survey that allows some aspects of the main series to be taken forward to 2016, and outlines the statistical techniques that the book uses to analyse them. The subsequent chapters then consider eight broad aspects of educational and social change in the second half of the twentieth century. Chapter 3 investigates the transition to comprehensive schooling, paying attention also to the ways in which the historical origins of schools continued to influence pupils' experiences long after the initial reforms had been put in place. Chapter 4 looks in particular at a central idea of Scottish comprehensive schooling, the aim to give everyone access to a broad curriculum, to what was called by

Matthew Arnold – the great nineteenth-century English Liberal – 'the best that has been thought and said'. Chapter 5 then asks whether pupils enjoyed this experience.

Chapter 6 investigates young people's experiences upon leaving school, both the pathways available to relatively high achievers who took part in the expanding system of post-school education, and also the fluctuating opportunities offered to less successful leavers for whom the collapse of the youth labour market in the 1980s severely disrupted their transition to adulthood. Chapters 7 and 8 investigate further the main aspect of that post-school expansion: the growth of higher education, first in the consequences of the Robbins reforms, and then in the even larger changes from the late 1980s. Chapter 7 concentrates on the affinities between school histories and university histories, and thus continues the theme of historical legacies that is developed in Chapters 3 to 6. Chapter 8 continues the theme of curricular breadth, not only in the transition from school to university, but also in the relationship of school breadth to graduation and to the kinds of employment which graduates entered.

Chapters 9 and 10 investigate the impact of all these reforms and social changes on the wider development of Scotland. Chapter 9 is about social mobility, including its link to learning that happens well after the period of initial education; this chapter compares the Scottish experience with that of England and of Wales. Chapter 10 asks how the expansion of education has interacted with politics, because all these educational and social changes have been happening at a time when Scotland's constitutional status in the UK has been brought into question as never before.

The book is thus a work of recent social history. It is not about current policies, although some comments on these are made in the concluding Chapter 11. It is also not about deep history, not even about the pre-war period that lies immediately behind the world that was created from 1945 onwards. Nor is it a narrative: it is a focus on specific themes, the importance of which is explained in detailed in the introductory parts of each of Chapters 3 to 10. The book is thus part of the social history of one aspect of the welfare state, the belief that democracy needed well-educated citizens if it was to thrive. Well-conducted social surveys are the closest that social science gets to scientific objectivity. This book is also then an attempt to show what that can mean.

Acknowledgements

The research was funded by a Leverhulme Major Research Fellowship (grant number MRF-2017-002), for which I am very grateful to the Leverhulme Trustees.

I am grateful to Dr Linda Croxford, of the Centre for Educational Sociology, Edinburgh University, for data from the surveys of school students 1963 to 2003, and to Dr Croxford and Dr Cathy Howieson, also of the CES, for advice on using the data. I am grateful to Professor Ian J. Deary, former director of the Lothian Birth Cohorts, University of Edinburgh, for data from the 1947 survey, and to the MRC Unit for Lifelong Health and Ageing, University College London, and the principal investigators of the MRC National Survey of Health and Development (doi: 10.5522/NSHD/Q101), for data from the survey of people born in 1946. I am grateful to the UK Data Archive for data from: the 'Education and Youth Transitions' series (study number 5765); the birth cohorts of 1958 (study numbers 5565, 5566, 5567, 5578, 5579, 6137 and 7669), 1970 (study numbers 2666, 2699, 3723, 3535, 3833, 5558, 5585, 6557 and 7473) and 2000 (study numbers 4683, 5350, 5795, 6411, 7464, 8156, 8582 and 8172); the National Survey of 1960 University Graduates (study number 67036); the Universities' Statistical Record (study number 3456); the UK Household Longitudinal Study (study number 6614); the Scottish Social Attitudes Surveys (study numbers 4346, 4503, 4804, 4808, 5076, 5298, 5617, 5840, 6262, 6638, 7018, 7228, 7338, 7519, 7599, 8188 and 8628); and the Scottish Election Surveys (study numbers 3889, 3171 and 1604).

For the long-term follow-up of the 1947 Scottish Mental Survey (used in Chapter 9), the help provided by staff of the Longitudinal Studies Centre Scotland (LSCS) is gratefully acknowledged. The LSCS is supported by the UK Economic and Social Research Council, the UK JISC, the Scottish Funding Council, the Chief Scientist's Office of the Scottish Government, and the Scottish Government.

I thank the study participants in all these surveys for their data, and also members of the scientific and data collection teams who have been involved in the data collection. All respondents to the original surveys took part voluntarily, and gave their informed consent to doing so. The details are in the sources cited in Chapter 2. Ethical approval for the secondary analysis reported here was given by the research ethics committee of the School of Social and Political Science, Edinburgh University, on 27 March 2017.

I am grateful to Professor Andrew McPherson and Professor J. D. Willms for information on when each school made the transition to comprehensive education (used mainly in Chapter 3), and to Professor Adam Gamoran for information on when each public-sector school adopted the Standard Grade reforms in the late 1980s (mainly in Chapter 4).

Versions of several of the chapters were given as seminars or public lectures at Edinburgh University School of Social and Political Science (2018, 2019 and 2022), Edinburgh University School of Education (2018 (the David Raffe memorial lecture) and 2021), the British Educational Research Association (Newcastle, 2018), the Scottish Catholic Historical Association (Glasgow, 2018), Gonville and Caius College, Cambridge (for the project Secondary Education and Social Change, 2019), Institute of Historical Research (London, 2020), Stirling University (2021) and Nuffield College, Oxford (2021). I am very grateful to the organisers for their invitations, and for many insightful comments made by people who attended.

CHAPTER 1

Scottish Education since the Middle of the Twentieth Century

SETTING THE CONTEXT

The purpose of this chapter is to set the context by telling the story of Scottish education and society since 1945. This account is no more than a summary – the changes of policy, the changes in how students, teachers and parents responded, and the wider social transformation that took Scotland from the aftermath of nineteenth-century industrialism to the post-industrial society that has replaced it. Much fuller accounts of these processes in this period are widely available – notably the general histories by Cameron (2010), Devine (1999) and Smout (1986), the general sociological account of McCrone (1992), and the educational histories of Gray et al. (1983), which used some of the same data as here, and Mandler (2020), who sets the Scottish story in a wider British context. McPherson and Raab (1988) and Humes (1986) provide the details of policy making during the crucial period of school reform between the 1960s and the 1980s. The present author's previous book on this topic is, in one sense, more comprehensive than is attempted here (Paterson, 2003), in that it deals with all the sectors of education, and stretches back to the beginning of the century, but it does not have the focus on detailed statistical evidence that the present book offers.

This introductory chapter has four themes. The main two relate to secondary schools and higher education. These are the sectors that changed the most during this period. Behind them – the third theme – lie the transformation of the Scottish economy and, with that, the up-ending of all sorts of aspects of the social structure – employment, the role of women, the nature of social hierarchy. Influencing all this are questions of identity and politics, which have in turn been shaped by these vast social changes. These four aspects of social change are the context for the educational changes, but the influence was also reciprocal. The question for this chapter is what successive waves of educational reform respond to; for the whole book, the aim is to understand also how the outcomes of these educational intentions shaped the way in which the society was developing.

SECONDARY EDUCATION

School Structures

The question of how Scottish secondary education should develop for a democratic age provoked the most eloquent expression of post-war idealism to come from any official body in Scotland. The Advisory Council on Scottish Education had been established by the Education (Scotland) Act of 1918. The aim had been to bring professional advice to bear on policy, advising government in an authoritative way. After a bold start in the early 1920s, its tendency to radicalism – to the extension of secondary schooling far beyond anything that the cautious officials of the Scottish government would contemplate – led to its being marginalised. But in 1942, as minds were turning towards a new wave of reconstruction, it was reconstituted by the Secretary of State for Scotland in the wartime coalition, the Labour MP Tom Johnston. He instructed it to consider itself a parliament on Scottish education (Lloyd, 1979, p. 369). Over the next decade, its reports in effect set the aims for educational reform of the next five decades, though it was not until the 1960s that most of them came anywhere near to being realised.

Specifically, the Council's report on secondary education, published in 1947, became a point of reference for radical reform thereafter (Scottish Education Department, 1947). It started by noting the very great progress that had been made since 1872, when the Education (Scotland) Act of that year laid the basis for a national system of compulsory primary education. That had been achieved by the end of the century, a success that encouraged thinking about secondary education for all (Paterson, 2018, 2021c). The next major legislation, the 1918 Act, offered a structure for secondary schooling, and established a proper framework for its professional governance. It also provided a way in which the primary and secondary Catholic schools could be integrated into the mainstream (Fitzpatrick, 1986; Treble, 1978, 1980). The Advisory Council then suggested that this new opportunity for post-war optimism would be a way of reviving the idealism.

The new reason to plan for fundamental change in 1947 was a theme that has lasted to the present: the newly democratic need to educate all citizens. The report referred to the 'proper concern of the state with the direction of social change', which it said had two aspects. One was 'to see that the schools inculcate those virtues without which democracy cannot survive'. The other was to ensure, 'especially at a time of great economic stress like the present, that boys and girls are taught the basic skills and cultivate the special aptitudes which will ensure the maximum productivity of the country' (Scottish Education Department, 1947, p. 13).

These ideals had two main aspects, organisational and cultural. The Council was ahead of its time in advocating a single kind of secondary school for everyone, what was then called in Scotland an omnibus school but which later acquired the common international term of comprehensive school: 'the case for the omnibus school is that this is the natural way for a democracy to order the post-primary schooling of a given area'. The reason was that 'it mitigates, though it does not wholly solve, the vexatious problem of selection and grading', and that it makes the school into a community (ibid., p. 36). Equally important in achieving these ends was the question of what the school should teach 'within its free yet ordered bounds' (ibid., p. 14). Its answer was that everyone should have access to the full range of human thought and experience, providing 'general secondary education for all . . . children in all their variety' (ibid., p. 61).

All of these ideas came to fruition in some form in the next half-century, even though imperfectly. But the first response by government to the question of secondary education in the late 1940s was to consolidate what had already been achieved on the basis of the 1918 Act and of policy in the two decades that had preceded it. No new foundational legislation was needed in Scotland: the 1944 Act that created a common system of secondary schooling in England and Wales had its parallel in that Scottish Act of three decades previously. Some kind of secondary education for all was established in Scotland between the early twentieth century and the mid-1930s, leading to the selective system of the 1940s and 1950s.

At the beginning of the twentieth century, Scotland had only around 60 full secondary schools. Some of these were managed independently of public authorities, but received some public grants. However, there was also a tradition of teaching advanced classes to a few boys (and a tiny but growing number of girls) in the parish schools that had been established throughout the country by the late eighteenth century, some of which continued to do so until the 1920s (Anderson, 1985; McPherson and Willms, 1986; Paterson, 2004). Between the beginning of the new century and the early 1920s, the government sought to extend the opportunity for a full secondary education by creating a new category of around 200 'Higher Grade' schools, many of which were extensions of the parish schools, but some of which were also new foundations to provide secondary schooling in urban districts that were populated by lower middle-class and upper working-class families. All of the Higher Grade schools were managed by public authorities, and some of the formerly independent schools were absorbed by that public system because their inherited financial endowments were insufficient to allow them to fund a more modern and complex type of education.

The expansion was halted after 1921 because of a series of economic problems facing the UK exchequer, but about two-thirds of the Higher Grade schools were recognised as full secondaries. Some new secondaries continued to be built, bringing that proportion to just under one-half. So there were essentially four historically defined sectors of schools providing full secondary education: pre-1900 schools in the public sector; schools founded in the public sector up to the 1920s; such schools founded after the 1920s; and the schools that were not managed by public authorities. These were the highest-status parts of the selective system in the period after 1945. Entry to them was based mainly on tests of intelligence and attainment taken in the final year of primary school at ages 11–12.

Most of the other third of Higher Grade schools were still recognised as secondaries, which meant being equipped and staffed to full secondary standards, but their courses lasted only three years, so that students would have to transfer to a full secondary if they wanted to take the school Leaving Certificate (discussed below). There were also some other former parish schools that had some experience of teaching students for the Leaving Certificate. The largest group of schools providing post-primary courses were the lowest status. They had grown out of successive attempts from the 1890s onwards to create satisfactory opportunities for pupils who were not selected for a full secondary education. The quality varied, and improved only gradually.

The 1936 Education (Scotland) Act brought all post-primary courses into a common framework of secondary education for all. It formally recognised two kinds of secondary course: senior secondary (5 years) and junior secondary (3 years). In practice, this tended to lead to two kinds of school: senior secondaries and junior secondaries. The Catholic schools that were brought into the public sector after 1918, or that were created under public authorities after that, developed as part of this same system. There were Catholic schools in all six categories.

Almost all these schools survived well into the post-war period. The relative sizes in later years of the schools that had belonged to these six sectors is shown in Table 2.3 (Chapter 2). The next major structural reform – and the best-known in the whole period since 1945 – was the ending of selection between different kinds of school in the public sector. Some experiments in comprehensive schools had been made before the 1960s, notably in Glasgow (McPherson and Raab, 1988), but the systematic reform started in 1965. It achieved universal coverage in the public-sector schools by the beginning of the 1980s (McPherson and Wilms, 1987, p. 511). After that, the only selection was for admission to the independent schools, educating about 5 per cent of secondary pupils. About 9 per cent of schools in the public sector continued to provide only four years of secondary education, mainly in sparsely populated rural areas. They contained about 5 per cent of pupils, who would transfer at age 16 to a full secondary school for a fifth and sixth year.

The agencies which managed the public-sector schools were called Education Authorities throughout the period covered by our surveys. These were the 35 elected councils of counties and cities until 1975, the 12 elected regional and islands councils from then until 1996, and the 32 elected local councils thereafter. The whole system was overseen by the arm of central government that was called the Scottish Education Department for most of the century. The official term for schools managed by Education Authorities was (and still is) 'public school', in line with terminology in other countries, but not the rest of the UK (Education (Scotland) Act 1980, s. 135).

Curriculum and Certification

There were two main political motives for the comprehensive-school reform (Paterson and Iannelli, 2007a). One was explicit attention to equal opportunities; the other was economic efficiency, enabling the country to draw upon all sources of talent (McPherson and Willms, 1987; Reynolds et al., 1987, pp. 16–21). Both of these required attention to what was taught and learnt, and so questions about the curriculum and about assessment followed inevitably: these were, in effect, the attempted policy responses to the Advisory Council's questions about how to educate all pupils to become democratic citizens.

A Leaving Certificate had been founded in 1888 to measure the standards in the evolving secondary system (Paterson, 2004, 2011; Philip, 1992). By the 1920s it had two main types of courses and assessment, at different levels of depth: Higher Grades and Lower Grades (colloquially referred to as Highers and Lowers). From 1908 until 1950, the only way in which a pupil could have their attainment recognised was through a Group Certificate, which required passes in a specified range of courses. The rules varied, but the group always required English, mathematics, a natural science and a language, and typically required at least three Highers and two Lowers. From the 1920s, one of the Highers had to be in English. Although the grouping requirement came to an end after 1950 – and thus was not formally in place for any of the surveys which are used in this book – the prestige of the group remained, partly because the Scottish universities continued to insist on their entrants' having something like the former grouping until the mid-1960s.

Throughout the periods of reform after 1945, the Highers remained in place, although their syllabuses and modes of assessment were frequently modified. The symbolism of this continuity was important in maintaining a sense that standards were being maintained during a period of great structural change to both secondary schooling and higher education (McPherson and Raab, 1988, p. 360). The specific curricular response to the comprehensive reform was the changes associated with the introduction of the Standard Grade courses in the 1980s (Croxford, 1994, 2015; Gamoran, 1996; Tinklin, 2003).

They were the implementation of proposals made in 1977 (Scottish Education Department, 1977; Consultative Committee on the Curriculum, 1977). The need to develop courses for the full range of ability and interests had become especially urgent after the raising of the minimum age at which pupils might leave school from 15 to 16 in 1973. The challenge then was to provide opportunities for credible assessment, while also not consigning lower-ability pupils to lower-status courses that might have been as invidious as the old junior-secondary courses before the 1960s. The ingenious device that was adopted was, in the jargon of the day, 'differentiation by outcome'. In principle, everyone might take the same course, but be assessed at the end of it by different levels of examination. In practice, matters did not work out as smoothly as this, but the ideal of a common assessment framework remained. In almost all subjects, there were three levels of assessment – Credit at the top, General in the middle, and Foundation. The awards were made on a common scale, stretching from 1 and 2 at Credit, through 3 and 4 at General, to 5 and 6 at Foundation. The awards 1 to 3 were stipulated to mean a pass. A practice that helped to reinforce the sense of a common framework was that, in most schools, everyone taking a subject sat the General paper, with the differentiation being implemented by their also sitting either Foundation or Credit assessments. In theory, therefore, everyone had the opportunity to gain a pass, a quite remarkable change from the practices since the advent of public certification in 1888.

The new courses were consolidated into a 'curriculum framework' in the 1990s, the explicit purpose of which was to require breadth of study (Scottish Consultative Council on the Curriculum, 1989). In achieving this breadth, the Standard Grades and this framework were influenced by the ideas of the educational philosopher Paul Hirst (1975): the curriculum was defined in terms of domains of knowledge to which everyone should have access. The core domains were English, mathematics, science, social studies, religious and moral education, aesthetic education, and physical education. Modern languages were added to the core later, in response to the widespread feeling that Britain needed better language skills if it was to flourish in the European Union. Religious and moral education, physical education and aesthetic education were never part of the core examined curriculum, though they were usually compulsory in the early years of secondary school.

The Standard Grades themselves superseded the Ordinary Grades (or O Grades), founded in 1962 to replace the Lower Grade courses. The O Grades also had sought to widen access to a liberal curriculum, although at first only for the most able third of students: one reason for the Standard Grade reform in the 1980s was that, by the late 1970s, double that proportion was actually taking Ordinary Grades.

There were several other curricular reforms in this period. At the very end of the century, courses called Intermediate were introduced, below the level of Higher and overlapping with Standard Grade. Though these courses did not become widespread until after the end of the main period covered in the book, a few students took them in our final main surveys. These in turn came to an end in 2015; Standard Grades ended in 2013. They were replaced from 2014 by courses called 'Nationals', which are discussed in Chapter 4. In this academic mainstream, there was also a curricular reform in 1968 at the level beyond Higher, with the introduction of courses for the Certificate of Sixth Year Studies. Before the 1990s, these were attained by fewer than 10 per cent of students, and were significant only for entry to university. So we postpone discussion of them to Chapter 8.

More sporadic, but also of more potential significance for a large proportion of pupils, were curricular reforms that attempted to provide vocational preparation. These changes varied greatly in their extent and importance. In the early 1960s, there was a brief attempt to develop a properly conceived vocational track that might include both general education and the acquisition of specific skills. It was superseded by planning for comprehensive schooling with its tendency to consider only general education (Gray et al., 1983, pp. 106–7), but the need for such courses continued to be felt before the Standard Grade reforms. One response was to use the Certificate of Secondary Education, an English scheme that could be adapted to the Scottish context because it allowed schools to devise their own syllabuses. Standard Grade brought that to an end, but new vocational courses were developed in parallel to that reform, the National Certificate from 1984 (Raffe, 1985). The details of these various vocational courses are analysed more fully in Chapter 6. The main point here is to set them in context. Important though they were for many pupils, they were never more than supplementary to the main curricular developments of Highers, O Grades, Standard Grades, and their successors.

Student-centred Education

The aims of the reformers was never only to deal with structures, the formal curriculum, and assessment. Indeed, the 1947 report of the Advisory Council most famously said this (Scottish Education Department, 1947, p. 10):

> the good school is to be assessed not by any tale of examination
> successes, however impressive, but by the extent to which it has filled
> the years of youth with security, graciousness and ordered freedom.

This kind of sentiment was influenced by thinking about what was called the 'new education' in the previous few decades, ideas that were most closely associated internationally with the New Education Fellowship which had been founded in 1921. It had a Scottish branch as early as 1924, and prominent among its early leaders internationally was William Boyd of Glasgow University, who in due course wrote a history of it (Boyd and Rawson, 1965; Paterson, 1996).

The ideas had a diffuse influence on the general growth of child-centred education after the 1950s, the belief that pupils were to be treated with respect not only because that was pedagogically effective, but also for ethical reasons (Duffield et al., 2000). The Advisory Council had invoked this principle in its insistence on the 'primacy of the individual' (Scottish Education Department, 1947, p. 9), which became in due course the assertion of children's rights (Stewart, 2006). The shift was part of the wider attention to rights in legislation of the 1960s and 1970s, notably in relation to sex and to race (Brown and Riddell, 1992; Croxford, 1994). The outlawing of invidious sex discrimination had particular implications for the school curriculum, because it had some influence on the long-standing sex differences in the studying of particular subjects. One aim of the new curriculum framework in the 1990s was to go beyond the prohibition of segregation by insisting on this broadening of access in a formal way. We look in detail at this throughout the book, especially in Chapters 4 and 8.

The most visible influence of the growing attention to individual needs and rights was on primary schools, especially after 1965, ultimately influenced also by a report on primary education in 1946 from the Advisory Council (Scottish Education Department, 1946; Scottish Education Department, 1965; Paterson, 2003, pp. 114–17). The changes at primary level then inevitably influenced thinking about the ethos of secondary schools, again – as with Standard Grade – especially because they now had to cater for a much greater diversity of pupils. One influential aspect was in the development of school guidance, the first proposals for which were made in 1971, in the middle of the move to comprehensive schooling (Scottish Education Department, 1971). The policy was formalised in 1986 into the version that lasted beyond the end of the century (Consultative Committee on the Curriculum, 1986). The nature and effects of this changing ethos are discussed in Chapter 5.

HIGHER EDUCATION

Higher education expanded only modestly before the 1960s, partly because the rate of participation in Scotland was already higher than in the rest of the UK (Paterson, 2003, p. 156). Scotland's four oldest universities dated from the late Middle Ages and the Reformation: St Andrews, Glasgow and Aberdeen in the fifteenth century, and Edinburgh in the sixteenth. They had been supplemented from the late nineteenth century by various technological colleges which the government in Scotland had established with the intention of emulating the role of science and technology in Germany at that time. Many of the courses in these were not truly at university level, but the largest gradually increased their truly advanced provision, notably the Royal Technological College and the Scottish College of Commerce in Glasgow, and Heriot-Watt College in Edinburgh. All of these became universities as part of the general UK expansion of higher education in the 1960s, the first two merging to form Strathclyde University. In the same decade, Dundee University was created from the part of St Andrews University that was based in the city. The only wholly new foundation was Stirling University. Scotland also took part in the development of the Open University from 1969 (discussed briefly in Chapter 9; it was not available to entrants directly from school).

After the broad stability of the 1950s, numbers of students then grew, in two main phases: the 1960s to the late 1970s, and the 1990s. From the 1960s to the early 1990s, there were four sectors: the eight universities, the various technological colleges, the colleges of education (the main role for which was training school teachers and social workers), and the local technical colleges that had been founded mainly in the 1950s and that gradually and then rapidly increased their provision of advanced courses (being renamed further education colleges in the 1980s). Throughout, the expansion was greater in the non-university sectors than in the universities. For example, in each of the decades of the 1970s and the 1980s, entrants to full-time undergraduate courses rose by around 20 per cent in the universities, but by around 60 per cent in the other sectors combined (Scottish Office, 1992, table 4).

In 1992, most of the technological colleges were retitled universities, or merged with neighbouring universities. In the 1990s, entrants to full-time undergraduate courses in this combined university sector rose by around 40 per cent, but the growth of advanced courses in the further education colleges rose by far more: from around 6,000 full-time entrants in 1990 to over 22,000 in 2000 (Scottish Executive, 2002, table 11). The consequence was that around four out of ten entrants to full-time undergraduate courses entered a further education college. This growth was partly because the former colleges that had become universities had given up most of their teaching at levels below degrees: almost all of the massively expanded higher education courses in the further education colleges were at levels below degrees, and in fact far more of it was part time than full time. Altogether, by the end of the century, one-half of people had entered a full-time course of higher education by age 21, having been 18 per cent in 1981, and 9 per cent in 1962 (Paterson et al., 2004, p. 108; Paterson, 2003, p. 164).

The growth led to much debate about the nature and purpose of higher education, drawing on two strands of thinking. One was from the international discussions of a similar kind, because higher education was expanding everywhere (Schofer and Meyer, 2005). In the middle of the twentieth century, in economically developed societies such as Scotland, universities and higher education colleges had provided the experts that would staff and lead the new welfare state – not only the much-expanded traditional professions such as doctors, lawyers, higher civil servants, and teachers themselves, but also the burgeoning new ways in which the state sought to guide society: social workers (who in some respects replaced another traditional, university-educated profession: religious clergy), planners, economists, scientists, and in due course also other groups whose training was upgraded, such as nurses and community workers. One writer has called this role for universities the creation of a professional society – a society supported by professionals who had been educated in a much more systematic way than had ever before been thought necessary for social leadership (Perkin, 1989). The admiration for expertise in the service of the state had indeed several influential Scottish origins, such as from the Liberal politician R. B. Haldane, who sought to bring Germanic ideas of educated efficiency into British thought about the nature of the democratic state (Campbell and McLauchlan, 2020). As expansion replaced this elite system, the international debate was about whether a system that had been developed for these needs could cope when it was five times larger. Would there be appropriate opportunities for employment?

The other debate was an older Scottish one, which was reinterpreted in the light of this expansion and of the international changes. It was the claim that Scottish universities had traditionally sought to develop the 'democratic intellect', a resonant term made popular by the philosopher George Davie (1961). He argued that the generalism of Scottish study had gradually succumbed to the pressure for specialisation. The breadth of a general education, he argued, better prepared people to be citizens. He represented this as being akin to Adam Smith's idea that we learn to live in society by seeing ourselves through others' eyes: thus the specialist is also a citizen through having understood the world outside the specialism. The historical accuracy of Davie's account is very much in doubt (Anderson, 1983; Paterson, 2015b, 2015c), and he failed to notice the large gap between the rhetoric about breadth at university and the reality of education for most school pupils. But none of his critics disagrees with his philosophical description of the social significance of the Scottish tradition of breadth. Moreover, although his claim that the pre-twentieth-century universities were open to all social classes was not based on any systematic analysis of evidence, it resonated in Scottish political debate in the 1980s, when there was a perception that the policies of the UK Conservative government were widening educational inequalities; indeed, Davie himself broadly took that view (Davie, 1990). An incidental aspect of all the empirical chapters of this book is to examine whether that accusation against the UK government was accurate.

This debate then absorbed some of the international debate from the 1960s onwards, notably on the question of specialism. Davie returned to the themes in a 1986 book, where he posed the wider question about expertise in terms of the Scottish tradition:

> The words 'democratic intellect' offer a twentieth-century formulation of an old problem. Does the control of a group . . . belong, as of right, to the few (the experts) exclusively, and not at all to the ignorant many? Or are the many entitled to share the control, because the limited knowledge of the many, when it is pooled and critically restated through mutual discussion, provides a lay consensus capable of revealing certain of the limitations of interest in the experts' point of view? Or thirdly it may be held that this consensus knowledge of the many entitles them to have full control, excluding the experts. (Davie, 1986, p. 262)

The debate was thus not only about opportunities for participation and for employment, but about the role of expertise in a democracy. It thus relates not only to our Chapters 7 and 8, where higher education is discussed, but also to the earlier chapters relating to the radically reformed secondary schooling which now every citizen experienced, and also Chapters 9 and 10, which investigate the implications of the expansion for the character of Scottish society and government. One way of interpreting the half-century of educational change is as an attempt to shift the answer to Davie's problem from his first group – the technocrats who managed the welfare state in the immediate post-war years – to a much wider group, potentially in fact the majority in an increasingly democratic polity. The general scope of Davie's questions about educated expertise is why his title has been taken as the present book's sub-title.

EMPLOYMENT, THE ECONOMY AND SOCIAL MOBILITY

Two other aspects of the context for the book's later chapters are worth noting: the changing character of employment faced by people leaving the education system in the half-century after 1945 (in this section), and the changing character of Scottish democracy, which may be thought of as the civic analogue to the economic changes (the final section).

The economic changes are often described as the end of industrial society, and the creation of a new one based on services, and certainly there were very large shifts that could be described in this way (Kendrick, 1986; Peden, 2012). The percentages of economically active people who worked in services – including 6–8 per cent in transport – was around 45 per cent in 1931 and 1951, rose to 52 per cent in 1971, 68 per cent in 1990, and 74 per cent in 2001 (Payne, 1996, p. 14; Paterson et al., 2004, p. 47). Nevertheless, the changes to employment also happened within sectors, reducing the amount of manual work and increasing the role of professionals (Paterson et al., 2004, p. 86).

So, rather than describing the change as being about the shift from an industrial to a service economy, the most important change sociologically is in the reduction in the size of social classes that are broadly described as being based on manual work, and the growth of these which are non-manual (Iannelli and Paterson, 2006, p. 523). The skilled manual group (in the official classification called socio-economic group) had 31 per cent of employment in 1931, and remained at a similar level till 1961, after which it fell steeply to just 11 per cent in 2000. The groups consisting of semi-skilled and unskilled workers fell from 28 per cent in 1931 to 15 per cent. In contrast, the proportion who were employers and managers was under 10 per cent until 1971, and then rose to 17 per cent at the end of the century. Professionals rose to 7 per cent from under 5 per cent until 1971.

There was a pronounced effect of this change on sex differences, because the declining groups were dominated numerically by men and the rising groups by women. The rising rate of female participation in the paid labour force was itself of very great significance. In 1951, 34 per cent of women aged 15 or older were economically active (McCrone, 1992, p. 83). In 1981, the rate among women aged 16–74 was 48 per cent. By the end of the century it was 60 per cent, whereas in that same two decades the male rate fell from 81 per cent to 74 per cent (Paterson et al., 2004, p. 44). All these process interacted with educational growth: the growing social classes required many more credentials than the declining ones, and the growth of female employment depended on the growth of girls' and women's educational attainment.

These stories are of expansion and opportunity. But the economic changes also brought new forms of disadvantage. The labour market for school leavers collapsed in the late 1970s and early 1980s not just for temporary reasons. If the problems had been cyclical, then they would have gone away when the economy recovered from the recession at that time. The collapse was also for irreversible reasons, mainly the ending of previous forms of employment where apprenticeship was the way in which young people – especially young men – could be inducted into respected and stable employment.

A similar explanation of long-term change applies to the slowing down of upward social mobility from the 1980s onwards (Erikson and Goldthorpe, 1992; Iannelli and Paterson, 2006). Since the middle of the twentieth century, upward mobility had been growing mainly because there was more room at the top (as it has been called): non-manual jobs grew, while manual jobs shrank, and so the children of manual workers were sucked upwards. But when expansion at the top slowed down from the 1980s, people born in the 1960s and later found fewer new opportunities than their parents had experienced. At the same time, the growth of London as the wealthiest and most economically vibrant part of the UK attracted well-educated people from the periphery, such as Scotland (Fielding, 1992, p. 1). This had two implications for how the distinctive Scottish system of education related to structures of opportunity. Those school leavers who could not compete in a UK-wide labour market had fewer opportunities because the best opportunities were in London. Those who did try to enter a UK-wide labour market depended on the wider competitiveness of Scottish credentials.

NEW DEMOCRACY?

All of this was happening while Scotland was moving from being a fairly contented part of the multinational United Kingdom to a position of increasing dissatisfaction. The first evidence was in the rise of the Scottish National Party in the 1970s, culminating in a referendum on limited legislative autonomy for Scotland in 1979. Although just over 50 per cent voted in favour, the rules of the referendum meant that no legislative devolution resulted. Resentment of the Conservative governments of the 1980s and 1990s – which were able to command a generally diminishing share of the Scottish vote – led to the next referendum on autonomy in 1997, when three-quarters voted in favour. This time change did happen, and a new Scottish Parliament was set up in 1999. Among its legislative responsibilities were almost all aspects of education. After the SNP rose again, forming a minority government in the Scottish Parliament in 2007 and a majority in 2011, the next referendum was on independence (2014), in which 55 per cent voted against secession. The relative narrowness of that result, the continuing majority support for the SNP in Scottish elections, and the subsequent political events across the UK – notably the vote to leave the European Union in 2016, when 62 per cent in Scotland voted for the UK to remain – meant that the question of independence came to dominate Scottish politics.

For the purposes of the discussion in this book, the intriguing paradox is that all of this was taking place as the country becoming increasingly educated. At each particular moment in time, higher levels of education have been associated, on average, with lower levels of support for independence. Yet, over time, higher levels of education have not stopped independence support rising. The paradox is made all the more acute by recent political science theories of national populism in many countries, which would also lead us to expect that a movement for national sovereignty would be based mainly on the support of people with minimal education.

These are not the only political implications of rising levels of education. Education in general makes people more civic: the better-educated tend to have more liberal views than people with less education. They also tend to be more socially engaged – more likely to sign petitions, join things, and take on responsible roles in the local community. Renewing democracy in this way was one of the sources of ideas that led to the Scottish Parliament after the referendum of 1997. In that sense, the growth of education might be said to have furthered the idealistic goals of the parliament's founding principles, by diffusing responsibility throughout society. Yet at the same time, internationally, the growth of populism has been claimed to be due to resentment by the less educated against educated elites. The more that people with advanced education staff the organisations and networks that underpin democracy, the more that people with less education feel alienated.

So the question which the final chapter seeks to answer is what, if any, are the implications for the future of Scottish governance and civil society of all the educational expansion which the earlier chapters of the book analyses.

CHAPTER 2

Sources of Evidence: Scotland's Unique Social Surveys

EVIDENCE

This chapter is mainly about the evidence which is used throughout the book. But it is also a story that is less technical than that. Scotland pioneered the use of social surveys in education in the 1930s. It led the world in the use of statistics to understand what students learn and how their learning relates to their social context and opportunities. That distinctive history attracted international admiration, and was sustained to the end of the twentieth century as a highly creative though often tense partnership among government, school teachers, and academic researchers. These surveys always sought to enable understanding and explanation, rather than routine monitoring of the kind that governments have to do. Although the main series of surveys ended at the beginning of the new century, a further survey (of people born in 2000) allows the story of some aspects of secondary education to be taken forward to 2016.

So the first part of the next section is an explanation of where the data come from. The rest of that section is a more technical description of the other sources of data. The remainder of the chapter is about the statistical measures that are used in several chapters (leaving to each succeeding chapter those measures that are particular to it), and about the statistical methods that were used to analyse and summarise the evidence which the surveys provide.

SURVEYS

There are five main series of data used in the book:

- The first provides the major part of the evidence. This is the series of surveys of school students undertaken between the early 1950s and the end of the century by three organisations: the Scottish Council

- for Research in Education (up to 1962), the Centre for Educational Sociology (1971–91), and ScotCen Social Research (1997–2003). They are the foundation of Chapters 3 to 8.
- The second series consists of Britain-wide surveys of people born in 1946, 1958, 1970 and 2000. Along with the data from the Scottish cohort of people born in 1936 that is also used in the first series, these are used at several places in Chapters 3 and 4, and are the core of the comparative analysis of social mobility in Chapter 9.
- The third series consists of the Scottish part of a UK-wide survey of people who graduated from university in 1960, along with annual data on people who graduated between 1980 and 1993. Along with the survey of school students in 1996 (who were followed up to age 22 in 2002), these provide information on graduates in Chapter 8.
- The fourth is the large survey called the UK Household Longitudinal Study, which has been interviewing a panel of people annually since 2009 (and some of them since 1991). This is used mainly to bring the analysis of social mobility in Chapter 9 into the second decade of the present century.
- The final series gives access to information about adults' civic values and social engagement in Chapter 10: the mostly annual Scottish Social Attitudes Survey (1999–2016), and the Scottish Election Surveys of 1997, 1992 and 1979.

The data for all but the first and part of the second series came from the UK Data Archive, details of which are in the Acknowledgements part of the Preface. Data from most of the first series – the 13 surveys of school leavers from 1963 onwards – were held in 123 separate databases, kindly supplied by Dr Linda Croxford, of the Centre for Educational Sociology at Edinburgh University, who – working with her colleague Dr Cathy Howieson – has painstakingly curated this invaluable archive. Data from the survey of 11-year-olds in 1947, and its extension to 1963, were kindly supplied by Professor Ian J. Deary. He has led their conversion into digital form as part of his pioneering research into the topic of cognitive ageing – following up some of the survey members half a century or more later – but incidentally also thus giving a means of studying the school system in the 1940s and 1950s.

Scottish Surveys of School Students (Chapters 3 to 8)

These are the unique source for this book, and their context is illuminating of the education story that the book seeks to explain. All the surveys started with policy and remained closely tied to policy. At the same time, in order to be able to provide valid comment on policy, they had to be well-informed academically –

historically, sociologically, statistically. The surveys also had to eschew academic fashion, because of the hostility to statistical measurement that nearly overwhelmed the social sciences in the UK from the 1970s onwards.

All of this made education surveys controversial, and controversy was present from the start, in the surveys carried out by the nascent Scottish Council for Research in Education (SCRE). When – as we noted in Chapter 1 – the Scottish Education Department suppressed the incipient radicalism of the Advisory Council in 1921 over the issue of secondary education for all, SCRE was created in 1928 as an autonomous source of research and ideas. It was founded under the auspices of the teachers' professional association (the Educational Institute of Scotland), and the directors of education in the locally elected Education Authorities. SCRE became the main source of authoritative research on Scottish education, especially in its pioneering surveys of school children. The first was in 1932, as part of the international interest at the time in the nature of intelligence, and also in how measures of intelligence might be used to allocate pupils fairly to different courses at secondary school. That survey was not designed as the beginning of a series, and did not include educational or sociological measures that would have been relevant to this book, but the example that it set allowed the inauguration in 1947 of what in effect became the half-century-long series that provides this book's core. The 1947 survey was pioneering in its subsequent development into a longitudinal sociological survey. Approximately 1,200 of the sample members were followed up annually to 1963, when they were 27 (Macpherson, 1958). There was then a gap of three decades, when the longitudinal collection resumed as noted below.

The final SCRE survey in this series belongs to the next part of the story – school leavers. This survey covered all pupils who passed at least one Higher Grade examination in 1962. It then inspired the series of school leavers' surveys which were conducted by the Centre for Educational Sociology (CES) at Edinburgh University. The first such surveys were in 1971 and 1973, of leavers from 1970 and 1972, again restricted to people who had passed at least one Higher Grade examination. A survey then took place nearly every two years from 1977 to 2003. The 1977 survey covered pupils with the full range of attainment only in five regions of Scotland, which included around three-quarters of all pupils (Gray et al. 1983, pp. 16–23); where the full range of pupils is being considered in this book, only that part of the survey is used. From 1979, the surveys covered all levels of attainment. All these leavers' surveys took place approximately nine months after their members had left school. After 1985, the survey was longitudinal, starting about nine months after their members had left school fourth year and following them to age 19 and, in some of these surveys, to ages 22 or 24. These surveys varied somewhat in their design, but they were all random, and all based on postal questionnaires (though also, after 1992, linked to data on the assessments run by the Scottish Examination Board and its successor, the Scottish Qualifications Authority). The sampling fractions ranged from under one in ten to four in ten. The sampling was often complex, for example to make sure that low-attaining pupils were adequately represented.

For succinctness, we label all the surveys by the year in which their members turned age 16, and thus we have 15 surveys referred to as 1952, 1960–2, 1968–70, 1970–2, 1974–6, 1976–8, 1978–80, 1980–2, 1984, 1986, 1988, 1990, 1996, 1998 and 2002. For most of our purposes in this book, we do not use the 2002 survey because it did not record certain core variables in the same way as for the other surveys (notably social class, parental education and the main subject studied at university), but it is used for some descriptive purposes. The surveys 1960–2, 1968–70 and 1970–2 may be used only where we are restricting attention to students who had passed at least one Higher (mainly in Chapters 7 and 8 on entry to higher education), but there were too few people in the 1952 survey with this level of attainment to allow it to be included in that series. For some limited purposes an alternative survey of the full spectrum of people aged 16 in 1962 is available from the Scottish part of a Britain-wide cohort survey of people born in 1946 (explained below). Some extension of the series to people aged 16 in 2016 is available similarly from a UK survey of people born in 2000 (mainly Chapter 4). Thus we have two main series of surveys:

- Thirteen surveys of all students: 1952, 1962, 1974–6, 1976–8, 1978–80, 1980–2, 1984, 1986, 1988, 1990, 1996, 1998 and 2016. The sample sizes are in Table 2.1 below.
- Thirteen surveys of students who passed at least one Higher: 1960–2, 1968–70, 1970–2, 1974–6, 1976–8, 1978–80, 1980–2, 1984, 1986, 1988, 1990, 1996 and 1998. The sample sizes are in Table 7.2 in Chapter 7.

Burnhill et al. (1987) noted that the leavers'-survey series was being developed at a time when academic social science in Britain was turning away from the use of large-scale surveys of this kind (a predilection that remains strongly prevalent). That critique of surveys claimed that research which uses surveys tends to take the problems of governments as given, paying little attention to the way in which social development was perceived by the respondents. The leavers'-survey series sought to offer a response to these criticisms. The main context of the CES surveys was indeed made up of the dominant policy concerns of the time: the development of comprehensive secondary schooling; the growth of unemployment among school leavers; the expansion of higher education; the sometimes radically different approach to education provoked by the Conservative government of the 1980s and 1990s. Behind all that were the social and economic changes that we noted in Chapter 1. At the time, however, the analysis of the surveys often led to sharp conflict between the CES and the government, because the surveys in fact never did take governments' framing of the problems as given.

Yet, in a striking instance of the pluralism of government attitudes even in the highly polarised 1980s, the survey was jointly funded by the Scottish Education Department and various other organisations – notably the UK Economic and Social Research Council (and its predecessors) – for nearly two decades. When the series was eventually taken away from CES in the early 1990s, it nevertheless survived as a public resource until it came to an end in the early years of the new century, surveying its final group of people who were in school fourth year in 2002. One explanation of the decision to end the series was declining response rates, which are a particular problem where a survey is longitudinal. Gone are the days when the 1947 survey could still have a follow-up rate of 91 per cent in 1963 after 17 annual sweeps, having been 98 per cent at the age-16 sweep in 1952. The later surveys had response rates around 80 per cent from 1968–70 to 1980–2 (McPherson and Neave, 1976, p. 130; McPherson and Willms, 1987) and around 65 per cent for the surveys from 1984 onwards (Croxford et al., 2007).

This series is unique. Research in other countries on educational change over time has mostly used one of three kinds of data. The most common is to construct synthetic cohorts from a single cross-sectional survey, basing cohort on age: so, for example, a survey carried out in 2009 would base its information on 16-year-olds in 1970 on the memories of people who were aged 55. There are disadvantages to this: some people will have moved out of the country, some will have died, and most will have selective memories for all but the most general aspects of their educational experiences. Our surveys of school students, in contrast, were carried out close to the ages for which they record experiences.

The second method is to use birth-cohort studies, for example the very high-quality British cohorts of people born in 1946, 1958, 1970 and 2000, which we describe below (Bukodi and Goldthorpe, 2016; Gugushvili et al., 2017; Kerckhoff et al., 1996). Dronkers (1993) did the same for the Netherlands, and Lindbekk (1998) for Norway. Cohort analysis avoids problems of memory, and, at least for education in childhood and adolescence, largely avoids the problem of selective migration and mortality. But they are rare because keeping track of people over a long period of time is very expensive. So, although such cohort studies are invaluable, they are never frequent enough to be able to measure the impact of policy changes.

Surveys of school leavers, such as our series, are of the third kind. They are a sort of cohort study, insofar as they interview people at more or less the same age, with the possibility of following them up subsequently. But very few of the previous research studies in other countries that have used leavers' surveys have had long enough time series to investigate changes. A rare exception is Ichou and Vallet (2011, p. 176), who analysed surveys of people who entered lower secondary school in France in 1962, 1980, 1989 and 1995. Breen (1998) analysed annual surveys of school leavers in Ireland between 1984 and 1993. But even these do not have the coverage of the surveys used here.

We describe the other sources of evidence more briefly, because in most respects they are not unique to Scotland: they are based on extracting the Scottish data from surveys that cover the whole of Britain or the UK. This wider British context reminds us also, however, that the UK is, by international standards, unusually rich in sources of good-quality data.

Birth-cohort Surveys: Born in 1946, 1958, 1970 and 2000 (Chapters 3, 4 and 9)

The full titles of these are the National Study of Health and Development, the National Child Development Study, the British Cohort Study, and the Millennium Cohort Study. The first three seek to follow almost everyone born in Britain in, respectively, a specific week in early 1946, early 1958 and early 1970. In Chapters 3 and 4 we use the Scottish data from the age-16 sweep of these three surveys to match as closely as possible the series derived from the surveys of school students, but the educational data are restricted to general measures of attainment: the surveys did not collect information on the school attended, on full details of the curriculum, or on attempts at passing formal assessment (as distinct from success). They also did not record destinations immediately after leaving school in a form that may be compared to the school leavers' series. The 2000 cohort is a representative sample of births covering the whole year; at present, it gives full information only for the subjects which students studied, not for their final attainment upon leaving school.

We use later sweeps of the 1958 and 1970 cohorts in Chapter 9 to compare lifelong learning and social mobility in Scotland, England and Wales. The survey sweeps used are ages 23, 33, 42, 46, 50 and 54 for the 1958 cohort, and 26, 30, 34, 38 and 42 for the 1970 cohort. The age-27 sweep of the 1936 survey adds a further time point for this comparison. We also can stretch the Scottish data over a longer scale by using a further extension of the full 1947 survey (not just the sub-sample who were originally followed to age 27). Its surviving and traceable members were linked by the Longitudinal Studies Centre Scotland to the Scottish Longitudinal Study (Huang et al., 2016). That is a 5.3 per cent sample of records from the population censuses of 1991, 2001 and 2011. So this gives us information about the respondents' highest educational attainment at ages 55, 65 and 75.

Although birth cohorts have the advantages of being roughly contemporaneous with experiences described, their disadvantage is attrition: people do not stay the course, and those who drop out might not be typical, so that, over time, the sample becomes increasingly biased. Nevertheless analysis of the 1936, 1946, 1958 and 1970 cohorts has suggested that attrition is not as biasing as might be feared

(Hawkes and Plewis, 2006; Kuh et al., 2011; Nathan, 1999; Paterson, 2022f). That is especially true when analysis includes a statistical adjustment for measures of intelligence or educational attainment, because the main predictor of drop-out are these factors. Most of our cohort analysis here does include such measures.

Programme for International Student Assessment (Chapter 4)

This triennial survey – usually referred to by its acronym, PISA – has become an influential means by which countries around the world assess their educational performance (Grek, 2009; Schleicher, 2017). It is managed by the Organisation for Economic Co-operation and Development, and has been running since 2000. The age of the students who are assessed is 15, and so the data correspond approximately to our mid-secondary measures. We use data from these surveys to say something about how Scottish education since 2006 compares with the absolute standard that is defined by the PISA tests.

Surveys of Graduates (Chapter 8)

Part of the analysis in Chapter 8 uses three sources of data on graduates from first degrees at one of the eight older universities, covering the years 1960, annually 1983–93, and 2002; for descriptive contextual purposes, we can also include 1980–2, and 2011.

The most extensive source consists of annual data from the Universities' Statistical Record (USR) for students who graduated from 1972 to 1993 (Mancini, 2003; Smith and Naylor, 2005; Smith et al., 2000). These records are in effect a census of all students graduating in each year, linked to a survey of their first destination; the survey had a response rate of around 80 per cent every year (Mancini, 2003, p. 11). The USR data on curriculum and employment from the 1970s is coded in inconsistent ways, and so cannot be used. We restrict attention to students whose main school-leaving qualifications were either from the Scottish school examinations or from those used in the rest of the UK (A levels, and AS levels for 1988–93).

Before that, we have data from a survey in autumn 1966 of all women and half of men who graduated in 1960 from faculties other than medicine, dentistry and veterinary surgery (Kelsall et al., 1970, pp. 1–7). We use weights to take account of this design. As well as the four oldest Scottish universities, this survey also included the Royal College of Technology in Glasgow.

After 1993, we use data on graduates from the survey of school students who were first surveyed in spring 1997. They mostly left school in 1997–8, and were followed up in 1999 (April to June) and 2004 (May to August). We confine the data to people who had entered the eight older universities by the time of the 1999 sweep. The response rates, as percentages of the original target in 1997, were 68 per cent in 1997, 39 per cent in 1999 and 16 per cent in 2004; statistical weighting compensates for the attrition (Dobbie and Jones, 2005, pp. 9–10). In that chapter alone, we refer to this survey as 2002, which is the modal year of university graduation for this cohort.

For contextual information, and to check that any difference between the 2002 survey and the earlier time points is not an artefact of that survey, we also use data from the Futuretrack survey, which has tracked students from entry in 2006 to beyond graduation in 2010–11 (Purcell et al., 2012, pp. 195–203). We use data from sweep 4 (November 2011 to February 2012), when the response rate in terms of the original target in 2006 was 12 per cent. Weighting compensates for non-response. We refer to this survey as 2010.

UK Household Longitudinal Study (Chapter 9)

This survey started in its present form in 2009–11, annually tracking a large sample of households (University of Essex, 2020). The latest wave used here was the tenth, in 2018–20. At its second wave, it subsumed the earlier British Household Panel Study, which tracked households from 1991 with annual follow-up to 2008. The samples were stratified and clustered, with weights to compensate for different sampling fractions for different ethnic groups and the different countries of the UK. The weights also compensate for differential non-response. How the data were put into a form that could be compared with the birth-cohort studies is described in Chapter 9.

Scottish Social Attitudes Surveys and Scottish Election Studies (Chapter 10)

The Scottish Social Attitudes Survey has been carried out every year since 1999 (except 2008) by ScotCen Social Research, a branch of NatCen Social Research which has been managing the annual British Social Attitudes Survey since 1983. Before 1999, election surveys in 1997 and 1992 were run as part of the British Election Surveys of these years, as was the oldest survey which we use here, in 1979. The target sample in each year was selected from the postcode address file and designed to be representative of all people eligible to vote. The election surveys used the postcode address file for 1997 and the electoral register for 1992 and 1979. The designs were similar to those later used in the attitudes surveys. For all the surveys from 1997 onwards, the sampling used multi-stage clusters, stratified at the cluster level. All but the 1979 and 1992 data sets include weights in order to take account of the cluster sampling and to make the data representative with respect to sex and age. We use only respondents who were aged 25 or over at the date of survey, in order to have a reasonably complete estimate of their initial education. The questionnaires were administered by interviewers in respondents' homes. They covered the full range of topical political issues and also collected demographic information on respondents. Further details of all these attitudes surveys are in Curtice et al. (2002, Appendix) and ScotCen (2021).

STATISTICAL MEASURES

Outlined here are the statistical measures which are used in several chapters.

Sex

A variable recording sex is available in all the surveys.

Parental Education

The only measure of parental education that was available for the whole of the series of surveys of school students, and for the largest number of the other surveys, was the age at which each parent left full-time education. The categories in the surveys of students are shown in Table 2.1. For the 1946 birth cohort (the 1962 time point in the table), we approximate this by equating primary education to 15 or younger, secondary education to 16, and advanced education to 17 or older.

Social Class

The only measure that can be derived for the whole series of surveys of school students is what is called Registrar General Social Class. This was the official measure of class in the UK from 1911 until the end of the century, when a new measure was introduced, the National Statistics Socio-Economic Classification (NSSEC). Both of these are derived from occupations. Registrar General class was originally developed to measure social inequalities in health. It was described by government statisticians as being based on the social prestige of occupations, to which was added in the 1980s their skill requirements (Rose et al., 2005; Brewer, 1986). The scheme was never based on any empirical analysis of actual skills, nor any more than a fairly intuitive sense of prestige. Nor did it have a firm basis in any theoretical analysis by sociologists. Debate about these perceived weakness led eventually to the new scheme at the time of the population census of 2001.

Undoubtedly, for the study of social class as a topic, the new scheme is preferable conceptually to the old one. On the other hand, in research on

Table 2.1 Distribution of ages at which parents left full-time education, 1952–2016

% in rows	Both 17 or older	One 17 or older	Maximum 16	Maximum 15	Both unknown	Total sample size
Year when respondent was aged 16	% of at least one parent known				% of total sample size	
1952	1	3	5	92	6	1,204
1962	2	4	8	87	6	528
1974–6	5	7	10	79	11	16,424
1976–8	6	9	14	71	11	8,834
1978–80	4	8	15	72	10	21,872
1980–2	4	8	18	69	8	7,149
1984	5	11	18	65	10	3,952
1986	5	12	22	61	11	4,009
1988	7	14	25	54	12	3,516
1990	10	16	29	45	12	2,692
1996	15	22	39	25	16	2,372
1998	16	24	40	20	16	4,751
2016	36	34	26	4	1	933

Notes:
Percentages are weighted.
'Maximum 16' means one or both 16, neither older. 'Maximum 15' means neither older than 15.

socio-economic inequality – such as in the investigation of educational outcomes – the conclusions reached have tended to be broadly similar using either measure (and similar also to the scheme developed by John Goldthorpe and his associates, which itself became the main source of ideas for NSSEC). That is research where social class is merely an indicator of advantage and disadvantage, rather than the focus of the analysis. Perforce, in order to be able to analyse the whole series, we use the Registrar General scheme. However, in the series of surveys of school students from 1984 onwards, NSSEC was retrospectively created as part of a research project at the Centre for Educational Sociology (Croxford et al., 2007). In Chapter 3 we show that, for this truncated series, the two measures gave similar results.

The Registrar General scheme has five categories, shown in Table 2.2. The titles of each category, and examples of the occupations in them, are:

I Professional
   For example: lawyer, accountant, doctor, scientist, engineer, university teacher.
II Intermediate
   For example: manager, technician, school teacher, nurse.

III Skilled
    For example: secretary, sales, police, hairdresser, electrician.
IV Partly skilled
    For example: waiter, domestic staff, machine operator, building.
V   Unskilled
    For example: porter, labourer, refuse collector.

Class III was often broken down into a 'non-manual' and 'manual' part, as was class IV in some analysis, but our earliest surveys did not record that distinction. For many purposes we combine I with II, and IV with V, because, at the beginning and end of the series, there are not enough sample cases in each of the full five categories to allow their complex cross-classification with other measures.

Table 2.2 records the distribution of the social class of the fathers of the respondents in the surveys of school students. The earlier surveys (up to the mid-1980s) mostly did not ask about mother's class, partly because, at that time, a large proportion of mothers were not in paid employment when the survey member was leaving school. For consistency, we use father's class for the whole series, and incorporate information about mother's social standing through the measurement of parental education. Table 2.2 shows the large changes in the distribution of these classes over the six decades from the early 1950s to the second decade of the new century. The proportion in the two

Table 2.2 Distribution of Registrar General social class of father, 1952–2016

% in rows	I	II	III	IV	V	Unknown
Year when respondent was aged 16			% of known			% of total sample size
1952	2	10	53	17	17	2
1962	2	8	51	31	8	25
1974–6	5	15	56	19	5	13
1976–8	6	21	51	17	5	15
1978–80	5	20	53	17	5	15
1980–2	4	20	55	16	4	17
1984	5	24	50	16	5	21
1986	6	24	51	13	4	21
1988	6	29	45	15	4	18
1990	7	29	45	15	4	17
1996	9	27	44	14	5	22
1998	10	29	45	13	3	24
2016	8	48	35	6	3	40

Note:
Percentages are weighted. For total sample size, see Table 2.1.

highest classes doubled in the 30 years to the early 1980s and doubled again in the next 30 years. The proportions in the lowest classes declined from a third to under a tenth, as the share of low-skilled employment declined markedly (Paterson et al., 2004).

The Registrar General scheme is available for all the cohort studies, though for the 2000 cohort it is necessary to construct an approximation to it from the full version of NSSEC (Office for National Statistics, 2004). It is also available in the data sets for the social attitudes and election studies. However, for the UK Household Longitudinal Study (UKHLS) and for the surveys of graduates, more complex approximations to it had to be developed.

In the UKHLS, for the respondents' own class we could use the same approximation from NSSEC to Registrar Class as was used in the 2000 cohort. However, this could not be done for the parental class because it was not recorded in enough detail (only in the eight-category NSSEC rather than the full version). An estimate of the Registrar General class of the parents was therefore based on statistical imputation, which essentially involved using NSSEC and parental education to predict the most likely value of parental Registrar General class for each respondent. The calculations are summarised by Paterson (2022e), which also shows evidence that the technique gave quite a reliable approximation to Registrar General class.

In the 1960 survey of graduates, we code Registrar General's class from father's occupational title and whether he had any managerial responsibility (General Register Office, 1960). The resulting tables corresponded closely to those derived by Kelsall et al. (1970). The data set from the 2002 survey already included the Registrar General's class of the father. The data from the Universities' Statistical Record required imputation again. The available information was father's occupational title coded to a list that was based on the official scheme of occupational classification that underlay Registrar General class. To convert this to Registrar General class would have required also information about status at work (for example, being a manager). In the absence of that, we imputed the most likely value of class for each occupational code; the imputation used data from the Labour Force Survey of 1984 (for students entering 1980–93) or 1979 (entry 1972–9), along with the official classification tables then in force (Office of Population, Censuses and Surveys, 1980, 1990). This is analogous to the method used by Elias and Gregory (1994, p. 13), and Mancini (2003, pp. 28, 158), and is also how these USR data were reported annually (for example, Universities Central Council on Admissions (1975) and Bolton (2010)).

In Chapter 9, this same measure of social class is used to record the class destinations of respondents, so as to be able to compare these with the class in which they grew up. The immediate occupational destination of university graduates (in Chapter 8) is classified according to the classification of occupations in 1960, 1980, 1990 (as above) or 2000 (Office for National Statistics, 2000).

Religion and Ethnicity

Individual religion is not available from the surveys of school students, but denomination of school is; this is discussed below. Individual religion is discussed in relation to social mobility, adult education and civic values in Chapters 9 and 10. None of the surveys had adequate sample sizes to allow specific minority ethnic groups to be studied. In the surveys of school students, ethnicity was not regularly asked, because the numbers in minority groups in Scotland before the 1990s were too small to allow reliable statistical measurement in general sample surveys of these kinds: the proportion of around 1 per cent or fewer until the 1990s would have given only a few dozen sample members. However, by the time of the 2002 survey, the proportion had risen sufficiently to allow minority groups to be studied in total, and so this is done in Chapter 3. For the same reason, the connection between Scottish education and the social mobility of minorities cannot be studied in Chapter 9, because, even when the numbers in minority groups rose, the majority of adults had not received their initial education in Scotland. Their civic views can, however, be analysed in Chapter 10, again as a single group.

School Attainment

School attainment is measured in relation to the certificates available at the time of each survey. These are mainly the Higher Grade assessments at the end of five or six years of secondary schooling, and the various kinds of assessments at mid-secondary level that might be taken at any point between mainly the fourth and the sixth years of schooling: Lower Grades until the 1950s, Ordinary Grades from 1962 until the late 1980s, Standard Grades from then until 2012–13, Intermediates from 1999 till 2014–15, and Nationals from 2013–14. The history of all these courses was outlined in Chapter 1, and their specific features are discussed in later chapters where these measures are used. A pass is defined to be: an award at Higher or Lower (1952); grades A–C in Highers (1960s onwards); an award (up to 1972) or grades A–C (from 1973) in Ordinary Grade; grades 1–3 in Standard Grade; and grades A–C in Intermediates. The definitions for 2016 are discussed in Chapter 4. The data available here cannot say anything about the validity of these assessments in an absolute sense – for example, whether a Higher Grade pass in 2002 meant the same as a nominally similar pass in 1952. The evidence is sociological, not psychological: that is what society, at each point in time, and through its governing institutions, judged to be an appropriate level of attainment at mid-secondary and senior-secondary level. Nevertheless, the comparison in Chapter 4 with the Scottish results in the PISA study does give some absolute yardstick for the period since 2006, and the comparison in Chapter 9 with England and Wales gives some indication of wider standards back to the early 1960s.

Intelligence

There was no measure of intelligence in the Scottish surveys of school students, except in the 1936 cohort. For some analysis, mainly in Chapters 3 and 9, we also use, along with that cohort, the 1946, 1958 and 1970 birth cohorts to analyse attainment and progression controlling for intelligence measured at ages around 10–12. Ideally we would have had the same test on each occasion, but having to reconcile different measures is the price that is paid for being able to compare over a long period. The measures available are:

- 1936 cohort: Form L of the Terman-Merrill revision of the Stanford-Binet scale, administered at age 11 (Deary, Whalley and Starr, 2009).
- 1946 cohort: test of general cognitive ability at age 11 that included verbal and non-verbal items (Pigeon, 1964).
- 1958 cohort: test of general cognitive ability at age 11. Shepherd (2012, p. 6) explains that this test consisted of 40 verbal and 40 non-verbal items, and that children were tested individually by teachers.
- 1970 cohort: tests from the British Ability Scales at age ten, using the mean of the scores on the word-definitions, similarities and matrices scales (Elliott, Murray and Pearson, 1978).

Because the tests are different, we standardise each of them to have mean 0 and standard deviation 1 in the sample that is being analysed. Goisis et al. (2017, p. 87) did the same for the 1958 and 1970 surveys to investigate the association between low birth weight and intelligence, noting that the standardisation is equivalent to ranking the children by intelligence within cohort. By standardising the measures within year, we also will have controlled for any changes over time in average scores. Although we will continue to refer to this measure as 'intelligence', it would be better described as 'relative intelligence', where the comparison is with peers within the same year of birth. This variable is thus being used as a control for the many ways in which primary schooling, family environment and genetic endowment influence attainment in secondary school and in later life. Secondary-school attainment is itself used as a control when analysing attainment and destinations after leaving school.

Schools

Part of the analysis in Chapters 3 to 8 relates to the history of secondary schools. The surveys of school students provided information about the school that sample members were attending when they left school. (There is no information on schools at earlier ages.) Schools were then classified in five ways.

The first is the longer-term history of their founding, as explained in Chapter 1. The schools are classified into six groups according to their date of founding and whether they had experience of teaching courses that might lead to the main school-leaving examinations (which are referred to here as certificated courses). All but the second category were managed by public authorities. The sectors are:

1. old secondaries, dating from before 1900, providing certificated courses by the early twentieth century;
2. schools not managed by public Education Authorities, all providing certificated courses;
3. new secondaries, founded between 1900 and 1924 in the initial phase of extending secondary education to all children, providing certificated courses by 1924 (Paterson, 2004);
4. new secondaries founded or upgraded between the 1920s and 1950s in order to provide certificated courses;
5. two groups of school that, though not teaching a full range of secondary courses, nevertheless had some experience of providing part of some these: (a) schools created as part of the same reforms as category (3); (b) former parish schools that had some experience of providing certificated courses between the beginning of the century and the late 1930s;
6. schools that, on the eve of the ending of selection from the mid-1960s, had no experience of teaching certificated courses.

The relative sizes of these categories is shown in Table 2.3.
The second classification was by denomination: Roman Catholic (17 per cent of pupils across the series) and non-denominational. The key resources in creating both these classifications were lists of schools compiled by the Scottish Examination Board and its predecessors and successors, and the regular inspection by the schools Inspectorate (National Records of Scotland, 2022; Paterson, 2004; Paterson, 2011). These were supplemented by websites of individual schools, published histories of individual schools, local history websites and public Facebook pages of former pupils of individual schools. For the fourth category in Table 2.3, we could also use the survey in 1962 of people who left school in 1961–2 with at least one Higher. Because that survey was in effect a census of such students, it gave a full list of all schools that were

Table 2.3 School sectors, defined by origin

Short description	Percentage share of pupils over the survey series*	Percentage share of average number of schools over the survey series†
Old secondaries, dating from before 1900	11	10
Grant aided or independent	4	7
Full secondaries founded as Higher Grade schools, 1900–early 1920s	22	19
Full secondaries founded late 1920s or later	11	9
Academic junior secondaries: former Higher Grade schools offering only short courses, and former parish schools with experience of leaving certificate	12	15
Other junior secondaries: no experience of leaving certificate	36	36
New schools after 1970s	4	4

Note:
*Weighted. †Unweighted. For sample size of pupils, see Table 2.1; for number of schools, see text.

offering full certificated courses before the transition to comprehensive education. Thus the fifth category is strictly schools that, although having some experience of teaching academic courses before the advent of comprehensive schooling, did not yet have experience of the full range of certificate courses.

In the 1950s, the schools in the first four categories were generally referred to as senior secondaries, and those in the fifth and sixth as junior secondaries, although – as explained in Chapter 1 – the official distinction was between courses, not schools, and most schools in the senior-secondary category also offered junior-secondary courses (Paterson, 2003, pp. 134–5). After the shift to comprehensive education was complete, the only remaining academic selection between schools was into the schools in the second category, which charged fees. We refer to the fifth category as 'academic junior secondaries' and the sixth as 'other junior secondaries'. As long ago as 1957, the academic junior secondaries were recognised informally as an educationally plausible way of developing secondary education for everyone (ibid.; see also Gray et al., 1983, pp. 235–9).

The schools that were not managed by public authorities – in the second category here – had a complex history in this period (Walford, 1987, 1988). The largest sub-group – containing about three-quarters of pupils in the category – were schools which had received some public grants. These were schools that had been founded in the nineteenth century or earlier on the basis of endowments, the size of which had enabled them to remain independent

(Anderson, 1983, pp. 172–201; Scotland, 1969, pp. 64–72). By the 1950s, over half of the income of these schools came from public grants, but the Labour governments of the 1960s and 1970s gradually reduced that subsidy (Paterson, 2003, pp. 140–2). It ended in the late 1970s, at which point all but two of these schools chose to become fully independent; as a result, their fees rose. Almost all the schools in this second category used the Scottish curriculum and examinations. Throughout the analysis of the surveys of school students, we have removed 16 schools whose curricula were based mainly on non-Scottish examination systems (A levels from elsewhere in the UK): this removed 0.8 per cent of all pupils in the surveys. In the retained schools in this category, 86 per cent of pupils were in those which had been grant aided.

The third classification is an indicator of whether, early in the twentieth century, a school had been the only school in its community that provided any kind of secondary course: this was defined as a school that, in 1924 or 1935, provided secondary courses and was the only such school that, in 1908, had served the area governed by one of the approximately 1,000 school boards (Paterson, 2004; Scotch Education Department, 1908); for this purpose, Catholic schools are taken to serve different such communities from non-denominational schools. Details are in Chapter 3.

The fourth classification of schools was based on information on their transition to comprehensive education. This was a simplified version of the classification compiled by McPherson and Willms (1987, pp. 516–17), into the categories: whether a school became comprehensive before the mid-1970s, between then and the late 1970s, or later, or was an independent school (thus not comprehensive), or was founded after the early 1980s. The earliest survey to have members who could have been affected by the reform was in 1976. All members of the 1986 or later surveys in public-sector schools entered a non-selective system. Details are in Chapter 3.

The final classification recorded the rate at which schools adopted the new Standard Grade courses in the late 1980s (Gamoran, 1996). This recorded whether a school had adopted the new courses in English in time for these to be taken by the 1988 cohort survey; the information is not available for independent schools. We use this engagement with English as an indicator of the school's general engagement with the reform at that date. Details are in Chapter 4.

STATISTICAL ANALYSIS

This is the most technical part of the chapter (and the book). The analysis was done in the statistical environment R (The R Project for Statistical Computing, 2022). Because the data came from surveys that had complex designs, almost all the analysis was done using the R package 'survey', which allows clustering and stratification to be taken into account (Lumley, 2010). The main such complexity relates to the fact that students in the same school would tend to resemble each other more than students in different schools. Technically, what would happen if we did not take account of this clustering is that standard errors would be underestimated. As a result, we would infer that specific differences probably did not occur by chance, whereas the opposite would be more correct.

This R package also allowed weights to be taken into account. Most of the survey data sets included weights that enabled some compensation for differential non-response. In the surveys of school students, these weights were defined in terms of sex and school attainment (Gray et al., 1983; Croxford et al., 2007, p. 7). The weights also took account of the differential sampling fractions for some sub-groups of students. Thus the weights ensured that the estimated distribution of attainment would match the national distribution in the relevant year.

Because nearly all the outcomes are dichotomies – for example, passing or not passing at least one Higher – we model them as logistic regressions. This is a technique that allows the valid and reliable comparison of proportions in particular categories – for example, comparing the male and female proportions passing at least one Higher. The relevant R function for this is 'svyglm'. The models for the lifelong learning part of Chapter 9 are slightly different, recognising the clustering of time points within respondents rather than respondents within schools, but the principle is the same; for this, the R package 'lme4' was used. The evidence from the PISA study in Chapter 3 is analysed using the specialist R package called 'intsvy', which was developed for international surveys of this kind by Caro and Biecek (2017). The full technical summary of all these various forms of analysis is not shown in this book, but may be found in the online papers cited for each chapter (as listed in the 'further information' section immediately before the bibliography).

Most of the tables and graphs in the book are summaries of the substantive conclusions of the statistical models. Modelling in this context, despite the word, is better thought of as a kind of smoothing. It is a way of drawing out the main trends in the data, disallowing most of the random fluctuations that any statistical series throws up. We present these findings as estimates from the models at specified values. An example is the estimated proportion of female students from class III who passed at least one Higher in 1988, which may be seen in Figure 3.4 in Chapter 3 (the answer is 31 per cent). There is one recurrent technicality that should be borne in mind. In many tables and graphs throughout the book, we show these estimates separately for different social classes (as in Figure 3.4). In calculating these estimates, we specified also the values of parental education. There are in principle two ways in which this could be done. One would be to average the estimate for each social class across all levels of parental education, weighted by the proportion at each such level (a technique sometimes called 'average marginal effects'). The problem with that approach is that it might include combinations of class and parental education that are very uncommon, such as working-class people in the 1970s both of whose parents left school at age 17 or older. So we do not use this technique. Instead, we specify the parental-education value to be the most common in each class in each year (as estimated from the surveys themselves). These values are shown in Tables 2.4 and 2.5. Table 2.4 is for models where we can include all five social classes, and where we estimate for classes I, III and V. Thus it may be seen that estimates for class V specify that both parents left school at age 15 or younger, until the 1996 survey where the evidence suggested that the most common parental education in this class category was to have at least one parent who left school at age 16 (but where neither left at older ages). Table 2.5 is, similarly, for when we had to combine class categories in order to have sufficient sample sizes; this is the most common situation throughout the book. This table shows the parental-education values for all students, and also for when the analysis was restricted to students who passed at least one Higher, a restriction that is used when we are analysing entry to higher education (Chapters 7 and 8).

All the estimates are subject to sampling error, which is technically measured most appropriately by estimated standard errors. However, to avoid cluttering the tables and graphs with standard errors for every point estimate, we show only average standard errors, sometimes as a single value for the whole

Table 2.4 Combinations of parental education and father's social class for percentages estimated from statistical models: students at all levels of attainment, and social classes I, III and V

	Social class		
Year when respondent was aged 16	I	III	V
1952	15	15	15
1974–6	Both 17	15	15
1976–8	Both 17	15	15
1978–80	Both 17	15	15
1980–2	Both 17	15	15
1984	Both 17	15	15
1986	Both 17	15	15
1988	Both 17	15	15
1990	Both 17	15	15
1996	Both 17	16	16
1998	Both 17	16	16

Note:
The cells show the values used to estimate from statistical models: the ages at which parents left full-time education at each level of social class. From Table 2.1: '15' corresponds to 'maximum 15'; '16' corresponds to 'maximum 16'.

Table 2.5 Combinations of parental education and father's social class for percentages estimated from statistical models: grouped social classes, for all students and for students who passed at least one Higher

Year when respondent was aged 16	Social class					
	I, II		III		IV, V, unclassified	
	All	At least one Higher	All	At least one Higher	All	At least one Higher
1952	15	-	15	-	15	-
1962	-	16	-	15	-	15
1968–70	-	Both 17	-	15	-	15
1970–2	-	Both 17	-	15	-	15
1974–6	15	Both 17	15	15	15	15
1976–8	15	Both 17	15	15	15	15
1978–80	15	Both 17	15	15	15	15
1980–2	15	Both 17	15	15	15	15
1984	15	Both 17	15	15	15	15
1986	15	Both 17	15	15	15	15
1988	15	Both 17	15	15	15	15
1990	16	Both 17	15	15	15	15
1996	One 17	Both 17	16	16	16	16
1998	One 17	Both 17	16	16	16	16
2016	Both 17	-	One 17	-	One 17	-

Note:
See footnote to Table 2.4.

table or graph, and sometimes for sets of estimates where the standard errors varied a lot (usually as a consequence of varying numbers of sample members in different parts of the data, such as in England compared to Scotland or Wales in Chapter 9). These standard errors of estimation were calculated using the R function 'vcov'. This presentation of averages is a compromise, but gives a rough sense of reliability; fuller statistical assessment may be found in the online papers listed in the further information section. In most cases, the standard error for the comparison of two values can be approximated by the square root of the sum of the squares of the separate standard errors as shown. Only differences that are unlikely to have occurred by chance are discussed in the text. The descriptive tables which merely describe trends over time in specific measures (such as Table 3.1 for basic attainment) do not show standard errors. The reliability of the percentages in them may be calculated directly from the sample sizes shown in Table 2.1 (and in a few other tables throughout the book as appropriate). The standard error of a percentage p is the square root of p multiplied by (100-p), and divided by the sample size. For a sample size of 4,000 (the median in Table 2.1), this is about 0.8 per cent.

The sources of data in the tables are, unless specified otherwise, the surveys that are being used in each chapter, as defined near the beginning of the chapter. Where data come from other sources, these are explicitly noted in a footnote to the table.

CHAPTER 3

The Impact of Policy and Social Change on Schools

WHAT HAS HAPPENED TO INEQUALITY IN OTHER COUNTRIES?

The educational reforms that were outlined in Chapter 1 took far longer to have an effect than the typical period of office of politicians or even of senior civil servants. Implementing the reforms was also a partnership between national agencies and local schools. This chapter analyses the resulting complexity of pupils' experience: how were the intentions of policy makers modified by the legacies of the selective system that they were trying to replace?

The main theme here is changing patterns of social inequality. The question of social disparities has been the dominant concern of educational sociology since the 1960s, and so the Scottish surveys provide a uniquely rich body of evidence to contribute to an important international debate. That debate has gone through three phases since the 1960s.

First, so-called modernisation theory proposed that inequality would decline as the labour market became more meritocratic. The argument was that the education system would have to draw on previously untapped pools of talent in order to supply enough skilled workers for an increasingly technological economy. Beliefs of this kind then became a core part of education policy in the two or three decades after the end of the second world war (Halsey et al., 1980). Democratic pressure forced both the expansion and the opening up, as newly enfranchised citizens saw education as a source of personal economic security.

However, evidence by the 1980s suggested that that initial prediction was too optimistic, which led to the second phase of debate. The most thorough comparative study that demonstrated the pessimism was led by Shavit and Blossfeld in 1993, with a title that summed up the conclusion from 13 countries: persistent inequality. Only for Sweden and the Netherlands was a reduction of inequality found. Heath and Clifford (1990, p. 15) concluded from such findings that perhaps 'education policy can have more effects on the overall levels of education than it can on class inequalities'. General expansion would eventually lead to a reduction of inequality only when the most advantaged social groups had reached an upper limit of participation or attainment: any further expansion could then not but benefit groups of lower status, even when that was not the deliberate intention. This theory was labelled maximally maintained inequality by Raftery and Hout (1993).

There was also a more deterministic interpretation of the persistence of inequality, most associated with the highly influential French sociologist Pierre Bourdieu. The kind of liberal education that had become the standard curriculum in the expansion could never be accessible to everyone, he said, because it was based on cognition rather than experience, and was grounded in the privileges, culture and language of middle-class or aristocratic education (Bourdieu and Passeron, 1977). As Goldthorpe (2007) has pointed out, Bourdieu's ideas are not really a theory of inequality, but rather a claim that there is an absolute barrier which prevents low-status people from having access to high-status culture.

Nevertheless, the consensus among researchers has changed in the past decade, notably influenced by a reply to Shavit and Blossfeld by Breen et al. (2009). Using more extensive data than had been available in the middle phase, the conclusion has become that inequality has changed. In a refinement of the original modernisation theories, Breen and his colleagues pointed out that the conditions for narrowing inequality were indeed in place for people growing up in the period 1945–75. Absolute poverty had been reduced. There had been expansion of institutional child-care and of pre-school education. There had been a strengthening of preferences to remain in full-time education beyond the legal minimum age. On the whole, the weight of evidence from large-scale surveys tends to support the conclusion reached by Breen et al. (and also Marks (2014, pp. 113–34)). Inequality has fallen in France, Germany, Ireland, Italy, the Netherlands, Poland, Sweden and the USA. Most of this research has concentrated on social class as the measure of social circumstances. Gugushvili et al. (2017) and Bukodi and Goldthorpe (2013) show the importance of treating social origins in a multi-dimensional way, especially of including parental education. The conclusion from research which has examined this is that inequality with respect to parental education has probably fallen in some countries, but less than for class (Ganzeboom and Treiman, 1993; Pfeffer, 2008; Shavit et al., 2007, p. 4; Triventi et al., 2016).

The trajectory of the debate about sex differences has in one respect been simpler – from a belief that they were quite impervious to change, to an understanding that female attainment has now firmly surpassed male attainment (Buchmann et al., 2008; van Hek et al., 2016). Furthermore, it has generally been found that changes in social-class inequalities have been similar for women and men (Breen et al., 2010). But there remain sex differences in specific parts of the curriculum, notably natural science and languages, and in what happens beyond the compulsory stages of schooling and in the labour market; we return to these topics in later chapters.

Policy makers have been influenced by the academic debate but during this period not by its recurrent pessimism: they have continued to believe that opportunities could be widened by reforming the structures of schooling and by making the inherited curriculum widely available. As we noted in Chapter 1, Scottish policy in the past century has followed common international trends, and so Scotland is a potentially revealing case study for these wider questions about disparities.

PROGRESSION AND ATTAINMENT

Before looking at inequality, we can set the context by tracing the sheer extent of the expansion. Table 3.1 illustrates this in terms of six measures

Table 3.1 School progression and attainment, 1952–2016

% of sample Year when respondent was aged 16	Attempt 1+ mid-secondary	Pass 1+ mid-secondary	Stay on beyond 4th year	Pass 1+ Higher	Pass 3+ Higher	Achieve 1+ A pass at Higher
1952	11	10	14	9	6	NA
1962	NA	24	21	15	10	NA
1974–6	60	49	30	22	15	7
1976–8	68	58	33	26	17	8
1978–80	75	59	45	27	17	8
1980–2	80	64	45	27	16	8
1984	80	67	45	32	20	10
1986	87	69	46	33	21	10
1988	88	72	52	37	25	13
1990	90	70	55	41	30	15
1996	97	85	67	50	36	22
1998	97	85	68	52	39	24
2002	98	90	70	51	37	26
2016*	96	96	88	62	44	NA

Notes:
Percentages weighted. For sample sizes, see Table 2.1 (along with 3,220 for 2002). Percentages for Highers are of the whole leaver-cohort or age-cohort (not only those who entered the senior years). NA=not available.
*Attainment and staying-on data for 2016 is public-sector schools only, and so probably underestimates the true proportion by 1–2%. Mid-secondary in 2016 is National 4 or 5.
Sources: 1952–2002: survey series, as described in Chapter 2, including 1946 birth-cohort data for 1962.
2016: attempt 1+ mid-secondary from Millennium Cohort.
2016: staying on from Table 3.3 in Scottish Government (2016).
2016: attainment from Publication Table 5a in Scottish Government (2017).

of the progression and attainment of school leavers. The first two record attempting and passing any examinations at mid-secondary level. The third is attending school beyond age 16. The remaining three are about success at senior-secondary level: the minimal criterion of passing at least one Higher, reaching the threshold of entry to university (passing at least three Highers), and achieving the highest award (grade A) in at least one Higher. Most of these measures cover the full half-century, and can be extended to 2016.

At the most basic level, access to meaningful certification rose very strikingly. Only one in ten sat or passed at least one external examination in the early 1950s. This had risen to a quarter passing on the eve of the comprehensive reforms. The reforming period rapidly extended proper courses at this level to over three-quarters of the age group, reaching 80 per cent in 1984, just before the fundamental reform to the courses which took place in the late 1980s. That reform, and the subsequent curriculum framework, gave almost all pupils access to properly planned and assessed courses for the first time, a level of provision that lasted well beyond the end of these reforms (96 per cent or more right up to 2016). Attainment in some form at these levels rose similarly, giving almost all pupils some recorded evidence of what they had studied at school.

Some of these new courses were at modest or low levels of intellectual demand that were simply not catered for in the system of assessment that was in place in 1952, nor even in the 1960s and 1970s. So the rise in attainment at what was officially classified as mid-secondary does not in itself necessarily show a rise at all levels of attainment. Nevertheless, one of the first effects of the better provision of mid-secondary courses was an encouragement to stay on in school for more. We return to the motivational aspects of this in Chapter 5, but here we may simply note the result in terms of commitment. In the 1970s, still only one-third stayed on; this reached one-half by the late 1980s, 70 per cent by the end of the century and around 90 per cent more recently. That then encouraged growing attainment at more advanced levels of study. The proportion of school leavers who passed at least one Higher grew from one in ten to one-half in the second half of the century, rising further to nearly two-thirds by 2016. The proportion passing at least three Highers went from 6 per cent to 44 per cent in that same period. At the end of the century, a quarter of leavers were gaining at least an A pass at Higher – the same as had just one mid-secondary pass four decades previously.

The main questions are then whether these changes were widely shared, and whether they did actually relate to policy.

The broad conclusion is that the equal spread of opportunity took a while to be evident, but did gradually come about. For those outcomes which reached near-saturation, inequality indubitably declined. Figure 3.1 illustrates this point for sitting any mid-secondary examination, showing inequality in terms

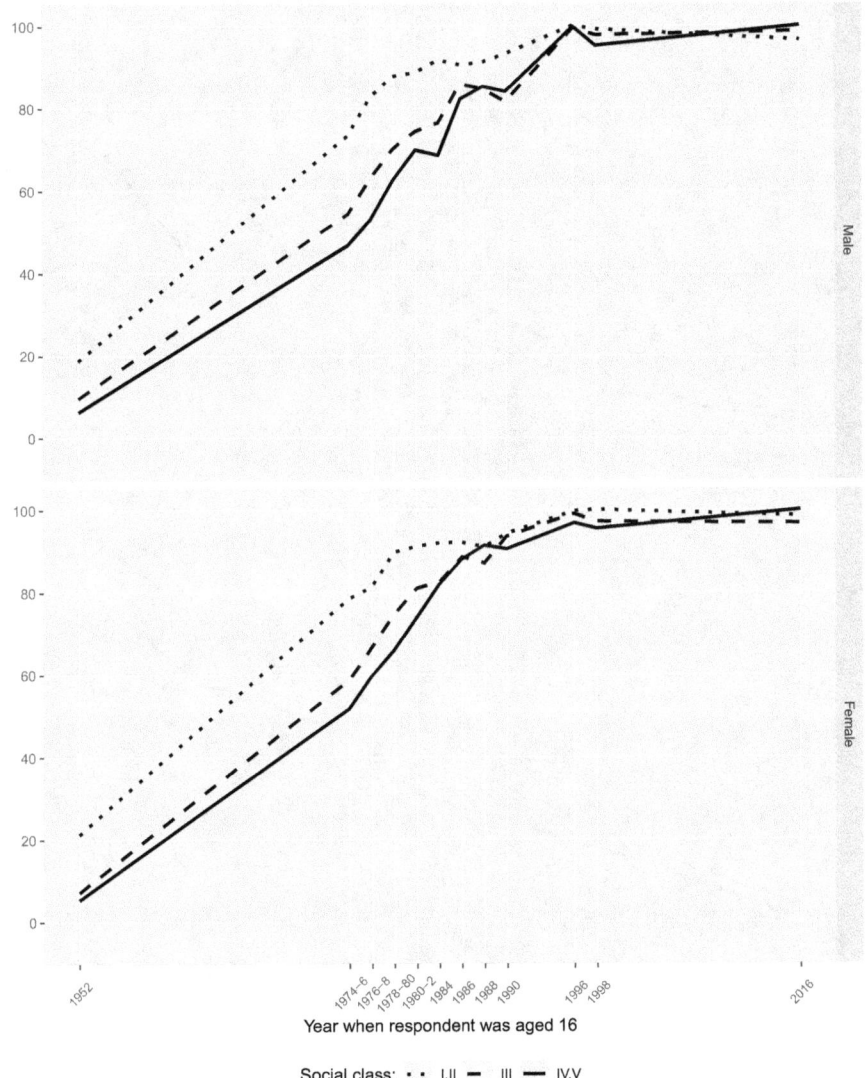

Figure 3.1 Percentage sitting at least one mid-secondary course, by sex and social class, 1952–2016
For each class, parental education is set to the modal value in each year: see Table 2.5.
Average standard error: 2.1.

of broad social-class groups. All three class groups reached over 90 per cent by the mid-1990s and remained there by 2016. This was partly but not only a consequence of the compulsory curriculum framework in the 1990s: the largest rise in the low-status group happened in the late 1970s and early 1980s. Passing any course at this level is shown in Figure 3.2 (for which the data on inequality

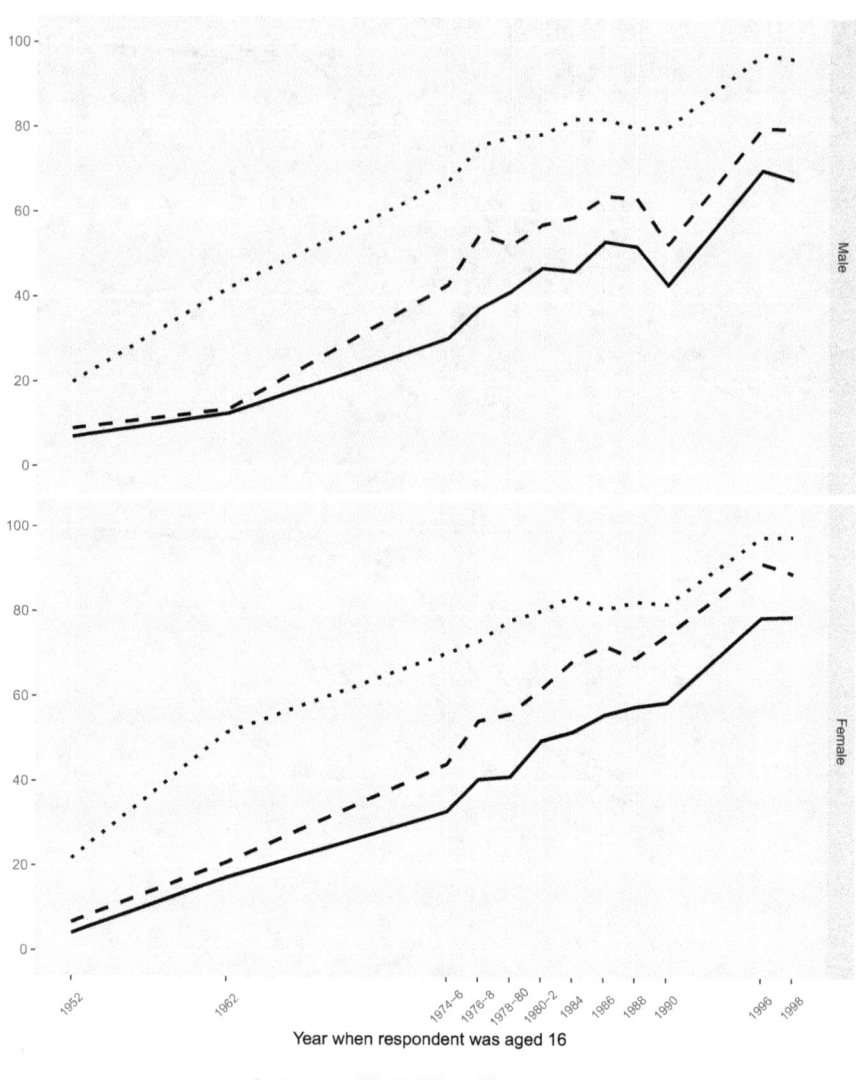

Figure 3.2 Percentage passing at least one mid-secondary course, by sex and social class, 1952–98
For each class, parental education is set to the modal value in each year: see Table 2.5.
Average standard error: 3.0.

are available only for the half-century 1952–98). Inequality widened at first, up to the late 1970s, but then gradually reduced, especially for girls.

The same was then true for staying on beyond age 16: widening at first, little change until the 1980s, and narrowing, with the narrowing at the end clearer for female students than for male: for example, low-status males rose from 9 per cent in 1952 to 44 per cent in 1998, whereas low-status females rose from 5 per cent to 59 per cent. For sitting one or more Highers (in Figure 3.3) a similar description applies, but with the initial widening not happening until the 1990s and the convergence not evident until 2016. The pattern of inequality for

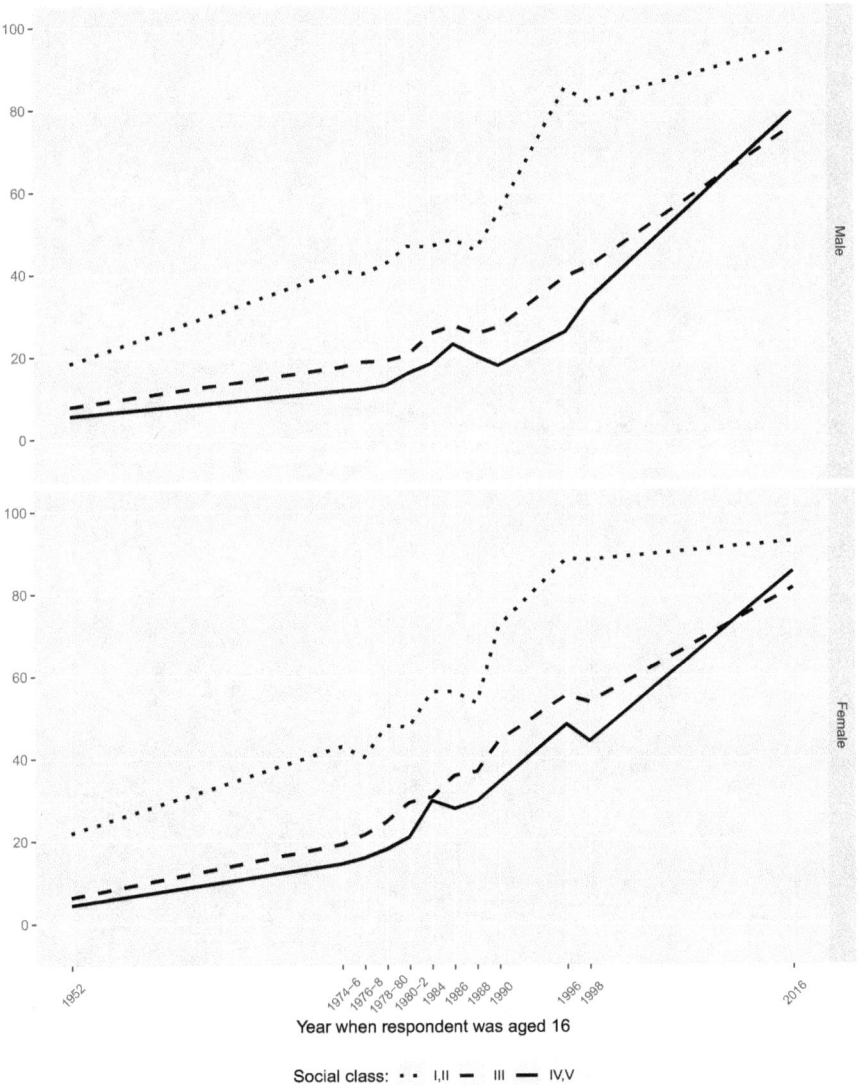

Figure 3.3 Percentage sitting at least one Higher, by sex and social class, 1952–2016
For each class, parental education is set to the modal value in each year: see Table 2.5.
Average standard error: 2.9.

passing at least one Higher (in Figure 3.4) showed little narrowing in the period 1952–98.

So if we date the beginning of the major reforms to the 1960s, we can say that the earliest point at which they were having a measurable impact even on inequality in mid-secondary attainment was three decades later, and that the

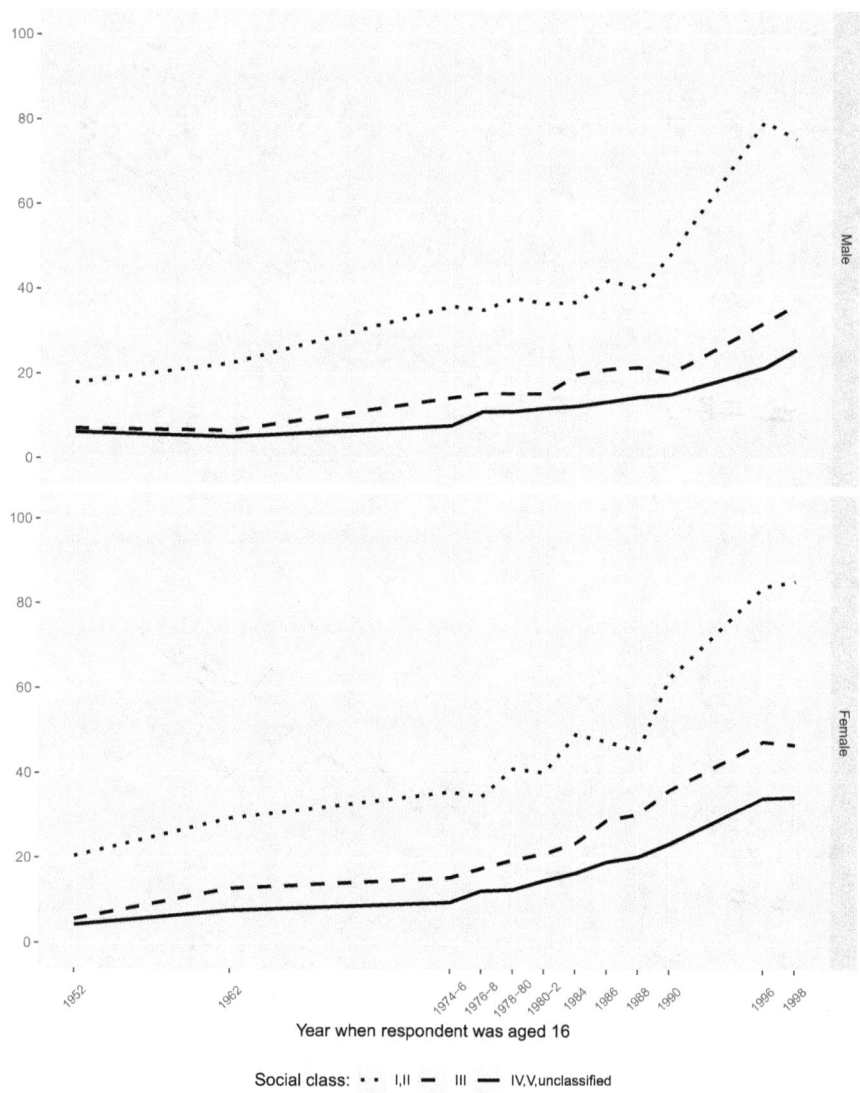

Figure 3.4 Percentage passing at least one Higher, by sex and social class, 1952–98
For each class, parental education is set to the modal value in each year: see Table 2.5.
Average standard error: 2.6.

IMPACT OF POLICY AND SOCIAL CHANGE 45

impact on inequality at more advanced levels was only beginning to be felt half a century after change was inaugurated, in the second decade of the new century.

There was change in attainment also with respect to measured intelligence. Figure 3.5 shows the percentage passing at least one Higher by social class, sex and intelligence measured at the end of primary school (represented in the

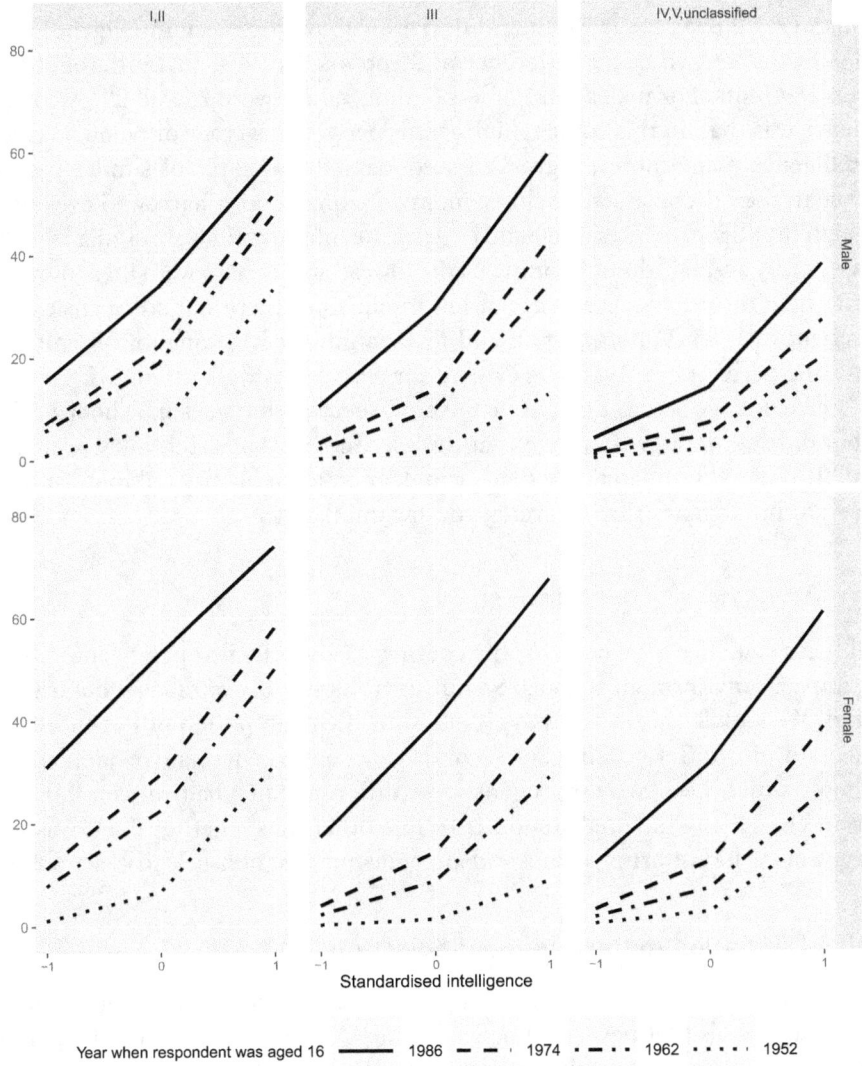

Figure 3.5 Percentage passing at least one Higher, by sex, social class and intelligence at age c. 11, 1952–86
For each class, parental education is set to the modal value in each year: see Table 2.5.
Average standard error: 5.1.

graphs as the mean and one standard deviation above and below the mean). For people who were aged 16 in 1952, 1962 or 1974, the slope on intelligence steepened between 1952 and 1974, especially for females. That is, between the 1950s and the 1970s, attainment in secondary came to depend more on attainment at the end of primary. For people aged 16 in 1986, the slope was maintained for the class groups III and IV, V, unclassified, but flattened somewhat for I, II. For example, among female students in that class group in 1986, the proportions were 74 per cent at 1 standard deviation above the mean intelligence, and 53 per cent at the mean, a difference of 21 points. In 1974, that difference had been 28 points. For males, the corresponding values were 25 and 29. A consequence was that, in this cohort, high-status people of average or below-average intelligence made more progress in secondary than people of similar intelligence in the other classes. Socio-economic inequality also narrowed over time at high intelligence: the right-hand ends of the lines for 1986 are similar for the classes I, II and III, though for males the lowest-status class was still somewhat lower than the others. At average or low intelligence there was still a clear class gradient in 1986. For staying on and for attaining at least one mid-secondary pass, the flattening in 1986 was evident for class III as well as I and II.

The evidence so far, then, is that overall social differences in school attainment did fall, to a greater extent at mid-secondary than later, but eventually (in 2016) not absent later, and that socio-economic inequality fell more at high levels of intelligence than at average or low intelligence.

THE IMPORTANCE OF SCHOOLS

All these statistics have been for the country as a whole. But policy could have an impact only through schools. So our next question is whether schools mattered. We look at this in two ways. One is for the main period of the ending of selection into different kinds of secondary school: is there any evidence that schools which became comprehensive at different rates had measurably different effects on students' attainment? The other asks whether there was any legacy of earlier reforms during and after the move to non-selective schooling.

School Variation in the Ending of Selection

For the first question, we look only at public-sector schools, omitting the independent schools that never stopped selecting. At first, we focus on the period when the comprehensive change was happening – recorded in the surveys of leavers between 1976 and 1984. We classify schools according to the rate at which they became comprehensive by the late 1970s, restricting attention initially here to those schools which were fully comprehensive when respondents in at least one of the surveys of 1974–6, 1978–80 and 1984 entered secondary school (containing 77 per cent of all sample members in the surveys at these dates). In this restricted sample, 61 per cent of students were in schools which were comprehensive in all three of these surveys (which we refer to as 'early comprehensives'), 33 per cent in schools which were not comprehensive for the 1974–6 survey but were comprehensive in 1978–80 and 1984 ('middle comprehensives') and 6 per cent in schools which became comprehensive between the 1978–80 and 1984 surveys ('late comprehensives').

As explained in Chapter 2, this classification closely follows McPherson and Willms (1987, pp. 521–3) in assessing the ending of selection as a quasi-experiment. Controlling statistically for social class, parental education and sex is then a substitute for random allocation. If, after these controls, students' attainment grew between the 1974–6 and 1978–80 surveys more in the middle comprehensives than in the late comprehensives, then we might attribute that to the move to non-selective status in the middle comprehensives. Similarly, the early comprehensives act as a control for the other two because their non-selective status is constant.

Table 3.2 provides detail on these patterns for the criterion of at least one mid-secondary pass. It uses the 1976 and 1980 surveys, comparing schools that changed their status between these two surveys (the middle comprehensives) with the control group that was not comprehensive until after the second survey (the late comprehensives). Inequality is measured as the difference in attainment between the highest-status and lowest-status classes, in order to bring out the effects of what happens when the most advantaged class reached

Table 3.2 Percentage passing at least one Ordinary Grade, by sex, social class and stage of becoming comprehensive, 1976 and 1980

	1976 survey		1980 survey	
	Middle comprehensive*	Late comprehensive†	Middle comprehensive*	Late comprehensive†
Male				
Class I	95.8	99.4	96.4	99.0
Class V	24.4	31.9	43.1	37.5
Difference	71.4	67.5	53.3	61.5
Female				
Class I	95.0	99.5	97.4	99.5
Class V	29.9	47.9	35.9	39.6
Difference	65.1	51.6	61.5	59.9

Notes:
* Middle comprehensive: not comprehensive for 1976 survey, comprehensive for 1980 survey.
† Late comprehensive: not comprehensive in either 1976 or 1980 survey.
For each class, parental education is set to the modal value in each class in each year: see Table 2.4.
Average standard error for percentages: 1976: 4.1; 1980: 3.4.

an upper ceiling of attainment. For male students, the reduction of inequality in the schools which became comprehensive was greater than the reduction in the schools that did not (71 per cent to 53 per cent, compared to 68 per cent to 62 per cent). For female students, inequality increased in the control group and fell in the group that became comprehensive. This analysis suggests that some part of the reduction of inequality might be attributable to the change of status from selective to non-selective, analogously to the finding by McPherson and Willms (1987).

We reach a similar conclusion if we then look at what happened to the late comprehensives when these schools, in turn, became comprehensive in time for the 1984 survey: Table 3.3. We can compare them with the group of early reformers that were comprehensive throughout this period. Over the whole period, the late comprehensives do show a fall of inequality. So becoming comprehensive after 1980 compensated for any stagnation or increase of inequality before that (as in Table 3.2). The early comprehensives had a greater fall of inequality than the late comprehensives, which is consistent with a maturing effect of the earlier comprehensives.

However, these tables also show that the reduction of inequality was mainly because the high-status social group was already at a ceiling of nearly 100 per cent. So inequality at mid-secondary level probably narrowed as an immediate result of the ending of selection, by a localised version of maximally maintained inequality. That was not the case at the senior-secondary level. In the middle comprehensives, the percentage in the high-status groups in 1976 left plenty of room for further improvement, which then happened by 1980, rising from

Table 3.3 Percentage passing at least one Ordinary Grade, by sex, social class and stage of becoming comprehensive, 1976 and 1984

	1976 survey		1984 survey	
	Early comprehensive*	Late comprehensive†	Early comprehensive*	Late comprehensive†
Male				
Class I	96.2	99.4	93.6	98.4
Class V	24.4	31.9	45.1	45.8
Difference	71.8	67.5	48.5	52.6
Female				
Class I	96.2	99.5	98.9	99.8
Class V	33.2	47.9	58.7	65.0
Difference	63.0	51.6	40.2	34.8

Notes:
*Early comprehensive: comprehensive for 1976 survey.
†Late comprehensive: not comprehensive in 1976 survey, comprehensive in 1984 survey.
For each class, parental education is set to the modal value in each class in each year: see Table 2.4.
Average standard error for percentages: 1976: 4.1; 1984: 5.9.

69 per cent to 83 per cent for males, and 76 per cent to 86 per cent for females. The low-status group also improved (5.6 per cent to 11 per cent for males, and 7.1 per cent to 11 per cent for females), but the gap thus widened from 64 points to 72 points for males, and 69 to 75 for females. It remained unchanged (at the even higher level of around 90 points) in the late comprehensives.

Moreover, whatever happened in this short span of the reforming period, the change directly associated with structural reform can be seen to be quite small in the longer context of half a century of gradual change. Figure 3.6 illustrates the differences, returning to the outcome of having at least one mid-secondary pass, and for each of the three groups of schools that we have been considering. The reforming period that was the subject of the tables is marked by the vertical lines. There is quite a lot of random variation here, especially for the small group of late comprehensives. Inequality did decline in all three groups of school, following the national pattern of Figure 3.2, but in a long process that continued over the half-century as a whole. The differences among the three groups associated with the reforming period itself were small.

The same point may be made about the probable widening of inequality at senior-secondary levels during the reforming period. When set in the long-term perspective analogous to Figure 3.6, the widening for holding at least one pass at Higher between the mid-1970s and the early 1980s was compensated for by the narrowing that took place a decade or two later. In the category of 'middle comprehensive', the proportion passing at least one Higher in the male class V group rose from 11 per cent in 1980 to 23 per cent in 1998, while the class I male group in these schools was stable at 83 per cent in 1980 and 82 per cent in 1998; thus inequality, though rising between 1976 and 1980 from 64 per cent to 72 per cent, fell to 59 per cent by 1998. Likewise for female students: the class V female group in these schools rose from 11 per cent in 1980 to 38 per cent in 1998, while the class I female group went from 86 per cent to 94 per cent, and so the rise of inequality between 1976 and 1980 from 69 per cent to 75 per cent was followed by a fall to 56 per cent by 1998.

So the ending of selection marked no more than a few steps on an upward ascent. With sex differences, not even that can be said. For example, the proportion of female students passing at least one Higher rose to equal male attainment by the 1970s in class I (both with 88 per cent in the 1976 survey). It overtook males in the early 1980s in class III (female 20 per cent against male 16 per cent in 1980), and in the late 1980s in class V (for example, female 17 per cent, male 11 per cent in 1986). There was no straightforward connection with any aspects of the structural reforms to schools, and indeed there was no official attention to equal sex opportunities in the policy shift to comprehensive schools (McPherson and Willms, 1987). It could be that what helped change sex differences was not the ending of selection but the subsequent reforms to the curriculum (Croxford, 1994), and so we return to this point in the next chapter.

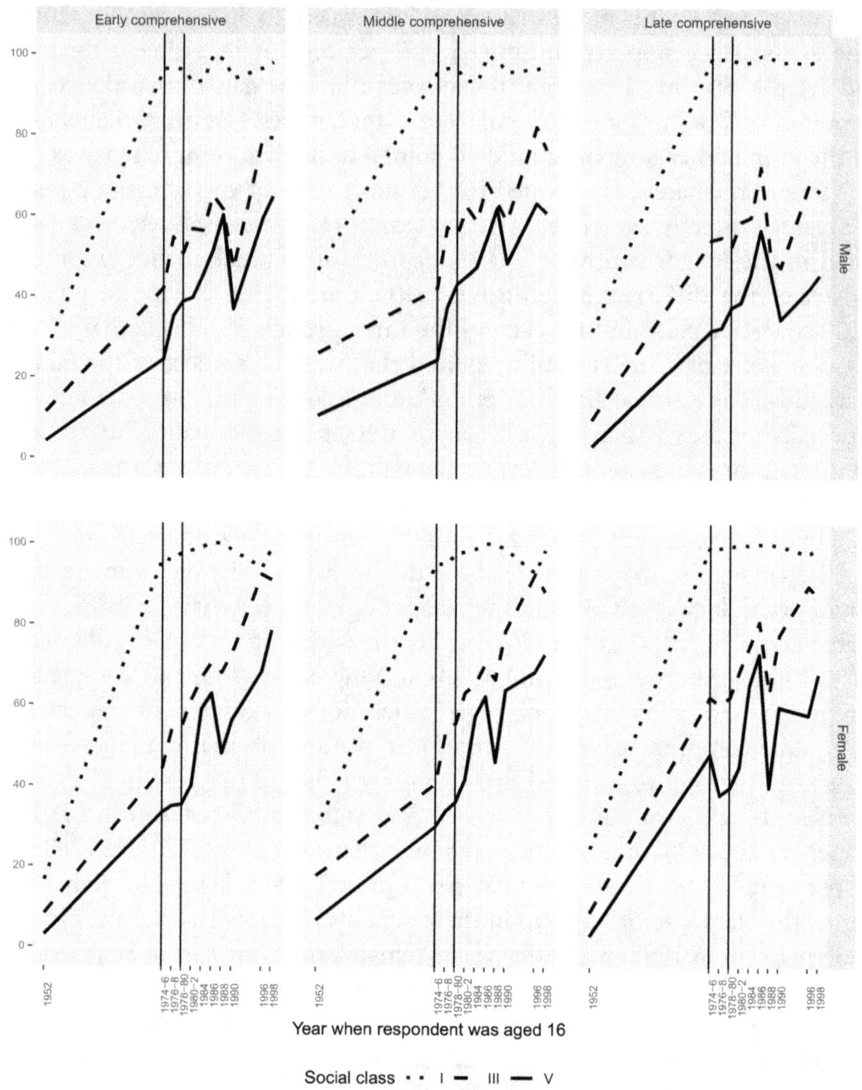

Figure 3.6 Percentage passing at least one mid-secondary course, by sex, stage of school's becoming comprehensive, and social class, 1952–98. Vertical lines note main reforming period
For each class, parental education is set to the modal value in each year: see Table 2.4.
Average standard error: early comprehensives, 6.3; middle comprehensives, 7.3; late comprehensives, 8.3.

Legacies of School History

So the policy of ending selection may be thought of as an intervention in a historical trajectory. This is seen even more clearly if we then examine how that policy interacted with the older legacies that were described in Chapter 1.

IMPACT OF POLICY AND SOCIAL CHANGE   51

One effect of the comprehensive reforms was to make the historical sectors more similar socio-economically, as Figure 3.7 illustrates for their social-class composition in the 1952, 1978 and 1998 surveys, along with the national distribution of all pupils as a yardstick at the right. At the first date, the old secondaries had much higher percentages of pupils in the top two classes than the other public-sector schools, and the non-academic junior secondaries had far lower. The differences were much less in 1978, and had all but vanished in 1998. The success of the early twentieth-century reforms is reflected in the closeness of

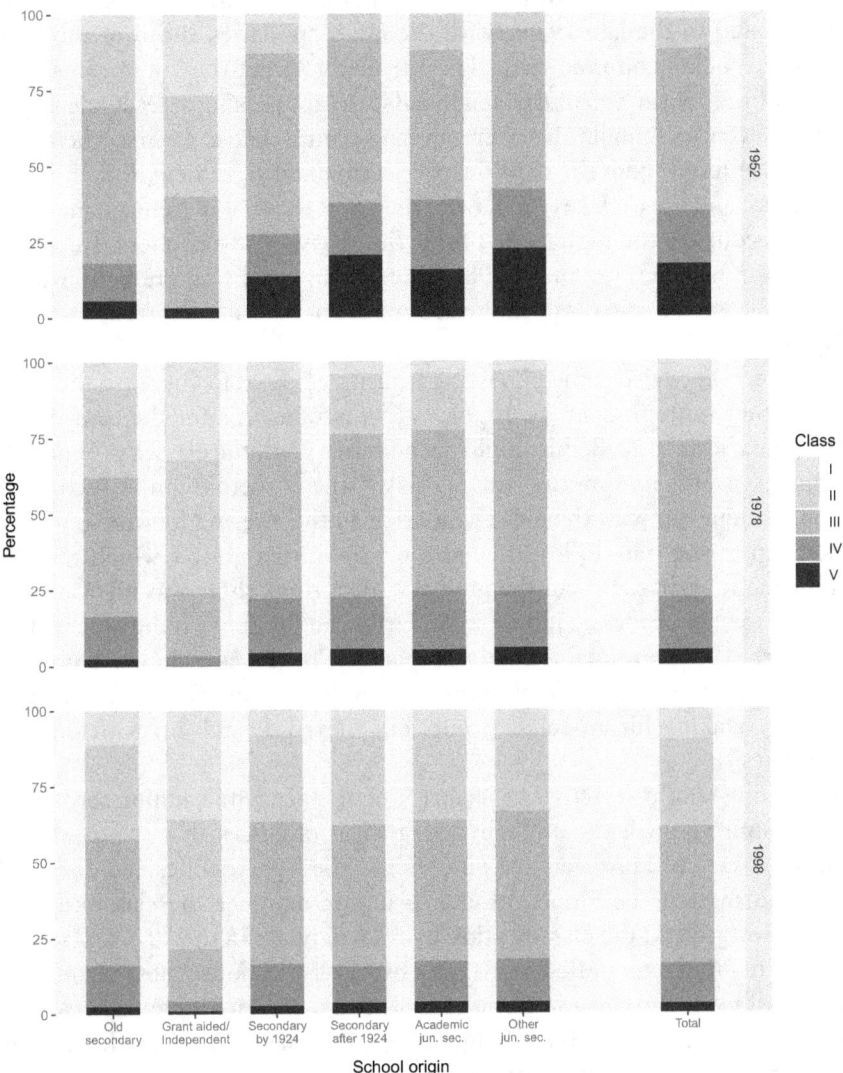

Figure 3.7 Father's social class by school origin, 1952, 1978 and 1998

the 'secondary by 1924' category to the national-average class distribution as early as 1952. In contrast, the schools that were independent of public management were increasingly dominated by the high-class groups. All this social convergence among the historically defined public sectors is an instance of the wider reduction of social segregation among schools in the 1980s and 1990s (Croxford and Paterson, 2006; Smith and Gorard, 2002). Scottish secondary schooling became then one of the least-segregated systems in the economically developed world, quite contrary to the fears that the 1980s policy of strengthening parental rights to choose a school would increase segregation.

In most respects, the differences of attainment among these historical sectors lasted to the late 1970s, with the old secondaries ahead of the others even when socio-economic status is controlled for; but they then vanished by the end of the century, as illustrated in Table 3.4 for passing at least one Higher. In 1976, even in schools that were already comprehensive when the sample members entered them (in 1970–2), there remained a gradient at each level of social class, and for each sex: generally, the older the school's engagement with academic courses, the higher the proportion passing any Highers. But for the fully comprehensive system in 1998, there was no consistent gradient, whether in all public-sector schools or in the group that had been comprehensive in the 1976 survey.

But there were also some persisting legacies of the reforms from the beginning of the twentieth century. Figure 3.8 illustrates this for the categories of old secondaries and academic junior secondaries, with the classes grouped. For the highest-status and middle-status classes, the academic junior secondaries not only caught up with the old secondaries: in the aftermath of the reforming period, up to the mid-1990s, they also overtook them, after which the older sector caught up in turn. For the lowest-status group, there was no overtaking, but these former academic junior secondaries caught up with the older schools in the early 1980s and maintained that parity. There was a similar but weaker trajectory for the non-academic junior secondaries (not in the graph): there was no overtaking for any class group, but they did catch up with the older secondaries.

Explaining the distinctive trajectories of the academic junior secondaries would require knowledge of their pedagogical practices that is not available from the data sets. However, one clue to how the legacies operated during the 1970s reforms may be found through bringing together the classification of school by origin and the classification by reform phase in the 1970s. There was evidence of interactive effects of these two classifications, most strongly for students of middling class status in schools that were early comprehensives, as may be seen from Table 3.4. In 1998, for people in class III, the academic junior secondaries that had been comprehensive for the 1976 leavers were ahead of all the other historically defined sectors. More detailed inspection showed that

Table 3.4 Percentage passing at least one Higher Grade, by sex, social class and school origin, 1976 and 1998

	Male			Female		
	1976 survey (schools already comprehensive)	1998 survey (same schools as in 1976)	1998 survey (all public-sector schools)	1976 survey (schools already comprehensive)	1998 survey (same schools as in 1976)	1998 survey (all public-sector schools)
Class I						
Old secondary	89	90	91	93	97	97
Full secondary by 1924	80	85	84	87	96	95
Full secondary after 1924	67	78	78	78	93	93
Former academic junior secondary	68	88	87	77	96	96
Former other junior secondary	63	85	84	71	95	94
Class III						
Old secondary	20	33	35	21	48	49
Full secondary by 1924	21	33	33	23	51	50
Full secondary after 1924	17	29	29	19	44	46
Former academic junior secondary	14	42	38	14	57	53
Former other junior secondary	10	31	32	10	44	45
Class V						
Old secondary	8	19	20	11	36	35
Full secondary by 1924	5	11	13	7	25	25
Full secondary after 1924	5	13	13	8	27	26
Former academic junior secondary	4	20	19	5	37	34
Former other junior secondary	4	18	20	5	32	33

Notes:
For each class, parental education is set to the modal value in each class in each year: see Table 2.4.
Average standard error: 1976: 5.2; 1998 (1976 schools): 7.2; 1998 (all schools): 6.4.

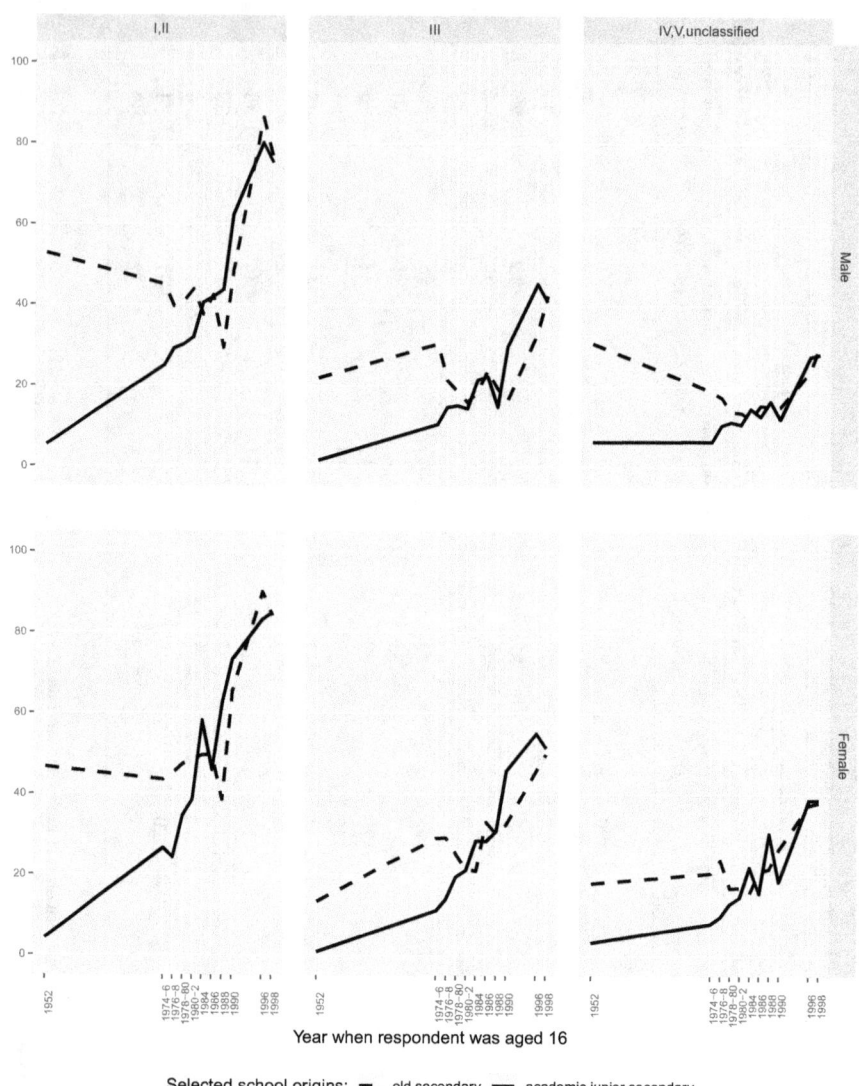

Figure 3.8 Percentage passing at least one Higher, by sex, social class and selected school origins, 1952–98
For each class, parental education is set to the modal value in each year: see Table 2.5.
Average standard error: 4.5.

this pattern emerged in the late 1970s. The suggestion here therefore is that those academic junior secondaries which became comprehensives soon after the reform were particularly effective with students of middling social status.

A further hint in explanation of this interaction of policy with institutional legacies may be had from the typical geographical location of the former academic junior secondaries. Earlier in the twentieth century, fully 80 per cent of those which survived to the 1980s had been the only school in their community that had provided any kind of secondary course, compared to one-third of surviving schools overall (and only two-thirds in the next-highest categories – old secondaries, and secondaries founded by the early 1920s). It could be that a community with a single school that had a record of providing academic study while also serving the needs of the full range of students would be likely to be most committed to maintaining that combined tradition into the comprehensive era (Gray et al., 1983, pp. 248–66; McPherson and Willms, 1986, pp. 261–7).

There was also some convergence between education authority and independent schools for students whose parents were in high-status occupations and who had high levels of education. For example, in the 1990s, the proportions passing at least three Highers were, for female students, 87 per cent in the independent schools and 61 per cent in the public-sector schools. This difference of 26 points, though large, was notably smaller than it had been in the 1970s (55 per cent and 21 per cent). For male students, the corresponding proportions were 84 per cent against 52 per cent in the 1990s, and 63 per cent against 23 per cent in the 1970s. This convergence happened around the time, in the early 1990s, that the typical parents of the highest-status classes start to have more than minimal education. This then suggests that part of the pressure towards making a common system of schools was not policy on institutions – because the independent schools were barely affected by that – but rather a combination of a common system of curriculum and assessment and those aspects of social change by means of which growing proportions of school pupils came from relatively affluent families in which the parents had themselves benefited from previous waves of educational expansion.

Ethnicity and Religion

Our final analysis in this chapter is to consider how ethnicity and religion interacted with school history. For ethnicity, the only survey with adequate numbers in minority groups was of people aged 16 in 2002 (as explained in Chapter 2). Even in that year, there were too few in the minority group to allow social class to be included reliably, and, for the same reason, ethnicity itself had to be grouped into very crude categories – Scottish, other British, and an amorphous group consisting of people of any Asian or African family origin. On average, minority attainment was ahead of attainment in the Scottish group: for example, 64 per cent of minority students had passed any Highers, compared to 50 per cent of Scottish students. Mostly that difference did not vary by school sector, but there was some evidence that minority students had higher average attainment in the schools classed as 'other junior secondary'. For male minority students, 65 per cent in these schools passed at least one Higher, compared to 53 per cent in the former senior secondaries. For females, these percentages were 76 per cent and 65 per cent. For Scottish students, there was almost no difference between these sectors. Somewhat distinctly from social class and the academic junior secondaries, then, these other former junior secondaries may have been particularly open to encouraging the attainment of minority students. The main point again is that understanding the experience of this dimension of disparity requires that we pay attention to school history.

We can investigate the denomination of schools over a much longer period. One consequence of the improvement of Catholic schools following the transfer of responsibility to the state after 1918 was a slow increase in the educational level of successive generations of parents after the middle of the century. This became evident in our surveys as a greater rise in parental education in Catholic schools than in non-denominational schools. In 1952, the percentage where one or both of the parents had left full-time education at age 17 or older was 3 per cent in non-denominational schools but 1 per cent in Catholic schools. The ratio declined to about 2:1 in 1978 (13 per cent and 7 per cent), and to 1.2:1 in 1998 (33 per cent and 27 per cent). By that last date, the proportion who had parents with minimal education (leaving school at 15 or younger) was almost the same in the two sectors (17 per cent and 19 per cent). There were similar trends for social class. This social convergence was thus analogous to the convergence of historically defined sectors that was illustrated in Figure 3.7, and indeed the two were interrelated because of the differential impact on the Catholic sector of the move to comprehensive secondary schooling between the mid-1960s and the late 1970s. Before the 1960s, the Catholic sector had a lower proportion of students in senior-secondary schools than did the non-denominational public sector: in the 1952 survey, 36 per cent compared to 45 per cent. The discrepancy was even greater for the non-academic junior secondaries schools: in 1952, these contained 57 per cent of students in Catholic schools compared to 37 per cent in non-denominational schools.

The two sectors converged also in student attainment and progression because Catholic schools improved more rapidly than non-denominational schools, especially in the 1980s: Table 3.5. In all respects, there was convergence between the sectors. So this, too, is analogous to the changes with respect to the sectors defined by school history.

MEASUREMENT OF SOCIAL CLASS

We noted in Chapter 2 that the measure of social class which we have used in this book is not ideal sociologically, and that we have used it because it is the only version that is available for the whole series of surveys. However, as explained there, for the surveys from 1984 onwards, our analysis can be re-run

Table 3.5 School progression and attainment, by school denomination, 1952–98

% of each denomination	1+ pass at mid-secondary		Stay on voluntarily after 4th year		1+ pass at Higher		Pass 3+ Highers	
Year when respondent was aged 16	Non-denominational	Roman Catholic	Non-denominational	Roman Catholic	Non-denominational	Roman Catholic	Non-denominational	Roman Catholic
1952	11	6	13	7	9	4	6	2
1974–6	51	39	29	24	22	16	14	10
1976–8	59	49	33	26	25	19	17	11
1978–80	60	51	45	41	26	22	17	13
1980–2	65	58	43	45	26	24	17	13
1984	68	55	44	39	31	27	19	16
1986	68	64	44	44	32	28	20	16
1988	70	71	49	53	34	34	23	22
1990	69	63	53	54	38	38	27	26
1996	85	81	67	64	49	43	35	30
1998	85	84	67	66	50	48	37	34

using the newer National Statistics Socio-Economic Classification (NSSEC) in place of Registrar General class. In the estimates corresponding to the graphs, parental education was set now to be the modal values in the NSSEC classes (which were the same as in Table 2.4, except that, in the top class, the values were 'one 17' in 1988, and 'both 17' thereafter).

All the results were similar to those reported above. For example, in Figure 3.2 (attaining at least one mid-secondary award), the average difference for male students between the top and the middle classes in the years 1984–98 is 21 percentage points, and between the top and the lowest classes is 32 points. Using the three-class version of NSSEC, the corresponding differences were 21 points and 28 points. For female students, the average differences in Figure 3.2 are 11 and 24 points, and 14 and 21 points using NSSEC.

Another example is the comparison of school sectors in Figure 3.8 (attaining at least one Higher.) For male students in class III in Figure 3.8, the average proportion in the years 1990 and 1996 was 38 per cent in the former academic junior secondaries, and 25 per cent in the old secondaries, a difference of 13 points. The corresponding proportions for the intermediate category in the three-class version of NSSEC were 39 per cent and 27 per cent, a difference of 12 points. For female students, this difference was 11 per cent both in Figure 3.8 and using NSSEC.

Probably the main reason why the results have not been fundamentally affected by how we measure social class is that our models also include parental education. The combination of class and education probably gives greater validity to the principle underlying the Registrar General scheme that it measures social status and skill.

CONCLUSIONS

In a general sense, therefore, both social-class and sex differences narrowed significantly in the half-century covered by our surveys. For mid-secondary attainment, for staying on voluntarily beyond age 16, and for attainment in the senior years of secondary school, disparities narrowed, often markedly. The changes with respect to social class were mostly the same for female and male students. Even where there did remain social-class differences in overall attainment – such as in attaining any meaningful certification at senior-secondary level – the rise in attainment at low levels of social status was striking.

The secondary-school system probably became more meritocratic during the half-century, as we saw in the steepening of the slopes that related attainment in secondary school to intelligence measured at the end of primary. Moreover – despite recurrent utopian complaints (Sandel 2020) – merit-selection was, in this period, consistent with extending access (as shown more widely by Wooldridge (2021)). The ending of selection for secondary school could be interpreted in the same way. Doubts about the justice of merit-selection tend to ignore the possibility that, at successive stages of schooling, it is not a permanent policy, but part of a transition to universal access. The reducing levels of inequality contradict the pessimistic academic theories which have claimed that inequality never changes. Inequality may shift, may open up at advanced levels when it has been reduced at lower levels, and may change from being a form of segregation among schools to being a matter of what happens within them. But any such shifts open up new opportunities for students who would not have had them in a previous dispensation – such as the opportunity to learn at mid-secondary levels, the opportunity therefore also to compete at levels beyond that, or the opportunity at school to follow courses that used to be available only in highly selective institutions. Whatever may have happened at later ages – a question to which we return in Chapters 6 to 10 – these new experiences and opportunities at school reached a very large segment of the population.

However, the evidence that deliberate policy did any more than facilitate processes that were happening for other reasons is scant. There was no evidence that varying rates of schools' ending of selection had more than a small and transitional effect. This finding is not inconsistent with that by McPherson and Willms (1987), who concluded that the ending of selection led to some reduction of inequality with respect to social class and sex, because our results suggest that the ending of selection was one means by which long-term social changes had their effect. At the very end of the period, there may also be evidence that former low-status schools were particular effective at raising the attainment of students of Asian or African family origin. But, on the whole, the long-term changes were more striking than anything that could be attributed to policy. Conclusions of these kinds are also consistent with previous research on other countries, where a trajectory of steady change has been more commonly found than change forced by institutional reform.

We can also conclude that change was not driven solely by exogenous social change, because large shifts were evident in each of the social-status groups that we have included in the analysis. If, for example, rising levels of parental education and greater participation in non-manual employment had explained the changes over time, then, in each class group, there would have been minimal change over time. That is not what was observed. The educational consequences of social categories such as class and sex changed profoundly.

So there are implications of the analysis also for how to understand the ways in which policy operates. Policy can take a very long time to have its intended effect, and in the short term might even seem to have failed. For example, we noted that during the initial shift to comprehensive schooling the social-class gap in attainment at senior-secondary levels widened. But, 20 years later, there had been a clear narrowing. No short-term evaluation could have picked this up. Indeed, by the 1990s, the political arguments about comprehensive schooling in Scotland were long past (Murphy et al., 2015), and so any evaluation of it then would have had little effect on policy. The analysis also suggests that policies which work with the grain of a school's ethos are more likely to succeed in that school than policies which seek to transform it. The academic junior secondaries were perhaps closer than any other group of schools to the national Scottish policy of a comprehensive education that was firmly based on widening access to academic courses.

That then brings us to the final policy conclusion of this chapter, which is also a conclusion about history. Policy is rarely cast in isolation: it proceeds incrementally (Hill, 2004, pp. 147–50). The institutional effects of the 1960s and 1970s could be understood by paying attention not only to slow social change, but also to the legacies of older reforms. The legacies of secondary-school foundation early in the century persisted to the late 1970s, and in some respects to the 1990s in the success of the former academic junior secondaries. These schools had provided access to fully secondary-level courses as long ago as the early 1920s, at times in the face of discouragement from government (McPherson and Raab, 1988, p. 359). Our data cannot provide an explanation of how this probable academic ethos prepared them for a non-selective era, but, in the light of the statistical findings, it seems plausible that the schools had built up a tradition based on the core Scottish liberal premise that secondary education for all meant academic education for all (Gray et al. 1983, pp. 235–9; Neave, 1976). If that is the explanation, then it would be an instance of the power of what Meyer and Rowan (1977) call institutional myth, the collective belief that a distinguished record of academic success can offer advice on how to deal with successive waves of policy that seeks to modernise.

CHAPTER 4

School Curriculum: Liberal Education for Everyone?

DEMOCRATISING THE SCOTTISH TRADITION

Scotland has always prided itself on the breadth of its curriculum (Paterson, 2015a). Nevertheless, until the middle of the twentieth century, the humanism of this tradition was confined to a small, highly selected elite. What changed from that point – as we saw in Chapter 1 – was the gradual strengthening of a belief that democracy required broad education for every citizen. This principle did draw on respectable Scottish antecedents, in the so-called common-sense school of philosophy which grew in the late eighteenth century and dominated Scottish thinking about education in the nineteenth century (Paterson, 2015b). But never before had the task been faced of having to interpret that for all pupils.

In any society, the school curriculum is worth studying because it is the means by which the officially sanctioned aspects of its culture are handed on. One function of this is highly instrumental: pursuing a high-status curriculum tends to lead students into high-status universities and to highly influential and respected social roles in later life (Arum and Shavit, 1995; Duta et al., 2018; Iannelli, 2013; Iannelli and Duta, 2018; Klein et al., 2016; van de Werfhorst et al., 2002). Through former students' later civic and political engagement, the curriculum also can ultimately sustain the values which underpin democracy and a wide range of cultural activities (van de Werfhorst and Kraaykamp, 2001; Paterson, 2009b). In later chapters, we look at these long-term implications of what people do at school. Here, we use our surveys to investigate whether Scottish policy and practice on the curriculum were able to provide to everyone the kind of liberal breadth of learning that the Scottish tradition had extolled. The main empirical section of the chapter investigates the extent of successful access to a liberal curriculum as a result of the several waves of curricular reform between the early 1950s and the end of the century, looking at breadth, at liberal culture and also at vocational courses as a way of assessing whether relevance to employment was compatible with the liberal ideals.

LIBERAL CURRICULUM AND SOCIAL INEQUALITY: INTERNATIONAL EVIDENCE

A recurrent critique of comprehensive schooling in many countries has been that it has imposed on working-class children a curriculum that had been devised for an elite (Hargreaves, 1982), and that there has been, as a result, a strong association between academic success and social class. Liberal education, far from being liberating, has been thought to be alienating. The common conclusion has been scepticism about any attempts to broaden access to a liberal curriculum. This pessimism was influenced by the writings of the French sociologist Pierre Bourdieu – whose ideas we have already discussed in Chapter 3 – and the English sociologist of education Basil Bernstein. Bourdieu described a curriculum of this kind as symbolic violence, imposing an elite culture on subordinate social groups (Bourdieu and Passeron, 1977). Bernstein (2003) saw the school as a place where abstract language is the unquestioned norm, and yet is inaccessible to working-class children. According to these views, there is no possibility of widening access to liberal education (Ball, 1990; Hargreaves, 1982). One common inference was then the belief that a curriculum that would be relevant to everyone had to have vocational aims at its heart (Favretto, 2000), partly on the grounds that, as Arum and Shavit (1995) have shown, vocational courses could protect low-attaining students against unemployment upon leaving school.

Against these views was the long-standing advocacy of liberal education that informed a wide range of British political views in the twentieth century (Paterson, 2015a; Young, 2007). A quite different kind of French sociologist, Raymond Boudon (1974, p. 109), noted that one of the main functions of schooling has been precisely to overcome the traditional inequalities of access to liberal education. This does not mean, however, that liberal education has stagnated. Kamens et al. (1996) observe a worldwide tendency in the twentieth century to discard the old classical curricula of secondary school (which throughout Europe was centred on Latin) in favour of modernised versions of liberal education, emphasising mathematics, science and modern languages. One of the main divides was then between systems where students have very open choice of subjects (the paradigm of which is the USA), and those where a full secondary education requires that students follow a quite tightly prescribed combination of subjects (the epitome of which is the academic versions of the French baccalauréat). Similar modernising tendencies that have the aim of bringing about what DiMaggio (1982) called cultural mobility have been noted in England, France, Italy and the Netherlands (Barone, 2009;

Davies et al., 2008; de Graaf et al., 2000; Ichou and Vallet, 2011; Triventi et al., 2016). Cultural mobility is when children who have grown up in households in which the parents themselves left school at a young age can nevertheless have access to liberal culture through a school that seeks to provide it to everyone. Concomitantly, there has been a general decline in vocational programmes at secondary school, because these were believed to be incompatible with liberal education (Benavot, 1983).

The empirical question raised by these debates is whether educational reform has had any impact on the inequalities of access to the full liberal curriculum. The most common conclusion from research on many countries is that this kind of inequality has fallen, though not uniformly across curricular areas. The main effect has been through postponing selection into distinct tracks (Benavot, 1983, p. 74): indeed, as Barone (2009, p. 95) notes for Italy, a common policy has simply been to enforce a common curriculum during the compulsory phase of schooling. Ichou and Vallet (2011) found that, in France, the development of a wider range of baccalauréat programmes led to a decline of inequality of access to them. Gamoran et al. (1997) – discussing the USA – concluded that providing 'a serious, meaningful curriculum' could rise the attainment of low-achieving students from families in low-status social classes. This general tendency in curricular reform can be interpreted through the concept of opportunity to learn, which in practice is providing to students an adequate syllabus and teachers with the knowledge and skills to teach it effectively. When these aspects of opportunity to learn have been measured by researchers, the impact in reducing inequality has been confirmed (Boscardin et al., 2005; Reeves, 2012).

Despite these tendencies, inequality of successfully completing a liberal curriculum does remain. Ichou and Vallet (2011) found that inequality in access to the highest-status programmes in France (mathematics and science) has widened, reinforcing the inequality that had belonged to the traditional baccalauréat. Davies et al. (2008, p. 237) found persistent differentiation by social class in the ostensibly common curriculum of England that has been in place for students aged 14–16 since the 1980s. While tracked programmes, such as the baccalauréat, can maintain inequality, so also can apparently free choice.

Explanations of these remaining inequalities have proposed mechanisms that avoid the cultural determinism of Bourdieu and his followers. Ichou and Vallet (2011) adapt from Lucas (2001) the idea of effectively maintained inequality. According to this, when access to a particular level of education becomes very widespread, inequality takes the new form of distinctions among informal or formal tracks within it. Thus, whereas the advantage of the highest-status social classes in France used to be represented by their access to the baccalauréat, it is now expressed through their dominance of particular versions of it – especially the literary and scientific versions, as distinct from the technical ones. Davies et al. (2008) note that, within the common national curriculum in England, students from low-status social classes tend to opt for subjects that have easier examinations.

A version of these debates applies to sex differences, but with the contrast that there is no doubting the extent of change in the last quarter of the twentieth century. In most countries where evidence is available, invidious associations between subject choices and sex have largely vanished (Buchmann et al., 2008, p. 324). Moreover, the influences which confer remaining advantages on high-status students might also do the same for female students, because they have been found by Dumais (2002, p. 44) to be more likely than males to take part in high-status cultural activities.

Liberal Education in Scotland

Scotland provides a test of the claim that access to a liberal curriculum could be widened to social groups that have traditionally been excluded from it. During the transition to comprehensive schooling, the strong consensus was to widen access to a modernised but essentially unchanged structure and content of school subjects (Croxford, 1994; Gamoran, 1996; McPherson and Willms, 1987, p. 532). That curriculum had always emphasised academic breadth and liberal culture, as we saw in Chapter 1, even though traditionally this had been restricted to a small elite (Gray et al., 1983, pp. 86–102). The early twentieth-century reforms had extended the core liberal curriculum to those secondary schools that became the academically selective part of the school system in the middle of the century. Through competition with these schools, the ideal of a broad curriculum also came to lie at the heart of most of the grant-aided and independent schools. Since these schools had students who were predominantly from high-status social classes, this tended to reinforce the high social status of a curriculum that was academic and broad.

The mechanism by which the Scottish curriculum was enforced traditionally was mainly through the examinations for the Leaving Certificate. The essential feature of that Certificate – as noted in Chapter 1 – was that it tried to combine a structure based on individual subjects that was characteristic of the English and US systems, with the enforced breadth that was typical of the main systems of continental Europe (Paterson, 2011). In order to understand how Scotland responded to the international democratising pressures on the curriculum in the 1970s and after, it is necessary to measure the curriculum in ways that are consistent with this ambivalent tradition. Therefore our main criteria for assessing access to the curriculum relate to breadth, while also paying attention to specific individual subjects.

Until 1950, breadth was defined in official regulations as the required group of subjects that a student had to pass at either Higher or Lower level in order to be awarded a Leaving Certificate. As we noted in Chapter 1, this required English, mathematics, a science and a language, with the highest-status version having two languages. However, changes to subjects and syllabuses make this anachronistic for our period. The subjects that came to be called history and geography used to be examined as part of English, but now were distinct; and a new subject called modern studies (essentially politics and sociology) was inaugurated in 1962. There was the same slow shift away from Latin and Greek to modern languages as was found in other countries (Cha, 1991), and a decline in the incidence of taking two languages (Gray et al., 1983, pp. 87–9). The science subjects were changing (for example with growing numbers of students taking biology, leading to a decline in botany and zoology). So we will use what Gray et al. (1983, p. 88) call modified breadth: English, mathematics, at least one science, and at least one of a language, a social science and an aesthetic subject (music, art, etc.). This breadth is then our definition of a modernised liberal curriculum. Completing such a programme is defined here at two levels: as having attained that combination of awards in the mid-secondary-level courses that were in existence in the survey year (Lower, Ordinary Grade, Standard Grade, Intermediate 1, Intermediate 2), or as having attained it at the Higher level (or, in 1952, Higher or Lower to reflect the grouping practices that had ended only one year previously). In the surveys up to the end of the century, the data include information on all the subjects which students took. In the survey used for 2016 (people born in 2000), subjects taken by fewer than 35 people in the survey are not recorded, in order to protect the anonymity of the respondents to the survey. Some of the percentages in Table 4.4 below may thus be underestimated, but the discrepancy will be slight because all the main school subjects that contribute to the curricular categories in that table were taken by more than 35 survey respondents.

Important though breadth has been, we also consider three further aspects of the curriculum in order to understand how it related to opportunities and to cultural aims. One concerns the core place which the subject of English played in Scottish schooling. In Scotland until the 1990s, this subject was much more than the study of language even after the removal of history and geography from its syllabus (Paterson, 2004). It was what a government paper on it described in 1952 as the inculcation of a liberal culture (Scottish Education Department, 1952, p. 24). The core of the syllabus was always the study of literary texts, and, through these, reflection on society, culture and ethics. It was an introduction to humanistic learning, and thus was somewhat akin to philosophy in the French system. So, for the second half of the twentieth century, we also record attaining awards in English, while also investigating the experience of the social subjects now that they had come to be independent of English.

Much debate about sex differences in the curriculum internationally has concentrated on science and languages. When given the choice, girls have been much more likely than boys to study languages (Croxford, 1994). Generally, boys have been more likely to study science, although, within the main science subjects at school, girls have preferred biology, boys have preferred physics, and chemistry has moved towards parity (Buchmann et al., 2008). The question therefore arises of whether the Scottish aspiration towards a broad curriculum for everyone managed to even out these sex differences in languages and science.

The final curricular topic which we consider is the relationship between liberal education and vocational study. As in other countries, a concern with vocational relevance lasted right through the Scottish introduction of comprehensive education (Raffe, 1984a). So we also consider achievement of vocationally relevant certificates, defined as awards in those courses which came under the heading 'technological studies' in the Standard Grade framework (Tinklin, 2000). This includes not only technical courses strictly defined (such as engineering, woodwork or metalwork), but also those more commonly called home economics or secretarial studies. We do not include computer science, but rather group it with mathematical subjects. There were barely any such vocational courses in 1952, and so this series starts with the 1974-6 survey.

In constructing each of these measures at the mid-secondary level, we assume that anyone who passed a Higher Grade in a subject had in effect passed at least one course at that lower level. The reason we have to do this is that some students (especially in the early years) bypassed the lower grades of examination on the way to attempting Higher Grades.

Running through all the debate on this topic is an assumption that deliberate policy is what makes a difference to the curriculum that pupils experience. But in a curricular structure that attempted to combine pupil choice with breadth, and that tried to enforce breadth for all pupils only towards the end of the century, the question of how influential policy actually is remains open. The introduction of Standard Grade gives an opportunity to test this, because schools implemented it at different rates between 1986 and the early 1990s. In this connection, we build on the work of Gamoran (1996) and Croxford (1994) to assess whether the reform was responsible for changes in the social distribution of breadth of study.

Extension of the Curriculum

For most of this analysis, we look only at the half-century from the early 1950s until the end of the century. The data source for 2016 does not allow a measure at mid-secondary level to be constructed that would be comparable to the data for that period, mainly because it surveyed students at around age 17, when those who were still in school would have been in school sixth year. The survey thus missed the results of the approximate 13 per cent of students who sat mid-secondary courses in that school year (Scottish Qualifications Authority, 2016, table SCQF5). So we postpone discussion of what happened in the new century until the end of this chapter.

The changes over time in these various measures of the curriculum are shown in Tables 4.1 (for mid-secondary) and 4.2 (for Higher). All the measures show large increases from the 1950s to the end of the century, but to varying extents. At mid-secondary level, only 2 per cent attained breadth in the early 1950s. That rose to 17 per cent in the mid-1970s, and to a quarter in the mid-1980s on the eve of the Standard Grade reform. It then doubled to one-half with that reform by the end of the century. The jump between 1990 and 1996 shows the effect of the new curricular framework. English – the core of the liberal curriculum – included three-quarters of pupils at the end of the century. The increase in languages was similar to that for breadth, while mathematics outstripped that of breadth until the subject of arithmetic was dropped in the Standard Grade reforms of the late 1980s. Social subjects rose in a similar way to mathematics, helped by the addition of modern studies to history and geography after 1960. The change in natural science was the most striking of all, from 5 per cent in 1952, through only one in four or five during the shift to comprehensive schooling, but reaching two-thirds at the century's end.

The rise of breadth at Higher was gentler, through 8 per cent in the mid-1980s to 15 per cent by end of century (Table 4.2). By that date, at Higher, four out of ten gained English. So in that sense liberal culture, having become pervasive at mid-secondary, was quite common at levels beyond that. One-quarter passed Higher mathematics, a similar proportion to those passing science and social subjects, and a rise from 3–5 per cent in half a century. But in languages, after an initial doubling to the mid-1970s in line with the other changes at Higher, there was little further change thereafter.

This extension of the academic curriculum and of breadth at mid-secondary and at Higher was not at the expense of attainment in vocational subjects. At mid-secondary, until the 1990s, the proportion with a vocational qualification was in every year at least as high as the proportion with breadth. Vocational attainment at Higher rose very similarly to breadth. These firm trends show that the system as a whole could combine a broad, liberal curriculum with opportunities for vocational attainment. The same combination was true for a quarter of individuals at mid-secondary level by the end of century (Table 4.2): the proportion with both breadth and vocational attainment at mid-secondary rose through the comprehensive reforms, with a boost from the curricular framework. Nevertheless, only very small proportions had both breadth and vocational attainment at Higher: under 2 per cent to 1990s, rising only to 4–5 per cent in the final years.

Thus participation in a broad, liberal curriculum did grow markedly at mid-secondary. This did not happen at the expense of vocational attainment.

Table 4.1 Aspects of passes in the mid-secondary curriculum, 1952–2002

% of sample passing each subject or group of subjects	Breadth	English	Mathematics*	Natural science	Language	Social subject	Vocational	Both breadth and vocational
Year when respondent was aged 16								
1952	2	10	9	5	8	8	NA	NA
1974–6	17	38	36	22	17	27	23	5
1976–8	22	44	45	27	20	33	30	8
1978–80	20	41	44	28	20	33	29	6
1980–2	24	45	48	30	21	36	35	10
1984	26	45	50	33	23	38	37	11
1986	28	50	52	37	22	41	38	14
1988	31	51	53	40	23	43	39	15
1990	30	55	42	41	28	45	33	13
1996	47	70	55	66	51	54	47	27
1998	50	73	56	68	55	57	47	29
2002	57	80	67	68	63	67	63	40

Notes:
*Mathematics O grade included arithmetic O grade, which ended after 1990.
Breadth means holding a pass at mid-secondary level in English, mathematics, a natural science, and at least one social subject, language or aesthetic subject.
Percentages weighted. For sample sizes, see Table 2.1 (along with 3,220 for 2002). NA=not available.

Table 4.2 Aspects of passes in Higher curriculum, 1952–2002

% of sample passing each subject or group of subjects	Breadth	English	Mathematics	Natural science	Language	Social subject	Vocational	Both breadth and vocational
Year when respondent was aged 16								
1952	2	8	5	4	4	3	NA	0.4
1974–6	5	18	9	10	8	12	5	0.5
1976–8	6	20	12	13	8	14	6	0.6
1978–80	6	20	13	14	7	14	7	0.6
1980–2	6	19	12	12	7	12	8	1.1
1984	8	24	14	16	7	15	9	1.3
1986	8	22	16	17	7	17	10	1.5
1988	10	28	17	19	7	19	10	1.9
1990	11	32	19	22	8	23	11	3.5
1996	14	38	26	26	9	25	17	4.3
1998	15	39	27	27	9	27	18	5.0
2002	13	32	25	25	10	29	21	

Notes:
*Breadth in 1974–98 means holding a Higher pass in English, mathematics, a natural science, and at least one social subject, language or aesthetic subject. Breadth in 1952 is defined across Lower Grade and Higher Grade courses.
Percentages weighted, and are of the whole leaver-cohort or age-cohort (not only those who entered the senior years). For sample sizes, see Table 2.1 (along with 3,220 for 2002). NA=not available.

However, if the highest-status version of breadth is taken as the yardstick – its attainment at Higher Grade level – then it still was reaching only about one in seven students in the late 1990s. The rate of increase of breadth at Higher had not slowed, but it remained at only on average a percentage point every two years. Even if we generously say that the core of liberal education could be encapsulated in Higher English, we still have to conclude that only a minority of students attained that. In both these senses, the ideal of academic learning for everyone was far from being realised.

Changes in the Social Basis of the Curriculum

If theories of the kind promulgated by Bourdieu and others are correct, then it would be expected that the expansion of breadth and of the liberal curriculum would be dominated by people with well-educated parents who were in professional occupations. The proportion of students in these groups grew, as we saw in Chapter 2 (Tables 2.1 and 2.2).

Figure 4.1 shows the trends in attaining breadth at mid-secondary level, classified by sex and social class. There was a rise in all classes, but the rise was strongest in the highest-status class, reaching over 80 per cent for females and over 70 per cent for males. The rise was far behind, though not insubstantial, for the other class groups, to at least about a quarter for both male and female. For English at mid-secondary – the rudiment of liberal culture – there was much less class differentiation than for breadth (especially for females), with the lowest percentage at the end of the century (for low-status males) being around 50 per cent, compared to over 90 per cent at that date for both sexes in the highest-status classes. But there was no narrowing over time. There was then a clear sex gap by 1998 in the middling and lowest classes: 80 per cent female compared to 60 per cent male for the middle group, just under 70 per cent compared to just under 50 per cent for the lowest class. The pattern for social subjects resembled that of English, with slightly greater social-class inequality than English for girls in the 1990s.

Mathematics and science were broadly similar to English. In mathematics, the high-status class moved ahead first, reaching 60 per cent or higher for males in the mid-1970s and for females in the early 1980s. The other class groups caught up somewhat by the 1990s, but then were left behind as people from the highest class moved further ahead. Within each class group, by the late 1990s the sex difference had vanished. On science, there remained sex differences in the sense that the specific sciences taken by boys and girls varied. Girls were much more likely to gain a biology certificate than boys (47 per cent against 20 per cent in 1998), physics was almost the mirror image (21 per cent against 40 per cent), and in chemistry by the 1990s the sex difference had disappeared (36 per cent and 35 per cent), having been 11 per cent against

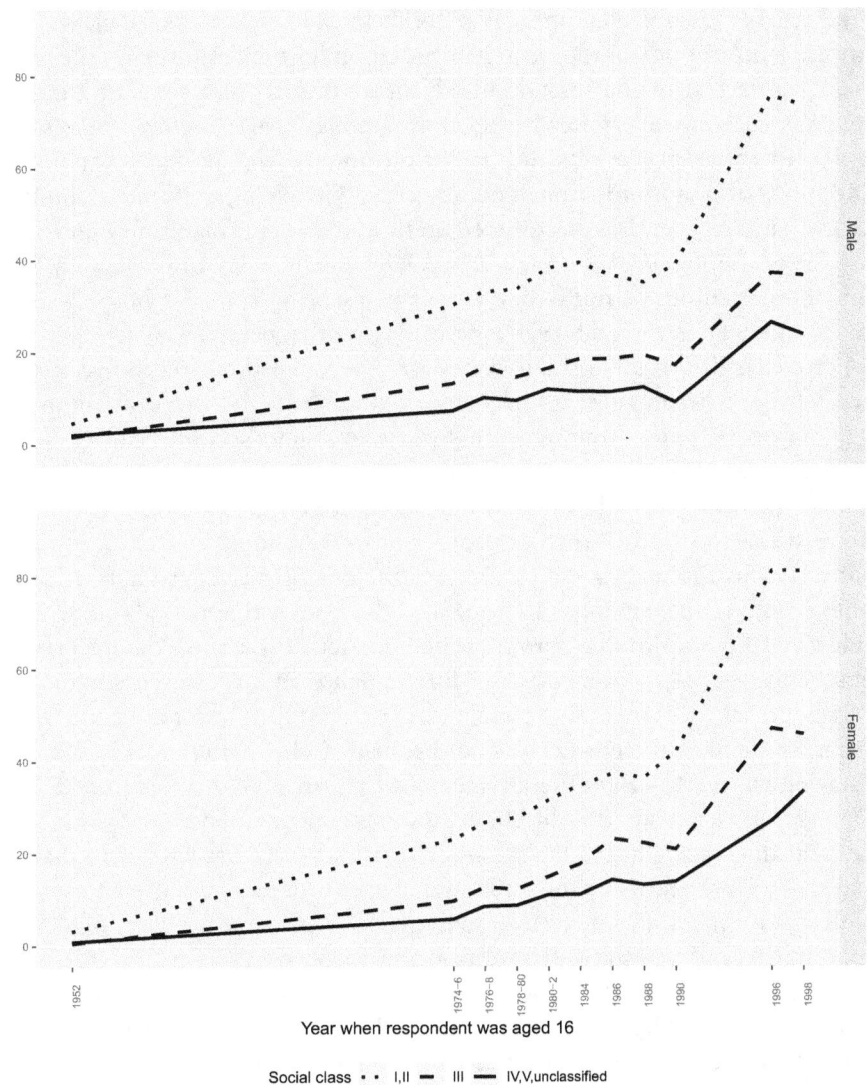

Figure 4.1 Percentage attaining breadth at mid-secondary, by sex and social class, 1952–98
For each class, parental education is set to the modal value in each year: see Table 2.5.
Average standard error: 2.1.

18 per cent in 1976. The new subject of general science, invented in the 1980s, played only a very minor role, just 7 per cent gaining a pass in it in 1998. In languages, by contrast, the overall sex difference did not vanish, and the class difference remained high, but here, too, there was an increase in all the social groups.

The curricular changes in the compulsory period of schooling thus present a paradox. On the one hand, access to a broad curriculum steadily widened, as did access to its main components. Pupils from low-status social classes had unprecedented opportunities to gain recognition for their study of a wide range of subjects. Most of the historic disadvantage of girls had gone, and indeed the lowest attainment of breadth was now among boys from low-status social classes. In that sense, access to breadth did indeed widen. Yet, on the other hand, inequality not only remained but grew. The changes at mid-secondary, and the paradox, can thus be summed up by a simple contrast from Figure 4.1. Girls from the lowest-status classes in 1998 were as likely to be successful in a broad curriculum at mid-secondary level as boys from the highest-status classes had been in the mid-1970s (percentages of respectively 34 per cent and 30 per cent). But in 1998, high-status girls were 3.4 times more likely to be successful in a broad curriculum than low-status boys (81 per cent compared to 24 per cent). Thus, although access widened at mid-secondary level, it also became more unequal.

At Higher, the class differences were even clearer (Figure 4.2). By far the strongest rise in breadth from the late 1980s to the end of the century was for students from the highest-status classes, reaching 30 per cent for both sexes. Other groups remained under 10 per cent, a rise from earlier periods but with no evidence of any specific boost from the new curricular framework in the preceding school stage. This widening class differentiation in breadth was also evident in analysis that was confined to people who had stayed on beyond the minimum leaving age, and so the change was not because of class differences in the rates of staying on. Social-class differentiation for English at Higher was greater than at mid-secondary; again this differentiation was similar among those who stayed on. As at mid-secondary, the pattern for social subjects was similar to that for English – a large rise for high-status students (to around one-half), and an only gentle rise for medium-status (to at most about 15 per cent for boys, and 24 per cent for girls) and low-status (10 per cent and 16 per cent).

Passes in Higher mathematics followed a similar trajectory to mathematics at mid-secondary. Higher science resembled mathematics in this respect, and also in the sense that the sex difference had all but vanished by the 1990s. There remained a difference in the kinds of science which male and female students took. In biology, the proportion of high-status female students who attained a Higher pass grew more than the proportion of high-status males: between 1976 and 1998, the rate rose from 6 per cent to 36 per cent for females, and from 4 per cent to 18 per cent for males. But the class gaps were much greater than this twofold sex difference: the ratio of high-to-low classes went from 5:1 to 4.5:1 for females, and from 4.5:1 to 6:1 for males. In physics, the proportion passing rose from 17 per cent to 35 per cent for high-status males, and from 5 per cent to 17 per cent for high-status females. The high-to-low-class ratio went from 6:1 to 4:1 among males, and from 8:1 to 5:1 among females. In chemistry, the class ratio was fairly stable at 5:1 among males, and at 6:1

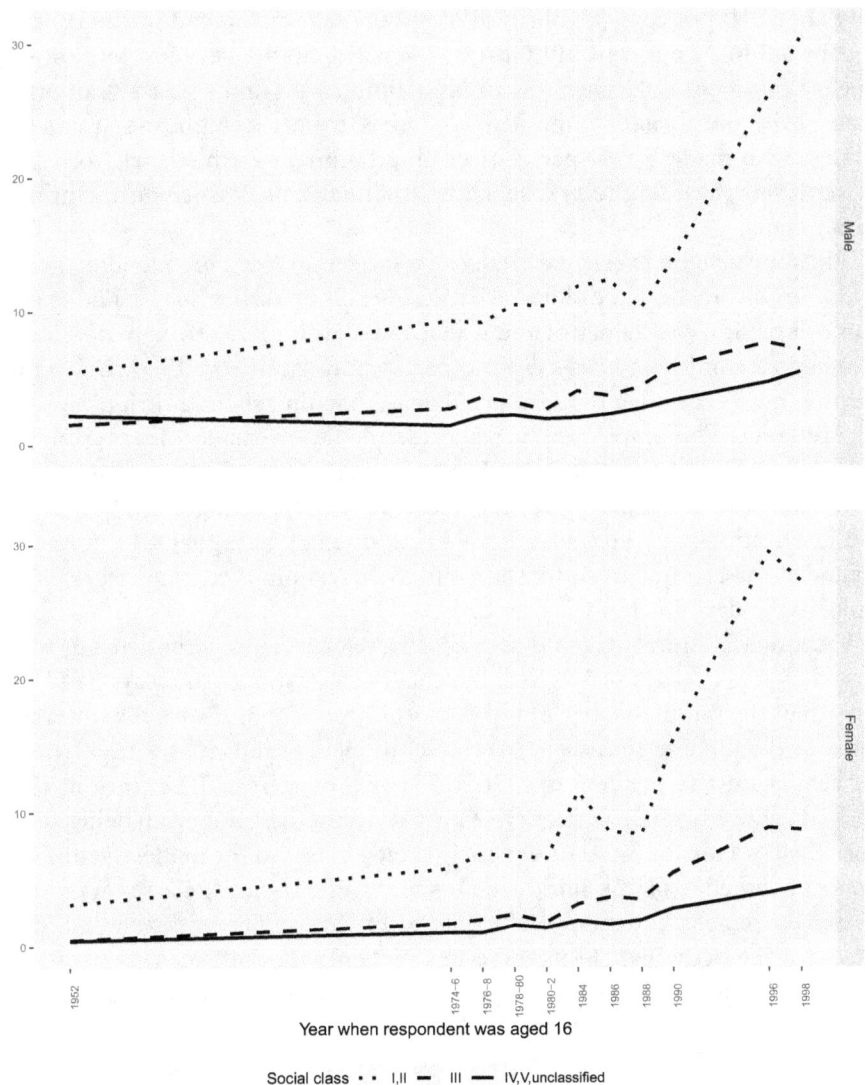

Figure 4.2 Percentage attaining breadth at Higher, by sex and social class, 1952–98
For each class, parental education is set to the modal value in each year: see Table 2.5.
Average standard error: 1.4.

from among females, while in 1998 there was very little sex difference in the percentages passing Higher chemistry among high-status students: 28 per cent male and 24 per cent female. Thus, in all these respects, the sex difference at the end of the century was much less than the class difference.

Higher language showed the largest sex difference of any of these subjects, though at low levels even for female students. Even high-class males had only about 10 per cent passing a Higher language at the end of the century, in contrast to 24 per cent of high-class females. So the very low level of language attainment at Higher was an issue both of sex and of class. Languages came to be dominated numerically by girls from the highest-status social classes, who made up 40 per cent of all attainment at this level from 1984 onwards, far ahead of the next social group (medium-class females, at around 20 per cent).

Thus the general curricular changes in the senior years of secondary school could be said to have amplified what happened in earlier years. The expansion of breadth, mathematics and science was even more strongly dominated by students from high-status classes than at mid-secondary. English was only slightly more accessible than these subjects, reaching about a fifth of low-status students. Therefore, however successful the extension of a meaningful curriculum at mid-secondary level, it remained largely the preserve of quite privileged students at senior levels. These curricular changes at Higher level had implications for the social distribution of entry to higher education as it expanded massively, and so we return to the question of curricular breadth at senior-secondary level in Chapter 8.

Vocational attainment at mid-secondary level was less differentiated by social class than was breadth or English, but the lowest-status class always had lower rates than the middle-status and high-status groups. For males, the difference between the highest-status and lowest-status class groups rose gently from 31 per cent against 16 per cent in 1976 to 53 per cent against 30 per cent in 1998; class III moved from 22 per cent to 45 per cent, thus shifting from being somewhat closer to the lowest-status group to being closer to the highest-status one. This convergence of the middle-status and highest-status classes was much clearer for female students, reaching almost identical percentages in the mid-1990s (in the high 50s). Thus there was certainly no evidence that vocational attainment was disproportionately for low-status groups. That class reach of vocational attainment was confirmed by the capacity to combine breadth and vocational courses: all class groups showed a rise, and by the mid-1990s all had a greater percentage with this combination than the high-status groups had in the mid-1970s. At Higher, vocational attainment was a distinctly high-class experience, especially among male students. Because this reinforced the same pattern in attaining breadth at Higher, the same high-class dominance was also true of those who achieved both, although at very low levels (in 1998, only 12 per cent of high-status males and 8 per cent of high-status females, in contrast to just 1–2 per cent in other classes, and 1–2 per cent in all classes up to 1990). So we can say that vocational attainment did not suffer from the development of a broader academic curriculum in the middle years of secondary schooling, and also that vocational attainment was not at all confined to low-status social groups.

The Effects of Policy

Our final topic is whether any of these changes may be attributed to policy. We have reached one such conclusion already, relating to the clear evidence that mid-secondary breadth increased following the implementation of the curricular framework from the late 1980s. A subsidiary aspect of that relates to the associated introduction of Standard Grade which Gamoran (1996) and Croxford (1994) have shown led to a widening of the social basis of access to English, mathematics and science considered as individual subjects.

Following Gamoran's research, we look at whether schools which were early adopters of Standard Grade had any distinct effect on curricular breadth. Gamoran classified each school according to when it adopted Standard Grade for each of the main subjects. We use his classification of adopting English Standard Grade in 1988 because of the centrality of that subject and because that date was at the height of the reforming period; so this information about English is used merely as an indication of the schools' general orientation to curricular innovation. On this basis, we define three categories of schools: those which, for English, had fully adopted Standard Grade in time for the survey of 1988, those which had not yet adopted Standard Grade for any pupils, and those which combined Standard Grade and Ordinary Grade at that date. We call these early, late and middle adopters of the reform. This information is available only for education authority schools, not for independent schools.

There are two broad patterns corresponding to the stage at which each school made the transition to Standard Grade. One is for the non-vocational outcomes, illustrated in Table 4.3 for mid-secondary breadth. On the one hand, after the reform had started (that is, in the period 1986–98), the social-class gap in attainment of breadth by male pupils was lower in the early adopters (a gap of 28.2 percentage points) than in the late adopters (36.8 points), a difference of 8.6. The same was true for female pupils (31.3 points compared to 36.7, a difference of 5.5). But this difference of inequality was probably already present before the reform (though less strongly): the corresponding differences in the class gaps in the period 1952–84 were 3.3 for males and 4.1 for females.

Moreover, the lower gap in the early adopters in 1986–98 was mainly due to poorer performance by high-status pupils in these schools than in the late adopters: 41.4 per cent compared to 52.5 per cent for males, and 51.3 per cent compared to 56.9 per cent for females. This, too, was a pattern which pre-dated the reform. For the medium-status and low-status students, there was no reliable evidence of differences in either period between the early and late adopters. For passing English at mid-secondary, and breadth and English at Higher, the pattern was similar to Table 4.3 though less pronounced: after the reform, lower inequality in the early adopters than in the late adopters, explained by lower attainment by high-status students.

Table 4.3 Percentage attaining breadth at mid-secondary level, by social class, sex, and stage at which school made the transition to Standard Grade. Education-authority schools only

Male

Class	1952–84			1986–98		
	Early adopter	Late adopter	Difference	Early adopter	Late adopter	Difference
I, II	23.8	29.0	5.2	41.4	52.5	11.1
III	11.0	13.8	2.9	22.5	24.8	2.4
IV, V, unclassified	7.0	9.0	1.9	13.2	15.7	2.5
Class gap (high–low)	16.8	20.0	3.3	28.2	36.8	8.6

Female

	1952–84			1986–98		
	Early adopter	Late adopter	Difference	Early adopter	Late adopter	Difference
I, II	19.0	24.7	5.8	51.3	56.9	5.6
III	9.2	11.9	2.7	32.8	31.5	-1.3
IV, V, unclassified	6.2	7.9	1.7	20.0	20.2	0.1
Class gap (high–low)	12.8	16.8	4.1	31.3	36.7	5.5

Notes:
Early and late adopters of Standard Grade reform in 1988: see text.
For each class, parental education is set to the modal value in each class in each year: see Table 2.5.
Average standard error of differences: I, II: 2.7; III and IV, V, unclassified: 1.7; class gaps: 2.5.

For the vocational outcomes at mid-secondary level, by contrast, there was no reliable evidence of any difference of inequality between the early and late adopters: the observed differences could have occurred by chance. There was weak evidence that the early adopters were more effective than the late adopters in getting low-status males to achieve vocational qualifications: after the reform, the proportion of that social group with this attainment was 30 per cent in the early adopters but 24.6 per cent in the late adopters (standard error about 3), whereas before the reform there was no difference in this respect between these two groups of schools.

In short, the early adopters of Standard Grade were perhaps relatively less effective than other schools at providing a broad liberal curriculum to students from high-status classes, and were no different from other schools in providing that for lower-status groups, or in providing vocational attainment to any class group except possibly for low-status males. The pre-existing difference in these early adopters probably tells us more about the process by which Standard Grade was implemented than about its effects, being adopted first in schools which had relatively low attainment for all social groups.

A second way in which we ask the question about the effects of policy is by investigating any legacies of reforms to schooling before the comprehensive period. In Chapter 3, we investigated these legacies for general attainment and progression. Here we look again at breadth, English and vocational attainment. The analysis now includes the independent schools. Figure 4.3 illustrates, for breadth, how long it took for the curricular legacies of the earlier policy changes in the public-sector schools to be ended, just as in Chapter 3. Consider first the public-sector schools, exemplified by the two categories of these schools which are picked out in the figure: pre-twentieth-century secondaries and the academic junior secondaries. As in Chapter 3 with overall attainment, the merging of the historical sectors of the education authority schools happened by the early 1980s after a persisting hierarchy between the early 1950s and the mid-1970s.

Similarly to Figure 4.3, this was also true for other outcomes – attaining mid-secondary English, and attaining breadth or English at Higher. Comprehensive schooling merged these legacies into a common curriculum for the first time, by the mid-1980s. There was one partial exception: in vocational attainment at Higher, for both male and female high-class students, the gap between these two historical sectors did not vanish until the 1990s. With this exception, therefore, the convergence of sectors happened before the Standard Grade reforms.

Now consider also the independent schools in Figure 4.3. Being smaller, there is more random fluctuation from year to year in the sample data from them, but it is clear that, at each level of social class, they had higher attainment of breadth than the other schools, probably mainly because of selection that is not fully allowed for by controlling for class. But for high-status students, the public-sector schools had almost caught up by end of century, especially for female students. That pattern was similarly true of mid-secondary English, breadth at Higher, and English Higher. The pattern was very different for vocational attainment, where, by the 1990s, the independent schools were no better than the academic junior secondaries at mid-secondary for all levels of social class and both sexes. For example, in the lowest-status class group, the average 1990s percentage for low-status male students was 35 per cent in the former academic junior secondaries and 29 per cent in the independent schools. For female students, the percentages were 48 per cent and 44 per cent. In classes I and II, the independent schools were firmly behind both the old secondaries and the academic junior secondaries, with around 30 per cent compared to over 50 per cent (average standard errors 5.3). So the independent schools might be said to have inherited the traditions of liberal breadth, but only for a highly selected minority and – unlike in the public-sector schools – at the expense of vocational attainment. The former academic junior secondaries, by contrast, had managed to combine both types of curriculum.

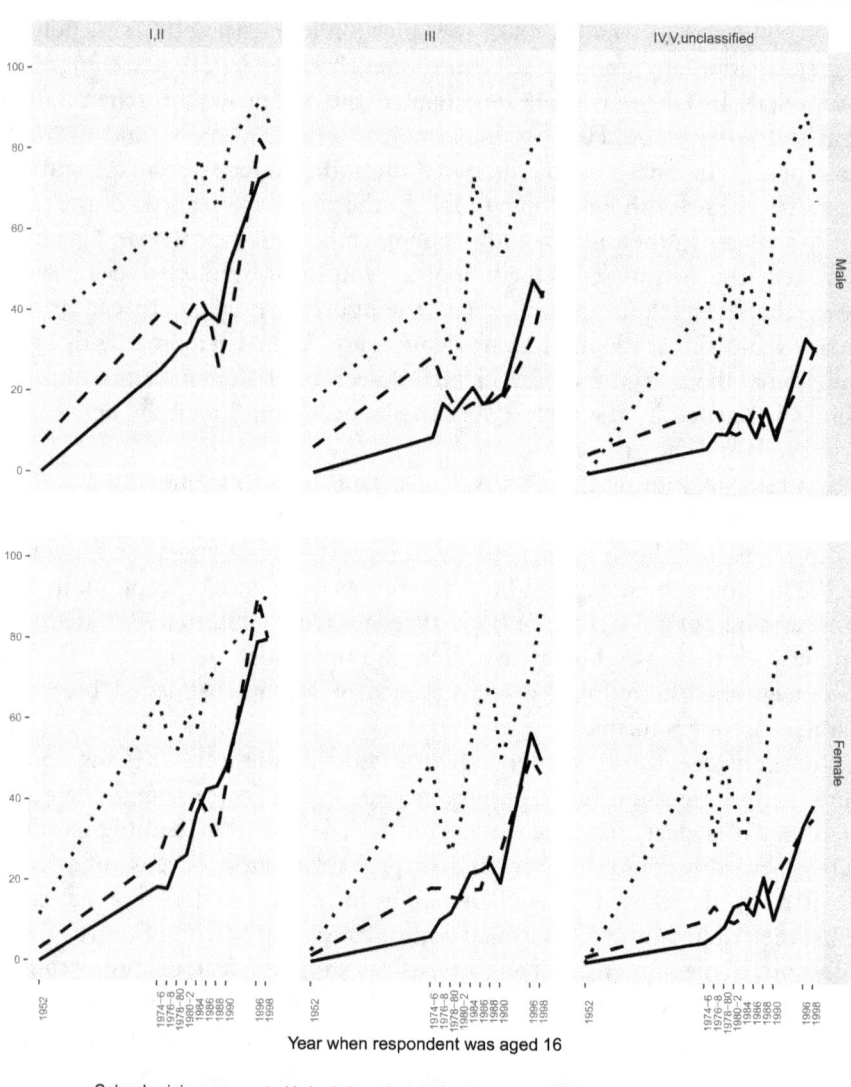

Figure 4.3 Percentage attaining breadth at mid-secondary, by sex, social class and selected school origins, 1952–98
For each class, parental education is set to the modal value in each year: see Table 2.5.
Average standard error: grant-aided or independent, 12; old secondary, 4.1; academic junior secondary, 4.0.

The institutional legacies also concerned Catholic schools. Chapter 3 showed that the aim of integrating pupils in Catholic schools into the mainstream was achieved so far as broad attainment was concerned, with the Catholic sector benefiting particularly from the move to comprehensive schooling after the 1960s. Something the same was true for breadth. Before the ending of selection, non-denominational schools had higher percentages attaining breadth than Catholic schools, especially among high-status pupils. That distinction disappeared after the late 1970s. For vocational attainment, the convergence took about a decade longer.

What Happened in the New Century?

The reforms to the curriculum which took place in the second decade of the new century make it impossible to construct a consistent series at mid-secondary level. The main reason is the replacement of the levels of Standard Grade with different courses and modes of assessment. Instead of the unified system in which, in principle, every pupil took part, with outcomes differentiated into Credit, General and Foundation, there were now three kinds of course, with National 5 corresponding approximately to Credit, National 4 to General and National 3 to Foundation. This fragmentation was the first deliberate reversal to the slow tendency since the advent of the Ordinary Grade in the early 1960s to bring all pupils into a common framework of learning and thus a common experience of school.

In order to cast the recent reforms in the best possible light, however, we look only at National 4 and 5, and redefine 'sitting' in Standard Grade up to 1998 as having gained an award at levels 1–4. For the certificates before Standard Grade, we simply define 'sitting' as the same as in Chapter 3. This is a conservative measure of the achievements of the Standard Grade policy in that, in the definition of 'sitting', it does not count people who attempted assessment at the General or Credit level of Standard Grade and failed to gain an award at any level 1–4; but it allows somewhat valid comparison with having sat National 4 or 5 in 2016. The result of defining sitting in this way is in Figure 4.4, which suggests that there was broad stability in the new century, perhaps with some decline in the highest-status class. In other words, there was a halt to half a century of expanding access to a broad liberal education at mid-secondary level, and no convergence of the highest-status and lowest-status social classes after the rise of inequality in the 1990s.

Measuring breadth at Higher does not suffer from this problem of comparability. Again, the 2016 survey allows us to consider only studying, not passing. The results for breadth and the subjects that constitute it are shown in Table 4.4 (which is for sitting subjects, not passing them as in Table 4.2). The increase of the 1980s and 1990s continued, but at a slower pace: for example, whereas in the 18 years from 1980 to 1998 the proportion sitting a breadth of subjects more than doubled (a rise of 11 percentage points), the increase in the following 18 years was a rise of only 15 per cent (or 3 percentage points). Similar comments can be made about each of the subject areas. There was also little change in the social distribution of breadth, shown in Figure 4.5 for attempting a broad range of Highers. As in Figure 4.4 for the mid-secondary

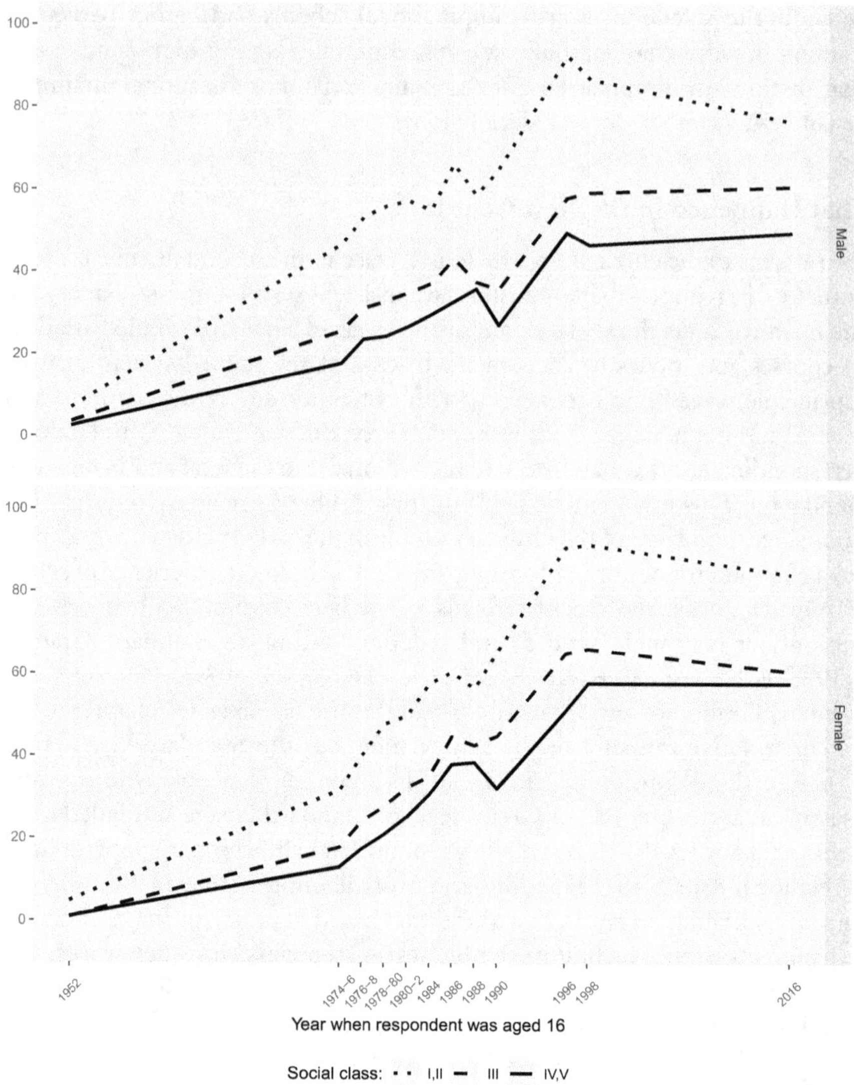

Figure 4.4 Percentage attempting breadth at mid-secondary (excluding Foundation-level Standard Grade*), by sex and social class, 1952–2016
*That is, an award at Foundation level is not counted as having sat the subject.
For each class, parental education is set to the modal value in each year: see Table 2.5.
Average standard error: 3.4.

level, the sharp rise of social-class inequality which occurred in the 1990s was not mitigated.

There is a final reason to be somewhat pessimistic about developments after the turn of the century. The triennial results for Scotland of the Programme

Table 4.4 Aspects of sitting Higher curriculum, 1952–2016

Percentage sitting	Breadth*	English	Mathematics	Natural science	Social subject	Language	Aesthetic subject
Year when respondent was aged 16							
1952	2	9	5	4	3	5	1
1974–6	8	25	14	14	16	10	3
1976–8	9	28	17	17	18	10	3
1978–80	9	28	17	18	17	9	4
1980–2	9	28	17	18	17	9	4
1984	14	34	22	24	22	10	7
1986	12	29	23	24	23	9	8
1988	13	36	21	24	23	9	11
1990	16	41	26	28	29	11	13
1996	19	49	32	34	31	11	19
1998	20	49	33	35	32	10	21
2002	18	44	32	33	35	12	20
2016	23	64	39	41	44	10	24

Notes:

Percentages weighted. For sample sizes, see Table 2.1 (along with 3,220 for 2002).
*Breadth means sitting English, mathematics, a natural science, and at least one social subject, language or aesthetic subject.

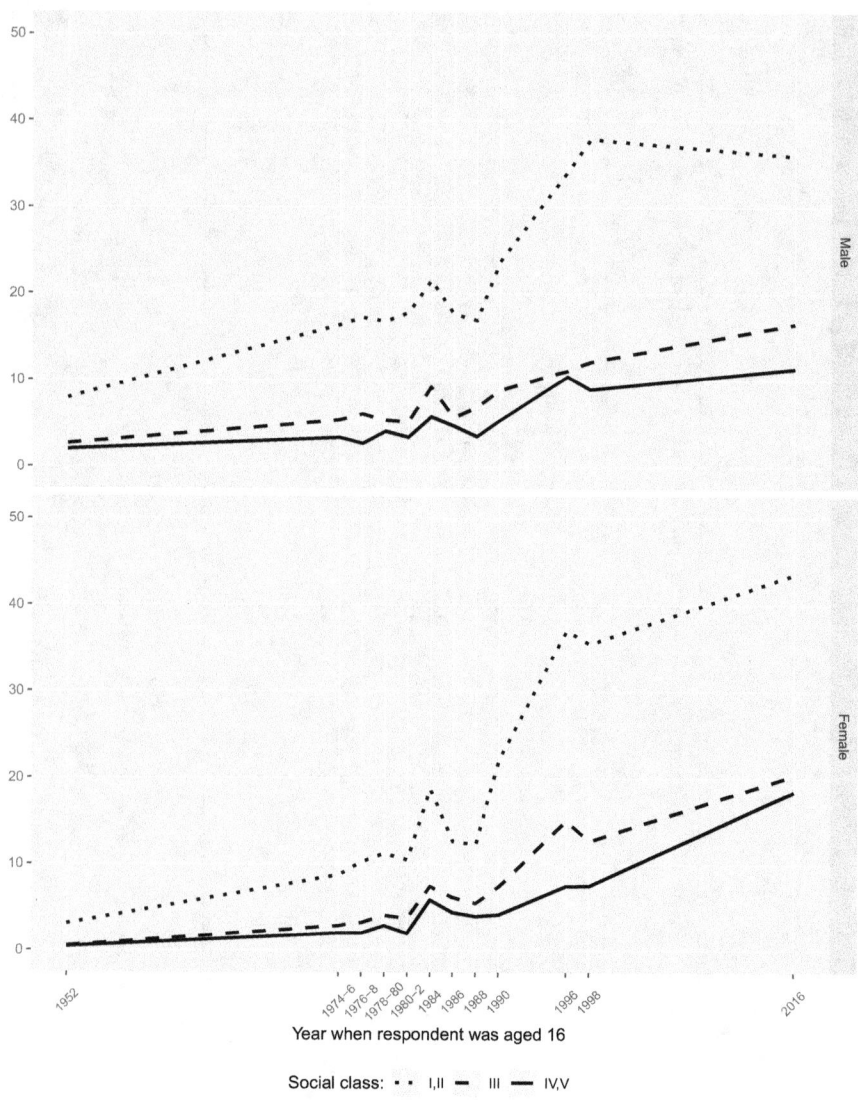

Figure 4.5 Percentage attempting breadth at Higher, by sex and social class, 1952–2016
For each class, parental education is set to the modal value in each year: see Table 2.5.
Average standard error: 2.3.

for International Student Assessment since 2006 are shown in Table 4.5. (Changes to the design of the PISA survey makes comparison with earlier years less valid.) The strength of this analysis is that the PISA measure provides a common standard across all countries. The table shows that Scotland has declined, and thus offers some independent confirmation of the slowing-down of improvement.

Table 4.5 Scottish results in the PISA studies, 2006–18

	2006	2009	2012	2015	2018
Reading					
Male	486	489	493	483	497
Female	512	516	520	504	511
Average standard errors: 2006, 4.6; 2009, 6.6; 2009, 3.4; 2015, 2.9; 2018, 3.7					
Mathematics					
Male	514	506	506	495	497
Female	498	492	491	488	481
Average standard errors: 2006, 4.1; 2009, 4.0; 2009, 3.1; 2015, 3.2; 2018, 5.2					
Science					
Male	517	519	517	497	494
Female	512	510	510	496	486
Average standard errors: 2006, 4.6; 2009, 4.2; 2009, 3.4; 2015, 3.0; 2018, 5.0					

Note:
The scale of assessment is fixed (in each year) to have an average of approximately 500 across all pupils (male and female) in economically developed countries (OECD, 2019, p. 16).

PISA does not measure inequality in the same way as we do in this book, but it does have an index of economic and social status (Avvisati, 2020). This records not only the economic situation of the household, but also parental education and such matters as the number of books in the home. One way to look at inequality over time is to divide the index into four quarters in each year, and to trace the trajectory of attainment within each. Figure 4.6 shows this for science. There may have been some narrowing of inequality, insofar as the lines for the most and least advantaged are closer together in 2018 than they were in 2006, but this was entirely because of a fall in the attainment of students in the most advantage group. In the light of the random error associated with the estimates, the safest and most relevant conclusion is that the position of the least-advantaged groups has not improved. Analogous graphs for reading and for mathematics showed similar patterns.

CONCLUSIONS

Our first conclusion is that there was a growth over the half-century in the proportion of students who experienced a broad, liberal curriculum. This was especially notable in the middle years of secondary, where, by the late 1990s, nearly one-half of students had successfully followed a broad curriculum, and three-quarters had passed the core liberal subject, English. The growth at higher levels was also definite, to over four out of ten for English and to one in six for breadth. Whatever else we may conclude, these changes are of unprecedented importance. For the first time in history, near to a majority of young Scots were gaining access to at least the introductory levels of the main

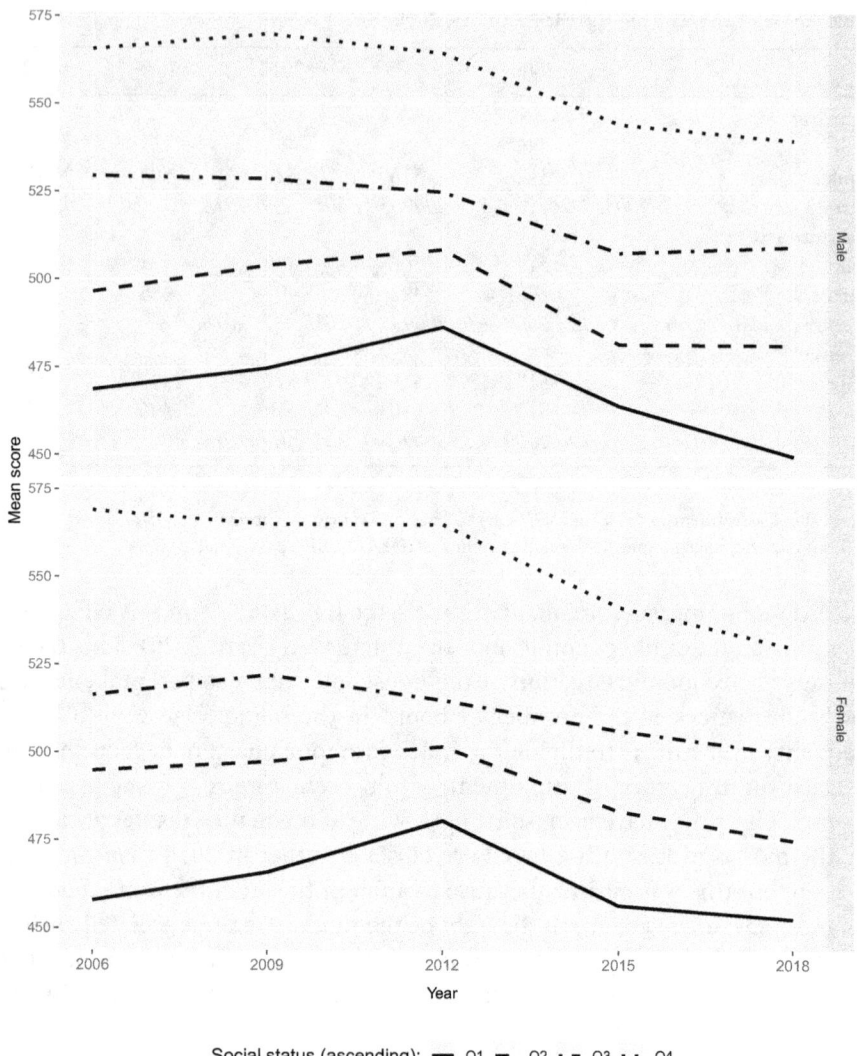

Figure 4.6 Scottish results in science from the PISA study, by sex and social status, 2006–18
Average standard error: 2006, 6.5; 2009, 5.7; 2012, 5.5; 2015, 5.4; 2018, 7.2.

traditions of European culture. The success of Catholic schools in that regard is a particularly Scottish contribution to our understanding of the potentially integrating effects of a broad curriculum. That legacy of the democratising school reforms of earlier in the century – whether the liberal reforms of the first few decades, or the social-democratic reforms of the 1960s – is as important as any other aspect of the twentieth-century welfare state, showing its catering for citizens' minds as well as their material well-being.

Our second conclusion, moreover, was that this growth was not at the expense of vocational achievement, despite the recurrent assertion in public debate that more attention had to be paid to it. At both mid-secondary and Higher levels, the proportion of students who passed a vocational subject was similar to the proportion who achieved breadth. This institutional combination of a liberal and vocational curriculum was true also of a quarter of individual students at mid-secondary level.

The social distribution of the broad, liberal curriculum changed. On the one hand, it grew at all levels of social class. However, the expansion was much greater for students from high-status classes than for others, with females ahead of males in all groups. So, despite the expansion for everyone, the social differentiation of this curriculum had widened. The social basis of vocational attainment was not so differentiated. In particular, that meant that there was no evidence that vocational courses were dominated by low-status students. Indeed, at Higher level, the proportion who passed vocational courses was higher in the high-status group than in lower-status groups; this class difference was especially large among males.

Policy was certainly responsible for creating the conditions under which expansion could happen. Thus the Ordinary Grade courses that were inaugurated in 1962 were the means by which the broad, liberal curriculum could begin its expansion in the 1970s. The Standard Grade courses took on that role in the 1990s, and, as Gamoran (1996) showed using part of the survey series which has been analysed here, probably directly furthered access to core subjects. However, the analysis here shows that the proportion of students who achieved a broad curriculum was already growing before Standard Grade appeared, and the sharpest increase in that extension was probably caused by the curriculum framework of the 1990s, not by the courses directly.

Schools were the conduits for policy, and some school characteristics seemed to incline them to take most advantage of reforms. The schools which pioneered Standard Grade had long been less effective with high-status students than with others. In that sense, they were places where low- and medium-status students did well, but only relative to their peers in the same school. The most visible of the effects of policy on schools was when the ending of selection for secondary schools in the public sector rapidly eroded the curricular distinction between schools that had and had not provided full secondary courses.

Yet older school differences remained. The schools that were independent of local councils were very successful at promoting liberal breadth, notably for the minority of their students who came from low- or medium-status families. Highly selected on academic grounds though these students were, their achievement of breadth at both mid-secondary and Higher does show that access to that kind of curriculum was not necessarily constrained by social class. In this sense, the independent schools became one of the strongest carriers of the dominant Scottish tradition in the curriculum.

Nevertheless, the independent schools achieved all this at the expense of somewhat neglecting vocational courses. Even more striking therefore is the trajectory of schools which started as academically inclined junior secondaries. Over the three decades from the mid-1960s they were at least as successful as the older secondary sectors in promoting liberal breadth for all social groups, and also achieved the same with vocational courses. Many of these schools owed their origin – and their experience of academic teaching – to reforms as far back as before 1914, but their academic characteristics then were achieved despite official doubts. If their success after the 1960s may be attributed to deliberate government intention, it is policy in one era interacting with the legacy of resisting policy in a previous one.

These changes suggest that a liberal curriculum was not intrinsically inaccessible to students outside social elites. Students from low-status and medium-status families achieved liberal breadth at the end of the century to an extent that had been confined to high-status students only a quarter of a century earlier. As we noted in Chapter 3, Goldthorpe (2007) has pointed out that the sheer fact of educational expansion belies the strongest versions of Bourdieu's theories. The data presented here tend to confirm this point: a high-status curriculum can be accessible to non-elite students, and the former academic junior secondaries showed that a curriculum could combine academic breadth and vocational relevance for all social classes. Nevertheless, the schools which, after the Standard Grade reforms, had the highest attainment of breadth among low-status students also had the highest gap between them and high-status students. It may be then that the price that was paid for such expansion of cultural opportunity was widening inequality.

CHAPTER 5

Student Choice and Respect

THE CHANGING EXPERIENCE OF SCHOOL

Educational reform in the twentieth century is most often discussed in terms of structures or attainment. Statistical attention to the subjective experience of schooling has been less common. The survey series included evidence on students' attitudes towards schooling. Although few of these questions were asked in every survey year, enough of them were asked in a sufficiently standard form over a long enough period of time to allow an assessment of long-term change.

The early twentieth-century advocates of a more democratic structure of schooling were as concerned with students' experience of school as with the outcomes. These campaigners were influenced by what was then called the 'new education', a body of ideas that later evolved into 'child-centred' education. The core aim was to make schools more humane. The international New Education Fellowship was the main source between the wars (Lawson, 1981; Brehoney, 2004), and the Scottish section of it was active from the 1920s onwards. Primary education did become gradually more child-centred from then, to some extent through official policy but also, in practice, because teachers responded directly to the international movement (Paterson, 2003, pp. 43–50). From the 1960s – as summarised in Chapter 1 – child-centred ideas were officially adopted as the guiding principles of Scottish primary schooling (Paterson, 2003, pp. 109–18).

Reforming Scottish secondary education in similar ways then became a natural corollary of extending secondary schooling to everyone in the 1930s, but the main impetus came with the development of comprehensive schooling (Howieson and Semple, 2000; Murphy et al., 2015). The ideas tended to be grouped under the heading of 'guidance', used in its educational rather than merely in its medical or vocational senses; the term generally covered the same ideas as 'pastoral support' came to mean in other countries (Watts and

Kidd, 2000, p. 488). The practice of educational guidance also had quite a long history in Scotland, dating from the 1920s (Stewart, 2006), and being adopted as policy in the 1980s (Consultative Committee on the Curriculum, 1986; Scottish Education Department, 1971). Guidance was thus the core policy idea that sought to shape the ethos of comprehensive schools, treating students with respect and seeking to give them a voice (Duffield et al., 2000; Howieson and Semple, 2000; Watts and Kidd, 2000; Wilson et al., 2004). A particularly salient aspect of these developments was the decline and final ending of corporal punishment in schools (Pollock et al., 1977, p. 34).

In practice, the principle of individual respect meant that pupils would expect to receive advice of four kinds: on personal problems, on the curriculum, on gaining employment, and on post-school education. Although some of this advice was intended to come from teachers with a specialist remit for guidance, it was also widely interpreted in Scotland as being a responsibility of all the staff in the school (Duffield et al., 2000; Howieson and Semple, 2000, p. 375; Wilson et al., 2004, p. 63). Guidance was also to be for all pupils, regardless of attainment or social background (Howieson and Semple, 2000, pp. 64–5, 385).

The wholesale change in school ethos that was sought was thus about much more than a specialist area of work called guidance. Congruent with it were the various reforms to the curriculum and examinations which we have discussed in the previous two chapters. The Ordinary Grade courses from 1962 were the first attempt to cater for an educationally wider range of pupils. Standard Grade courses went much further, and thus may be interpreted as the first systematic attempt to adjust schooling to meet the needs of all almost pupils (Croxford and Howieson, 2015; Croxford, 1994; Gamoran, 1996; Paterson, 2003, pp. 143–4). Vocational courses that were developed from 1984 onwards had similar aims (Raffe, 2009). Hartley (1987, p. 125) argued that a stronger attention to student motivation was intended to counter alienation from school.

The Ordinary and Standard Grade courses probably contributed to the steady rise in the rate of staying in full-time school education after the minimum leaving age (analysed in Chapter 3). Rising staying on generated new work for guidance, as choices had to be made about courses in post-compulsory schooling. Moreover, as the youth labour market collapsed in the 1980s, a new set of challenges emerged for those school leavers who were not going to university. Various training schemes were set up by government, initially of poor quality but steadily improving (Raffe, 1987). Navigating these options, too, required guidance, but questions about motivation and thus also about student behaviour never went away (Munn et al., 2004). Nevertheless, by the end of the century there was a growing sense that school was indeed for everyone: in the mid-1970s, hostility to school among low-attaining students was widespread (Gow and McPherson, 1980). A couple of decades later, three-quarters of students were happy in school (Wilson et al., 2004, p. 48).

THE MEASUREMENT OF SCHOOL EXPERIENCE

For school experience, we use only those measures that were available from the surveys over quite a long period that includes the late 1990s, at least the early 1980s, and preferably also the 1970s. For a few measures, there is also information from 2016. The only exception was for corporal punishment, which was recorded only up to its abolition (and thus not in surveys after 1982). Only questions that are relevant to a fully representative sample of the target population in the specified years are included. However, for several topics, the question was asked only of people who had stayed on in school beyond age 16. These are converted into measures that describe all respondents by expressing them as a percentage of the whole sample who gave a particular reason for staying on. For example, we then have a measure which shows what percentage of the sample not only enjoyed school but also stayed on because of that.

Some questions in some years were asked only of a randomly selected subset of the sample. This does not affect representativeness, only sample size. The sample sizes for each measure in each year are shown in Tables 5.1, 5.2 and 5.3 below. The measures may be grouped under three headings. Each measure is re-coded in the way indicated to give a dichotomy.

Engagement with School

There are two measures available for the whole series 1976–98:

- Whether or not the respondent stayed on in school beyond age 16 (which is available also for 1952). This is shown in Table 3.1 in Chapter 3, and provides the most clearly behavioural confirmation of attitudes to school.
- Whether the respondent truanted (even for 'a lesson here and there'), asked about the fourth year of secondary school. For 2016, truanting is defined to be ever having 'missed school without parents' permission', and was asked when the respondent was in third year of secondary school. It should be remembered therefore that, unlike the other surveys, the 2016 data do not count as truancy absences that have been condoned by parents.

The remaining measures are recorded only in the specified years:

- Whether or not school was worthwhile (1980, 1990, 1996, 1998). Typical wording (from 1980) was: 'On the whole, do you feel your last year at school was worthwhile? Yes/No'.
- Stayed on to study specific subjects (1980, 1986, 1988, 1990, 1996, 1998). Typical preamble (from 1980) was: 'Why did you start a fifth year?', with an option 'I planned to do subjects for Highers'.

- Stayed on because enjoyed school (1980, 1986, 1988, 1990, 1996, 1998). Typical preamble was as for the previous measure, with option 'I enjoyed school life'.
- Stayed on because always assumed would stay on (1980, 1986, 1988, 1990, 1996, 1998). Typical preamble was as for the previous measure, with option 'I had always assumed would start a fifth year'.
- Was the respondent happy or unhappy at school? Although this was asked in only two years, they are six decades apart – 1952 and 2016 – and so the comparison is an indicator of long-term change. For the 1952 survey, the question was asked at age 18 looking back over the whole experience of school, with the response options 'not very happy/fairly happy/very happy'. For 2016, the question was asked about unhappiness when the respondent was in the third year of secondary school (aged approximately 14–15), with options 'all of the time/most of the time/some of the time/never'.

School Environment

- Teachers helped student to do their best (1976, 1978, 1980, 1990, 1996, 1998). Typical wording (from 1980) was: 'My teachers helped me to do my best: true/untrue'.
- Teachers gave student confidence to be independent (1976, 1996, 1998). The wording in 1976 was: 'How much did your teachers help you to become independent?' (grouping 'a lot' and 'quite a lot'). The wording in 1996–98 was: 'School has helped to give me confidence to make decisions: agree/disagree'.
- Friends took school seriously (1980, 1990, 1996, 1998). Typical wording (from 1980) was: 'My friends took school seriously: true/untrue'.
- Too many troublemakers in classes (1980, 1990, 1996, 1998). Typical wording from 1980 was: 'There were too many troublemakers in my classes: true/untrue'. In 2016, the question was 'How often do other pupils misbehave in lessons', with response categories 'all of the time/most of the time/some of the time/never'. Here, 'all' and 'most' are equated with 'true' from the older series.
- Whether respondent had ever received corporal punishment (1976, 1978, 1980, 1982).

Preparation for Life after Leaving School

- Teachers taught student things useful in a job (1976, 1996, 1998). Typical wording from 1976 was: 'How much did teachers help you to

learn things that would be useful to you in a job' (grouping 'a lot' and 'quite a lot').
- Stayed on to improve qualifications (1980, 1986, 1988, 1990, 1996, 1998). The preamble was as under 'engagement' above, with option 'I wanted to get more or better Ordinary grades'.
- Stayed on because no suitable jobs or training available (1980, 1986, 1988, 1990, 1996, 1998). The preamble was as above, with option 'There were no jobs available'.
- Stayed on because not yet decided own future (1980, 1986, 1988, 1990, 1996, 1998). The preamble was as above, with option 'I hadn't decided on my future'.

IMPROVING EXPERIENCE

Table 5.1 shows clear evidence of growing engagement. The proportion who truanted decline from 64 per cent in 1976 to 43 per cent in 1998, and then fell further to 14 per cent in 2016. Serious truanting of staying away for days or weeks at a time also fell, from 15 per cent in 1976 to 6 per cent in 1998. In 2016, a mere 1 per cent reported truanting '2–3 times per week or most days'. Even bearing in mind that the 2016 definition of truanting did not include absence that was condoned by parents, this trend is consistent with the trajectory of staying on. As we discussed in detail in Chapter 3 (Table 3.1), the choice to stay on beyond age 16 rose from 14 per cent in the early 1950s (when the minimum leaving age was 15), through a third in the 1970s, and reached a half in the late 1980s, two-thirds at the end of the century and nearly nine out of ten by the second decade of the new century. The detailed reports of experience to which we now turn should be interpreted in the light of these basic measures of behaviour: however enthusiastic or disgruntled, pupils chose to be in school for longer.

The reasons which people gave for staying on are consistent with a growing attachment to school. The proportion who stayed on because they enjoyed school rose from 15 per cent in 1980 to nearly three times that in the late 1990s. That was partly because a similarly large minority had come to think that staying on was the norm, in the sense that they could not imagine doing otherwise.

Although these variables indicate improvement, the one variable in Table 5.1 which shows no change – judging school to be worthwhile – is stable at a level of widespread approval of school. The stability of broad satisfaction despite very extensive social and educational change in this period is striking. Leaving school at the first opportunity in the earlier years was perhaps more to do with economic necessity than with attitudes to school. We return to this point about stability below.

Table 5.1 Engagement with school, 1974–2016

% of sample Year when respondent was aged 16	School worthwhile 1	Truanted* 2	Stayed on to study specific 3	Stayed on because enjoyed school 4	Stayed on because assumed would 5	Sample size Col. 1	Sample size Col. 2	Cols 3–5
1974–6		64					15,808	
1976–8		58					8,564	
1978–80	82	57	32	15	22	5,183	10,418	5,299
1980–2		56					6,922	
1984		54					3,761	
1986		53	17	17	24		3,767	3,830
1988		48	24	23	30		3,247	3,318
1990	86	53	32	27	36	2,506	2,498	2,530
1996	84	44	54	40	37	2,216	2,224	2,230
1998	84	43	55	38	39	4,412	4,414	4,431
2016		14					933	

Notes:
* In 2016, does not include truanting condoned by parents.
Percentages weighted; sample sizes unweighted.

The pattern for staying on to study specific subjects may confirm this. It fell and then rose, from one-third in 1980 to one-sixth in the mid-1980s, then reaching over one-half in the late 1990s, after the new, broad curriculum had been fully developed. The pattern of this variable may suggest that, in the 1970s, for the minority who stayed on, the main reason to do so had been the intention to study specific subjects of an academic kind. When staying on rose from the mid-1980s, the reasons were initially more diffuse than they had been. In the late 1980s, however, the new courses gave a new kind of subject-related reason to stay on, no longer predominantly academic but now also, for example, to gain qualifications for employment (as we will see in connection with Table 5.3).

One reason for the generally growing attachment to school may have been a strengthening sense that school valued students and that students valued school (Table 5.2). The proportion who said that teachers gave them confidence doubled to around 70 per cent between the mid-1970s and the end of century. The proportion who were in social circles that took school seriously rose to over one-half, probably one reason why, in column 5 in Table 5.1, there was the rise in staying on because that was the norm.

As with the persistently high proportion who judged school to be worthwhile, there was no change in the percentage reporting that teachers helped them do their best, remaining at the very high level of three-quarters from the mid-1970s to the late 1990s. So the more positive evaluation of the school ethos

Table 5.2 School environment, 1974–2016

% of sample	Teachers helped students do their best	Teachers gave confidence	Friends took school seriously	Too much disruption	Sample size		
Year when respondent was aged 16	1	2	3	4	Col. 1	Col. 2	Cols 3–4
1974–6	74	35			6,944	6,864	
1976–8	78				4,506		
1978–80	74		47	33	5,134		5,094
1990	76		51	45	2,488		2,450
1996	78	70	50	46	2,213	2,213	2,206
1998	78	73	55	48	4,403	4,399	4,394
2016				59			933

Note:
Percentages weighted; sample sizes unweighted.

in Table 5.2, and the greater engagement with school noted in Table 5.1, may be due to greater attention by teachers to students as whole people – giving confidence to be independent (an all-round quality) rather than just helping with study. On the other hand, respondents seem to have been able to distinguish between the educational practices of the school as a source of teaching and potential learning, and the social context in which these activities took place. Thus, alongside these increasingly positive evaluations of teachers, there was also a slowly growing sense that there was disruption from other pupils. Only one-third reported this in 1980. The proportion grew to just under one-half in the late 1990s, and to well over a half (59 per cent) in 2016.

This sense of being valued personally by the school was no doubt helped by the fall and then the abolition of corporal punishment (not in the tables). The proportion who reported ever having been punished in this way fell from 79 per cent in 1976 to 62 per cent in 1982, on the eve of the abolition. Yet having received corporal punishment was quite consistent with positive evaluation of school. In 1978, for example, 74 per cent of people who had received corporal punishment reported that teachers helped them to do their best, not much lower than the 85 per cent among people who had never received corporal punishment.

A growing proportion of students also felt that school was preparing them for life, despite policy makers' recurrent concern that this was not happening (Munn et al., 2004). In Table 5.3, the proportion who reported that teachers taught things that would be relevant to jobs more than doubled from 34 per cent in 1976 to 76–7 per cent in the 1990s. The proportion who stayed on beyond age 16 to improve qualifications for employment or further study rose from under one-half in the 1980s to nearly two-thirds in the late 1990s. Contrary to many beliefs at the time (summarised by Paterson and Raffe, 1995), the rise in staying on was not due to the rise of youth unemployment or to the inadequacy of the training schemes which government put in place to try to deal with that: in Table 5.3, fewer than one in 20 gave that as a reason even in the period of high youth unemployment in the 1980s.

For a growing minority of students, school gave them unprecedented choice over their own futures, enabling them to postpone decisions by staying on: this rose from 18 per cent in 1980 to around one-third by the late 1990s. That there was a rise in the early 1980s in all the reasons for staying on except to study specific subjects does tend to confirm further that a change was taking place in students' attitudes to post-compulsory school. As well as being for pursuing further study, school was also becoming a route into the labour market, an opportunity to reflect on future life, and an experience to be enjoyed with friends who felt similarly about it. These trends are all consistent with the growth of student-centredness, fostered by the spirit of guidance.

Table 5.3 Preparation for life after leaving school, 1974–98

% of sample	Teaching relevant to jobs	Stayed on for qualifications	Stayed on because no jobs or training	Stayed on because not decided future	Sample size	
Year when respondent was aged 16	1	2	3	4	Col. 1	Cols 2–4
1974–6	34				6,769	
1978–80		15	5	18		5,299
1986		42	4	20		3,830
1988		46	4	25		3,318
1990		49	4	28		2,530
1996	76	62	7	35	2,218	2,230
1998	77	62	11	33	4,409	4,431

Note:
Percentages weighted; sample sizes unweighted.

ATTAINMENT AND SCHOOL EXPERIENCE

The next questions are whether this improving experience was shared equally, first with respect to attainment, and second in relation to sex and social class. All the measures of engagement with school showed strong evidence of an association with attainment (measuring that as one-half of a standard deviation above and below the mean mid-secondary attainment in each year). Where the level was already very high at high attainment, the level at mean and at low attainment gradually caught up. A typical example is the belief that school was worthwhile: at low attainment, the percentage rose from 77 per cent in 1980 to 84 per cent in 1998, while at high attainment it rose from 87 per cent to 91 per cent. Notably, though, over three-quarters of even quite low-attaining students already in 1980 saw school as worthwhile.

Where satisfaction was not already high, improvement at low attainment was greater than at mean or higher attainment. An example is staying on because of enjoying school. At low attainment, the proportion was merely 8 per cent in 1980, was still below 20 per cent up to the mid-1980s, but then rose to around 36 per cent in the late 1990s, more than a fourfold increase. At high attainment, the relative increase was about half that (23 per cent to 53 per cent). There was a similar pattern for staying on for the reason that doing so was always assumed. On staying on to study specific subjects, the dip in the mid-1980s (in Table 5.1) did not happen with students of low attainment. This was also true of truancy, for which we can take the analysis forward to 2016 by measuring it in relation to numbers of mid-secondary courses sat (rather than passed). There was a sharp fall at all levels of sitting, with a similar rate of decline at each. The rates at high and low sitting (analogously to the definition of attainment) were, at two-decade intervals: 56 per cent and 65 per cent in 1976, 36 per cent and 45 per cent in 1996, and 12 per cent and 15 per cent in 2016.

On school environment, there is again strong evidence of a relationship with attainment and of change in the relationship. Improvement at low attainment was greater than at high levels. An example is the proportion who reported that teachers helped them to do their best. The level was high at all levels of attainment, but improved most at low attainment, from 69 per cent in the late 1970s to 78 per cent in the late 1990s (while being stable at 82–3 per cent at high attainment). A similar pattern was evident for the proportion who reported that their friends took school seriously, which rose from 55 per cent in 1980 to 62 per cent in 1998 at high attainment, but more steeply from 40 per cent to 54 per cent at low attainment. The pattern for reporting that teachers gave the respondent confidence was only weakly related to attainment (rising from around one-third in 1976 to around three-quarters in 1998). For disruption in class, the attainment differences narrowed because reported conditions worsened most at high levels of sitting (27 per cent in 1980 to 45 per cent in 1998 and 59 per cent in 2016 at high levels, but 36 per cent to 48 per cent to 60 per cent at low levels).

In the analysis of views about how school related to the student's future life, there is again evidence of an association with attainment, and of a change over time. Staying on to improve qualifications became more important at all levels of attainment: at low attainment, the proportion rose from 11 per cent in 1980 to 60 per cent in 1998; at high attainment the change was from 21 per cent to 88 per cent. Not yet having decided about the future grew much more at low attainment (10 per cent to 32 per cent) than at high (29 per cent to 45 per cent), reinforcing the point that a greater range of students was being given the opportunity to choose a future life.

Staying on because of a lack of immediate employment prospects was rare at all levels of attainment: at low attainment, this reason was given by 3 per cent in 1980 and 11 per cent in 1998; the proportions at high attainment were 7 per cent and 13 per cent. There was only weak association of attainment with reporting that school had taught things relevant to jobs.

SEX, SOCIAL CLASS AND SCHOOL EXPERIENCE

So in most respects the improvements were at all levels of attainment. Our final body of evidence then relates to whether this was also true for both sexes and at all levels of social class. The estimates control for attainment by showing values at mean attainment.

The statistical effects of attainment and change in these effects are mostly stronger than the independent effects of sex or social class or any interactive effect of these with attainment. For example, the percentages who thought that school was worthwhile are shown in Table 5.4(a). The main difference was that, in 1980, the satisfaction among female students was about 6 percentage points higher than among male students, but generally all the levels were high, and sex difference disappeared. In particular, among students from low-status social classes, the level reporting that school was worthwhile was always at least around 80 per cent or higher.

The proportion who stayed on because they enjoyed school rose for both sexes and at all levels of class, but with no reduction of the differences: see Table 5.4(b). The same was true for staying on because that was always assumed to be appropriate. The proportion of males from low-status classes who stayed on to study a specific subject rose from 27 per cent in 1980 to 54 per cent

Table 5.4 Engagement with school, by social class and sex, 1980–98

(a) Percentage who thought school was worthwhile

Calculated at mean attainment within year	1980	1990	1996	1998
Male				
I	86	90	89	92
III	79	90	87	88
V	78	92	81	80
Female				
I	93	92	89	92
III	86	92	86	87
V	84	93	80	79

Average standard error: 3.9.

(b) Percentage who stayed on because enjoyed school

Calculated at mean attainment within year	1980	1986	1988	1990	1996	1998
Male						
I	29	31	32	39	53	55
III	11	18	24	30	39	44
V	11	8	22	15	31	36
Female						
I	35	35	38	47	59	58
III	18	22	30	37	46	47
V	17	12	29	22	37	39

Average standard error: 4.4.

Note:
For each class, parental education is set to the modal value in each class in each year: see Table 2.4.

in 1998. Females from low-status classes had a similar trajectory, but about 4 points higher. In the highest-status class, the rise was 59 per cent to 80 per cent for males, and 63 per cent to 83 per cent for females.

On perceptions of the school environment, the statistical effects of attainment and the change in these effects are again greater than any of the effects of sex or social class. Nevertheless, there is here some evidence of a widening in the 1990s of the differences with respect to class. For reports that friends took school seriously, among female students from high-status classes there was a rise from 54 per cent in 1980 to around 69 per cent in the 1990s; for males from these classes, the rise was from 44 per cent to around 64 per cent. But in the other classes, although there was a rise it was smaller: in class III, for example, from 51 per cent to around 60 per cent for females, and from 41 per cent to just over 50 per cent for males. All groups reported high levels of support from teachers: by the late 1990s, around 77–84 per cent in each sex-by-class group reported that teachers helped them to do their best (much the same as in the 1970s), and around 78 per cent reported that teachers encouraged their confidence (about double the proportion in the 1970s).

In some other respects, however, the environment was perceived to have deteriorated, a conclusion reinforced where the series can be taken forward to 2016. An example is reports that there was too much disruption in class. The percentages for both males and females in all social classes rose from around 30 per cent in 1980, through the mid-40s in the 1990s to over 50 per cent in 2016. The deterioration was worst for the lowest-status classes, reaching over 60 per cent in 2016 for both males and females.

If this deterioration of behaviour in the new century may indicate a reversal of the improvement in students' engagement with school, especially students from low-status social classes, then the emergence of social-class variation in truancy may reflect the same problem. Until the late 1980s, there was hardly any class-related variation in truancy rates: for all class groups, the truancy rate among male students with average attainment fell from around 65 per cent in the mid-1970s to 45–50 per cent in the late 1980s; the corresponding female rates were the same in the late 1980s, and about ten points lower in the 1970s. But then a gap opened up, though within a slowly falling trend, so that in 1998 the rates in the lowest-status classes were higher than those in the highest-status classes (32 per cent compared to around 50 per cent for both males and females, with standard error 2.5). Even when the rates had fallen much further in 2016 – with the caveat that it now excluded absence that had been condoned by parents – the class gap probably remained (4 per cent compared to 7 per cent for males; 7 per cent compared to 10 per cent for females).

Over the long term – 1952 to 2016 – there was also probably a reversal in the sex difference in how happy pupils were at school. In 1952, 44 per cent of girls but only 28 per cent of boys said they were 'very happy'. In 2016, the proportion saying they were 'never unhappy' was 25 per cent of girls and 33 per cent of boys. These percentages were similar at all levels of sitting courses (as an indicator of attainment), and in all social classes. The change in the question asked (from happiness to unhappiness) should make us cautious in how we interpret the absolute levels of happiness reported, but the contrast of female and male pupils is unlikely to be affected by that. Even as they became more educationally successful than boys, girls tended to become less happy at school.

For experiences relating to life after school, sex and social class are, again, less important statistically than attainment. The proportion staying on to improve qualifications rose for both sexes and all social-class groups: among females between 1980 and 1998, from 28 per cent to 86 per cent in class I, and from 23 per cent to 64 per cent in class V; the male trends were very similar. Staying on because the respondent had not decided on their future rose for both sexes and all class groups, as did the reports of learning material relevant to jobs, and (at rates of 16 per cent or lower for all groups) staying on because no suitable job or training place was available.

The main point about sex and social class is then that attainment mattered far more than these in a direct sense. Although, in this period, attainment was itself related to these demographic variables, as we saw in Chapter 3, the statistical explanation of attitudes to the school experience was much more strongly attainment than demography. Differences with respect to sex fell to negligible levels by the late 1990s. However, there is also evidence that social-class differences in some aspects of the experience of school widened in the 1990s and after, having closed in the previous decade.

SCHOOL SECTOR AND SCHOOL EXPERIENCE

There were no systematic differences in these reported experiences of school according to the history of the schools: the reforms created a common system in the public sector in this respect, just as they did for attainment and the curriculum (Chapters 3 and 4). However, there were differences between the public-sector schools and the independent schools, only partly explained by attainment.

On only one measures were the reports from independent schools more negative than from public-sector schools: in the 1970s, public-sector schools were reported to be more likely than independent schools to teach material that would be relevant to employment. This difference vanished by the 1990s, and in any case might not have been seen as a criticism of independent schools. As we saw in Chapter 4, the view that the curriculum ought not to be tied too closely to employment was historically a strong feature of Scottish educational thinking.

The most common pattern across the measures was that the independent schools had better ratings than the public-sector schools at all levels of attainment. This was true of truanting, friends taking school seriously and too much disruption. It was true, too, of staying on because of enjoying school, because that was always assumed, in order to improve qualifications, and because of not having yet decided what to do after leaving school. This most common pattern is illustrated for disruption in Table 5.5(a) (grouping years and the sexes in order to have adequate sample sizes in the independent sector).

On a few measures, the more positive evaluation of independent schools was seen most clearly at low or average attainment. This was true of finding school worthwhile, staying on to study a specific subject, and reporting that teachers helped pupils to do their best, or gave pupils confidence. The pattern is illustrated for studying a specific subject in Table 5.5(b).

We might sum up the differences between public-sector and independent schools by saying that, on average, the independent schools had an ethos that was more uniformly favourable to academic study, helped by the attitudes of families that sent their children there (as indicated, for example, by the assumption about staying on, by having friends who took school seriously, or by being affluent enough not yet to have decided what to do after leaving school). On several of these measures, the public-sector schools, catering for a much more educationally diverse group of pupils, nevertheless did close the gap for the highest-achieving students.

Table 5.5 Comparison of education authority and independent schools, by attainment, 1980s and 1990s

(a) Percentage who reported that there was too much disruption

Mid-secondary attainment	School status	1980s	1990s
0.5 s.d. below mean	Education authority	38	48
	Grant aided or independent	25	27
Mean	Education authority	33	45
	Grant aided or independent	22	24
0.5 s.d. above mean	Education authority	28	41
	Grant aided or independent	20	22

Average standard error: Education authority: 0.75; Grant aided or independent: 4.1.

(b) Percentage who stayed on beyond age 16 to study a specific subject

Mid-secondary attainment	School status	1980s	1990s
0.5 s.d. below mean	Education authority	10	45
	Grant aided or independent	15	61
Mean	Education authority	15	57
	Grant aided or independent	19	67
0.5 s.d. above mean	Education authority	20	70
	Grant aided or independent	23	73

Average standard error: Education authority: 0.47; Grant aided or independent: 3.8.

CONCLUSIONS

The aims of educational reform in the twentieth century were not confined to raising attainment or reducing structural barriers to opportunity. The purposes also came to include making schools more congenial and more encouraging of effort and achievement. The strength of the analysis in this chapter of these themes about experience is that it is based on an unusually long time series of survey data. Even though we confined attention to variables that were available in the late 1990s and at least as far back as 1980, and for about half of our measures back to the mid-1970s, we still were able to analyse in detail 13 indicators of students' experience.

There are, however, weaknesses in the data used here. Although the variables cover 25–30 years of schooling, they are mostly intermittent, with quite long gaps for some of them. The variables also try to capture in a small number of categories (usually just two) the complexity of students' experience of school. A fuller picture would require a range of other measures, whether from qualitative interviews or from ethnographic studies of schooling. Examples of such non-statistical studies from this period of Scottish education are Gow and McPherson (1980) on the 1970s, and Duffield et al. (2000), MacBeath (2006) and Wilson et al. (2004) for the turn of the new century. The analysis in this chapter pays the price of loss of subtlety for the capacity to compare many thousands of students over a long period of time.

The findings generally confirm that the aims of treating students with greater respect and individual attention were achieved, though in many respects not till some three decades after the initial move to a comprehensive system in the mid-1960s. The proportion of students who were committed to school gradually rose, whether measured by behavioural indicators such as staying on beyond age 16 or not truanting, or by measures of attitudes, such as enjoying school. There was evidence that policy played a role: for example the reform to the curriculum may have encouraged increasing proportions to stay on in order to study specific subjects. But perhaps the most extensive influence was from professional practice, seen in the growing appreciation by students that teachers provided both encouragement to attainment and also pastoral support. In several ways, schools were already providing levels of support to students in the 1970s that were widely appreciated: large majorities were already finding school to be worthwhile at that time, and were also appreciating teachers' help. It must also always be borne in mind that dissatisfaction among students was probably never as high as the reformers claimed: overall happiness at school was very high in 1952.

The beneficial changes extended to all levels of attainment, to both sexes, and to all levels of social class. The rate of improvement was greater for students with low attainment and students from low-status classes. Some of this convergence of experience might be attributable to ceiling effects in the sense that the proportions in one category might have reached as high a level as could be expected, so that any further change would be bound to lead to some reduction of inequality. This is analogous to the concept of maximally maintained inequality which we discussed in Chapter 3 (Raftery and Hout, 1993). For example, the proportion reporting positive attitudes in the high-status or high-attainment group was at around 90 per cent or greater in the late 1990s for school being worthwhile, for teachers helping the respondent to do their best, and for staying on to improve qualifications. But that is only three of the 13 measures. As we have illustrated with several of the graphs, for most measures there was steady improvement in all social-class groups, and so the high-attaining or high-class groups had not reached any apparent limit. Moreover, in the case of the high-attaining students, the improvements were so great as to bring students' satisfaction of the public-sector schools close to that of students in the independent schools.

There was some evidence that the gains by students from low-status social classes were not advancing further at the end of the century, and for the few measures available in 2016 there was some indication that this widening gap might have intensified more recently. But in no respect was there a fall back to levels that were common in the late 1970s. This conclusion is shown most clearly by the trend in truancy: the slight increases of inequality from the mid-1990s to 2016 still left more acceptance of school among students from low-status classes than students from high-status classes had reported in the 1990s.

In short, Scottish secondary schools became more humane in the last quarter of the twentieth century. For the advocates of universal secondary education in the 1920s and later, this outcome would have been as welcome as the increase in attainment that we have looked at in previous chapters, or the rising rates of entry to higher education that we will consider in the chapters that follow. The ethos of schools might be used, these reformers thought, to shape the character of citizens in a democracy. If being treated with respect by teachers, and returning that appreciation, are signs that these aims were being met, then we may conclude that Scottish schools at the end of the century were fulfilling some of these pioneers' most ambitious hopes.

CHAPTER 6

Young People and the Labour Market

SCHOOL REFORM AND SCHOOL LEAVERS

Young people's transition from school in the second half of the twentieth century was shaped by two aspects of social change and the resulting policy response. One of these influences consisted of changes to the labour market for school leavers that started in the economic recession of the late 1970s, proceeded apace with the contraction of manufacturing industry in the 1980s, and were sustained by the growth of service-sector employment from the 1990s (Furlong and Cartmel, 2007; Howieson and Iannelli, 2008). These changes fundamentally altered the relationship between sex and progression, and also pushed to the margins the prospects of school leavers with low attainment whose families were of low social status. The policy response to this mainly took the form of special training schemes for school leavers, which gradually improved in quality over the 1980s and 1990s (Dolton et al., 1994; Jones, 1988; Raffe, 1984b; Roberts et al., 1986).

The other set of changes is the reforms to the structure of secondary schooling that we have been looking at in this book so far. As we saw in Chapter 1, the ending of selection for secondary school between the mid-1960s and the late 1970s was responding to earlier social changes than those which led to the changing labour market, mainly an expectation of equal opportunities and also a perceived need for a better-educated workforce (Ball, 1990; McPherson and Raab, 1988). The thoroughness of the structural aspects of the reform led to the new system of curriculum and assessment that we analysed in Chapter 4. Because one of the main aims of that system was to cater for almost all students, we might expect that it would have an unprecedented impact on those school leavers – still the large majority – who did not go into higher education. Because their prospects were being transformed by the changes to the labour market for young people, there is good reason to expect that the curricular reforms would interact with the first set of contextual changes.

There is a further complication that is particularly important in Scotland. We have seen in previous chapters that the developing curriculum for comprehensive schools in Scotland was imagined by policy makers to be a development from the country's tradition of liberal, academic schooling, providing to almost everyone a modernised version of a tradition that used to be confined to a highly selected elite. The Scottish policy responses to the changing labour market was then to try to make new vocational training consistent with that liberal tradition.

Because of the long timescale over which both processes took place, any analysis has to take a long view. The comprehensive reforms may be said to have lasted from the 1960s until the final reforms to the curriculum of compulsory schooling in the early 1990s. The changes to youth transitions lasted from the mid-1970s until the end of the century. To be able to comment on either of these changes requires also a baseline before they started. Our surveys cover all these periods. They also allow us to use Scotland as a crucial test case of the central question of curricular reform internationally. Could an academic type of secondary curriculum respond to the labour-market changes in a way that would further the opportunities of students with the full range of attainment and social class? As we will discuss further in the following chapters (especially Chapters 7 and 8), Scottish education saw a large rise in the rate of participation in academic courses at school and in academic higher education. The question then is whether that kind of expansion was consistent with providing opportunities for all.

THE COLLAPSE OF THE YOUTH LABOUR MARKET

Until the early 1970s, the transitions which school leavers in the UK made were quite predictable (Bynner et al., 2002; Bynner and Parsons, 2001; Furlong and Cartmel, 2007). Apart from the minority who entered higher education, the immediate destination was work. Many then had the possibility of part-time training, whether at the training colleges that had been established after the late 1940s, or, especially for men, through an apprenticeship (Paterson et al., 2010). In this respect the formal training opportunities for young people in the 1950s were better than for previous generations (Hannan et al., 1995). A large proportion of women left the labour market in their twenties to form a family. These patterns for women and men were common to most developed economies, and so Scotland was quite typical (Furlong and Cartmel, 2007, pp. 36–7).

But then the labour market for school leavers collapsed, causing youth unemployment to rise rapidly from the late 1970s, in the UK reaching over 20 per cent in the early 1980s (Bynner, 2012). One reason for the economic problems was cyclical, with a rise of unemployment in the 1970s that was greater than any since 1945, followed by a fall during the economic boom in the late 1980s and then a rise again in the 1990s (Broadberry, 1994, p. 242). The experience was similar across economically developed countries (Furlong and Cartmel, 2007, p. 37), and affected young people more acutely than other groups – sharper rises of unemployment in recessions, and more rapid falls during expansions (Furlong and Cartmel, 2007, p. 37). Policy responses to this source of youth unemployment tended to emphasise the importance of education as a form of insurance against short-term unemployment. This became known (by economists) as the human capital argument, both for individuals and for a country as a whole. Investing in education in good times stored up a resource that could be spent later, whether for an individual to get a new job after being unemployed, or for a country to enable its economy to recover from a recession. For young people, moreover, remaining in education beyond the minimum leaving age during a recession might not only strengthen their qualifications (and thus their competitive position) but also postpone labour-market entry until the economy recovered (Hasluck, 1999; Shelly, 1988: 102–5).

The second reason for the more difficult employment market for school leavers in the 1970s and 1980s was not cyclical in this way. It related to the decline of manufacturing industry, with the loss of opportunities for training that were generally not replaced in the new service sector which grew from the 1980s onwards (Chisholm, 1999; Gangl et al., 2003; Paterson et al., 2004, pp. 47–9; Solga, 2008). Merely postponing entry to the labour market would not allow a school leaver to escape the consequences of these long-term structural changes. Because men had been concentrated in manufacturing, and women were more likely than men to work in services, there was a strong impact on sex differences in employment and training. In the 1980s, a larger proportion of male than of female school leavers were unemployed, but a lower proportion of women than of men took part in training (Crawford et al., 2011; Smyth, 2005) and the labour-market consequences of having low attainment from school were more severe for women than for men (Howieson and Iannelli, 2008, p. 286). The overall participation of women in the labour market grew rapidly in the 1980s, partly in a delayed form by means of rising female participation in post-compulsory education (Egerton and Savage, 2000).

A growing proportion of school students remained in education beyond the minimum leaving age, as we have seen in Chapter 3. Governments in many countries also tried to respond more deliberately with new training schemes for those school leavers who were not entering higher education (Bynner, 1999; Bynner and Parsons, 2001; Dolton et al., 1994; Furlong and Cartmel, 2007, pp. 41–2). In the UK, the first schemes (from 1975 onwards) were criticised as merely being a way of keeping young people out of unemployment. To an extent, that was indeed what they were intended to do, insofar as there was still an expectation that the recession was cyclical and that employment would in due course return to normal levels and patterns. When youth unemployment appeared to be more persistent, the training schemes became better organised, but still did not match the lengthy apprenticeships that had been a feature of predominantly male training in the 1950s and earlier. The Youth Opportunities Programme, introduced in 1978 by the UK Labour government, gave only six months of work experience, and the first version of the Youth Training Scheme (YTS), introduced by the Conservative government from 1981, gave only a year of training. The controversies around the inadequacy of these came to be linked with the controversies around the collapse of manufacturing industry which was happening at the same time. Critics of the government alleged that the problems of manufacturing were exacerbated, or at least accelerated, by the recession which had been provoked by that government's monetarist policies (Tomlinson, 2021). Because the government also placed strong emphasis on improving the supply of labour as a way of responding to the recession, they took these criticisms seriously, extending the YTS to two years from 1986 (Raffe, 1984b). Nevertheless, the scheme remained controversial because the pay for trainees was low, and because it did not lead to any guaranteed employment (Bynner, 2012). Versions of the scheme remained in place until the end of the century, but the Labour government elected in 1997 did introduce a minimum wage, and encouraged the development of modernised forms of apprenticeship. Through the cyclical economic expansion which had started from the mid-1990s, the employment prospects of people who had been on the YTS and its successors were improved (Bynner, 1999, p. 67; Croxford, 2015, pp. 130–1; Eurydice, 1997, pp. 82–5; Main and Shelly, 1988), although the effect may have been stronger for women than for men because the legacy of the structural changes remained (Dolton et al., 1994).

The conclusion of research on vocational training of this kind has been that it did help low-attaining young people to avoid unemployment and low-status jobs (Crawford et al., 2011; Arum and Shavit, 1995). For low-status and low-attaining young people, vocational qualifications even of a minimal kind were helpful in the labour market (Dearden et al., 2004). Even low levels of training could make a difference to young people's employment chances by their early twenties (Howieson and Iannelli, 2008). Solga (2008) found that, in the UK, the reason why the employment chances of young people with low-level vocational qualifications were poor was not related to the quality of that training. Rather, it was because of displacement – the jobs they might have entered being taken by the growing number of better-qualified school leavers – and because they lacked the social networks to enter the labour market effectively.

Therefore entering training of some kind after leaving school became, in the 1980s, a desirable goal in the UK for leavers who were not entering higher education. That goal was particularly relevant for students from low-status social classes because they were much more likely than high-status students to leave school with minimal attainment. The policy questions also then related to how schools could enable these changes to happen. In one sense, this was implicitly a goal of the move to a non-selective system of secondary schools, insofar as one of its aims was to improve the employment prospects of people from all social backgrounds (Kerckhoff et al., 1996; McPherson and Willms, 1987). As we have seen, that reform probably helped to increase attainment, encourage staying on beyond the minimum leaving age, and reduce social-class and sex inequality of attainment. However, the greater potential for direct impact on school leavers' prospects in the labour market came from the reforms to the curriculum.

Although school vocational education was never as coherently organised as that curricular reform, there were also other kinds of course that were directed especially at low-attaining students, as noted in Chapter 1 – courses without any formal certification in the late 1970s and earlier, the Certificate of Secondary Education until the mid-1980s, and the new National Certificate modules from then until the end of the century. The policy document which introduced these modules propounded, as Howieson et al. (1997, p. 13) put it, 'a liberal educational philosophy which rejected any abandonment of broadly-based education at 16', and thus was intended to be compatible with the principles of liberal education that underpinned the Standard Grade reforms.

There has been a large volume of research on all of these topics, but there has been very little – in any country – which has brought together evidence about the changing transition from school and evidence about the effects of comprehensive schooling. In Scotland, the analysis of comprehensive schools has concentrated on changes to progression and attainment within the core school curriculum (Croxford, 1994; McPherson and Willms, 1987; Gamoran, 1996); we discussed that previous research in earlier chapters. Analysis of reforms to vocational education has taken the comprehensive reform as a given part of the context rather than as an evolving system that potentially might shape in changing ways young people's transition to their first destination after leaving school (Croxford, 2015; Howieson et al., 1997). Yet the wider research on vocational training gives reason to believe that the structure of schooling and its courses might have an effect on school leavers' transitions. Many writers have noted that policy and tradition in the UK have preferred general rather than vocational qualifications at school as a preparation for entering the labour market (Gangl et al., 2003, p. 279; Müller and Shavit, 1998). The UK shares this with some other Northern European systems, though not with, for example, Germany and the Netherlands where secondary schooling is divided into academic and vocational tracks. Scotland is, if anything, even more firmly attached to general education than the rest of the UK (Howieson et al., 1997, p. 17). Iannelli and Duta (2018) have confirmed, for Scotland, that less academic curricula have no particular benefit for any social group, and Moulton et al. (2018) found, for England, that these harm the prospects of female students and of white students.

This chapter does not attempt to deal with the full range of changes in the second half of the twentieth century in school leavers' experience upon entering the labour market directly: that would require a book in itself, and there are already excellent examples which do so (notably Furlong and Cartmel (2007) and Müller and Gangl (2003)). We concentrate here on the relationship between education policy and these changes. So the topics which we address all relate to aspects of a single question: did the reforms to secondary schooling have any impact on the transitions which students made when they left school in a context where that transition was being deeply affected by economic transformation?

CLASSIFYING DESTINATIONS

For the whole series of surveys, we classify the destination of students within about a year of leaving school. To cover the whole half-century, we have to develop categories that are broad enough to embrace the changes that took place, while also being focused enough to capture the major differences in school leavers' experience at any particular point in time. We use six categories, recording the main activity which the respondent was undertaking within about a year of leaving school; the relative sizes of these over time are shown in Table 6.1 below:

1. Not education, training, employment or looking for work
2. Unemployed and looking for work
3. Employed without training
4. Employed with short training (including government training schemes)
5. Employed with long training
6. Education

The survey questions from which this is constructed varied, but had enough in common to allow a consistent definition at this level of generality. Category 6 was confined to people who said that their main activity was education, whether or not that was full time. (It thus includes the category which Wolbers (2003) calls 'working student', for example students who had a part-time job to cover their expenses, but does not include people training on the job, at whatever level of training.) Unemployed people were allocated to category 1 or 2 depending on whether they were looking for work. Anyone whose main activity was employment was allocated to categories 3, 4 or 5, even if the employment was part time; few of the surveys distinguished between part-time and full-time work. Categories 4 and 5 contained respondents who reported ever having been on any kind of training or course since leaving school. Because of the varying form which the survey questions about training took, the distinction between short and long training had to be something of a compromise. Long training consisted of apprenticeships (all years), attending courses at colleges or training centres (1984–98), or training that lasted longer than a year (1976–8). It also included professional learning, mostly in the earlier years when direct entry from school was still common in some professions (Paterson, 2003, p. 160). Thus short training consisted of courses lasting less than a year, on-the-job training, and – most notably, from the 1978 survey onwards – the special training schemes provided by government, of whatever length. Other researchers have investigated this distinction in detail by restricting attention to particular periods of time when such provision was changing (Dolton et al., 1994; Main and Shelly, 1988). Our intention here is to track over time the aggregate effects of these broad categories of opportunity for part-time training. Category 4 is defined as widely as possible, leaving category 3 to be strictly defined in a residual way as people in work who have done no sustained training or education of any kind since leaving school.

Our data do not allow us to investigate whether employment with training at this stage of young people's lives led to worthwhile employment later, but we return to this question, using different surveys, in Chapter 9. The category 6 here (entering education without work) is itself very broad, especially at a time when higher education was expanding, first gradually and then (from the late 1980s) massively. Exploring that radical expansion of higher education is the main topic of Chapters 7 and 8. The present chapter thus concentrates on the comparison of the other categories with each other and with any kind of education without work.

We add to the attainment variables which we have used in previous chapters a dichotomous indicator of whether the respondent took at least one low-level course. These were defined (as in Chapter 1) to be taking any non-certificate course (1974–6 and 1976–8 surveys), any Certificate of Secondary Education course (1980–90), or any National Certificate module (1984–98). Because no such courses existed for the 1952 school leavers, that survey is omitted from analysis which includes this measure. The analysis also continues to use the classification of schools' trajectories during the reforms of the 1970s and 1980s that were investigated in Chapters 3 and 4.

THE CHANGING DESTINATIONS OF SCHOOL LEAVERS

Table 6.1 summarises the large changes between 1952 and 1998 in students' immediate destinations after leaving school, separately for males and females. In the 1950s, over 90 per cent of leavers of both sexes entered employment, but, whereas 33 per cent of males had some training, only 4 per cent of females did so. There were two notable developments from the 1970s onwards. The more long-lasting was the growth of entry to education. By the late 1970s, the male proportion had risen from 6 per cent to just under 20 per cent, while the female proportion had risen from 2 per cent to over 20 per cent. There was a plateau in the 1980s, after which the proportion doubled to around one-half by the end of the century. These post-school education courses took a variety of forms, with a growing share in higher education, as we will see in later chapters.

The other main change in Table 6.1 is in employment with training. From the 1950s to the mid-1980s, there was a large rise in the proportion of leavers in work who had had some training. There were two influences here. One, for women, was the steady growth of employment with training before the 1980s, reaching around one-half of women entering employment in the second half of the 1970s. Most of that growth was in short training. The proportion for any training was much closer to the corresponding male proportion at that time (about two-thirds) than in the 1950s, but there continued to be a marked difference in long training. The other influence then came from the various policy responses to the growth of youth unemployment, which itself is evident from the table (unemployment reaching a peak of about one in six in the early 1980s). For both men and women, a large majority of those who entered employment had had some training in the mid-1980s, predominantly of a short kind. Short training fell by about a half by 1998 from its peak in the late 1980s. Over the whole series, the proportion of women with long training was always less than the proportion of men, but the gap reduced.

Changing Role of School Attainment

Our more detailed statistical analysis now investigates how these trends relate to socio-economic circumstances, and whether any of the changes might relate to policy on school structures and the school curriculum. Figure 6.1 summarises the statistical effects of school attainment on entering post-school education, showing this separately for males and females and for the three categories of social class. Unsurprisingly, students with higher school attainment had higher proportions entering education upon leaving school. However, the most striking feature of the graphs is the interactive effect with sex and social class. Between the 1950s and the 1970s, school attainment came to matter much more for female students at all levels of social class than it had done, insofar as the attainment lines become more separated. Thus, in 1952, hardly any female students in low-status social classes at any level of attainment entered formal post-school education. By 1976–8, a wide attainment gap had opened for low-social-status female students: 46 per cent with three Highers, but 5.6 per cent with no formal attainment. At medium status, the attainment

Table 6.1 Destinations around a year after leaving school, by sex, 1952–98

Year when respondent was aged 16	Not education, training, employment or looking for work	Unemployed and looking for work	Employed without training	Employed with short training	Employed with long training	Education	Sample size (=100%)
Male							
1952	0	0	61	0	33	6	554
1974–6	3	13	25	8	38	13	7,817
1976–8	2	7	21	16	38	15	4,170
1978–80	1	15	15	23	29	18	9,932
1980–2	4	17	7	32	21	19	3,528
1984	3	15	6	38	21	17	1,800
1986	3	15	11	39	14	19	1,702
1988	2	6	14	42	14	22	1,542
1990	4	11	12	33	12	29	1,083
1996	4	8	18	19	6	46	780
1998	3	11	9	21	13	44	1,835
Female							
1952	1	0	93	0	4	2	597
1974–6	4	12	30	21	14	19	8,115
1976–8	3	7	36	21	11	23	4,461
1978–80	2	12	26	28	7	26	10,944
1980–2	6	15	9	39	3	27	3,417
1984	4	13	10	35	17	20	1,989
1986	5	11	15	35	13	21	2,095
1988	4	6	15	35	11	28	1,759
1990	8	9	14	26	8	36	1,433
1996	6	7	19	17	5	46	1,189
1998	5	8	12	18	7	50	2,569

Note:
Percentages are weighted; sample sizes are unweighted.

gap rose from 17 points to 41, and at high status it rose from 23 to 48. These attainment gaps for females remained quite stable to the end of the century.

For male students, there was little change between 1952 and the 1970s in the attainment gap at any level of class status. At high and medium status there was also little change between the 1980s and the 1990s. But for low-status males

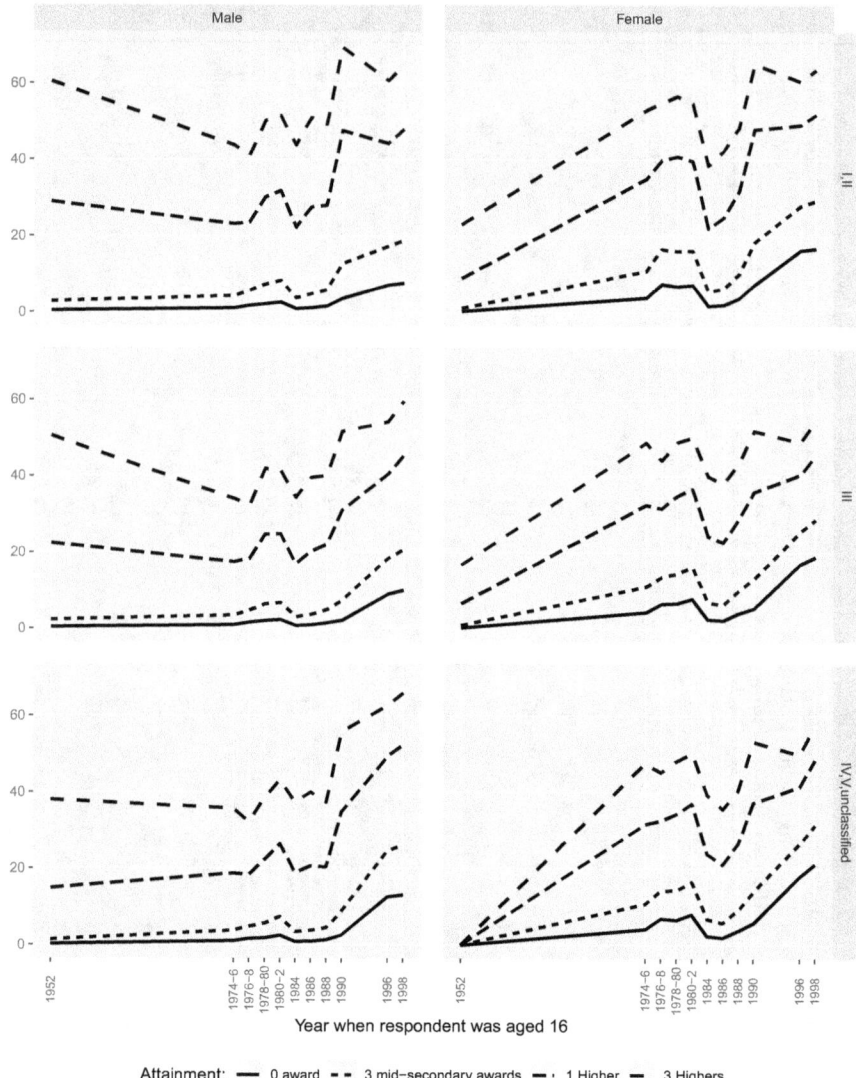

Figure 6.1 Percentage in post-school education, by social class, sex and school attainment, 1952–98
For each class, parental education is set to the modal value in each year: see Table 2.5.
Average standard error: 3.4

there was a rise in the attainment gap between the 1980s and 1990s that was similar to the change for female students in that period: a rise from 38 points in the 1980s to 52 points in 1990–8.

Figure 6.2 analogously summarises experience of entering employment with any kind of training among those people who were not in education a

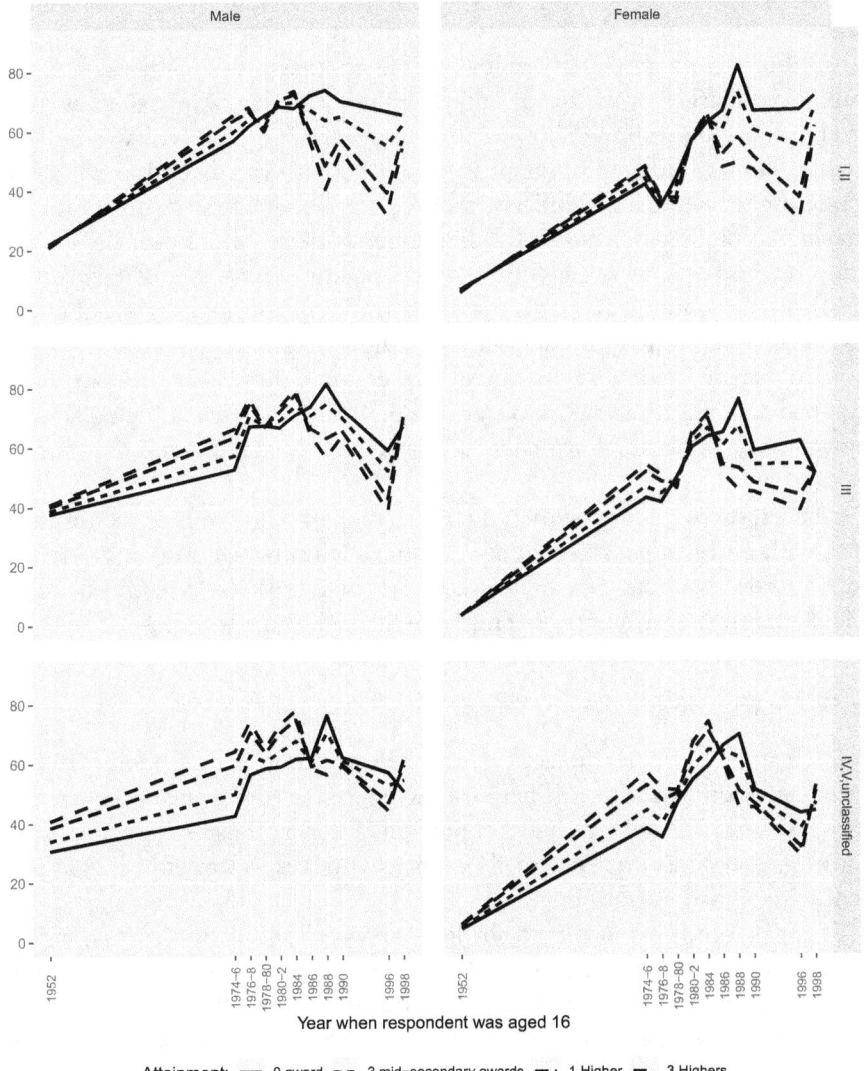

Figure 6.2 Percentage employed with any training, by social class, sex and school attainment, 1952–98, among people who were not in post-school education
For each class, parental education is set to the modal value in each year: see Table 2.5.
Average standard error: 3.9.

year after leaving school. There was little difference by attainment up to the early 1980s, although some indication in this period that, for students from low-status classes, having high attainment (the broken lines in the graphs) was somewhat more likely to lead to employment with training than having low attainment (the solid line). This position was then reversed in the late 1980s, when entry to employment with training became more common at low attainment than at high attainment, especially among people from high-status social classes.

But this greater propensity of lower attainers than of high attainers to enter training was largely a matter of entering short training. An analogous graph for entering long training showed no such reversal: the pattern was closer to that for entering education (as in Figure 6.1), with consistently higher rates among higher attainers. Similarly, the effect of school attainment on directly entering employment without training (among those who did not enter education or employment with training) was positive from the 1970s onwards, especially for school leavers from low-status or medium-status social classes. The average gap in this proportion (from the 1970s to the end of the century) between female students with three Highers and those with no awards was 32 percentage points at medium status and 39 at low status; at high status, the gap was only 17 points. For males, the gaps were 20 and 26, and only three at high status.

In short, there was a growth in the association of high levels of school attainment with entry to post-school education, to lengthy training, or to employment without training, but there was a decrease in the association of higher school attainment with entry to employment with short training.

End of Selection for Secondary School

As in Chapter 3, we next look at the variable which groups schools into three periods of ending selection. There was no consistent difference between these school sectors in the average proportion entering post-school education. However, there was evidence of differences with respect to entering employment with or without training.

There is some evidence that, for low-attaininmg students (that is, with no awards in the public examinations) the rate of entering employment with training was highest in the last group of schools to end selection, though only for students in low-status or medium-status social classes in the years immediately after the ending of selection (1982–6). The gap compared to the other schools was around 5 per cent for males and females (with standard error around 2.7). There was no difference between the early and middle reformers. But there is also evidence that these schools already had a good record in that respect for medium-status students before the reform, insofar as they were ahead for them also in 1976, by around 9 per cent. There was no such prior gap for low-status students. So the possibly beneficial effects on training opportunities which these schools conferred on medium- and low-status students who had very low attainment may have been an interaction between the reform and a longer-term history. Moreover, further analysis showed that there was no effect on entering long training. So any effect was on short training: the late-reforming schools were able to take advantage of the government training programmes in the mid-1980s, but seem to have had no such affinity with more substantial programmes of training.

What is certainly clear is that there is no evidence that pioneering comprehensive schools (the first group) were particularly effective in any respect, even when compared to schools that remained selective in the second half of the 1970s. This was true of getting their leavers into post-school education, or into employment with training or into employment without training.

Reform to the Curriculum and Assessment

Nevertheless, in response to these only weak conclusions on the relevance of the ending of selection to pupils' transitions from school, it might reasonably be expected that the more appropriate focus should be curricular reform, affecting the school years immediately before the leaving age of 16, rather than what happened at age 11–12.

Here, there is some evidence of an effect of the reform (confining attention to public-sector schools, as in the analogous evidence in Chapter 4). But this was only for low-status students with relatively high attainment in the sense of passing one Higher. There was no effect for entering post-school education. For entering a job with training immediately after the reform (in 1990) the advantage lay with the early-reforming schools. The proportion of low-status, high-attaining female students who entered a job with training (but not education) was 56 per cent in the early-reforming schools, in contrast to 46 per cent in the other schools. For low-status, high-attaining males, the gap was 8.9 points. These gaps rose slightly with higher attainment (respectively 11 and 9.6 points for people who passed three Highers). This was an effect in short training, because there was no similar pattern for entering long training.

There was a similar advantage for early reformers in directly entering employment (rather than any kind of training or education), now in every social-class group and at both low and high attainment. In 1990, for example, the gap between early and later reformers for female leavers with no formal certification was 16 points in high-status classes, 8.3 points at medium status and 8.0 points at low status. The corresponding gaps for males were 15, 11 and 12. For leavers who had passed one Higher, these gaps were similar at high and medium status, and probably were even greater at low status (13 and 16 points). Moreover, when we examine further the trajectory of these employment rates of leavers from these early reformers, we find that their advantage started around the time that Standard Grade was starting, the mid-1980s. But the advantage vanished by the mid-1990s as the other sectors caught up.

One of the purposes of the reform was to broaden the curriculum for all students, as we explained in Chapter 4 (following the policy context in Chapter 1). Table 6.2 suggests that this breadth then helped high-attaining students to enter educational courses after leaving school. The table shows the differences associated with breadth at mid-secondary level in the percentage of students entering post-school education. For each combination of sex and social class, these differences are shown at two levels of school attainment – passing four subjects at mid-secondary level (the minimum required to be able to have mid-secondary breadth), and passing three or more Highers. For example, consider the bottom-right cell of the table, which is for high-attaining female students in the class group IV, V and unclassified in the years 1990–8. Not shown

Table 6.2 Percentage in post-school education, by social class, sex and attainment: difference associated with mid-secondary curricular breadth, 1976–98

	1976–8	1980–8	1990–8
Male, low attainment*			
I, II	-6.4	-7.1	-17
III	-4.6	-5.2	-14
IV, V, unclassified	-4.5	-5.0	-17
Female, low attainment*			
I, II	-15	-11	-21
III	-12	-9.6	-18
IV, V, unclassified	-12	-9.2	-18
Average standard error: 1.1.			
Male, high attainment*			
I, II	4.1	8.7	9.4
III	3.6	8.1	9.8
IV, V, unclassified	3.7	8.1	9.7
Female, high attainment*			
I, II	4.3	8.6	9.6
III	4.3	8.5	9.8
IV, V, unclassified	4.3	8.4	9.8
Average standard error: 1.8.			

Notes:
For each class, parental education is set to the modal value in each class in each year: see Table 2.5.
* Low attainment is having passed four subjects at mid-secondary level (O Grade or Standard Grade); high attainment is having passed three or more Highers.
Cells show percentage-point difference: students with breadth minus students without breadth.

Table 6.3 Percentage employed with any training, by social class, sex and school attainment, among people who were not in post-school education: difference associated with mid-secondary curricular breadth, 1976–98

	1976–8	1980–8	1990–8
Male, low attainment*			
I, II	4.2	2.4	5.5
III	4.2	2.3	4.9
IV, V, unclassified	4.5	2.5	5.7
Female, low attainment*			
I, II	4.6	2.8	5.4
III	4.6	2.7	6.0
IV, V, unclassified	4.6	2.8	6.0
Average standard error: 2.2.			
Male, high attainment*			
I, II	-4.0	-5.8	-2.9
III	-3.4	-5.6	-3.0
IV, V, unclassified	-3.6	-5.8	-3.1
Female, high attainment*			
I, II	-4.4	-6.1	-2.8
III	-4.6	-6.0	-3.0
IV, V, unclassified	-4.6	-5.9	-2.7
Average standard error: 2.0.			

Notes:
For each class, parental education is set to the modal value in each class in each year: see Table 2.5.
* Low attainment is having passed four subjects at mid-secondary level (O Grade or Standard Grade); high attainment is having pass three or more Highers.
Cells show percentage-point difference: students with breadth minus students without breadth.

in the table is that the average proportion entering post-school education in this group was 54.8 per cent with breadth and 45.0 per cent without breadth. The difference between these two percentages is the figure of 9.8 shown in the table.

For high-attaining students in this table, breadth is consistently associated with a higher rate of entry to post-school education, an effect which may have grown slowly over time. The persistently positive effect of breadth, when combined with the evidence from Chapter 4 on the extension of breadth to large proportions of school leavers, suggests that the Standard Grade reform was successfully improving the educational opportunities of high-attaining students. Part of this effect was growing rates of entry to higher education, to which we return when we consider breadth in Chapter 8.

On the other hand, in this table breadth had a negative effect for low attainers. One possible explanation is that breadth of attainment in an academic curriculum may have detracted from a focused attainment in a very few subjects that low-attaining students may have required to enter any kind post-school education. Nevertheless, if they then left education to enter employment, breadth conferred some benefits, as Table 6.3 illustrates for entering training. In contrast to Table 6.2, the effect of breadth here is positive for low attainers. High attainers, by contrast, did not benefit from breadth if they did not enter post-school education (though the level of random variation here means that we cannot be sure that they were disadvantaged by it). There was a similar pattern to Table 6.3 in avoiding unemployment among school leavers who did not enter education or training.

So we may tentatively conclude here that broadening the curriculum benefited high attainers for entry to education after they had left school, but low attainers for entering training and employment.

A different way of thinking about the effects of curricular reform relates to the development of low-level courses, which in their various forms over the years were particularly directed at low attainers. Figure 6.3 illustrates the association of these courses with entering post-school education, confining attention again to public-sector schools and to the period from the 1970s onwards. In this graph, the effect of low-level courses is the contrast between solid and broken lines; the effect of formal attainment is the contrast between black and grey lines. The pattern is of steadily strengthening association of this outcome with having completed a low-level course, especially for leavers with no awards in the main school courses (black lines). When the low-level courses were only non-certificate (in the 1970s) or only the Certificate of Secondary Education (1980–2), the statistical effect was generally negative at high overall attainment (grey lines), in the sense that people who took a low-level course (solid line) had lower proportions entering education than people who did not (broken line). However, for female students with no awards in the main courses (black lines), the line in the graphs for having taken a low-level course (solid line) moved above the line for not having done so in 1978–80, which would be consistent with there having been a targeted use of CSE with such students. Especially from the advent of the vocational modules in 1984, the line for low-level courses shows an advantage, especially for students who had no formal attainment (black lines). This benefit to low-attaining students is in contrast to the effect of breadth (Table 6.2).

Low-level courses also had a positive effect on entering jobs with training among people with no formal attainment, though without the effect of CSE in 1980. Unlike with post-school education, there was a diminishing effect in the late 1990s. This was an effect on short training only, because it was not found for entry to long training. The same positive but reducing effect was true for entering jobs without training by people who had no formal attainment.

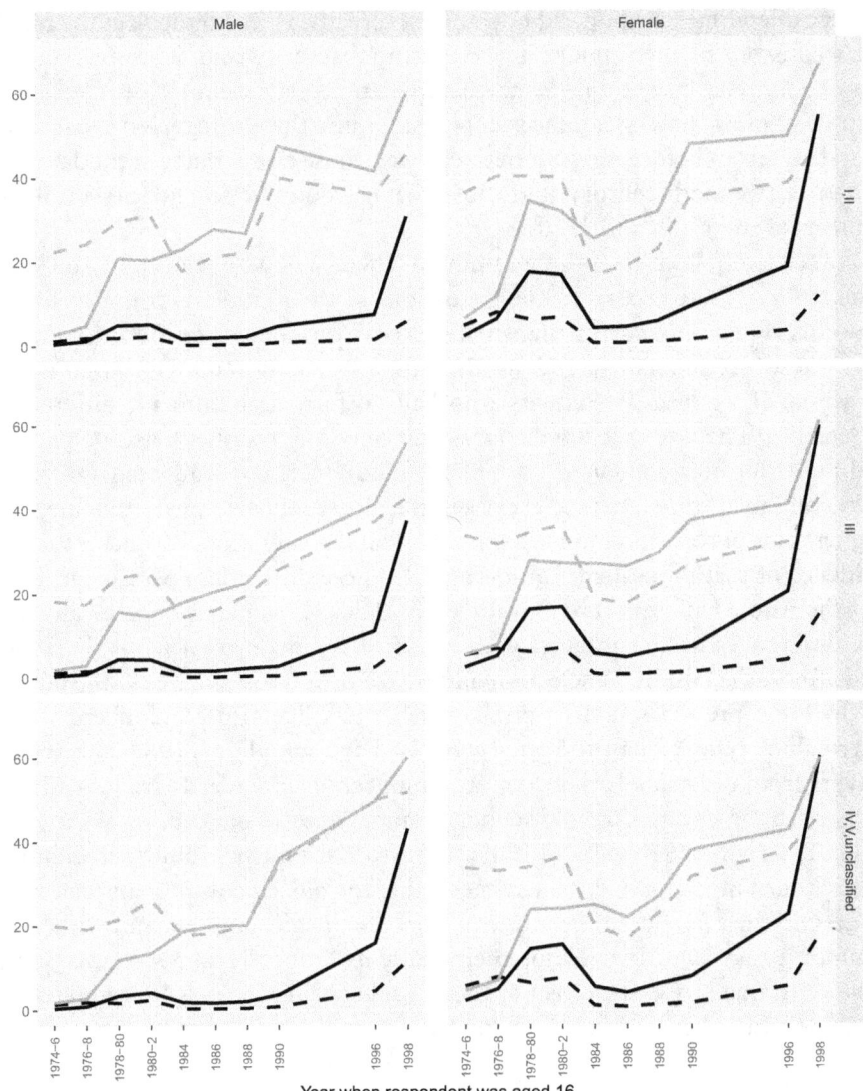

Figure 6.3 Percentage in post-school education, by social class, sex, attainment, and whether took a low-level course at school, 1976–98. Education authority schools only
Solid = any low-level course; broken = no low-level course
Black = no formal attainment; grey = passed 1+ Highers
For each class, parental education is set to the modal value in each year: see Table 2.5.
Average standard error: 3.1.

School History

Yet the conclusion about the effect of school reforms is not as straightforward as saying that the curriculum change had some effect while the structural change of ending selection did not, at least directly. If we now look at the much earlier history of the schools, as we did in Chapters 3 and 4, we find that it continued to have a residual legacy for transitions from school. To avoid small sample sizes, we now group the school history into three categories: the schools that dated from before the twentieth century, those that became secondaries in the early twentieth century, and those that were junior secondaries until the reforms of the 1960s and 1970s.

At relatively high levels of attainment, there was no evidence of any variation among these sectors in the transitions of their students from the 1980s onwards. This is not surprising when we recall the conclusion from Chapter 3 that these sectors converged at that time in their students' attainment. However, if we look at students who had no formal attainment, differences do emerge. The one that stands out is entering long training by students who did not enter post-school education: see Figure 6.4. For students from high-status and medium-status social classes, the oldest schools (the dotted line) had higher rates of transition to long training than the later schools. There was less evidence of that for students of low status. These differences persist throughout the whole half-century from the early 1950s. This persistence means that the differences do not interact with either of the main reforms of the 1960s and after – the ending of selection and the reform to the curriculum. Indeed, if anything, the old schools were somewhat less likely to be pioneers of the curriculum reform than the later schools. For example, in 1988, the school leavers from old schools that were also pioneers of Standard Grade made up 11 per cent of leavers from old schools, compared to 14 per cent from the early twentieth-century schools and 13 per cent from the former junior secondaries. The pattern in Figure 6.4 then suggests that the old schools perhaps had ways of getting their low-attaining students into worthwhile employment with good training prospects, though not their students from the lowest-status social classes. In that sense, the effect of the old schools in Figure 6.4 resembled the effect of a broad curriculum in Table 6.3.

CONCLUSIONS

Our surveys have provided coverage of several periods of very great change in the prospects facing school leavers, from the stability of the former selective system in the post-war expanding economy, through the transition to comprehensive schooling in the 1970s, the transformation of the youth labour market between the late 1970s and the mid-1980s, and the reforms to curriculum and assessment in schools in the late 1980s and 1990s. The surveys allow a broadly consistent classification of destinations in the year after leaving school. The main weakness of the analysis is any information on the local labour-market conditions faced by school leavers at each of these points in time. Local

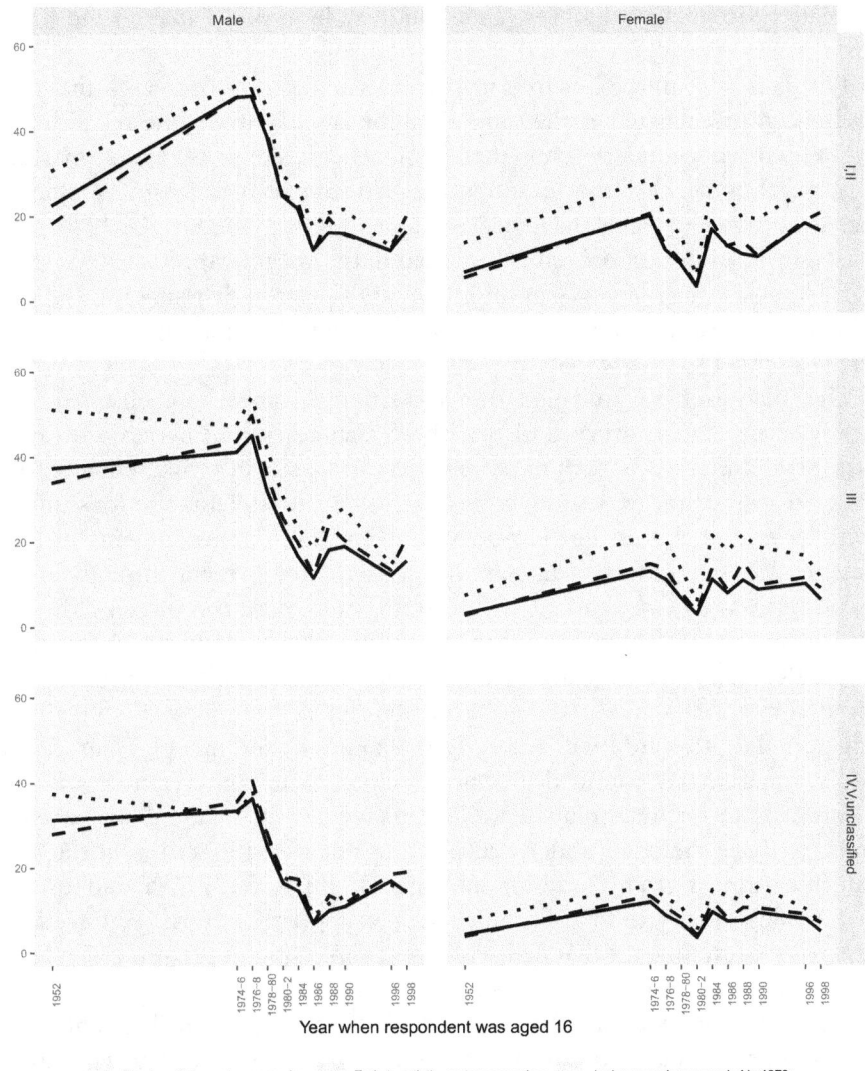

Figure 6.4 Percentage employed with long training, by social class, sex and school origins, 1952–98, among people who were not in post-school education. Education authority schools only; leavers with no awards at mid-secondary level
For each class, parental education is set to the modal value in each year: see Table 2.5.
Average standard error: 3.8.

conditions might be particularly relevant to leavers with low attainment from school. Nevertheless, previous detailed investigation of the 1980s, using the surveys of that period, has suggested that local conditions were not the main influences on leavers' decisions to leave school, which were more strongly associated with factors that were common to all localities (Paterson and Raffe, 1995).

The data have allowed us to bring together two areas of research that have rarely been investigated at the same time for any country – the transition to comprehensive secondary schooling and the changes to youth labour markets. We have thus been able to examine the educational precursors to entering vocational training when shortened versions of it expanded in the 1980s, and to ask how the educational reforms related to the vocational reforms. We were also able to set these changes in the context of the strongly rising rates of participation in post-school education as distinct from the training that was provided to school leavers who entered employment.

The analysis has confirmed that transitions from school changed very greatly in the half-century, and that these changes varied by sex and social class. School attainment became increasingly important in giving school leavers access to post-school education, especially for female students and for students from low-status classes. For low-status and medium-status students of both sexes, it also was important in gaining access to employment throughout the period. Access to employment with training was more complex: by the late 1980s, that was more common among low attainers than among high attainers, and in that sense training may be said to have successfully compensated for low attainment at school. But this contribution of training was only after a long period (in the late 1970s and early 1980s) when it did not play such a role, and in any case was confined to short training, mainly government schemes to compensate for unemployment. The inadequacy of many of the schemes which we have included under that heading was noted by critics at the time (a debate summarised by, for example, Jones (1988), Raffe (1984b) and Roberts et al. (1986)). Entry to long training, such as apprenticeships, reinforced the disparities of attainment that had arisen at school, a pattern that was similar to that for entering post-school education.

There was no evidence that the ending of selection into different kinds of secondary school had any particular effect on transitions to education, or employment with or without training. If anything, indeed, the strongest effects were from schools that were the last to reform, but these also had had similarly beneficial effects in the old selective system. Moreover, the effects of school reform were weaker than the effects of attainment: for low-attaining students, the gap in entering training in the 1980s corresponding to the reform categories (around 5 per cent) was less than the differences between attainment levels for the same outcome at that time (Figure 6.2). Nevertheless, there was some evidence that the schools which were the last to end selection were better able to take advantage of the new, short training opportunities in the 1980s. One possible explanation is that these schools, rethinking their courses in a non-selective way in the late 1970s and early 1980s, were doing so in the same context of the rapid rise in youth unemployment as caused government to develop new training schemes. By contrast, the earliest comprehensive schools, ending selection a decade previously, had less reason to make fundamental changes for their newly diverse school leavers. These early reformers then caught up with the late reformers when the short training schemes declined, but were not leaders in coming to terms with the unprecedented challenges of unemployment.

Reform to curriculum may have had a greater effect than ending selection. There was evidence that the schools which pioneered the transition to the new Standard Grade courses may have increased the proportions entering employment with or without training among students from low-status social classes who had relatively high attainment. Because this effect was found only for entry to long training, it may have been a more sustainable impact than had been ending selection. The Standard Grade reforms themselves may be interpreted as one aspect of the policy response to the growth in youth unemployment, even though, far from being deliberately vocational, they were in fact an attempt to extend a liberal curriculum to everyone. Indeed, as we saw in Chapter 4, these reforms were probably not associated with much change in the taking of vocational courses: the effect was entirely in the core curriculum. The breadth of that new curriculum may have helped high attainers to progress to educational courses after leaving school, but breadth also may have helped low attainers to enter training or employment. So these reforms extended general attainment as a direct means of increasing school leavers' chances in the labour market. Unlike with the ending of selection, the timing ensured that the schools which adopted Standard Grade first (in the mid-1980s) were doing so in the context of persisting high unemployment, and so would be most aware of any potential contribution that the new curriculum might make to school leavers' prospects. But that characterisation is not enough, because employment with short training became an important destination for people who had not attained highly in the general course. Low-attaining students did seem to benefit from the growth of mainly vocational, low-level courses alongside the core reforms – the National Certificate modules after 1984 – and continued to do so in the late 1990s, well after the Standard Grade reforms had been completed. On the other hand, as Jones (1988) noted, the very fact that what we have called 'short training' was entered by people with low-level courses from school tended to cause this training to be seen as being of low status. That kind of training might then be seen as a diversion of low-attaining school leavers away from worthwhile opportunities.

Throughout these policy responses to the crisis of youth unemployment in the 1970s and 1980s there remained also a legacy of much earlier reforms to schooling, dating back to the first few decades of the century. This is then a further appearance of something that we have noted several times before.

The old schools that had been founded before the twentieth century seemed to be better able than later secondary schools to get low-attaining school leavers into jobs that had worthwhile prospects of training, though only for students from high-status or medium-status social classes. Moreover, that old-school advantage persisted through the reforms of the 1970s and 1980s, right to the end of the century. This aspect of the legacy was thus sustained much longer than the effects on attainment or the curriculum that we observed in Chapters 3 and 4.

These results are consistent with both bodies of prior research from other countries that were summarised earlier, and thus place Scottish experience in the international mainstream. On the one hand, comprehensive schooling's extension of meaningful courses and assessment to a much wider range of students than in the previous system is reflected here in the growing importance of school attainment not only for gaining access to post-school education but also for entry to longer programmes of training or to employment. Changing levels of attainment were particularly important for students of low social status, and (to some extent at all social levels) females. On the other hand, the changes in schools can be seen in this analysis to have been an important part of the policy response to youth unemployment. Relatively high attainment at school became an increasingly important route into a post-school destination that might lead to stable employment. In that sense, our analysis is consistent with previous research which shows the increasing importance of credentials that accompanied the expansion of comprehensive schooling and the collapse of the youth labour market in the 1980s. But the analysis also shows that the expansion of vocational training in the 1980s was complementary to these school reforms. Employment with training was more likely to be entered by school leavers who had relatively low attainment, but this compensatory effect was confined to short training, mainly in the government training schemes that were widely criticised at the time as being inadequate. Access to employment with training did not compensate for the rise of unemployment that was caused by cyclical economic change – the recession of the 1970s and early 1980s – but at best may have helped to compensate for the structural changes that persisted through the economic recovery after that date. In a labour market from the late 1980s onwards where the service sector was expanding and manufacturing was declining, young people could strengthen their competitive advantage only by acquiring credentials after leaving school, whether in formal education or in lengthy training courses.

This complementarity of schools and longer types of training was argued at the time by Raffe (1985) in a prescient discussion of the new vocational modules that were introduced from the mid-1980s. The preference of the education systems of the UK for general education over vocational training has often been seen as a failure to prepare school leavers for employment. Scotland's predilection for general education has been especially strong, and the Standard Grade reforms of the 1980s ensured that Scottish comprehensive schooling at that time would be liberal rather than vocational. The analysis presented here might suggest that the implied dichotomy between academic and vocational preparation is too stark. Even in the depth of the recession of the 1980s, school leavers' opportunities were being shaped by the expansion of general education in the newly comprehensive schools rather more than by the training opportunities that were being offered beyond school, because these were mainly short rather than long. In that sense, the effects of comprehensive schooling were not so much in the specific ending of selection or even in the specific reforms to courses and assessment, but rather in the increase in general educational participation that it accompanied and probably encouraged. The analysis reported here suggests, then, that if we are to understand how a new labour market for young people was created after the 1980s, we need to take into account not only vocational training and policy on the labour market, but also schools and policy on the general curriculum.

CHAPTER 7

Schools and Higher Education

AFFINITY BETWEEN SCHOOLS AND UNIVERSITIES

The influence which secondary schools have on students' entry to higher education has attracted research interest in many countries in recent years, although our knowledge of it is less extensive than the abundant evidence relating to students' individual characteristics such as attainment, sex or socio-economic status (Taylor et al., 2018; Donnelly, 2015). The question is whether schools are influential over and above their effects through attainment. A subsidiary question is whether schools modify the direct effects on entry to higher education of sex and social class, beyond these demographic factors' effects on attainment. The main new evidence in the recent research has related to the role which is played by schools that are independent of public management, and also the role which school context plays, whether that is defined by socio-economic measures or by attainment (for example, Boliver, 2013; Sutton Trust, 2011). On the whole, independent schools and schools with high proportions of students from high-status social classes tend to have higher rates of entry to higher education, even after controlling statistically for attainment and individual-level social class.

In these debates, there has been little attention to how the effects of schools might change over time. That absence is quite surprising. One of the aims of reforms to secondary schooling in many countries between the 1960s and the 1980s was – as in Scotland – to widen access to officially recognised attainment and thus to meaningful opportunities in post-school education. Because higher education, too, was structurally reformed in that same period, and later, it might be expected that there would be some interaction of these two policy processes. One reason to expect that is the concept of 'institutional habitus' (Donnelly, 2015; Reay et al., 2001), which refers to the ways in which the ethos of a school might help its students to gain access to particular kinds of university. Reforms to secondary schools might be expected to modify the ways in which institutional habitus operates.

This chapter considers Scottish higher education in the second half of the twentieth century in the light of these questions. The school leavers' surveys allow us to study the interaction of two institutional reforms – to schools and to higher education – and how that interaction, in turn, was modified by the changing demographic distribution of social class, the changing differences between female and male students, and the rising attainment in school-leaving examinations. The school changes were described in Chapter 1 and their effects were analysed in detail in Chapters 3 to 6. The changes to higher education were also described in Chapter 1; here we concentrate on the distinctions among four broad sectors, based mainly on institutional history but also paying attention to the educational level of the courses which students were taking:

- The four old universities. Sometimes in Scotland they are referred to informally as 'ancient', but that word is ambiguous in the context of a sector of education that, in other parts of Europe and the Arab world, genuinely does stretch back to ancient times. The word 'old' is enough here.
- The four 1960s universities: only one of these was wholly new, the rest having independent institutional predecessors. The label is used here, slightly anachronistically, to refer to these predecessors in the early 1960s.
- The 1990s universities: these all had institutional predecessors, some dating back to the late nineteenth century. Again, the 1990s label is used for the whole data series.
- Non-degree courses and professional courses: by the end of the century, these were almost all provided in further education colleges, though until the 1980s some were in the institutions that became 1990s universities. We classify all these course together, whatever institution they were in; so the other three categories are defined to be degree-level courses only.

A few students attended universities outside Scotland: these were fewer than 1 per cent of school leavers in most of the surveys, rising slightly to 1.9 per cent in 1998. It would have been informative to have been able to analyse this movement out of Scotland, especially in relation to Oxford and Cambridge. However, most of the surveys did not distinguish between different universities outside Scotland. In those which did record that information (1976–90), the number of sample members who attended Oxford or Cambridge was tiny – between 5 and 11 sample members per year, which is not enough for reliable statistical analysis in a period of great change over time. The universities outside Scotland are included in the second category here, thus keeping the four oldest universities as a distinct sector.

THE EFFECTS OF SCHOOL ON ENTRY TO HIGHER EDUCATION

In the past decade and half, there has been a growth of research into the effects of secondary schools on entry to higher education. The earliest recent investigation of this topic was by Pustjens et al. (2004), who examined the effects of secondary school on students' choices of educational destination after school. These authors noted the sparsity of research on this topic, as did Espenshade et al. (2005, p. 270), Palardy (2015, p. 346) and Donnelly (2015, p. 1075). The general conclusion of the recent research has been that, although the main way in which schools have an effect on entry to higher education is through their effects on attainment in school-leaving examinations (Gorard et al., 2006), there is clear evidence also of direct school effects over and above that, and also over and above the effects of social class and sex. Pustjens et al. (2004, p. 297), with data from Flanders, found large school effects on the chances of entering higher education. Taylor et al. (2018, p. 591) found that, in Wales, the probability of going to university depended on the school that a student had attended. Anders and Micklewright (2015) found, for England, that the probability of a school leaver proceeding to university was influenced by schools' capacities to modify young people's aspirations, a similar finding to that by Chowdry et al. (2013) and Tymms (1995).

A recurrent finding in this research has been that the socio-economic composition of the school affects the probability of an individual student going to university. Smyth and Hannan (2007) found, in Ireland, a positive effect of attending a predominantly middle-class school, beyond the effect of individual circumstances. Shulruf et al. (2008) reached a similar conclusion for New Zealand. Iannelli (2004), comparing rates of transition to various post-school destinations in Scotland, Ireland and the Netherlands, found that variation among schools was greatest in the Netherlands, with its structurally divided school system, and least in Scotland, with its non-selective public sector. Thus in Scotland individual characteristics (attainment, social class and sex) explained a larger proportion of the variation in entry rates among schools than in the other two countries.

Donnelly (2015) noted that the most common finding on how the character of a school might affect the probability of entering higher education has related to the difference between independent schools and public-sector schools. Boliver (2013) found that independent schools in England increased their students' chances of applying to, and being accepted by, high-status universities. There were similar findings by Mangan et al. (2010) for England, Gayle et al. (2002) for England and Wales, Epenshade et al. (2005) for the USA, and Power and Whitty (2008) for high-attaining students in England. The Sutton Trust (2011) in the UK has used such research to campaign for fairer mechanisms of selection into higher education, noting also that public-sector schools with records of high attainment seem to be similar to independent schools in their positive effects on their students' likelihood of entering university.

Some of this research has distinguished among different categories of higher education. Closest to the classification which we use here is that by Taylor et al. (2018), who studied entry not only to degree courses at any university but also to shorter (usually two-year) courses, and, separately, to degree courses in the highest-status universities. The distinction between degrees and two-year diplomas – which is our distinction between the first three sectors of higher education and the fourth – is analogous to that between four-year and two-year programmes in the USA, school effects on entry to which were investigated by Palardy (2015). The conclusion of this body of work is that, on the whole, high-status schools tend to be associated with high-status universities or courses. Taylor et al. (2018) found that school effects were particularly strong for entering high-status universities. Power and Whitty (2008) even found that students from independent schools whose attainment was too low to allow them to enter elite universities tended to avoid university altogether, whereas similarly qualified students from public-sector schools would go to lower-status universities.

EXPLANATIONS

The main body of ideas which has been offered to explain school effects on entry to higher education relates to what has been called 'institutional habitus'. Though abstract theory is no substitute for empirical detail, it can be valuable as a way of interpreting the empirical findings. Smyth and Hannan (2007, p. 176) describe institutional habitus as 'the impact of a social group on an individual's behaviour as it is mediated through organisations such as schools'. Donnelly (2015, p. 1076) links this more explicitly to the ideas of Bourdieu, defining institutional habitus as 'a set of dispositions and behaviours that are the product of a school's past experiences, staff and pupils', a description that is analogous to Nash's summary (1999, p. 184) of Bourdieu's idea of habitus as 'a system of durable dispositions inculcated by objective structural conditions'. Though Bourdieu himself does not seem to have used the term, institutional habitus is central to his ideas of social reproduction, habitus in general being 'that system of dispositions which acts as a mediation between structures and practice' (Bourdieu, 1973, p. 72), the means by which 'structures ... reproduce themselves' through creating agents attuned to that reproduction. So the students become both the products of the reproduction and the agents of its further development. Part of that process is the affinity between secondary schools and particular tertiary institutions. In Bourdieu's work on

France, that was embodied in the connection between the highest status forms of the baccalauréat and the grandes écoles. Reay et al. (2005, p. 52) applied these ideas to understanding the links between particular kinds of secondary school in England and sectors of the university system. Forbes and Lingard (2013) invoke institutional habitus to explain the effects of an independent girls' school on its students' opportunities. Previous empirical development of the idea of institutional habitus has emphasised what Reay et al. (2001, paras 1.2–1.3) call its dynamic aspect: 'institutional habituses, no less than individual habituses, have a history and have been established over time'. Nevertheless, there has been little empirical attention to change of institutional habitus except as a slowly and autonomously evolving characteristic.

The questions which we investigate in this chapter are intrinsically about potential change in habitus – the ending of selection into different kinds of secondary school in the public sector, and the various reforms to higher education institutions. Therefore, although we invoke the concept of institutional habitus as a way of explaining empirical patterns, and although these previous writers' use of the term is illuminating, we have to turn to distinct bodies of ideas for suggestions about how that concept might be relevant to institutional change. The idea of institutional habitus is in some respects a way of representing what might be called the relationship between structure and agency (Archer, 1979). Previous studies of the historical legacies of educational institutions in Scotland have drawn on these older ways of thinking about their effects. The history of Scottish schools has been studied for its lasting effect on school attainment (Chapters 3 and 4 above, and also, for example, McPherson and Willms, 1986), by invoking ideas about institutions' persisting identity. Ocasio et al. (2016, p. 676) noted that all persisting organisations develop 'historically situated webs of meaning and significance'. These might be particularly strong in schools and universities, because attention to cultural meanings is part of these institution's basic purpose. Much of the previous study of institutional legacies in Scotland has paid attention to the ways in which schools contribute to defining the social-class identity of communities (McPherson and Willms, 1986): we noted an example of this towards the end of Chapter 3, in connection with communities that have had a single secondary school. All these historical studies have had change as their central focus. J. W. Meyer and Rowan (1977, pp. 340 and 355) describe how 'institutional rules function as myths' but 'may conflict with one another', provoking institutional change. H.-D. Meyer (2006, p. 52) goes further in noting that institutional myths might actually embody 'beliefs in the change process and the power struggles that always surround institutions'. Analysing the history of the common school in the USA in the late nineteenth century, he described how the advent of massive waves of immigration from central Europe elicited new political coalitions that could emphasise the egalitarian potential of the institutional tradition in order to shape it as the basis of a new system of schooling for the twentieth century. This US experience is an instance of the 'critical events' which Clemente et al. (2017, pp. 22–4) suggest are a common means by which 'slow-changing systems' adapt. Nikolai (2019, 377–8), while recognising that 'accumulated commitments and investments in the selected path make it difficult to effect any profound change', comments that a change in 'societal values' might 'delegitimise established institutional forms and practices'. She was studying the legacies of schools in the former East Germany even after the enormous disruption of reunification in 1990. Ocasio et al. (2016, p. 690) point out that this can happen when the gradual 'accumulation of historical events' leads to general 'societal transformation'. The influence of institutions and the wider society might thus be mutual.

There are two specific reasons to ask whether institutional habitus can change as well as the reasons which arise from the idea itself. One is change in the context. When the nature of social class has changed as profoundly as it did between the early 1950s and the late 1990s, we might expect some change in the connection between class and institutions; and if there is no such change, the stability would itself require to be explained. The other reason is the extensive policy changes in that same half-century. Because several of these policies were designed to modify the relationship between social class and educational opportunity, the question then arises as to whether institutional habitus has anything to contribute to understanding the changing links among institutions, social class and an expanding system of higher education. Few of the empirical investigations of the effects of schools on entry to higher education that were summarised in the previous section had data that allow any study of change over time, in contrast to our data.

Whether the concept of 'habitus' is useful here is open. We saw in Chapters 3 and 4 that Bourdieu's ideas almost axiomatically deny the possibility of change in the essence of social inequality, a denial that (as we quoted there) was subject to detailed theoretical and empirical critique by Goldthorpe (2007). Our analysis in these chapters thus tends to support Goldthorpe's doubts insofar as we have found very large changes in the social distribution of achievement. We return at the end of the present chapter to the question of whether, nevertheless, a different kind of habitus might be of some value in explaining the changing experience of whole institutions. For the time being, it should thus be taken as no more than a tentative metaphor.

CLASSIFYING HIGHER EDUCATION

Because we are now mainly looking at people who had some realistic chance of qualifying to enter higher education, we can use the fuller version of the survey series, the surveys with school leavers who turned 16 in: 1952, 1960–2,

1968–70, 1970–2, 1974–6, 1976–8, 1978–80, 1980–2, 1984, 1986, 1988, 1990, 1996 and 1998. For some preliminary analysis, to set the context, we continue to use the 11 surveys 1952 and 1974–6 to 1998. The main series is restricted to people who passed at least one Higher Grade course, and uses the surveys from 1960–2 to 1998 (omitting 1952 because it had too few such students for reliable estimates). The corresponding distributions of entry by school leavers to the four sectors of higher education are shown in Tables 7.1 and 7.2 below. The tables analyse entry to each of the sectors listed earlier in this chapter among students who did not enter the sectors above it in the list. This approach thus recognises the ordered hierarchy of institutions, somewhat analogously to how, in Chapter 6, we dealt with the full range of destinations after leaving school. One caveat should be borne in mind for the 1952 data when comparing this table with Table 6.1: because the evidence about entry to higher education is based on questions asked when the respondent was aged 27, it will include people who did not enter directly from school. Moreover, for that survey year, and to an extent right up to the 1970s, higher education also included people who combined advanced study with employment as an apprentice professional (as noted in connection with Table 6.1).

The explanatory variable on which we concentrate is a simplified version of the classification of school history (similar to that used in Figure 6.4, but now also including the independent schools). Thus the first two categories are the same as in Table 2.3 in Chapter 2. The third combines the two categories of secondary school founded in the first half of the twentieth century. The fourth category here combines the two categories of junior secondary school.

The other new explanatory variable is attainment in the senior years of school, measured as awards in the Higher Grade examinations, and standardised to have mean 0 and standard deviation 1 in each survey. For the models confined to people with at least one Higher Grade award, we measure both the number and the quality of attainment as

$$\text{(number of A–C awards)} + 0.5 \times \text{(number of A awards)}$$

It too is standardised in each survey.

EXPANSION

Table 7.1 shows the expansion of school-leaver participation in the four sectors of higher education in the second half of the twentieth century. The overall growth, shown in the 'all sectors' column, happened in two periods – a doubling to a quarter by the mid-1980s, and then an increase to four out of ten by the end of the century. That expansion masked broad stability until the late 1980s in both the oldest sector and, after their initial growth, the other

Table 7.1 Percentage entering sectors of higher education, 1952–98

Percentage	Old universities	Other pre-1990s universities	Degree courses not in pre-1990s universities*	Non-degree and professional courses[†]	All sectors[‡]
Year when respondent was aged 16					
1952	4	–	2	6	12
1974–6	4	3	2	4	13
1976–8	5	3	2	5	14
1978–80	4	3	2	4	14
1980–2	4	2	3	5	15
1984	4	3	5	6	19
1986	5	4	5	9	23
1988	7	4	8	9	28
1990	8	6	8	10	33
1996	9	8	12	10	39
1998	10	8	12	9	39

Notes:
Percentages weighted; for sample sizes, see Table 2.1.
* Degree courses in any institution that, until the 1990s, was a non-university higher education college. In 1952, 'degrees' include professional qualifications for high-status professions.
[†] Non-degree higher education courses in colleges not included in the first three columns, or courses while in professional employment. In 1952, includes nursing and other non-graduate professions.
Institutions outside Scotland are included in columns 2–5 (as proportions of all entrants in column 5: 0.03 or lower until 1984; 0.04 to 1990; 0.05 in 1996–8).
[‡] The 'all sectors' column is the sum of the others, apart from rounding error.

pre-1990s universities. Expansion until the late 1980s was more striking in the degree courses outside the then universities, and in non-degree courses in local colleges. As a result, the share of students taken by the two older sectors fell from around one-half in the 1970s to just over a third in the early 1980s, recovering back to just under one-half in the late 1990s.

Table 7.1 thus sets the context. Figure 7.1 shows the social class make-up of the student intake to the four sectors of higher education, and to higher education as a whole, covering the period from 1952 to 1998. Comparing the first and last columns in this graph, we can see that, until the 1960s, the old universities originally had intakes that were representative of all students, but that they took an increasing share of high-status students over the following three decades. The other pre-1990s universities, by contrast, were more inclusive in the 1960s and remained in line with overall intake, as did the sector of degree courses in the institutions that were higher education colleges until the 1990s and new universities thereafter. The low-status students were

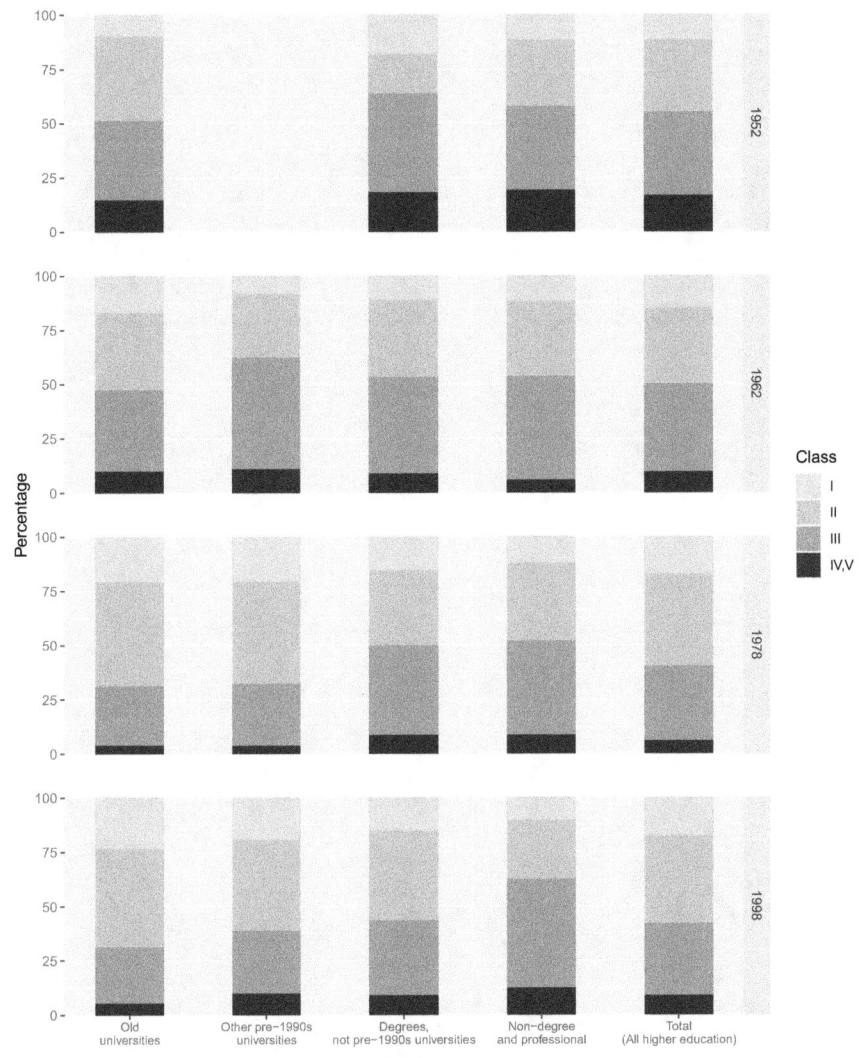

Figure 7.1 Social class of school-leaver entrants to sectors of higher education, 1952, 1962, 1978 and 1998

thus increasingly concentrated in the mainly non-degree programmes of the further education colleges. This segmentation contrasts with what happened to schools during the shift to comprehensive secondary education. As seen in Figure 3.7 in Chapter 3, the historically defined school sectors became more similar with respect to social class.

Whereas Figure 7.1 shows intake to higher education – what the students who arrive there from school look like – Figures 7.2 and 7.3 show the same

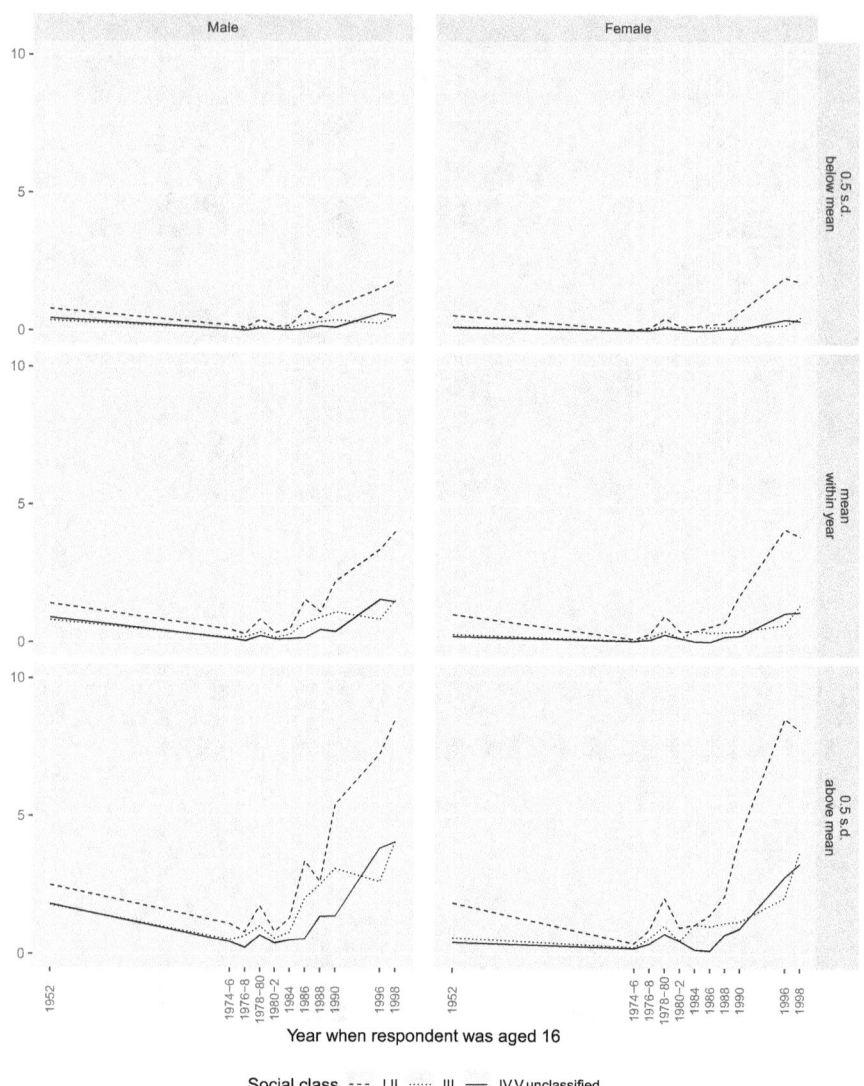

Figure 7.2 Percentage of all school leavers entering old universities, by attainment, sex and social class, 1952–98

For each class, parental education is set to the modal value in each year: see Table 2.5. The 1952 information was as recorded at age 27, and so will include some people who did not enter directly from school. Average standard error: 0.5.

story in terms of outflows from schools: what proportion of each social class, and each sex, go into specific kinds of university? The first of these shows entry to the old universities. The three values of attainment are the mean plus and minus 0.5 standard deviations. The greatest growth after the 1970s was

SCHOOLS AND HIGHER EDUCATION 137

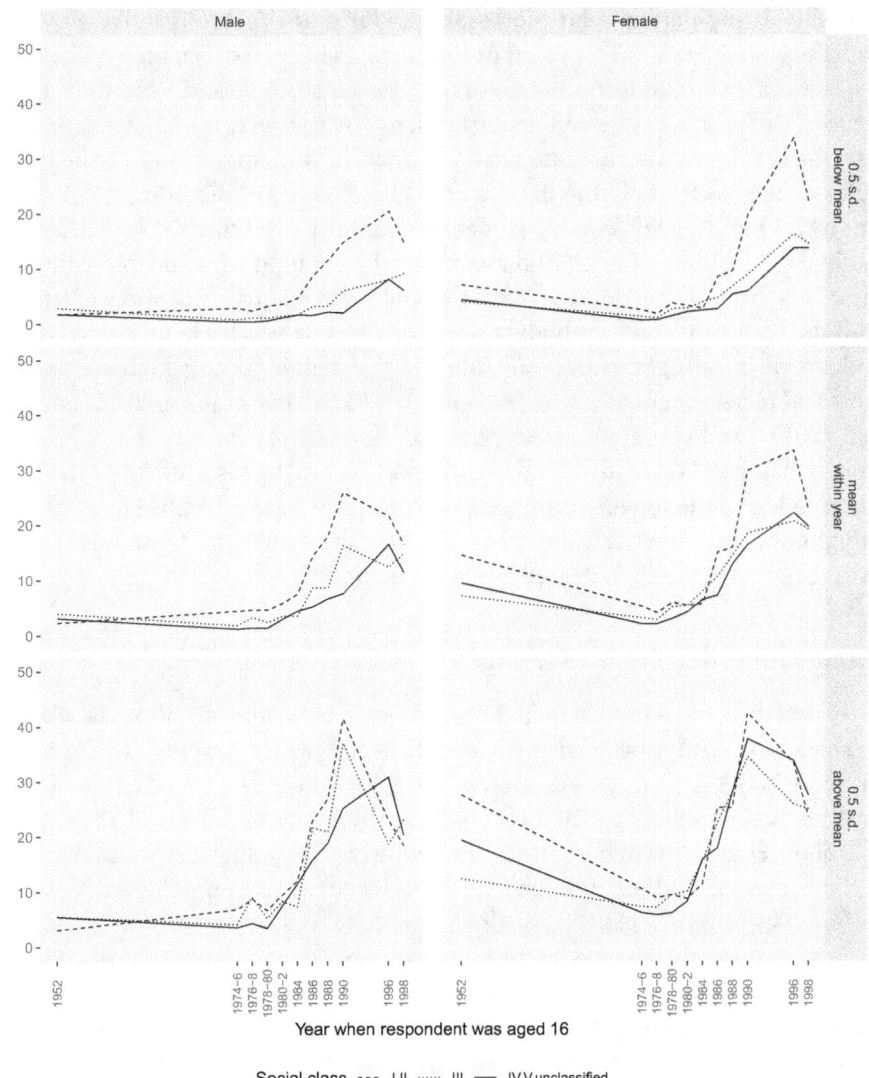

Figure 7.3 Percentage entering non-degree higher education among all school leavers who did not enter degree-level higher education, by attainment, sex and social class, 1952–98
For each class, parental education is set to the modal value in each year: see Table 2.5. Attainment is standardised across all school leavers (and thus means the same as in Figure 7.2). The 1952 information was as recorded at age 27, and so will include some people who did not enter directly from school.
Average standard error: 2.5.

for people with above-average attainment (bottom panels), most notably for students from high-status social classes (dashed lines).

The patterns for the other pre-1990s universities and for degrees outside these two university sectors (not shown) were similar, with greater inequality, especially at high attainment. For example, for entry to 1960s universities by students who did not enter the old universities, the gap between high-status and low-status males at high attainment grew between 1952–78 and 1996–8 from 0.1 per cent to 8.6 per cent, and for females from 0.1 per cent to 2.8 per cent. For entry to 1990s universities among those who did not enter either of the older sectors, the growth was from 0.7 per cent to 7.5 per cent for males, and 1.6 per cent to 7.4 per cent for females. But entry to non-degree courses was different, as Figure 7.3 shows. These students might be thought of as people who just missed out on entering degree courses. Social-class inequality of entry fell in the 1990s to a point at which, at high attainment, the rate was higher for lower-class students than for higher, essentially because the high-attaining, high-status students had taken advantage of the expansion of old and new universities (Iannelli et al., 2011), and so were less likely to enter non-degree courses. Although this process has been described as the diversion of low-status students into low-status colleges, the longer-term perspective shown in the graphs suggests that it might be more appositely described as a new aversion by high-status students from these colleges when degree courses expanded.

Public and Independent Schools

In this context of rising participation in higher education by all social classes and both sexes, but also of rising social-class inequality for entry to the highest-status universities, our question is what, if any, was the specific role of particular kinds of school in the process. Was there any institutional association of school sector with higher education sector, was any such association linked to social class, could any link be explained by school attainment, and did any of these associations change over time? Before taking attainment into account, there were large differences between the independent schools and the education authority schools. For example, in the 1990s, the average rate of entry to the old universities by female students in the highest classes was 29 per cent from the independent schools, but only 15–16 per cent from each of the sectors of public-sector schools. The corresponding proportions for male students were 25 per cent and 14–17 per cent.

Restricting attention to people with at least one Higher Grade award enables us to include the surveys of 1960–2, 1968–70 and 1970–2, but we have to drop the 1952 survey because its sample size of people with at least one Higher is too small for reliable inferences. The rates of entry by these students to the four sectors of higher education are shown in Table 7.2. We deal separately with: (1) grant-aided and independent schools compared to education authority schools, and (2) comparison among the categories of the latter.

The sample sizes for the independent schools are relatively small in the later surveys, especially for social classes other than I and II. For example, in the five

Table 7.2 Percentage entering sectors of higher education, among people who had passed at least one Higher, 1962–98

Percentage	Proportion with at least 1 Higher*	Old universities	Other pre-1990s universities	Degree courses not in pre-1990s universities	Non-degree and professional courses	All sectors†	Sample size for all but first column (=100%)
Year when respondent was aged 16							
1960–2	15	32	6	1	4	43	6,048
1968–70	25	24	11	2	12	49	2,482
1970–2	27	21	10	3	9	42	2,779
1974–6	22	20	11	7	16	53	7,079
1976–8	26	18	11	7	16	53	1,741
1978–80	27	16	11	8	13	48	6,667
1980–2	27	14	9	11	15	49	2,477
1984	32	14	10	14	17	55	1,695
1986	33	16	11	15	22	64	1,829
1988	37	18	12	21	18	69	1,731
1990	41	19	15	20	19	74	1,478
1996	50	18	15	23	13	69	1,459
1998	52	19	16	21	12	68	2,946

Notes:

Percentages weighted; sample sizes unweighted.
For definition of higher education sectors, see footnote to Table 7.1, and text. In 1960–2, 'Other pre-1990s universities' includes those colleges which became universities in the 1960s.
* Proportion of school leavers passing at least one Higher. Sources: Table 3.1 in Chapter 3, and SED (1973, p. 29).
† The 'all sectors' column is the sum of the others, apart from rounding error.

surveys 1986–98 taken together, a total of only 126 people from class III were in these schools, and only 100 from the groups IV, V and unclassified. Therefore, for illustrating the difference between independent and education authority schools, we confine attention to class I and II, and also group the years into four categories: 1962–72, in which period most students would have entered secondary school in the pre-comprehensive system; 1976–84, which is the period of ending selection in the education authority sector; 1986–90, the period of extending the mid-secondary curriculum to all students; and 1996–8, which reflects the stable reformed system in the education authority sector. Table 7.3 shows, for each of these periods, the proportion of students in class I and II who entered each of the sectors of higher education (conditional on not entering the sectors above it in the hierarchy), controlling for attainment and sex.

For the old universities, the entry rate from the independent schools remained consistently a few percentages points higher than from the education authority schools, widening in the 1990s for women. For the other pre-1990s universities and the institutions that became universities in the 1990s, there is a widening in favour of the independent schools after the mid-1980s for both men and women. In contrast, entry to non-degree courses is nearly always more common from the education authority schools than from the independent schools, the latter route falling away almost completely in the 1990s.

We can sum this up by saying that the independent school advantage has not been explained wholly by attainment. The long-established advantage in entry to the old universities was supplemented by a new advantage for independent schools in relation to the other pre-1990s universities and to those that were upgraded in the 1990s. So this is evidence of the maintenance of institutional affinity between independent schools and old universities, and the possible creation of a new affinity with other sectors.

School History

The remaining analysis is confined to education authority schools. The general trajectory for all social-class groups is illustrated in Figure 7.4, which is for entry to old universities: even after controlling for attainment, there was a distinction among the historically defined sectors of schools up till the 1970s, but that then diminished. For classes I and II – where the school distinctions in Figure 7.4 are greatest – the differences are illustrated in detail in Table 7.4, showing the three sectors of schools and also the four types of higher education. Until the full implementation of comprehensive schooling, the pre-twentieth-century schools had a distinct advantage for entry to the old universities. In the surveys 1962–72, the rate of entry by high-status males was 21 percentage points higher from the old schools than from those junior secondaries that were already making the transition to comprehensive status, and

Table 7.3 Percentage entering sectors of higher education, by sex and whether school was education authority or independent, 1960–2 to 1996–8. Class I, II only. Attainment set at mean among those who passed at least one Higher

	Old universities		Other pre-1990s universities[*]		Degree courses not in pre-1990s universities[*]		Non-degree and professional courses[*]	
	Education Authority	Grant aided or independent	Education Authority	Grant aided or independent	Education Authority	Grant aided or independent	Education Authority	Grant aided or independent
Male								
1962–72	30	33	20	22	8	9	23	17
1976–84	13	18	16	18	23	21	27	21
1986–90	16	19	11	19	46	58	45	24
1996–8	15	17	18	23	45	66	25	0
Average standard error	1.7	3.6	2.0	3.8	2.8	4.3	3.6	4.5
Female								
1962–72	22	27	12	15	2	0	18	16
1976–84	14	16	11	16	23	21	41	39
1986–90	13	18	11	27	45	59	55	60
1996–8	14	26	17	27	42	56	33	8
Average standard error	1.5	3.7	1.9	6.6	2.3	5.0	3.0	4.5

Notes:
Parental education is set to the modal value in this class in each year: see Table 2.5.
[*] The percentages are on successively restricted data sets, each pair of columns excluding those respondents who entered the sectors in the pairs to the left of it.

142 SCOTTISH EDUCATION AND SOCIETY SINCE 1945

13 points higher than from the newer. For females, the differences in rates were 18 and 10 points. The differences between the early twentieth-century secondaries and the former junior secondaries were also quite clear: 8 points for both males and females. Then all the differences disappeared by the 1990s. The percentages entering the old universities were smaller because the proportion

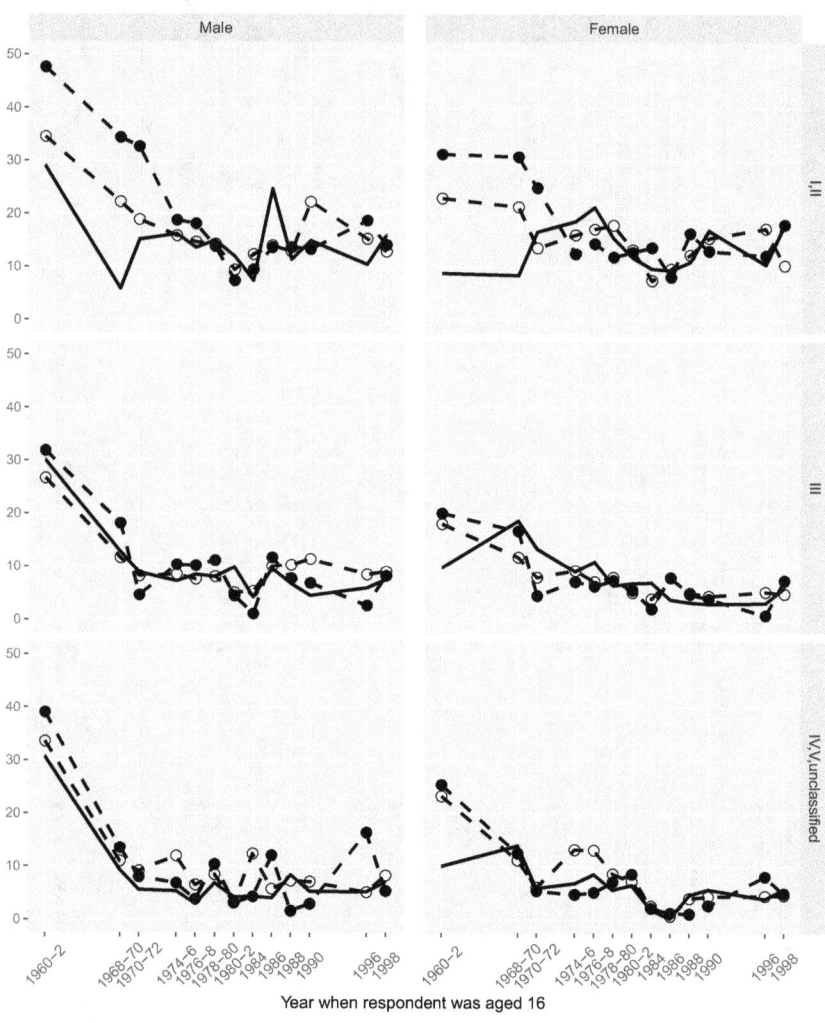

Figure 7.4 Percentage entering old universities at mean* attainment, by social class, sex and school origin, 1962–98. Education authority schools only
*Mean attainment among students who had at least one Higher Grade award.
For each class, parental education is set to the modal value in each year: see Table 2.5.
Average standard error: 3.4.

Table 7.4 Percentage entering sectors of higher education, by sex and school origin, 1960–2 to 1996–8. Class I, II only. Attainment set at mean among those who passed at least one Higher

	Old universities		Other pre-1990s universities*		Degree courses not in pre-1990s universities*			Non-degree and professional courses*	
	1962–72	1990–8	1962–72	1990–8	1970–2[†]	1990–8		1962–72	1990–8
Male									
Pre-twentieth-century secondary	38	15	21	16	6	44		27	40
Early twentieth-century secondary	25	17	21	18	10	44		21	34
Former junior secondary	17	14	21	20	8	42		18	26
Average standard error	3.6	2.7	4.2	3.2	3.9	4.5		4.5	6.1
Female									
Pre-twentieth-century secondary	29	14	13	18	2	52		21	47
Early twentieth-century secondary	19	14	13	13	1	47		16	38
Former junior secondary	11	15	9	17	3	42		17	40
Average standard error	2.8	2.1	2.6	2.8	1.9	3.9		3.2	5.0

Notes:
Parental education is set to the modal value in this class in each year: see Table 2.5.
* The models are on successively restricted data sets, each pair of columns excluding those respondents who entered the sectors in the pairs to the left of it.
[†] The earlier date range omits 1962 for the third group of higher education institutions because of very small sample size from the former junior secondaries (13 males and 15 females). The estimates for the other two school sectors including 1962 were very close to those in the table (respectively 5 and 8 for males, and the same as in the table for females).

of the age group with one or more Highers had tripled (Table 7.2), and because the other three sectors of higher education had vastly expanded, but the main point for our discussion here is that they were indistinguishable among the school sectors: 15, 17 and 14 for males; 14, 14 and 15 for females.

There probably never were any consistent differences by school origin for entry to the other university sectors by students from high-status social classes. Only for those men who did not enter university but who did enter sub-degree courses was there a possible persisting advantage of the oldest schools. These men in this social class had relatively low attainment from school: in the 1990s, on average a score of 2.5 (in the metric defined earlier in this chapter), compared to over 6 for similar men entering the oldest universities. This effect on students with relatively low attainment is reminiscent of the possible effect of these schools on high-status, low-attaining students which we saw in Chapter 6: the old schools seemed there to confer some advantage on them for entering employment with lengthy programmes of training. For the other two broad social classes here, there was no association with the school sectors (as was seen for the old universities in Figure 7.4). Further analysis showed that all these patterns were similar for attainment at half a standard deviation above or below the mean.

So there was probably an affinity between old schools and old universities for students from high-status social classes before selection for secondary school was ended, and before higher education started to expand. There was a weaker but still distinct affinity between these universities and the secondaries that had been created early in the twentieth century. The affinity was not due to school attainment (nor sex nor social class). It was brought to an end by the comprehensive schools, and showed no sign of re-emerging when higher education expanded in the 1990s. There was no such affinity evident for newer segments of higher education. This contrasts with independent schools, where there was evidence of persisting affinity with the oldest parts of higher education, and the emergence of a new affinity with the newer universities.

CONCLUSIONS: HISTORY AND POLICY

It is possible also now to see that the concept of institutional habitus, and its changing importance over time, does perhaps provide a way of giving some coherence to the conclusions. One set of answers related to change which happened autonomously from any deliberate policy intent. When the public-sector schools were ending selection between the 1960s and the early 1980s, the independent schools, serving predominantly students of high social status, maintained their association with the oldest parts of higher education. This constant association is then a typical instance of the consequences of institutional habitus that have been investigated by previous researchers (as summarised above). During the second phase of expansion of higher education, in the 1990s, new affinities emerged between these schools and other pre-1990s universities, and also with colleges that became universities in the 1990s. The independent schools' advantages were not explained by attainment, suggesting that, during the period when their apparent affinity with university entrance was strengthening, there was emerging the kind of institutional habitus which other writers have invoked as an explanation of independent schools' role. But the key point is that any such habitus emerged, and was not merely inherited: it emerged to link these schools with university sectors to which they had not previously shown any affinity. Change of this kind has not usually been traced in the literature on institutional habitus, but has been a theme (under different names) in the historical work that was also summarised earlier. To understand better how it emerged would require detailed, perhaps ethnographic, research on individual schools during the five decades covered by our surveys.

Understanding emerging habitus would also have to take into account the precisely opposite trajectory of the older schools in the public sector. The history of these schools was associated with entry to high-status higher education in subtly differentiated ways. It was not only that, during the transition to non-selective secondary schooling, students from the former senior-secondary schools remained more likely to attend the old universities than students from the former junior-secondary schools who had similar attainment and similar social status. Even within the category of senior-secondary school, the oldest schools at that time had an advantage over the schools that had been founded early in the twentieth century. These differences suggest, as with the independent schools, some aspect of institutional habitus which associated the older schools with the older universities. But then, quite unlike the independent schools, this distinction vanished as the comprehensive system settled down, and as the social-class distribution in the older schools came to resemble the social-class distribution of the system as a whole. As with the independent schools, explaining these changes in the effects of the older schools would require detailed archival work on their ethos and characteristics during the ending of selection (for example, as discussed in Chapters 3 and 4). But what can plausibly be said is that the association between school sector and university sector did change, and that the change could be represented as a declining role for social class as a dimension of stratification between historically defined school sectors. Perhaps of greatest interest for the theory of institutional habitus, these changes would not have happened without the deliberate policy intervention represented by the development of comprehensive secondary schooling.

Whether this is a vindication of the concept of institutional habitus is not clear, and of less concern than what this analysis suggests about the interaction of educational institutions with policy. Perhaps a simpler concept such as 'ethos' would be enough, the kind of thing which schools and universities tend to celebrate at those moments in their annual cycles where symbolically important aspects of their institutional identities matter. One of the best-known accounts of an old Scottish school is in Muriel Spark's *The Prime of Miss Jean Brodie*, where the school's use of history in the 1930s is palpable from the start:

> Marcia Blaine School for Girls was a day school which had been partially endowed in the middle of the nineteenth century by the wealthy widow of an Edinburgh book-binder. She had been an admirer of Garibaldi before she died. Her manly portrait hung in the great hall, and was honoured every Founder's Day by a bunch of hard-wearing flowers such as chrysanthemums or dahlias. These were placed in a vase beneath the portrait, upon a lectern which also held an open Bible with the text underlined in red ink, 'O where shall I find a virtuous woman, for her price is above rubies.'

That school was based on the real-world James Gillespie's School in Edinburgh, an example (in our terms) of a senior-secondary school that became a mixed-sex comprehensive after the 1960s. These sorts of celebrations of an illustrious identity that has been inherited from the past – and that was being radically reformed in a more egalitarian era – would be the kind of evidence that would be required by a fuller investigation of the patterns described here. What we may reasonably conclude from these patterns is that there would be something worth investigating. Whatever we call it, institutional habitus can indeed change, and not only slowly: in historical perspective, the period from the 1970s to the 1990s is relatively short. The change can be autonomous of policy, or fostered by policy. It can make inequality greater, as in the strengthening links of independent schools with university entry, or it can remove old social distinctions, as in the case of the old schools in the public sector. Schools and universities are not merely mechanisms by which policy makers provide places where people can teach and study. They have symbolic lives of their own.

CHAPTER 8

Higher Education and Breadth of Study at School

EXPANSION AND INEQUALITY

The social impact of the massive expansion of higher education in many countries since the 1960s is summed up in the idea developed by Lucas (2001) that we have encountered already in Chapter 4: effectively maintained inequality. As social disparities in rates of completing full secondary education narrowed, a new form of social inequality emerged between curricular pathways. The highest-status classes came to be over-represented in those types of curriculum which are most likely to give access to the highest-status universities. These results have come from several countries – Scotland, England, Ireland, Israel and the USA (as explained in the next section). Only where the curriculum in secondary school is standardised is the association with social stratification weakened.

The caveat about standardisation reminds us, however, that there have been two contrasting ways of understanding the social effects of the secondary-school curriculum, as also discussed in Chapter 4. The socially stratifying effect was argued to have arisen because the language and content of the high-status school subjects were more familiar to the children of high-status families than to others. The contrasting view is that which was taken by policy makers when they responded to the stratification by seeking to require all students to follow the same curriculum. As we have seen in Chapter 4, Scotland provides a clear instance of that view. Nevertheless, although access to a broad curriculum by lower social classes was significantly extended in the 1980s, inequality in that respect widened in precisely the manner which Lucas's theory would lead us to expect. The question now is how these changes related to higher education.

This very general question is highly relevant to Scotland, but is not enough, because there are also questions about the cultural tradition of educational breadth. Putting it very briefly at the outset, the two questions are these: to what extent is breadth of attainment at secondary school a mechanism of effectively maintained inequality, evidenced in a growing importance of breadth for entry to the highest-status universities, and to what extent, on the contrary, was breadth an inherited cultural characteristic that was eroded during the shift to mass higher education?

The next section reviews what is known from research internationally on the relationship between the secondary-school curriculum and entry to higher education. We then use the ideas from that research to guide our analysis of these questions in Scotland. Part of that links back to the themes of the previous chapter, asking whether breadth had any role in the affinity of school sectors with types of university.

THE SECONDARY-SCHOOL CURRICULUM AND ENTRY TO HIGHER EDUCATION

There has been surprisingly little research anywhere on the connection between the secondary-school curriculum and opportunities after school. Ayalon (2006, p. 1209) concludes that the highest-status school subjects not only lead to the highest-status post-school courses but also are most likely to be taken by students from the highest-status families. Iannelli et al. (2016) found that, in Scotland, subject choice at school was a strong mediator of social-class inequalities of entry to higher education, especially the oldest universities. Dilnot (2018) reported that, in England, taking high-status subjects at secondary school was associated with increased chances of entry to the highest-rated universities. Van der Werfhorst et al. (2003) and Schührer et al (2016) concluded that subject choice was a mechanism by which social inequality of entry to higher education was maintained.

These patterns of differentiation can be modified by two features of the school and university systems. One is where subject choice at high school is constrained, as in Ireland (Iannelli et al., 2016). The other is where choice of post-school specialism is postponed until well after university entry, as in the USA (Duta et al., 2018). In both these circumstances, overall attainment at secondary school is relatively a stronger predictor of university entry. Postponing choice has generally been seen as a way of reducing social inequality (Ayalon, 2006).

This situation is what would be expected from the theory of effectively maintained inequality (Lucas, 2001). As higher education has expanded, merely gaining access to it was no longer as strong a marker of status distinction as it used to be. So the expansion diverted a disproportionate number of lower-status students into lower-status institutions (Iannelli et al., 2011). In systems where subject-choice at the prior stage of secondary school was unconstrained, as in Scotland and the USA, this diversion came about partly through the pattern of choice of secondary-school subjects. The strength of Lucas's theory is that it allows for change in the association between social status and educational outcomes. Furthermore, it allows a distinction to be drawn between what Boudon (1974) called primary and secondary inequality. Primary inequality means overall differences of intelligence, economic resources and cultural aptitude. Secondary inequality relates to processes that operate among people who have successfully completed a particular stage of education. So secondary inequality might be the means by which inequality is effectively maintained.

Scotland provides a potentially illuminating case study, because of the school curricular reforms that we investigated in Chapter 4, and the large expansion of higher education in the 1990s. We saw in Chapter 6 (Table 6.2) that breadth of study at mid-secondary level was associated with entry to post-school education by high-attaining students. This context provides a reason why the Scottish case might give insight into the changing nature of social stratification by means of curricular differentiation. The historical pattern of university education until the 1960s was based on faculty entry rather than entry to a specialised programme, a principle that was the outcome of the mid-nineteenth-century debates about modernising the universities (Anderson, 1983, pp. 253–93; Paterson, 2015c). The principle of faculty entry was a compromise between modernisers who sought to raise the standard of entry and defenders of the tradition in which breadth of study corresponded, in aspiration, to breadth of social recruitment. The compromise entailed shifting the inauguration of breadth into the senior years of the secondary schools which served a more socially extensive clientele than the universities. This was, in effect, one of the roles that the new Leaving Certificate played from 1888. The pattern persisted in the four oldest universities until the 1970s, and marked off Scottish university education from the more specialist traditions that developed elsewhere in the UK. Until the 1970s, entry was guaranteed to anyone who attained what was called the 'attestation of fitness' (Withrington, 1992, p. 139), which was the means by which the breadth of school attainment was formally incorporated into decisions about admission. Breadth of study at school then corresponded to breadth of study in the first two years of university, followed by two years of specialist Honours study. Students also had the option of graduating after three years with what was called an Ordinary degree, in which breadth was mandatory, requiring students to take courses in science and humanities or social science, with philosophy as a core unification of the disparate modes of understanding. Unlike in England, these degrees were not, as it were, fail degrees for students who were not likely to succeed at Honours level; as we will see, nearly one-half of graduates from the universities took Ordinary degrees until the early 1980s, but this fell to a quarter in the late 1980s and merely one in 20 in the first decade of the new century.

Breadth was thus to some extent a cultural rather than a stratifying value, and defending curricular breadth became a focal point of much cultural campaigning in the 1960s and 1970s (Paterson, 2015b). As we mentioned in Chapter 1, the growth of specialism in the 1960s provoked re-evaluation of the Scottish generalist tradition, much of it centred on debate about George Davie's idea of the democratic intellect.

Gaining access to the rest of higher education was potentially different. Neither the new universities of the 1960s, nor the various specialist colleges, replicated the older pattern of faculty entry, using instead the model of specialist programmes that were common in the rest of the UK. In that sense, the growth of these new universities began to erode the historical distinctiveness of Scottish university education. The four oldest universities also came to adopt this curricular approach by the 1980s. Selection for entry came increasingly to depend on high attainment in a specialist curriculum rather than breadth (Paterson, 2003, pp. 160–4).

Our curricular focus in this chapter is on the effects of breadth of study in the senior years of secondary school, because that allows the historical Scottish debate about the curriculum to be related to the recent sociological debates about social stratification. This putative cultural role for breadth also raises questions about the kind of graduates which the universities were sending out into the community. A core part of the historical rationale in Scotland for breadth of study was the belief that it would widen graduates' cultural awareness (Paterson, 2015b, 2015c). So we also investigate here whether breadth at school was associated with levels of attainment at university or with the kind of employment that graduates entered. That will allow us to answer such questions as whether graduates entering specialist fields of employment had acquired some cultural breadth from their school preparation.

It is difficult to disentangle the effects of breadth from the effects of attainment, because having broad attainment necessarily entails also having quite high attainment in a system where, as in Scotland, the main measure of attainment is a count of the number of senior-secondary courses which the student has successfully followed. We attempt to deal with this problem by recording also the quality of students' performance at this level, and, for part of the analysis, by restricting attention to students who entered higher education with the intention of taking a programme in science. For such students, as explained when we consider that analysis, we can more unambiguously distinguish between the specialist attainment required to gain entry and the cultural value or status distinction associated with breadth of study.

CONTEXT: RISING SCHOOL ATTAINMENT AND EXPANSION OF HIGHER EDUCATION

We have seen in Tables 7.1 and 7.2 in the previous chapter the growth of participation by school leavers in higher education from the early 1950s to the end of the century. We also showed the changing social distribution of that participation, and the changing shares taken by the different sectors of higher education. In this chapter we look in detail at the links between the curriculum which students followed at school and their entry to these different sectors, and so a further part of the relevant context is the changing effects of attainment, sex and social class on entry to different kinds and levels of higher education institution.

For entry to the old universities, the striking feature was a fall over time at high levels of school attainment, as competition for entry became fiercer but also as other opportunities opened up. In the early 1960s, when these were the only universities available, around two-thirds of school leavers with five Highers entered them; this fell to 20–25 per cent in the early 1980s and under 20 per cent in the late 1990s. At this level of attainment, the levels and trends were similar for males and females, but the fall was greater for low-status and medium-status social classes (down to only around 10 per cent) than for the highest classes (still over 20 per cent). There was a similar fall at lower levels of attainment, but with lower rates thoughout: at four Highers, around 35 per cent in the 1960s to around 10 per cent in the 1990s; at three Highers, around 15 per cent to well under 10 per cent.

The pattern was similar for the other pre-1990s universities, though with more random variation from year to year and with no fall in the rates of entry for three or four Highers (which were already very low). Thus the relative contraction of both of these university sectors was mainly a matter for students with above-average school attainment. These displaced students went into degree courses in other higher education colleges. Participation there from this subset of students – that is people who did not enter the two kinds of older universities – rose for each class and sex at each level of attainment. For example, the rate among such students with five Highers reached around two-thirds in the late 1980s. It fell back at high attainment in the 1990s to around one-half, when new opportunities opened up in the newly expanding two older sectors. This was partly through mergers between some of the smaller non-university institutions – mainly those which provided teacher education – and universities in the two older categories (Kirk, 1999). But this can only have been a small part of the fall. In the early 1990s, among all school leavers who had passed five or more Highers, only 2 per cent entered the teacher-education institutions. Among these high-attaining school leavers who entered the degree courses outside the older universities, the proportion was only 8 per cent.

There were no consistent sex or social-class differences in these trends among the highest-attaining displaced students, but at lower levels of attainment participation by displaced students from high-status classes rose faster than in the other social-class groups. Thus inequality widened in entry to these degree-level courses outside the two kinds of older universities. Consider, for example, students with three Highers who did not enter these older universities. Among such students who came from the highest-status classes, the rate of entry to degree courses elsewhere reached around 40 per cent in the late 1980s and remained there. But among those from medium-status or low-status classes, the rates were only half that. The pattern of inequality for non-degree courses was similar, though with more random variation.

Breadth in Senior-Secondary Courses

The question is now whether curricular breadth adds explanatory power to this analysis of secondary effects. Breadth is as we have defined it in Chapter 4: that is, at Higher, English, mathematics, a natural science, and at least one social subject, language or aesthetic subject. In defining breadth in this way, we have omitted attention to the Certificate of Sixth Year Studies, which was usually taken in the final year of school and which had been designed to be preparatory for specialist study at university (McPherson and Neave, 1976). The reason we have not included this is that, in order to be allowed to take one of these courses, it was necessary to have passed a Higher in the same subject. So this Certificate could not add to any student's breadth of study. Moreover, students who left school at the end of the fifth year would not be able to take these courses. Another reason to exclude them from detailed attention here is that they were not provided in all schools. In each survey year, at least half of schools in the surveys – and usually over two-thirds – had no student sitting Sixth Year Studies mathematics. The same was true of all the sciences taken together. In contrast, by the 1990s, over 90 per cent of schools had students who sat Higher mathematics; again the same was true of science. Whatever the intention of the policy makers, schools and students (and universities) saw the Highers as the main route to further study.

As a preliminary, we look at the trends in attaining breadth among students who had sat or passed at least four Highers, supplementing the analysis in Chapter 4 of senior-secondary breadth across all students (for example, Figures 4.2 and 4.5). Four Highers is the minimum required to allow breadth as we have defined it to be feasible. Sitting or passing four or more Highers may be thought of as indicating a student who is likely to be a strong candidate for entering higher education. Indeed, in each survey from 1952 to 2002, the rate of entry from people who had passed four or more was at least 70 per cent, and from those sitting four or more was at least 60 per cent.

Table 8.1 shows the proportion with a breadth of subjects among the group who had attempted at least four subjects, and also the proportions sitting at least one Higher in each of the components of breadth. The proportion attempting breadth declined from one-half to four in ten in the 1970s. It rose again to around one-half, and then declined again in the new century. The proportion

Table 8.1 Aspects of attempted senior-secondary curriculum, among people who sat at least four Highers, 1952–2016

Percentage sitting / Year when respondent was aged 16	Sat at least 4 Highers*	Breadth†	English	Mathematics	Natural Science	Social subject	Language	Aesthetic subject	Sample size for all but first column (=100%)
1952	4	53	100	81	66	36	79	9	47
1960–2	8	53	99	79	66	56	77	9	3,422
1968–70	16	40	99	70	62	66	64	8	1,730
1970–2	18	38	98	70	64	66	56	9	1,939
1974–6	17	46	99	73	70	68	51	10	5,530
1976–8	20	47	99	77	73	68	44	11	1,315
1978–80	20	46	98	78	76	64	40	11	5,094
1980–2	19	48	98	78	75	64	40	13	1,859
1984	26	53	99	77	81	68	35	18	1,442
1986	25	47	87	78	81	70	34	20	1,420
1988	26	51	98	76	80	71	30	25	1,287
1990	32	50	98	72	79	74	31	27	1,206
1996	40	47	98	75	77	66	24	34	1,181
1998	41	48	97	74	76	65	23	37	2,385
2002	42	42	93	71	70	72	27	36	1,781
2016	58	39	93	62	65	69	18	36	553

Notes:

Percentages weighted; sample sizes unweighted.

* Proportion of school leavers sitting at least four Highers calculated from surveys described in Chapter 2. For 1962, 1970 and 1972, combines the percentages for passing at least one Higher (Table 7.2) with the percentages sitting at least four Highers from the surveys of these years (which were restricted to people passing at least one Higher). For these three years, this probably slightly underestimates the percentage of all students who sat at least four Highers, because it omits those who sat at least four but passed none (and thus did not appear in the surveys).

† Breadth means sitting English, mathematics, a natural science, and at least one social subject, language or aesthetic subject.

sitting English remained over 90 per cent. In most respects, however, there was a decline. The percentage sitting mathematics fell from around 80 per cent to two-thirds, most of the decline being from the 1990s onwards. In language the fall was steady and very large, from around 80 per cent to a third in the 1980s, a quarter in the 1990s and merely one in five in the new century. Natural science rose from two-thirds to around 80 per cent, and then fell back in the 1990s and after to two-thirds. Only social subjects and aesthetic subjects showed a rise that was sustained. The most common pattern, then, was a rise in the 1980s and a fall from the 1990s onwards. Subjects not shown in the table which also rose were vocational – 3 per cent in 1962 to 39 per cent in 2002 and 30 per cent in 2016 in commercial subjects, 7 per cent to 13 per cent (2002) and 11 per cent (2016) in technical subjects, and, from the 1990s, 10 per cent to 13 per cent (2002) and 20 per cent (2016) in physical education. The falls in Table 8.1 in the new century – for people who sat at least four Highers – contrasts with the modest rise in the analogous Table 4.4 in Chapter 4, for all school leavers. The contrast suggests that policy after the turn of the century began to cater less well for those students who were potentially high attainers (the base of Table 8.1). As we noted when commenting in Chapter 4 on Table 4.4, although there was improvement in the new century for school leavers as a whole, the rate of the improvement was much less than it had been in the 1980s and 1990s.

Much the same patterns are seen for passing among people who had passed at least four Highers: Table 8.2. For example, the proportion passing a breadth of subjects among people who passed at least four Highers is very similar to the proportion sitting a breadth of subjects among those who sat at least four. Two things may be inferred from this comparison of passing and sitting for these high-attaining students who had a good chance of entering higher education. One is that the decline in sitting in 2016 which was observed in Table 8.1 almost certainly will have translated into a decline of passing, especially since the beginnings of that decline is already evident for 2002 in Table 8.2. The other inference is that, in further investigating the effect of curricular breadth on access to higher education, it is probably sufficient to analyse passing, because sitting would be likely to yield similar patterns.

For the rest of the analysis, we omit 1952 because the sample size of people with four or more Highers is so small there (and we omit 2002 and 2016 as explained in Chapters 2 and 4). A further preliminary is then the social distribution of breadth among these high-attaining students. Although the social-class differences were relatively smaller in this group than among all students (Figure 4.2 in Chapter 4), they were nevertheless not negligible, and they grew after the 1960s. For female students in 1996–8 who had passed at least four Highers, the proportion with breadth was 55 per cent in classes I and II, but 30 per cent in classes IV, V and unclassified. This gap of 25 points had grown from 14 in 1979–6, and in 1962 there was probably no gap at all. That was

Table 8.2 Aspects of successful completion of senior-secondary curriculum, among people who passed at least four Highers, 1952–2002

Percentage passing	Passed at least 4 Highers*	Breadth†	English	Mathematics	Natural Science	Social subject	Language	Aesthetic subject	Sample size for all but first column (=100%)
Year when respondent was aged 16									
1952	3	52	98	83	62	31	79	7	42
1960–2	8	52	99	79	65	54	78	7	2,710
1968–70	13	40	98	69	62	63	64	8	1,393
1970–2	14	36	97	68	63	64	57	8	1,524
1974–6	11	44	96	72	69	67	53	9	3,611
1976–8	13	46	95	77	74	67	47	10	881
1978–80	13	45	94	77	76	64	44	11	3,492
1980–2	12	47	95	78	75	65	43	12	1,219
1984	16	51	96	78	81	67	36	13	897
1986	16	49	87	80	82	68	36	16	950
1988	20	48	96	75	78	71	30	22	1,009
1990	23	49	96	74	78	73	31	25	903
1996	30	47	97	76	75	66	27	31	900
1998	32	46	95	75	74	66	25	35	1,901
2002	31	41	88	71	70	71	28	34	1,379

Notes:

Percentages weighted; sample sizes unweighted.

*Proportion of school leavers passing at least four Highers calculated from surveys described in text. For 1970 and 1972, combines the percentages for passing at least one Higher (Table 7.2) with the percentages passing at least four Highers from the surveys of these years (which were restricted to people passing at least one Higher).

†Breadth means passing English, mathematics, a natural science, and at least one social subject, language or aesthetic subject.

true for men also in 1962, after which the gap reached a peak in the 1980s (16 points in 1980–4), then falling to 8.6 per cent in 1996–8. So if breadth confers an advantage on any aspect of entry to higher education, we might expect it to be increasingly beneficial to students from high-status social classes, but not to have had that differentiating effect in 1962, on the eve of the many educational reforms that we have been discussing.

Breadth and Entry to Higher Education

We can now investigate what, if any, association there was between curricular breadth at school and entry to higher education. The results are exemplified in Table 8.3. In Table 8.3, for entry to the old universities, the effect is positive, but mostly weakening over time. What is, nevertheless, striking is that breadth conferred an advantage on students from all social classes, even though somewhat less on the lowest-status classes. Of course, there were also strong class effects on attaining breadth in the first place, as we saw in Chapter 4. But, in the operation at what Boudon calls this secondary point of selection, the oldest Scottish institutions showed only limited further such distinctions.

For the other pre-1990s universities, the pattern of change was different from the old universities: the effect of breadth was positive for females in the 1960s and the early 1970s, generally narrowed up to the late 1980s, and then widened again in the 1990s. For males, the effect of breadth grew from the 1980s. The result was that, by the 1990s, for both males and females, the difference associated with breadth was 9–10 per cent in classes I, II and III, and 5–7 per cent in the lowest-status classes. Even more clearly than for the old

Table 8.3 Percentage entering old universities, by social class and sex: difference associated with school curricular breadth. Students with four Highers

	1962–72	1976–88	1990–8
Male			
I, II	16	6.5	5.3
III	16	4.3	5.3
IV, V, unclassified	10	5.4	4.8
Female			
I, II	9.7	4.8	7.4
III	10	2.9	4.4
IV, V, unclassified	4.5	3.7	6.2

Notes:
Parental education is set to the modal value in this class in each year: see Table 2.5.
Cells show percentage-point difference between students with and without breadth at Highers.
Average standard error: 3.0.

universities, therefore, breadth here offered opportunities to groups outside the highest-status social classes.

The pattern for degree courses in the 1990s universities was more complex. There was no reliable evidence of any effect of breadth in the 1960s and early 1970s, and for high-status and medium-status males this absence persisted until the 1990s. But between the 1980s and the 1990s, low-status males went from having a positive effect of breadth to having a negative effect. For female students, the effect of breadth became positive by the 1990s, which is similar to the trend for the 1960s universities. The negative effect of breadth among men was observed also for non-degree courses, where there was no effect at all for women.

We may say therefore that breadth was more than merely a dimension by which (in Lucas's terms) inequality was effectively maintained in response to rising participation in the 1990s. Although the growing importance of breadth between the 1980s and the 1990s for entering the 1960s universities would be consistent with that theory, as would the eventually growing importance of breadth for female students entering the 1990s universities, a straightforward interpretation along these lines is not consistent with the advantage of curricular breadth as long ago as the 1960s and 1970s for the 1960s and old universities, the declining effect of breadth in the latter, and the sex difference in relation to the 1990s universities.

Breadth and Entry to Science in Higher Education

A further test concentrates the focus further, by looking only at entry to courses in science, technology or medicine (which we refer to simply as science). For these courses, we can introduce tight controls for relevant attainment at school in natural sciences and in mathematics. If a prospective science student is very highly qualified in these respects, then any effect of breadth is likely to be an indicator of some wider characteristics.

Entry to scientific courses in higher education grew at a similar rate to entry in general, encouraged by the growth of science in schools that we considered in Chapter 4. Among all school leavers, entry to science by males doubled during the first wave of the expansion of higher education (from 4 per cent in 1952 to 9 per cent in 1980), but then rose only slowly until the 1990s expansion, when it doubled again to 20 per cent. Female entry to science rose quite steadily throughout, rising from a rate around one-half of that of males in the 1970s to 17 per cent in the late 1990s. Among school students who might have reasonable prospect of entering higher education – those who eventually passed at least one Higher – the growth was less steep, but again much greater for females than for males: from the period 1962–72 to the end of the century, the male rate rose by about a quarter (from around 32 per cent to 40 per cent), whereas the female rate nearly tripled, rising from around 10 per cent to 28 per cent.

We can then look at the effect of curricular breadth on entering science rather than non-science among those students who entered the old universities and who had strong scientific attainment from school. Specifically, we consider students who entered these universities, and who had passed five Highers, amongst which were mathematics and two sciences, with at least one of these three passes at level A. Thus attaining breadth means, for these students, having also passed a Higher in humanities or social science. There was a clearly positive association with breadth for female students before the 1990s. For example, in the lowest-status social classes in years 1962–72, the average proportion entering science was 96 per cent with breadth, and 81 per cent without breadth, giving a difference of 15 percentage points. The corresponding female differences in that period for the other two class groups were similar. The effect was weaker but still discernible in the 1980s, but had vanished by the 1990s. There was no effect at any date for males. The pattern for entering science in the other pre-1990s universities among those who entered these universities was similar but weaker. For the other sectors of higher education, the numbers entering were not large enough to allow reliable estimates.

So the conclusion here is even more emphatically that breadth did not disproportionately benefit students from high-status social classes entering old universities during the 1990s expansion. If it had any effect, it was a traditional means by which very high-attaining female students from low-status and medium-status classes had the opportunity to become pioneering women scientists. But breadth stopped conferring that advantage on female students in the transition to mass higher education.

Breadth, School Origin and Entry to Higher Education

The final topic on school breadth and entry to higher education brings together the main topics of this chapter and the previous: breadth and school origin. In Chapter 4 we investigated the relationship between school origin and breadth at mid-secondary level, finding that a gradient across school origins was eventually brought to an end as a result of the reforms of the 1960s and 1980s. Before the full development of comprehensive schooling, this link was also found at higher levels of attainment. In 1962, for each social class and both sexes, there was a gradient across the categories of school history in the proportion attaining breadth at Higher: the highest proportion with breadth was in the oldest secondaries, and the lowest in the former junior secondaries. Jumping forward four decades, there was no such systematic difference according to school history. Correspondingly, there was little differentiation by social class in 1962, especially in the two older categories of school, which were selective academic schools at that time. For example, among male students with four or more Highers, the proportion attaining breadth in the oldest secondaries was 65 per cent in the highest-status group of classes, 63 per cent in the medium-status class, and 69 per cent in the lowest-status group. Among female students, the corresponding proportions were 39 per cent, 39 per cent and 41 per cent. But four decades later the percentages for the highest-status group were higher than those for the other classes. In these oldest schools, among males, these were 51 per cent compared to 41 per cent and 45 per cent in the other two class groups; among females, 50 per cent, 35 per cent and 31 per cent. Further analysis showed that this switch from stratification by school origin to stratification by social class occurred in the early 1980s, in other words only after the comprehensive system had settled down.

Tables 8.4 and 8.5 then look at the statistical effects of breadth and school origin on entry to the old universities, respectively for two distinct class groups. The main point in Table 8.4 is that the link in 1962 between school history and the old universities is tightest for both males and females with breadth, especially the distinction between the oldest secondary schools and those which were founded in the early twentieth century. Any such association with school origin had been much reduced by the 1990s. Any association with breadth had also vanished, which is a version for each sector of school origin of the general point about breadth and entry to the old universities shown above in Table 8.3. The pattern was similar for students from the other two social-class groups who had passed at least four Highers, as shown for the lowest class in Table 8.5 – the gradient across school origins probably having vanished by the 1990s.

So the link which we drew between school history and university history in Chapter 7 is better interpreted as going via breadth. Breadth was the cultural

Table 8.4 Percentage entering old universities, by school origin, whether followed broad curriculum at school, and sex, 1962 and 1990s: Class I, II. Students with four or more Highers

	1962		1990s	
	Breadth	Not breadth	Breadth	Not breadth
Male				
Pre-twentieth-century secondary	67	43	26	22
Early twentieth-century secondary	51	44	24	22
Former junior secondary	33	24	19	17
Female				
Pre-twentieth-century secondary	51	36	23	19
Early twentieth-century secondary	34	36	23	20
Former junior secondary	13	12	21	18

Notes:
Parental education is set to the modal value in this class in each year: see Table 2.5.
Average standard error: male, 8.1; female, 6.3.

Table 8.5 Percentage entering old universities, by school origin, whether followed broad curriculum at school, and sex, 1962 and 1990s: Class IV, V, unclassified. Students with four or more Highers

	1962		1990s	
	Breadth	Not breadth	Breadth	Not breadth
Male				
Pre-twentieth-century secondary	61	36	16	13
Early twentieth-century secondary	55	47	10	9
Former junior secondary	42	31	7	6
Female				
Pre-twentieth-century secondary	39	26	15	12
Early twentieth-century secondary	34	36	11	9
Former junior secondary	15	14	9	8

Notes:
Parental education is set to the modal value in this class in each year: see Table 2.5.
Average standard error: male, 6.8; female, 7.0.

expression of that tradition which linked the old schools to the old universities. This institutional and cultural expression of tradition transcended social class and sex. The tradition was to some extent inherited by the first wave of new secondary schools, dating from the early twentieth century. But the tradition did not outlast the transition to comprehensive schooling after the 1970s.

Breadth at Secondary School and the Outcomes of Higher Education

Unfortunately, there is no data set that can allow us to investigate reliably the connection between school history and eventual university outcome. But we can look at school breadth and outcome at and beyond university, using the data sources described in Chapter 2 which relate only to the institutions that were universities before the 1990s, and covering people who graduated between 1960 and 2002 (with some limited information also for 2010). As explained in Chapter 2, we have confined this series on graduates to people who entered university more or less straight from school, in order to be consistent with the analysis in the rest of the present chapter and in Chapter 7 (and because the relationship between attainment at school and at university was different for older students (Brown and Webb, 1990)). We return in Chapter 9 to studying people who entered higher education later in life.

As with the school leavers' surveys, we thus have four decades of data, including the periods of the comprehensive reforms at school level, and the two major waves of university expansion – the late 1970s and the 1990s. We can analyse three types of outcome: the result of students' degree, their immediate destination after graduation, and, if they entered employment directly then, what kind of occupation they went into. We report the results separately by two broad faculty groups, Arts and Social Sciences (which we refer to as arts), and Science and Technology (referred to as science). No more refined grouping was possible with the sample sizes at the beginning and end of the series, but also because the disciplinary structure of the universities varied several times in this half-century. The data sets do not include information about subjects taken outside the main discipline in which a student graduated. Because medical students were not included in the 1960 survey, they have been omitted from the data used from all the surveys (about 10 per cent of all graduates in each year), but the results reported here for the period 1983–2002 were also found when medicine was included.

The proportion of graduates gaining an upper-second-class degree grew, from 6 per cent in 1960, through 12 per cent in 1980, over a third by the early 1990s, and reaching over a half by 2010. Combined with first-class degrees – a category that we refer to as 'good honours' degrees – the proportion moved from 14 per cent in 1960 to 69 per cent in 2010. That trend is familiar elsewhere in the UK (Yorke, 2009), but the decline of the Ordinary degree is specific to Scotland. That degree was the most common outcome until the mid-1980s, with over 40 per cent of graduates. Then the proportion fell to around a third in the late 1980s, 16 per cent between the early 1990s and 2002, and a mere 7 per cent in 2010. As participation expanded in the late 1980s and 1990s, the relative school attainment of people achieving the different classes of degree changed. (The scaling of school attainment is described in Chapter 7; it is analogous to the scaling which we have been using for the school leavers' surveys hitherto in this chapter.) For example, the mean relative attainment of people who graduated with first-class Honours fell from around 0.8 in the early 1980s to around 0.6 in the 1990s, and the mean for upper-seconds moved towards the overall mean as that outcome become the norm (around 0.1 in the early 1980s to 0.02 in 1993). The relative mean attainment of Ordinary graduates was always below average, but moved towards the overall mean as that degree become less popular (from -0.3 in 1983 to -0.2 in 1993).

The proportion in the two broad faculty groups was quite stable (about one-half in each, with a slowly rising proportion of women who graduated in science, from 26 per cent in 1960 to 42 per cent in 2010. The corresponding proportions of men were 60 per cent and 64 per cent.

The proportion who entered employment without further education or training rose from a third in 1960 to a half by the mid-1980s and two-thirds in 2010. Taking part in some kind of post-graduate education fell from two-thirds in the very select group of graduates in 1960, to a third in the early 1980s, and fluctuated around 25–30 per cent up to 2010. Within that, advanced education (MSc or PhD) at first fell to around 10 per cent, but then gradually rose; that may partly be due to re-grading (or merely re-classifying) some professional training as leading to an MSc. The proportion of graduates who did not enter employment or further education was generally between a sixth and a fifth.

For those who entered employment, the most notable trend was the reduction in the share taken by professional work (such as lawyer, scientist or accountant). It fell from 80 per cent of the small pool of graduates in 1960, to just under two-thirds in 1980, under a half in 1993, and one-third in 2002 and 2010. There was a concomitant growth of work as associate professionals (such as scientific and engineering technician, quantity surveyor, nurse, journalist or graphic designer), rising from 7 per cent in 1960 to around a fifth in the 1980s and 1990s, and 30 per cent in 2010. At the end of the series, there was also a large rise to over a third in the proportion entering other occupations (see also Purcell et al., 2006).

In all these respects, the 2002 data was consistent with developments between 1993 and 2010. Therefore curtailing the series at 2002 (in order to be able to use information about the school curriculum) probably does not distort the trends. Our focus is on the indicator of curricular breadth at secondary school, the trends for which in this data set were consistent with those which we have recorded from the school leavers' series earlier in this chapter. The proportion of female students with breadth rose from 25 per cent in 1960, only a half of the male proportion in that year (47 per cent), to well over a half in the 1990s, thus nearly converging with the male proportion. The percentages fell back slightly with the overall expansion to 2002, when they were 54 per cent of men and 51 per cent of women. One reason for the relative growth of breadth among female students was their growing participation in science: the proportion of female science graduates with breadth from school was always (from 1960) around two-thirds, very similar to the proportion among male science graduates. But there was a growth also among female graduates in arts and social science, from under a third up to the early 1980s to around a half in the 1990s (when the proportion of male arts and social science graduates with breadth was around two-thirds).

For gaining a good honours degree, there is no evidence of any effect of breadth at high attainment in arts nor, mostly, at low attainment in science. But in arts, for students with relatively low attainment from school, a higher proportion achieved a good honours degree without breadth than with it. For example, in the 1990s, the proportions were respectively 42 per cent against 39 per cent for women, and 39 per cent against 34 per cent for men. This suggests that specialising was perhaps the less risky route open to students of modest ability. In contrast, at high attainment in science, breadth was associated with a greater proportion achieving a good honours degree: in the 1990s, 68 per cent against 64 per cent for women, and a narrower 65 per cent against 63 per cent for men. As with entry to science courses (discussed above), this again tends to suggest that students – especially female students – who were scientifically accomplished also tended to have broad abilities, and could thus supplement their scientific achievements by also successfully studying humanities or social sciences.

Breadth was also positively associated with attaining an Ordinary degree in arts in the 1980s, but that association dwindled in the 1990s as the degree itself did. For example, for high-attaining students (of either sex), the proportions were respectively around 35 per cent and 27 per cent in the early 1980s, but around 16 per cent and 14 per cent in the decade to 2002. There was no association of school breadth with taking the Ordinary science degree.

Beyond graduation, there was no consistent pattern of any association of breadth with taking an advanced degree in arts. But in science, where advanced study was always more common, breadth along with high attainment from school was quite consistently associated with a greater proportion taking advanced degrees, especially among female students. For example, in high-attaining female students, the proportions entering advanced study in the decade to 2002 were 24 per cent with breadth from school and 19 per cent without, a difference that was stable throughout the 1980s and 1990s; the corresponding proportions for men were much closer, but consistently 1–2 per cent more among those with breadth. This is the same pattern as we have observed several times previously for female scientists.

Arts graduates showed, from the 1980s, a consistently positive association of breadth with entering professional employment: Table 8.6. This was also generally found for science graduates who had high attainment from school (here now also probably including 1960), but not for science graduates with lower attainment. The reverse was true for entering managerial employment. For example, among high-attaining graduates of each sex in arts, the percentage entering managerial employment was in the mid-20s without breadth and at most half that with breadth. That was also true for high-attaining science graduates in 1960, but that effect vanished from the 1980s onwards.

All these results on school breadth and graduation held also when controlling for university attainment, essentially because school attainment is a strong predictor of university attainment, and because school attainment is more finely graded. It also held regardless of the original social class of the graduate, and there was no difference after the 1980s between the old universities and those that were created in the 1960s. Thus social class of origin did not modify the effect of breadth on university outcomes or on the career which graduates followed.

CONCLUSIONS: THE END OF A TRADITION?

The main question for this chapter was about the role of curricular breadth at school in access to higher education and to progression beyond it. This is

Table 8.6 Percentage entering professional employment among graduates who entered employment directly, by sex, school attainment, broad university faculty, and whether followed a broad school curriculum, 1960–2002

		1960	1983–6	1987–90	1991–2002
Arts and Social Sciences					
Low attainment Male	Breadth	65	52	51	30
	Not breadth	81	45	43	26
Low attainment Female	Breadth	63	44	49	26
	Not breadth	79	37	41	22
High attainment Male	Breadth	68	71	68	58
	Not breadth	78	57	52	47
High attainment Female	Breadth	62	60	63	49
	Not breadth	72	44	46	38

Average standard error: 1960, 14; other year groups, 1.8.

Science and Technology					
Low attainment Male	Breadth	86	50	53	37
	Not breadth	77	57	59	41
Low attainment Female	Breadth	84	41	52	32
	Not breadth	75	48	57	36
High attainment Male	Breadth	87	69	70	68
	Not breadth	73	68	67	65
High attainment Female	Breadth	84	58	65	59
	Not breadth	67	56	62	55

Average standard error: 1960, 9.0; other year groups, 2.1.

Notes:
Omits graduates from medicine.
High attainment is one standard deviation above the mean within year; low attainment is one standard deviation below the mean within year.

what Boudon calls a secondary effect. The primary effects relate to school attainment, sex and social class, which are the main influences on entry. The question is whether, over and above these factors, breadth also influenced participation, achievement and progression.

Before getting to that question, the analysis established that there was variation among the higher education sectors in the patterns of participation, with attainment, sex and social class having different relationships to entry for different kinds of institution. For the pre-1990s universities, and the higher education colleges that became universities in the 1990s, the expansion was strongest among people with above-average attainment, and who were from high-status social classes. That was not so for non-degree courses: social-class inequality there fell because high-status students became less likely to enter.

The survey series then also showed that the social differentiation of secondary effects was similar to these primary effects. These are the influences on participation among students who successfully completed at least one senior secondary course. The rise in overall participation increased competition to enter the older universities, which thus became more differentiated than previously from newer institutions. For entry to the old universities, even at high attainment there was a remaining small effect of social class. The contraction of both sectors of pre-1990s universities in the early 1980s – the old universities and those founded or upgraded in the 1960s – pushed some students with above-average attainment into the colleges that became the new universities, especially students from high-status social classes. The net effect was that the overall expansion between the 1970s and the early 1990s disproportionately benefited high-status students who had middling or low attainment in the senior years of the secondary school. Only in the very large further expansion in the later 1990s did other groups benefit.

These patterns of expansion and differentiation were the context for the analysis of the effects of curricular breadth. For entry to the pre-1990s universities, breadth at secondary school had a positive effect on the chances of entry over and above that of attainment. On the whole, this breadth effect was similar for males and females, and was strong for all social-class groups. Although these are secondary effects, operating among people on the threshold of higher education entry, the findings do not contradict the cultural importance of breadth as it has operated within the dominant Scottish tradition. That was always what Boudon would call a secondary effect, a preference for the broadly educated above the specialist, but never doubting the importance of high attainment for competitive entry to university. The findings relating to this tradition of higher education are the main conclusions of the analysis, and the most important feature in that respect has been the general reduction in the importance of curricular breadth in an era of massive expansion.

That is not the whole story, however, for two reasons. One is a further insight into the importance of institutions, building on the discussion of schools and universities in Chapter 7. These institutional legacies interacted with the cultural role of curricular breadth. Institutions are not just physically persisting entities such as schools and universities, but also what UNESCO calls the intangible cultural heritage: the cultural institution of curricular breadth was inherited in Scotland at school level from more than a century of secondary-school reform, reforms which in turn, through the link to Scottish university history, go back to the cultural ideas of the eighteenth-century Enlightenment and to the sixteenth-century Reformation's modification of the medieval university curriculum. These very old ideas, originally for tiny, exclusively male elites, became the defining features of Scotland's much widened secondary-school curriculum in the late twentieth century. But understanding how that came about also required that we pay attention to the institutional reforms of the twentieth century, the ways in which the old schools that dated from before that century became the defining institutions first for the new, selective schools of the first half of the century and then, ultimately, for the radically democratised system of comprehensive schools after the 1970s.

In that process, the cultural distinctiveness of the old schools was lost. They were no longer the channels for the association between curricular breadth at school and entry to the old universities. Breadth thus became for the first time a socially differentiating feature of progression beyond school, an example of Boudon's secondary effects. Although breadth was indisputably more widely available than before the reforms of the 1960s and after, it had not previously had that secondary effect: among high-attaining students, there was very little social-class inequality in access to breadth in the early 1960s, especially in the oldest schools. Moreover, the relative inequality of access to universities via this route of old schools and breadth grew. For example, in 1962, the proportion of female students with breadth in the oldest schools who entered the old universities was 51 per cent in the highest-status class and 39 per cent in the lowest-status class. In the 1990s, these proportions were 23 per cent and 15 per cent. So as a fraction of the high-status rate of entry, the lowest-status rate fell from 39/51, which is 0.76, to 0.65. The analogous fall for men was from 0.91 to 0.62.

The other further aspect to the story is the kind of leadership class which was then formed by these graduates. The effect of school curricular breadth was not exhausted in the transition to university. It continued to have a legacy in the kind of attainment which students had there, and the careers which they subsequently entered. Breadth probably contributed to the university success of relatively high-attaining scientists, especially women, and likewise perhaps encouraged male and female arts graduates into the professions. Since the modern state and public services are largely staffed by professionals and scientists, there is an indication here of a breadth of cultural awareness that would not be evident if we neglected attention to the curriculum which graduates had followed at school.

Therefore there are two answers to the overarching research question that was posed at the beginning of the chapter, corresponding to two contrasting interpretations of the social significance of breadth. One answer is a confirmation of the theory of effectively maintained inequality. Breadth was as strongly associated with entry to the highest-status universities after the massive expansion in the 1990s as it had been in the 1980s before that phase of expansion started. Although that association did happen at similar levels for each social class (Table 8.3), the social-class disparities in breadth of attainment at secondary school (as we have also seen in this chapter as well as in Chapter 4) ensured that this pattern reinforced the high-status social classes' dominance of the older institutions.

But the other answer shows the opposite trajectory when looked at in longer-term perspective. Compared to the 1960s and early 1970s, breadth became less strongly associated with the older universities. This change was particularly stark for the four oldest universities, the defining feature of which since the late nineteenth century had been the affinity between breadth at school and breadth of university study. Although achieving breadth at school was socially differentiated, the association of breadth with entry to these oldest universities extended to all social classes in that old Scottish tradition. That is the sense in which the affinity between breadth and the university traditions may be described as marking breadth as a cultural accomplishment, not merely as a marker of status.

We noted at the beginning that the effects of secondary-school curricula on entry to higher education have recently been studied in many countries. The important work cited earlier has tended to view curricular differentiation as a new dimension of social stratification, with Lucas's theory of effectively maintained inequality as an appropriate explanation. In many circumstances that is the best way of interpreting the findings. But in some education systems, curricular breadth has been also a cultural characteristic, valued intrinsically beyond a certain level of attainment, and not merely as an expression of social status. Scotland is such a case. Our findings suggest that breadth, while being strengthened as a dimension of stratification by expansion, has been eroded in its traditionally classless cultural significance.

CHAPTER 9

Social Mobility and Lifelong Learning

SCOTLAND AND THE BRITISH CONTEXT

We now turn to setting Scotland in the wider context of the rest of Britain. Throughout the previous chapters, we have frequently referred to experiences from other countries – not just England and Wales, but further afield. But the advantage of concentrating on the countries of Britain is in what Raffe et al. (1999) have called 'home internationals' comparison. Similar approaches in other contexts have sometimes been referred to as comparing 'most similar cases' (Seawright and Gerring, 2008). The rationale is that, if we are wanting to understand the impact of education in different societies, it is more valid to make comparison in contexts where, for example, the labour market operates in similar ways, and where the structure of social classes is similar. For example, if we find that a particular level of education gives readier access to high-status occupations in one society than in another, we would want to know that the measures of status are reasonably comparable, and that we have constructed genuinely equivalent levels of educational attainment. That is more straightforward to do within Britain than between Scotland and elsewhere (for reasons we expand on below). The same might be said about the influences the other way round, from society to education. If we want to examine how socially unequal two education systems are in their outcomes, it is better to have similar measures of inequality and broadly equivalent measures of the outcomes.

Comparison is also over time, the dimension that has been present throughout this book. Here we come up against a fundamental problem of interpretation which we have not dealt with hitherto because we have not yet investigated the competitive opportunities that being educated might offer. Bukodi and Goldthorpe (2016) have pointed out the importance of distinguishing between absolute and relative definitions of educational attainment in the investigation of changes over time in the effect of education on social mobility. This is a problem when access is expanding. For example, in the data which we consider below, the proportion whose education by their late twenties was at midsecondary level or higher was 33 per cent for people born in Scotland before the Second World War, but 95 per cent for those born towards the end of the century. In that later group, 32 per cent had completed a university degree. So do we equate the nominally similar levels defined by secondary schooling, or do we equate the levels attained by similar proportions, so that secondary schooling in the middle of the century is functionally equivalent to university education at the end (Heath and Clifford, 1990)? Bukodi and Goldthorpe (2016) showed that how we answer this question can have a significant effect on our conclusions about the trajectory of inequality of opportunity. For Britain treated as a single society in the second half of the century, they found that with an absolute definition the association with education declined both for class origin and for class destination; but with a relative definition the association with origins declined far less, and there was no decline of the association with destination. They conclude that, to the extent that the labour market allocates a finite number of high-status jobs on the basis of a competition in which credentials are part of the sorting mechanism, it is likely to be relative rather than absolute attainment that will be more relevant. When studying the education system itself – as we have done up till now – the absolute definition is the main concrern, insofar as being educated brings intrinsic benefits – cognitive or cultural or (as we will see in Chapter 10) civic. But when we turn to the opportunities which that education leads to, the distinction between absolute and relative measures is inescapable.

These ideas provide the general framework used in the main analysis in this chapter. However, implicit in that approach is that the society over which the relative standing of credentials is measured is the same as that in which they are used to gain social rewards. When labour markets operate across borders while educational systems remain primarily defined by national governments and traditions, this assumption might be open to question. So the first large question for the chapter is to ask whether this disjunction of social referent might lead to more complex conclusions about the trajectory of inequality.

Questions of these kinds matter because of the general understanding of educational expansion and its relation to social mobility which abundant research has provided. The relevant changes in Britain may be summarised as two large, interacting processes. One is the expansion of education (Breen et al., 2009; Bukodi and Goldthorpe, 2016; Mandler, 2020; Murphy et al., 2015). From the mid-1960s, the proportion of people who completed a full secondary education expanded very greatly, as we have seen for Scotland, especially in Chapters 3 and 4. Higher education also then expanded, between the 1960s and the late 1970s, and even more markedly in the 1990s, a record that has been traced in Chapters 7 and 8. The other large process consisted of changes to the structure of employment, as manual work in predominantly manufacturing industry declined, and as professional occupations expanded (Gallie, 2000). We noted this for Scotland in Chapter 1, and that the change was partly also a change in sex differences, because women entered the new sectors of employment in larger proportions than men.

EDUCATION, SOCIAL ORIGINS AND STATUS ATTAINMENT

Research on educational inequality and social mobility in England, Scotland and Wales has found that these societies share experiences that are common across the economically developed world (Erikson and Goldthorpe, 1992; Müller and Karle, 1993; Paterson and Iannelli, 2007a, 2007b). Despite the initial optimism associated with the hope that modern societies would inevitably have rising mobility, the direct association of class origins with class destinations did not weaken in the second half of the twentieth century. Although the large rise in the share of employment taken by service-class jobs did depend on a strengthening of educational credentials, the persisting inequalities in access to these credentials maintained inequality of mobility at mostly unchanging levels (Bukodi and Goldthorpe, 2019, pp. 34–51; Buscha and Sturgis, 2018; Erikson and Goldthorpe, 1992; Gallie, 2000, pp. 285–6; Goldthorpe, 2014; Shavit and Blossfeld, 1993). When inequalities of attainment at a particular educational level did fall – usually because the attainment of the most advantaged social classes had reached a high plateau – the social-class inequality merely shifted to the next education level above that (Breen, 2004; Breen et al., 2009), yet another instance of Raftery and Hout's 'maximally maintained inequality'. The experience of men and women has mostly been similar in these respects (van de Werfhorst et al., 2018; Bukodi and Goldthorpe, 2019, pp. 191–202).

We have seen in previous chapters that these general trends apply to Scotland, suggesting that empirical findings from our data might be relevant to many other places, especially perhaps societies that are firmly part of the economically developed world but that are on the peripheries of the core metropolitan centres. The same general importance also attaches to the distinction between absolute and relative educational attainment. A useful set of ideas for interpreting that distinction in the labour market is labour-queue theory (Goldthorpe, 2014; Thurow, 1976, pp. 95–7). According to this, the role of credentials is mainly to sort people into a metaphorical queue, the best jobs going to those at its head. Credential inflation would then not affect people's position in that queue, even though their nominal attainment might be higher than someone in the same position in the queue several decades previously. We refer to these as the distinction between the job queue and the education queue.

The job queue is an entry queue – people seeking positions in the labour market. The education queue is an exit queue – people ranked according to their credentials. So the rationale for a relative measure of educational attainment is this idea of a queue.

But what if there are several education-queues contributing to the same job queue? Suppose that someone at, say, the 50th percentile of one education queue had nominal credentials that would place them at the 60th percentile in a different education queue, and suppose also that this latter queue was the main education queue for the labour market. Then that person's relative education standing, so far as the labour market was concerned, would be more strongly determined by that second queue (where they were above average) than by the one where they were merely average. In essence, enabling this switching to a metropolitan job queue has been one of the important roles which education has played in peripheral societies, allowing people to compete for better jobs in the core economy than they could do at home and, crucially, to out-compete people from the education system in that core economy (Findlay et al., 2008).

Transfer to a different education queue will work most smoothly when there is a common job queue across the whole territory – not only in the metropolitan centre – and where credentials in the different education queues are regarded as equivalent in a nominal sense. That is why studying England, Wales and Scotland can be illuminating here (Raffe et al., 1999). On the one hand, increasingly since the mid-twentieth century, the labour market has operated according to the same mechanisms throughout Britain, the main reasons being the growth in public-sector employment (conducted according to mostly the same rules throughout the UK), the growth of employment by multinational companies, and the increasing regulation of the labour market by the UK state (Raffe et al., 1999; Raffe and Courtenay, 1988). The regions of Britain converged in their industrial structure during the twentieth century (McCrone, 1992, pp. 70–4). The emergence of London as the strong driver of UK economic activity also imposed a greater homogeneity of recruitment practices, especially for entry to professional employment, even for labour markets outside London (Champion and Gordon, 2019; Fielding, 1992).

On the other hand, the education queues of Scotland and England have long been distinct, with historically higher rates of participation in post-compulsory schooling in Scotland (as confirmed by our data below). Welsh education, by contrast, was closely tied to that of England throughout the development of mass elementary and secondary schooling (also confirmed below), and has begun to diverge only since the devolution of some legislative autonomy to Wales from 1999. So there have been three education queues, but with reasons to believe that two of these (Wales and England) would behave in similar ways.

Furthermore, credentials in the different education-queues are regarded as being nominally equivalent. The boards which supervise school-leaving examinations in England and Wales have long sought common definitions of credentials (Newton, 2021; Tymms and Fitz-Gibbon, 1991), and that has extended to the different system of school-leaving assessment in Scotland (Philip, 1992). Similarly, the process of awarding academic degrees has been regulated by the system of external examiners of UK universities, and also, when there was a distinction between universities and colleges or polytechnics before 1993, by the Council for National Academic Awards (Barnett, 1987; Halsey and Trow, 1971).

The reasons why these standardised credentials can nevertheless produce different education queues include different institutional structures, different patterns of accessibility, and different quality of provision (Machin et al., 2013). Relative attainment may differ also because of different incentives arising from the very phenomenon we are studying here. If education is a means by which young people from economically peripheral regions may gain access to opportunities in a metropolitan core, then the incentive for high attainment may be greatest for students far from that centre (Findlay et al., 2008). It is a matter for empirical investigation, then, whether relative attainment measured on the same basis across different but connected education systems is a more cogent way of assessing inequality of attainment or of opportunity than when attainment is measured separately within each system.

SOURCES OF COMPARISON

This analysis uses data from five distinct sources, four of which allow Scotland to be compared with England and with Wales. The aim is to measure educational attainment after the respondent had completed their initial education, and to measure social class when they were in their early thirties. That choice of ages is consistent with work by other researchers on status attainment (Barone and Schizzerotto, 2011; Bukodi and Goldthorpe, 2016; Buscha and Sturgis, 2018).

The most straightforward sources are the three cohorts born in 1946, 1958 and 1970 (described in Chapter 2 as with all our sources). These give us information on people born in England, Scotland and Wales, from which we can measure their educational attainment in their late twenties and and their social class in their thirties. In the 1946 cohort, we use the age-26 measure of attainment and the age-36 measure of class. In the 1958 cohort, the respective ages were 23 and 33; in the 1970 cohort, they were 26 and 30. Our fourth source is the people born in Scotland in 1936. Their social class at age 27 gives as a straightforward extension back in time from the Scottish data in the three later cohorts. In this chapter, we refer to these surveys by the date at which class is measured (for example, 1982 for the 1946 cohort).

The fifth source is the UK Household Longitudinal Study (sometimes called Understanding Society). A precedent for using the UKHLS to study social mobility is by Bukodi et al. (2015), who compared people in it who were born in 1980–4 with people in the 1946, 1958 and 1970 birth cohorts. However, they were analysing Britain as a single society, whereas our attention is on comparisons among England, Scotland and Wales. In order to have adequate sample sizes to do this, we had to extend the range of birth dates. We selected every panel member who, at any of the first nine sweeps of the UKHLS (as described in Chapter 2), was within the age range 25–35, and then their highest attainment and class were recorded for those sweeps of the data when they were not older than 35. Thus the birth dates of this sub-sample ranged from 1975 to 1993 (the oldest and youngest people to be within the 25–35 range at some point within these sweeps). The median year of the oldest age at which information was recorded was 2014, and so in our graphs and tables we refer to this survey by that name.

In all the surveys, attainment in absolute terms was recorded at the seven levels shown in Table 9.1. In the analysis of absolute attainment, the two categories 'degree' and 'post-graduate degree' have been combined, as have the categories 'mid-secondary', 'low' and 'none'. For relative attainment we had to devise a measure that could be sensitive to different distributions in the three nations as a means of indicating each respondent's position in the different education queues. An ideal scale would rank every sample member, but

Table 9.1 Highest educational attainment before age c. 30, by survey year and nation of birth within Britain, people born 1936–c.1984

Survey year	Higher degree	Degree	Sub-degree higher education	Senior secondary	Mid-secondary	Low	None	Sample size
England								
1982	1	6	8	12	20	8	45	3,315
1991	3	9	15	14	35	14	10	6,236
2000	3	18	11	20	27	9	13	7,975
2014	8	23	10	28	23	3	4	9,385
Scotland								
1963	0	5	8	4	16	17	52	1,084
1982	1	6	5	14	12	9	53	498
1991	3	8	16	21	32	2	18	868
2000	4	17	13	20	23	8	14	915
2014	11	21	17	30	16	2	3	1,065
Wales								
1982	3	5	5	7	21	13	46	220
1991	4	9	12	10	37	10	18	425
2000	3	18	12	17	26	7	17	590
2014	7	21	11	29	23	4	5	865

Note:
Percentages in rows. 1982 and 2014 percentages are weighted.

in the absence of a finely differentiated measure of attainment we derive an approximation based on the distributions in Table 9.1. Consider as an example people in the category 'Mid-secondary' in the 1982 survey in England. They lie between the 54th and the 73rd percentile of the distribution of attainment in England in that survey, because 53 per cent of respondents had lower attainment (in the categories 'Low' or 'None'), and the next 20 percentage points are in this category 'Mid-secondary'. Then the score which is given to all those people in this category is mid-way between 54 and 73, in other words 63.5.

So, in this metric, a respondent's value reflects their relative standing in the distribution of attainment in a specific year in a specific nation, a higher value corresponding to higher levels of credentials. A second version of the metric used the distribution into the categories of attainment across all three nations. In this version, a respondent's value reflects their relative standing in relation to the whole of Britain. For the Scotland-only cohort of people born in 1936, the Britain-wide distribution was approximated from table 5.24 in Smith (2000).

Outcome was recorded in terms of Registrar General class. This is the same measure as in all the previous chapters, and is the only measure available for the 1963 survey. We followed the general approach of previous chapters in constructing measures of the socio-economic circumstances of the respondent's upbringing, combining parents' education with family social class. The age at which each parent left full-time education is available in the 1963, 1991 and 2000 data. In the 1982 data (as we noted in connection with Table 2.1 in Chapter 2), the information is recorded as whether the parent had primary education only, secondary only, schooling along with post-school technical education, or higher education. In the 2014 data, the categories are having left school with no certificates or with some certificates, having gaining post-school certificates below higher education level, or having a higher education certificate. These disparate measures were put onto a common scale by converting them into rank orders, ranked separately for each parent within each survey year but on the same scale in each year. The samples were restricted to cases where information on both parents' education was available, a restriction that would be unlikely to distort the comparison among the three nations because the extent of missing data was similar in each nation. It was also similar at each level of respondent's education and respondent's social class. The average of the two parents' ranking variables was used in the modelling. This approach also has the advantage of being analogous to the relative measure of attainment for the respondents.

In four of the surveys, the social class of upbringing was recorded as Registrar General class when the respondent was in secondary school, in the same categories as outcome class. In the 1991 and 2000 surveys, class of upbringing was defined to be the higher of father's and mother's class; in the 1963 and

1982 surveys, only father's class was available. In each of these surveys, cases were omitted where no information on the occupation of parents was recorded (again, a restriction that would not affect comparisons). For the 2014 data, a more elaborate approach had to be used to derive an approximation to this class scheme, as explained in Chapter 2.

For analysing absolute attainment after the respondents had completed their initial education, three indicators were created (reaching or not reaching the thresholds of senior secondary education, of any higher education, and of a university degree). These indicators were then the dependent variables in binomial logistic regressions (as explained in Chapter 2). The same was done for modelling entry to the managerial and professional class I and II. For the relative measures of education, the scores were treated as dependent variables in a linear regression. The explanatory variables in the models of education were year, sex, parental education, father's class (grouped into I and II, III, and IV, V and unclassified), respondent's age in the 2014 data, nation of birth, and interactive effects among these. Respondent's education was added to the models for entering classes I and II, giving five different models: the three thresholds, and the two relative measures. The results are presented as predicted values from the models, as in previous chapters. Parental education was set in the predictions to be the mean value in the sample within each of the social classes in each year, similar to the approach in previous chapters. Age in the 2014 survey was set to be 30 (the median).

EDUCATIONAL ATTAINMENT: SCOTLAND IN COMPARATIVE CONTEXT

The increase in educational attainment by age around 30 across the cohorts is clear in Table 9.1, showing that England and Wales experienced broadly the same educational expansion as we have traced for Scotland in the previous chapters. Correspondingly, there was a very large fall in the proportion with low or no formal attainment. The main difference among the nations is at higher education below a degree, where the percentage in Scotland reached higher levels than in England or Wales. The changing occupational structure is reflected in Table 9.2. The proportion with origins in classes I or II rose similarly in each nation. The rise in educational attainment and the changing occupational structures all confirm that these three societies are quite typical of economically developed societies in general, where – as noted in Chapter 1 – these trends are common.

Figure 9.1 illustrates that Scotland's higher rates of attaining full secondary education or better are seen for people in all classes except men in the routine and manual class. The Figure also shows that England and Wales mostly had similar percentages for each combination of sex and class, though with Wales behind England in the first two cohorts for people of intermediate-class origin.

Table 9.2 Social class of upbringing, by survey year and nation of birth within Britain, people born 1936–c.1984

Survey year	I	II	III	IV	V	Unclassified
England						
1982	2	6	43	22	6	22
1991	6	27	51	11	3	3
2000	7	32	47	7	1	6
2014	11	39	43	7	1	0
Scotland						
1963	2	9	54	18	17	0
1982	2	6	38	25	6	22
1991	4	19	55	17	4	2
2000	7	29	49	8	2	6
2014	11	39	42	8	0	0
Wales						
1982	1	9	40	15	9	27
1991	6	25	50	11	5	4
2000	5	32	45	11	2	5
2014	9	38	44	9	1	0

Notes:
Percentages in rows. For sample sizes, see Table 9.1. 1982 and 2014 percentages are weighted.
Father's class for 1963 and 1982 surveys; higher of father's and mother's class for 1991, 2000 and 2014 surveys.
2014 percentages include imputed data: see Chapter 2.

The patterns for attaining any higher education qualification were very similar to those in Figure 9.1. For degrees, the differences were generally much less: for example, the three national proportions in the intermediate class in 2014 were all in the range 23–26 per cent, in contrast to the range in Figure 9.1 of about 25 points for men and 10 for women. The only evidence of Scottish advantage in degrees was in the managerial and professional class, and any such advantage came to an end by 2014 for men, and by 1991 for women.

Measuring education relatively in a common way across all three nations produces a pattern of differences that is similar to that for secondary education or better, even though the overall trend is downwards rather than up: Figure 9.2. For women from the managerial and professional class, Scotland had a better outcome in each cohort, whereas England and Wales are similar. The same was true for men except in the last cohort. For the intermediate class, Scotland became better than England and Wales. For the routine and manual class, there was little difference, though women in Scotland probably moved ahead of women in England and Wales in the final cohort.

However, when the scale of relative education is defined separately in each nation, the differences are generally smaller, as may be seen by comparing Figure 9.3 (separate scales) with Figure 9.2, noting that the vertical axis

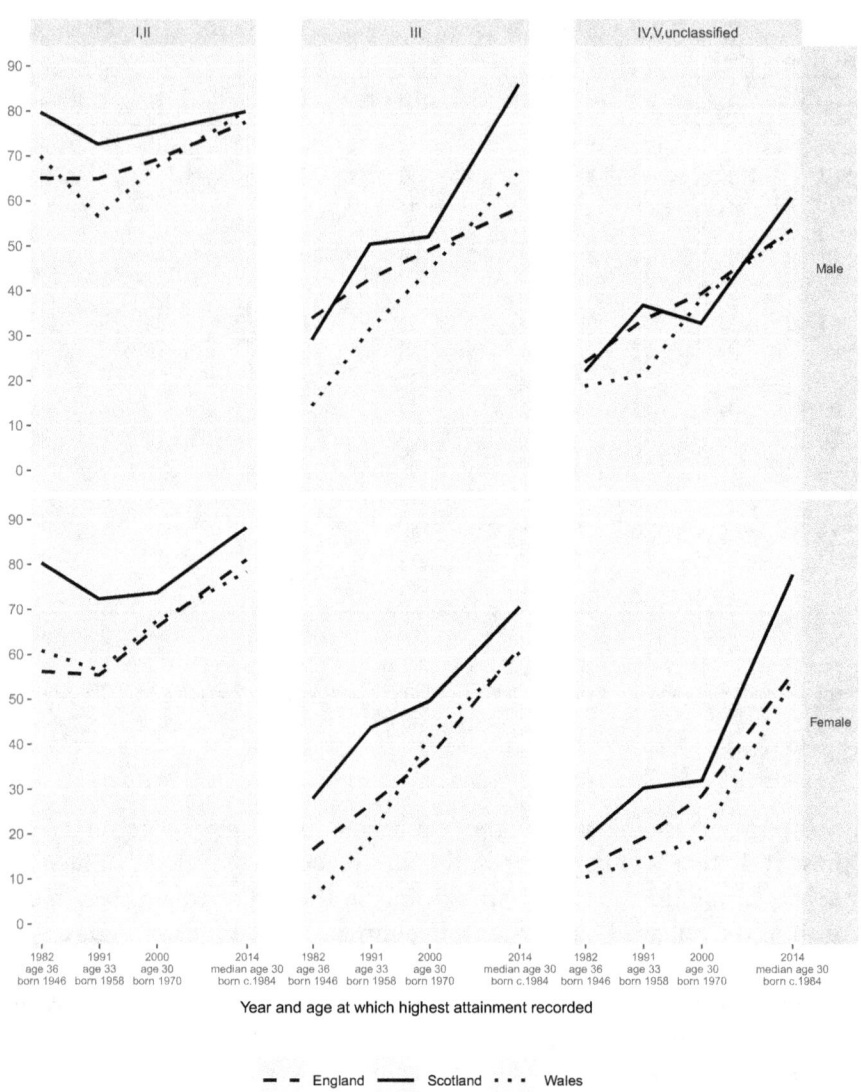

Figure 9.1 Percentage having attained full secondary education or better before age c. 30, by sex, class, survey year and nation of birth within Britain, people born 1946–c.1984
Average standard error: England, 2.0; Scotland, 4.9; Wales, 6.8.

has the same range in each graph. How this comparison may be interpreted can be illustrated by considering the relative values in relation to medians. Consider, say, a Scottish woman who is typical of origin class managerial and professional. In Figure 9.3, this woman is estimated to have on average across the cohorts a value of 66.7, in other words 16.7 points ahead of the Scottish

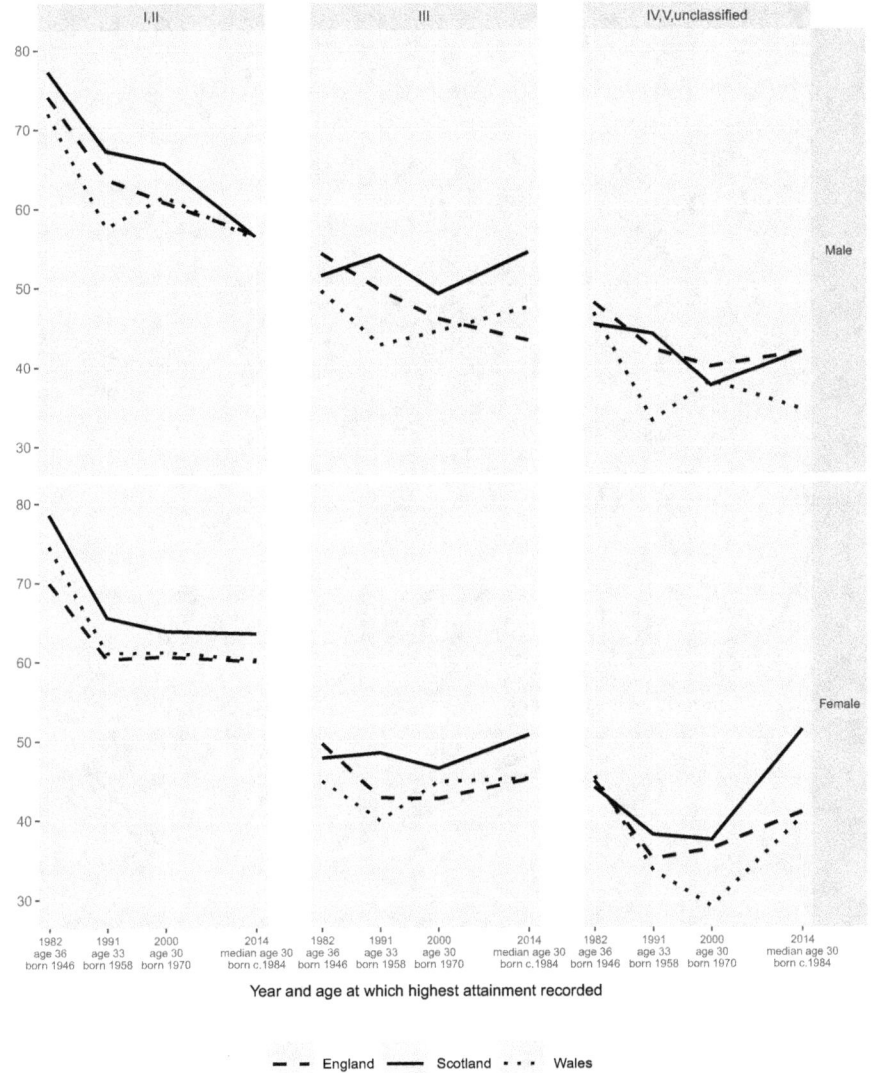

Figure 9.2 Education score (common metric) at age c. 30, by sex, class, survey year and nation of birth within Britain, people born 1946–c.1984
Average standard error: England, 1.1; Scotland, 2.8; Wales, 3.6.

median attainment (by definition a value of 50). A women of the same class in England has an average of 62.8, or 12.8 points ahead of the English median. So the difference is 3.9. But when these two women are compared to the common British median (Figure 9.2), the Scottish women is 17.9 points ahead while the English woman is 12.7 points ahead, a difference of 5.2.

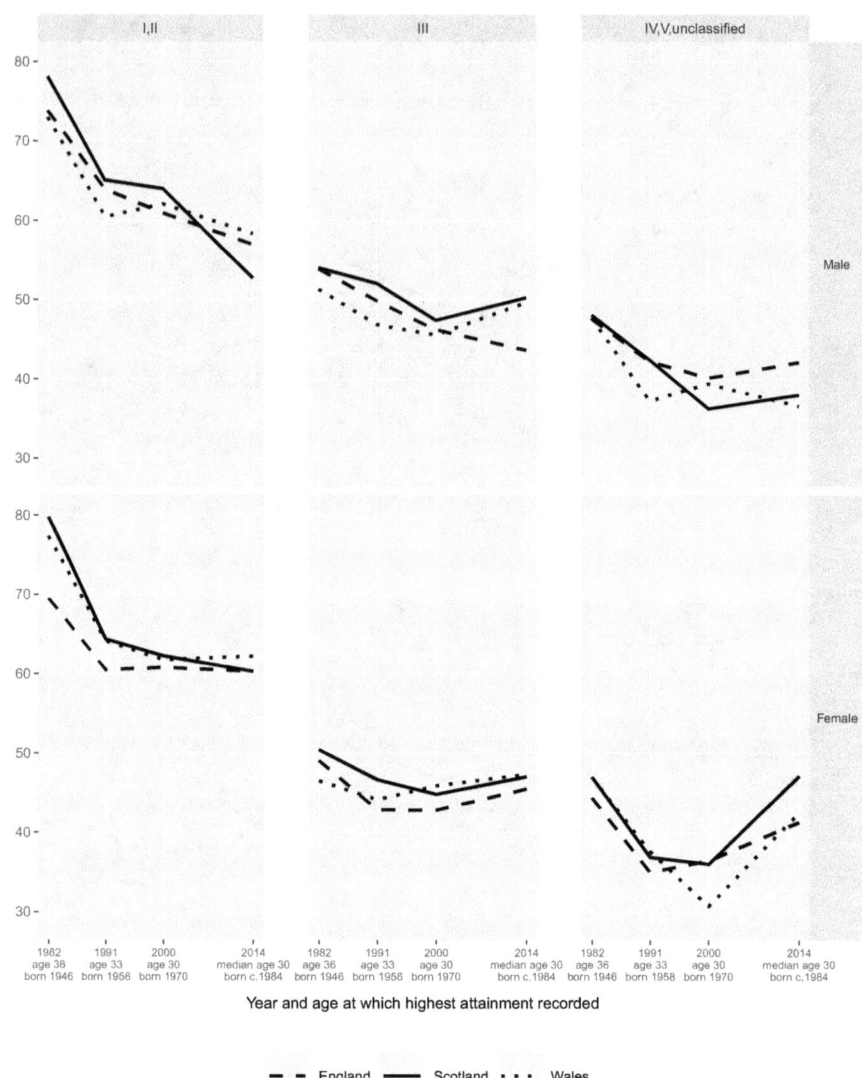

Figure 9.3 Education score (nationally specific metrics) at age c. 30, by sex, class, survey year and nation of birth within Britain, people born 1946–c.1984
Average standard error: England, 1.1; Scotland, 2.8; Wales, 3.7.

One consequence is that the comparison of inequality across the three nations depends on the measure of attainment that we use. For completing secondary education (Figure 9.1), Scotland was more unequal than England or Wales up to 2000. For example, in the first three cohorts, the difference between the top and bottom class is, for men, 11 points greater in Scotland than in England, and, for women, 9.4 points greater. Figure 9.1 also shows that this difference is not because of any poorer performance in Scotland by people from the routine and manual class, but rather because of a higher rate of completing secondary education by people from the top class. Indeed, the lowest class in Scotland mostly has a higher percentage in this graph than the corresponding classes in England and Wales. The fall of inequality in this measure between the oldest and youngest cohorts is greater in Scotland than elsewhere. The difference between the top and bottom class fell by 38 points (male) and 51 points (female) between the first and fourth cohorts in Scotland, but only by 17 and 18 points in England, and 24 and 26 points in Wales. Similar conclusions are reached from analysing the attainment of any higher education qualification and of attaining degrees, though the differences and the changes are less than for secondary education.

Moreover, when we take the Scottish picture further back in time (Figure 9.4), the importance of the top class in producing the relatively high inequality in 1982 is reinforced. Between 1963 and 1982, the line for that class rises more rapidly than the lines for the other two classes. Indeed, this graph is a further instance of maximally maintained inequality: when an education level expands, the first group to benefit is the most advantaged, and only when it reaches saturation do the other classes rise too, so that inequality falls. So the high inequality in Scotland in 1982 when compared to England and Wales may be seen as a consequence of Scotland's having embarked earlier on a process that eventually led to a reduction of inequality, but only after at least a further two decades had elapsed.

Inequality is also greater in Scotland when attainment is measured according to the common relative scale (Figure 9.2). In all three nations, there was reduction of inequality: the lines for managerial and professional fell more than the lines for the other two classes. But the fall is less than when using the criterion of attaining secondary education or better, exactly as we would expect from the work of Bukodi and Goldthorpe. In Scotland, the male gap here fell by 17 points, compared to 38 in Figure 9.1. The fall for women was 22 compared to 51. Moreover, again, if the Scottish data are taken back to the first survey, inequality is seen to widen before narrowing: for women, the difference between the highest and lowest classes went from 22 in 1963 to 35 in 1982, and then to 12 at the end of the series. The trajectory for men was 16 to 33 to 14. Nevertheless, the implications for opportunity are ambiguous, as with the absolute measure in Figure 9.1. In Figure 9.2, people from the two lower-origin classes in Scotland, though temporarily in the early surveys further behind people from the top class in Scotland, are equal to or ahead of people from the corresponding lower classes in England or Wales.

Thus we have a potential paradox, depending on whether we consider changes in attainment over time or differences in attainment between nations. On the one hand, within each nation the reduction of inequality in relation

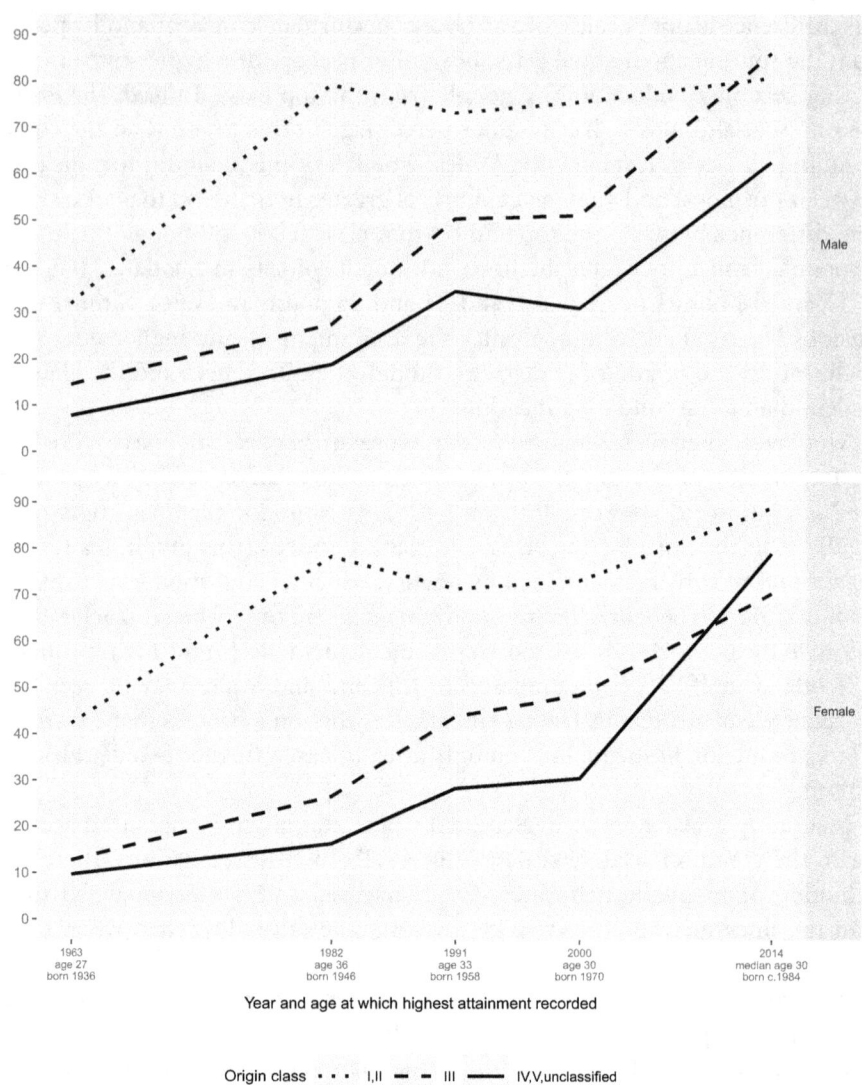

Figure 9.4 Percentage having attained full secondary education or better before age c. 30, by sex, survey year and class: people born in Scotland, 1936–c.1984
Average standard error: 4.8.

to attaining a full secondary education is much greater than the reduction of inequality when attainment is defined relatively. In that sense, higher absolute attainment over time does not much improve the standing of the lowest class. That is as true within Scotland as it is elsewhere. On the other hand, the greater inequality in Scotland than elsewhere is not because of lower attainment in the lowest class, and – when seen in the longer timescale available for Scotland – is transitional towards a reduction of inequality. If the lowest class in Scotland only ever competed with other Scottish classes of a similar age, then this point would be irrelevant to their opportunity, and they would face the situation of declining relative opportunity described by Bukodi and Goldthorpe. But where the labour market and the social networks extend across a wider territory than Scotland, then the comparison with the same class outside Scotland potentially is of great importance. One way we can assess these questions is our next step, by investigating entry to a high-status class.

CLASS ATTAINMENT: SCOTLAND IN COMPARATIVE CONTEXT

As a preliminary, Table 9.3 shows the social class of people at around age 30 in England, Scotland and Wales for each of the birth cohorts. The same trends towards the higher social classes appear here as for class of upbringing in Table 9.2, but very much magnified.

Figure 9.5 shows the rate of entry to the managerial and professional class by people who have attained full secondary education or better. The rate varies by social origin, despite this control for attainment. It also falls gently over time, which corresponds to the declining competitive advantage of education measured in this absolute way. But it does not vary systematically by national origin. Any such national variation is less than the corresponding variation in

Table 9.3 Social class of destination at age c. 30, by survey year and nation of birth within Britain, people born 1936–c.1984

Survey year	I	II	III	IV	V	Unclassified
England						
1982	6	21	48	11	1	13
1991	6	32	48	10	2	3
2000	7	34	38	8	1	12
2014	6	36	34	8	2	15
Scotland						
1963	4	14	58	15	9	0
1982	4	20	43	14	2	17
1991	6	33	44	12	3	3
2000	7	32	35	9	1	16
2014	7	31	37	10	2	13
Wales						
1982	4	22	48	14	2	9
1991	4	29	50	12	2	3
2000	6	31	33	8	2	20
2014	8	30	36	10	4	13

Notes:
Percentages in rows. For sample sizes, see Table 9.1. 1982 and 2014 percentages are weighted.

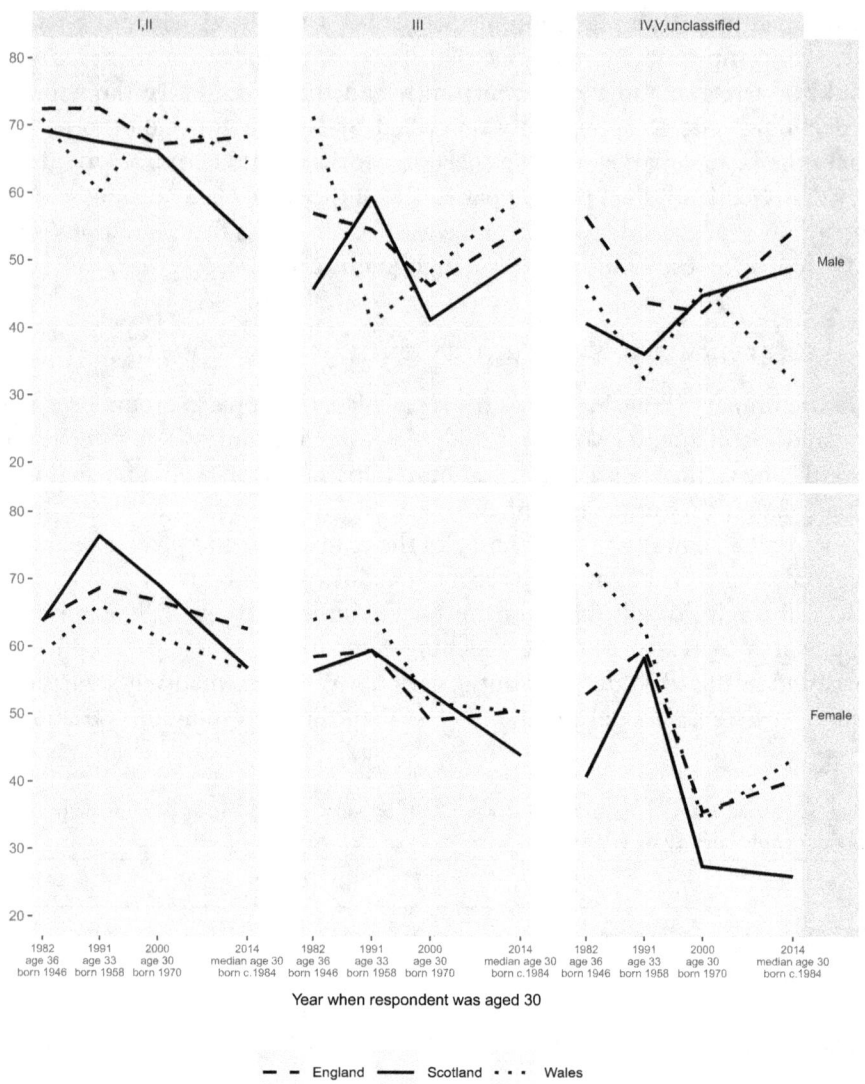

Figure 9.5 Percentage having entered class I, II before age c. 30, by sex, class, survey year and nation of birth within Britain: people who attained full secondary education or better, born 1946–c.1984
Average standard error: England, 2.8; Scotland, 5.8; Wales, 7.8.

this level of educational attainment (Figure 9.1). For example, in Figure 9.5, the Scottish rate for men whose origin is in the managerial and professional class is on average 6 points lower than the corresponding rate for people in England. From Figure 9.1, the rate of attaining this educational level among such men was 7.8 points higher in Scotland than in England. So, for Scottish men from this class with this level of educational attainment, even the small deficit of 6 points in the rate of entering the highest class does not cancel their advantage in attainment. Even where there is sustained or growing Scottish advantage in reaching this level of education in Figure 9.1, there is no sign of any reduction in the effect of that education on the chances of entering the highest class, as evidenced from Figure 9.5: this is true of intermediate-class men between 2000 and 2014 (growing educational advantage in Figure 9.1 and also growing rate of entry in Figure 9.5), intermediate-class women throughout (sustained educational advantage but almost identical to England in entry), and lowest-class women between 2000 and 2014 (growing educational advantage but stable rates of entry).

In short, Scotland's higher attainment at the absolute educational level of secondary or better did not lead to a consistently lower rate of return than for the same absolute level elsewhere, even though, within each nation, the growth of secondary education led to a declining rate of return to that absolute level of education. Similar conclusions were reached for those who attained any higher education qualification.

For people with a degree, there was, again, no systematic differences between the nations, especially in the last two cohorts. In these cohorts, among people from the highest-status origin classes I, II or III, around 80 per cent of male and female graduates entered class I or II, similarly for each nation of birth. The proportion from class group IV, V and unclassified was slightly lower – at the low 70s for men, and between 60 and 70 for women – but there was no clear difference among the nations of birth. This might be thought to be uninteresting because there was little such variation in attaining a degree, as noted above. But this combination of results acts as a kind of control for the conclusions relating to secondary education or better. In essence, we can say that degrees are similarly distributed and similarly rewarded in each nation, suggesting that educational credentials are of similar value in the Britain-wide labour market. So that reinforces the interpretation of the combination of Figures 9.1 and 9.5 that credentials are similarly rewarded despite variation among the nations in the distribution of secondary education.

Next, consider what happens to these conclusions about variation among the nations when education is measured relatively. Figure 9.6 shows the rate of entry to the managerial and professional class of people with high relative attainment (at the 75th percentile) in the scale measured in common across the nations. Recall from Figure 9.2 that Scottish people mostly had higher predicted values on this scale than similar people from elsewhere. In Figure 9.6, men from the managerial and professional class do have lower rates of entry to the highest class than similar men from England. But for all the other combinations of sex and class, the advantages in Scotland in relative attainment in

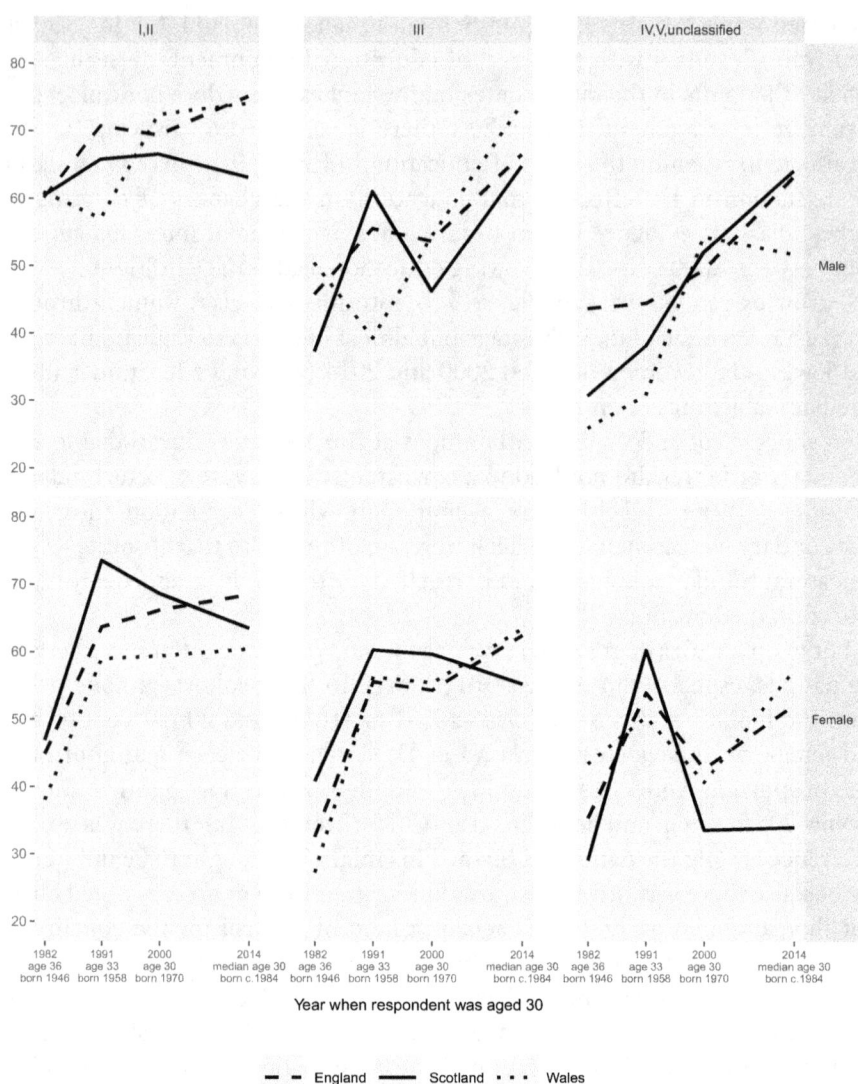

Figure 9.6 Percentage having entered class I, II before age c. 30, by sex, class, survey year and nation of birth within Britain: people at upper quartile of common metric of relative attainment, born 1946–c.1984
Average standard error: England, 2.5; Scotland, 5.7; Wales, 7.5.

Figure 9.2 are not systematically rewarded any less in Figure 9.6 than people of the same class and sex elsewhere.

We discuss the implications of these patterns in the final section of the chapter, after looking at the connection between lifelong learning and social mobility over a longer range of ages.

LIFELONG LEARNING AND SOCIAL MOBILITY

All the analysis so far in this chapter has been about a specific age, standardising that in order to make valid comparisons between birth cohorts. But the great strength of cohort data is that they provide insights into how people change as they age. In particular here, these data can tell us whether getting better formal qualifications might lead to better employment.

On adult learning itself – before we get to its relationship to employment – very much has changed over time. For example, in the three cohorts born in Scotland in 1936, 1958 and 1970 – and using the very long-term follow-up of the 1936 cohort described in Chapter 2 – the proportion of people who gained a higher education certificate rose steadily between the early 1990s and the second decade of the new century, and rose more for the youngest cohort than for the oldest. At the dates 1991, 2001 and 2011, the percentage in the 1936 cohort who had gained a higher education qualification grew from 9 per cent to 14 per cent to 17 per cent (ages 55, 65 and 75). In the middle cohort, the rise was from 29 per cent to 31 per cent to 34 per cent (at ages 33, 42 and 54). In the youngest cohort, the rise was from 34 per cent to 36 per cent to 42 per cent (at ages 26, 30 and 42). Thus not only do people learn more as they get older; the tendency to do so has been growing over time.

Unfortunately the 1936 cohort has the long gap between age 27 and age 55 that is explained in Chapter 2, and so we now concentrate on the other two. The loss of scope for investigating the relationship to social mobility is perhaps not too great, however. As we will see below for the 1958 cohort, upgrading of employment dwindles to very low levels statistically by the time that people are in their fifties (which is not surprising), and so the data from the 1936 cohort at ages 65 and 75 does not offer much information on this question. The further advantage of the 1958 and 1970 cohorts is also, again, that Scotland can be compared with Wales and England. (The 1946 cohort did not gather information about new educational qualifications obtained after respondents' mid-thirties.)

Tables 9.4 and 9.5 summarise information about educational upgrading. They show the percentage of people who upgraded their qualifications between each pair of ages, separately for men and women, and for each nation. For example, in the 1958 cohort, 10 per cent of women in Scotland upgraded their highest educational attainment between the ages of 23 and 33. There was a great deal of upgrading, and it probably increased between the two cohorts: for example, between the ages of 23 and 42, 18 per cent of men born in Scotland in 1958 increased their highest level of qualification (Table 9.4), compared to 30 per cent between 26 and 42 of men born in Scotland in 1970. The corresponding figures for women were 19 per cent and 29 per cent. In the 1958 cohort (Table 9.4), about one in eight people in Scotland improved their qualifications between ages 23 and 33; by age 54, the proportion had risen to about a quarter,

Table 9.4 Percentage upgrading their formal qualifications at various ages (23 to 54), by sex and nation of birth within Britain: people born in 1958

Male	England	Scotland	Wales
Ages			
23 to 33	15	13	13
33 to 42	9	6	13
42 to 46	2	1	2
46 to 50	2	2	3
50 to 54	2	1	1
23 to 54	26	22	28
23 to 42	22	18	23
Sample size	4,179	498	271
Female			
Ages			
23 to 33	9	10	6
33 to 42	12	9	12
42 to 46	7	5	6
46 to 50	5	4	5
50 to 54	3	2	1
23 to 54	31	28	27
23 to 42	19	19	17
Sample size	4,330	560	301

Table 9.5 Percentage upgrading their formal qualifications at various ages (26 to 42), by sex and nation of birth within Britain: people born in 1970

Male	England	Scotland	Wales
Ages			
26 to 30	24	21	27
30 to 34	5	7	6
34 to 38	3	2	2
38 to 42	5	4	4
26 to 42	33	30	37
Sample size	3,063	341	205
Female			
Ages			
26 to 30	22	17	21
30 to 34	7	8	6
34 to 38	5	4	5
38 to 42	6	4	5
26 to 42	35	29	33
Sample size	3,790	391	222

though with minimal changes after age 42. (The percentage for '23 to 54' is slightly less than the sum of the percentages between successive sweeps of the cohort survey because some people upgraded more than once.) Much the same can be said about England and Wales, bearing in mind the small sample size in Wales and thus the greater variability. There is not much systematic difference between men and women, though perhaps some evidence that women tend to upgrade later. For people born in 1970 (Table 9.5), the patterns are similar to those in the 1958 cohort, except that the overall percentage is higher, and that the Scottish rates are slightly lower than in England or Wales.

Figures 9.7 and 9.8 then illustrate, for Scotland, the association between this upgrading of qualifications and upgrading of social class between consecutive ages, for people who had been in class III or classes IV or V at the previous wave of the surveys, and who had average intelligence. To see what the graphs are showing, consider a specific example: the position at age 42 of a woman in the 1958 cohort who, in the previous sweep at age 33, had been in social class III and who, at that sweep, had a senior secondary education but no education higher than that. This woman is in the graph labelled III, in the category labelled on the horizontal axis '33 to 42', and in the lines marked with a cross. If she had not upgraded her qualifications between ages 33 and 42, her chance of upward class mobility between these ages is indicated by the dotted line: it is 23 per cent. But if she did upgrade her qualifications, her chance of upward mobility is indicated by the solid line: 48 per cent. To avoid clutter, the graph shows this only for two prior levels of education – low or none, and senior secondary. The patterns for others were intermediate between these.

In both cohorts, education has always a positive association with upward mobility, but to a diminishing extent as people age. Upward mobility was always greater at higher prior education (the lines for senior secondary are always higher than the corresponding lines for low or no qualifications). Indeed, upward mobility at senior secondary level but without upgrading is similar to upward mobility at low or none with upgrading (the dotted line with crosses is close to the solid line with circles). There were also greater rates of upward mobility from the lower class group shown here (IV, V) than in class III. (Class II showed very little upward mobility, and so is omitted from these graphs.) When comparing these rates, however, it should be noted that, in the 1958 cohort where this contrast is greater, the extent of education upgrading was less in the class group IV and V than in the others: for example, between ages 23 and 31 in the 1958 cohort, 7 per cent of people in that group upgraded their education, compared to 11 per cent in class III and 13 per cent in the group I and II.

The same broad patterns were observed for England and for Wales (not shown here): positive associations of educational upgrading with upward mobility across the lifespan, greater effects of this kind in the later cohort, and diminishing such effects as people aged.

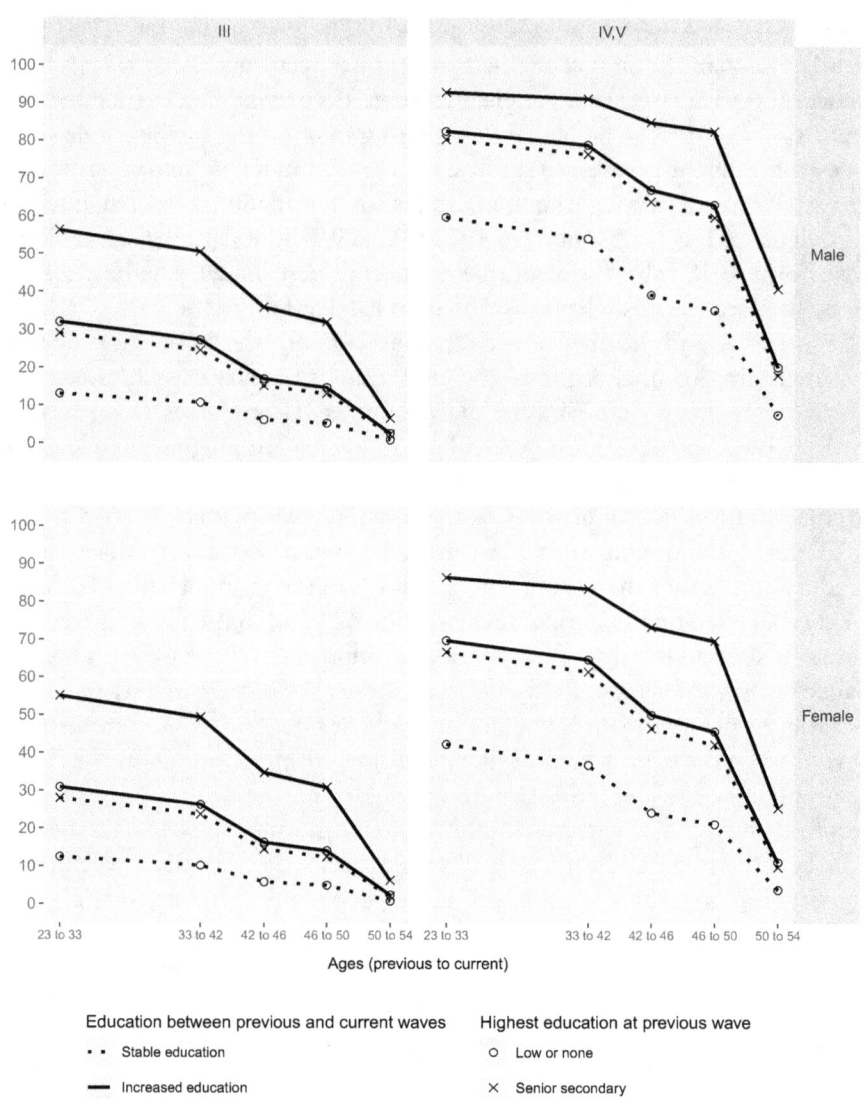

Figure 9.7 Percentage upwardly mobile between various ages (23 to 54), by sex, previous social class, and whether upgraded education: people with average intelligence at age c. 11, born in 1958 in Scotland
The columns of the array correspond to class at previous wave. Average standard error 4.1.

A final point about higher education across the life course relates to the Open University. Most of the data sources which we have been using have no information about this university. However, graduates in the 1970 birth cohort survey were asked a question when they were aged 42 about the name of the university from which they had graduated. In that year, about 2 per cent of

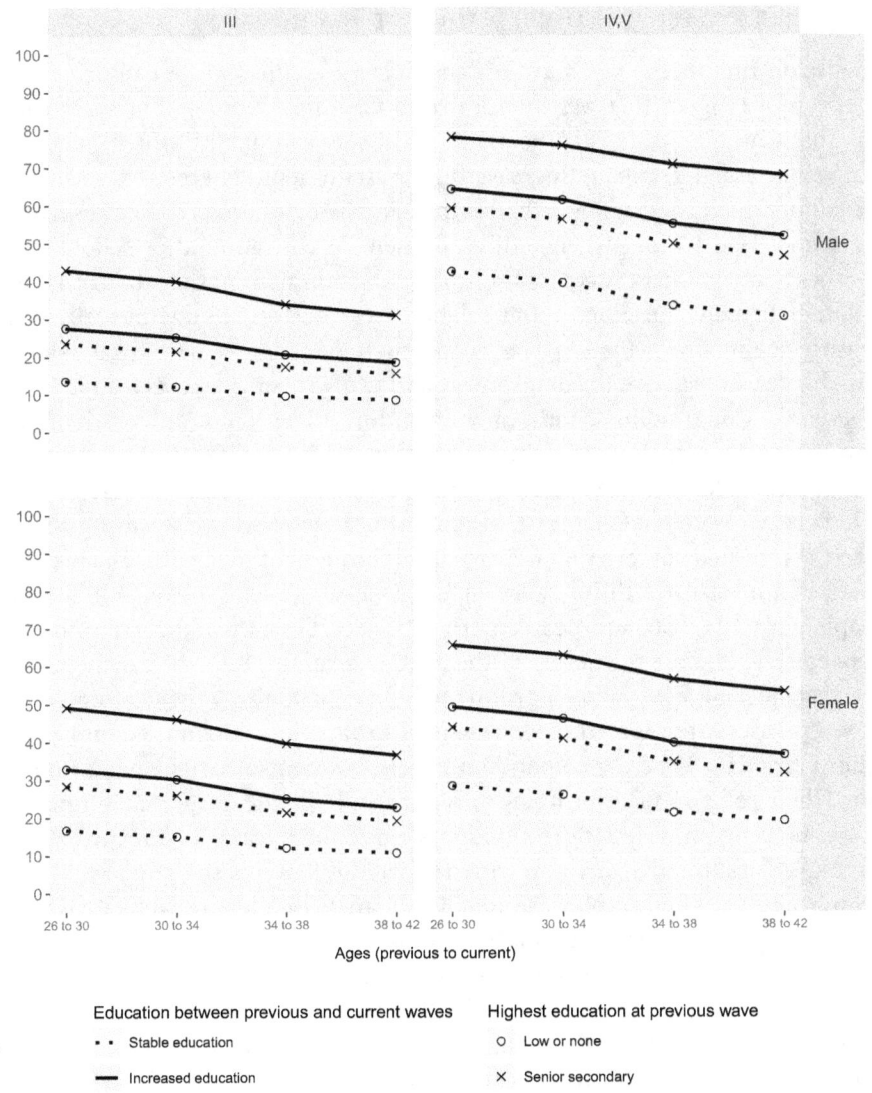

Figure 9.8 Percentage upwardly mobile between various ages (26 to 42), by sex, previous social class, and whether upgraded education: people with average intelligence at age c. 11, born in 1970 in Scotland
The columns of the array correspond to class at previous wave. Average standard error 5.5.

graduates who had been at secondary school in Scotland in 1986 had gained their degree from the Open University. This number is too small to allow any further analysis, but it does show that most of the higher education that was obtained between the ages of 26 and 42 (the rise from 34 per cent to 42 per cent noted above) must have come from the other institutions.

CLASS ATTAINMENT AND RELIGIOUS DENOMINATION

Finally on this theme of education and social mobility, we can return to the question of religion that was mentioned in Chapters 3 and 4. The story there was that Catholic schools in Scotland had been a means by which people of that religion had gradually increased their attainment. There are two further questions which we can now ask: did this equalising of opportunity at secondary school lead to convergence of attainment in education after school? And did these educational processes lead to equal attainment in the labour market?

Unfortunately, questions about religion were not asked systematically from an early age in any of the long-term cohort studies that we have been using in this chapter. So we have to compromise, and use synthetic cohorts from the UK Household Longitudinal Study (now including all ages, not only the younger people who were included in the earlier analysis in this chapter). A synthetic cohort is people in a survey of this kind who were born in a specified period (which, as we noted in Chapter 2, is a less satisfactory way of measuring change than the repeated surveys that we have used throughout the book). To have adequate sample sizes in different religious groups, we define two such cohorts: people born 1937–56, and people born 1957–86. Thus the older group mostly were educated before the period of the main educational reforms which we have been considering. The younger group might have been affected by these reforms.

We restrict attention to three religious groups: no religion, Catholic, and other Christian. Where a respondent described themselves as having no religion, their religion of upbringing was substituted, and so the remaining category 'no religion' refers to respondents' childhood years. The recorded data force us to assume that any currently reported religion is the same as religion of upbringing. The samples are much too small to allow reliable analysis of these questions in other religious groups.

Despite these various compromises and exclusions, the sample numbers remain quite low, with particularly few Catholics in Wales. So it is feasible to compare Scotland only with England. The proportion having attained a higher education certificate illustrates the marked improvement in the position of Scottish Catholics. In Scotland, Catholics in the older of these two cohorts had relatively low proportions with higher education: for men, 24 per cent, compared with 34 per cent of other Christians and 33 per cent of the areligious; for women, respectively 17 per cent, 30 per cent and 36 per cent. In the younger cohort, by contrast, Catholics fared much better: for men, 52 per cent compared to 45 per cent (other Christian) and 43 per cent (no religion); for women, 51 per cent, 59 per cent and 44 per cent. (The average standard error of all these Scottish percentages is 5.3.). In both birth cohorts in England, by contrast, Catholics were not behind the other two groups for either sex, even in the older cohort, in which the percentages were: for men, 34 per cent (Catholic),

35 per cent (other Christian) and 33 per cent (no religion); for women, respectively 33 per cent, 27 per cent and 28 per cent. This educational trajectory in adulthood is consistent with our findings on Catholic schools in Chapters 3 and 4. Then, for the younger cohort, Catholics could translate these credentials into high attainment in the labour market at no lesser a rate than the other two religious group. Among men, 78 per cent of Scottish Catholics with a higher education certificate had reached classes I or II, compared to 80 per cent of other Christians and 73 per cent of the areligious; the corresponding percentages for women were 78 per cent, 75 per cent and 68 per cent. (These percentages had average standard error 6.8.)

Fuller analysis of religious differences in social mobility in Scotland – including classes of origin – is provided by Paterson and Iannelli (2006), using the large Scottish Household Survey of 2001. Although the comparison with England is not available from that survey, the broad conclusions are consistent with what we have seen here. Younger Scottish Catholics had attainment and patterns of social mobility that were indistinguishable from those of other Christians and of people with no religion. Taken together with Chapters 3 and 4, all this evidence shows the importance of the Catholic schools in enabling Scottish Catholics to join the mainstream of social opportunity.

CONCLUSIONS

Education and Entry into Adulthood

This chapter has placed the outcomes of Scottish schools, colleges and universities in two comparative dimensions – over space and across ages. Both of these have also been compared across chronological time. The strength of the analysis of educational and social-class attainment at ages around 30 is the length of time which it covers and the capacity to consider distinct education systems serving a labour market that generally has operated in a common way. It has thus set Scotland in a context where we know that comparison is valid because the labour market operates broadly in the same way and because examination credentials broadly mean the same kinds of thing. By including the cohort born in 1946 we have been able to start the series of comparisons with people who attended school before the ending of selection for secondary school, and well before the expansion of higher education. By using the large UK Household Longitudinal Study to construct a cohort born in the last quarter of the twentieth century, we have taken the series forward to the second decade of the new century, while retaining a large enough sub-sample of people born in Scotland and Wales to allow comparison of both of these with England. For Scotland, we were able to take the starting point back to people who entered the stable selective system in the immediately post-war period.

Of course, any such investigation is doomed to be out of date, especially at older ages than 30: it is not possible to investigate, say, the lifelong learning of people aged 50 until half a century after they were born; to decide how that learning is changing in chronological time, some of the data have to be even older. Nevertheless, the long span of time that is covered by the cohorts gives some pointers to trends over a period of very extensive reform to the institutions that provide opportunities for learning.

The first set of conclusions resulted from applying the ideas of relative educational attainment to a situation where the social context for the relative measures might differ from the context for measuring the relative status of social-class outcomes. For attaining at least a full secondary education, Scotland had higher attainment than in England or Wales, except among men in the lowest class. The same was true of attaining a higher education qualification. When education was measured relatively to a common British norm, these Scottish advantages persisted, but not when the norm was specific to each nation. Inequality was consistently greater in Scotland than elsewhere except when all classes were close to saturation, which was only for secondary education in the later time points. But not only was the Scottish inequality not due to any poorer performance by the lowest Scottish class. Taking the Scottish data back to the 1936 cohort showed that it was also a temporary phenomenon associated with the initial period of expansion.

Then the crucial test was whether these differences in educational attainment were associated with different rates of entry to the managerial and professional class. Our data did show that over time, at each level of absolute attainment, its declining relative standing led to declining rewards in social-class outcomes. This was true of each nation considered separately (and confirms research by previous authors, notably by Bukodi and Goldthorpe (2016)). But that pattern mostly did not apply over space. There was no evidence that the higher relative share of, say, secondary school attainment in Scotland led to poorer class outcomes than the same absolute measure in England or Wales.

In all these respects, moreover, Wales was similar to England. So the greater distinctiveness of Scottish educational policy over many decades may have enabled its students to take advantage of education in the classic way that people from peripheral societies have been able to do. Wales, also peripheral, was not able to provide this advantage historically, being too tightly tied to the dominant educational model of England. In terms of Thurow's queuing theory for employment, the education queue produced by Scotland between the 1930s and the early years of the present century enabled people to join the pan-Britain job queue at a higher point than people emerging in the education queue in England or Wales.

These comments remain speculative, and testing them would require the analysis of specific occupational careers using much larger data sets for students from Wales and Scotland. The speculations may also be tested further in practice in the coming decades as education policy in Wales – as well as in Scotland – diverges further from that in England because of legislative devolution in 1999. We might also draw a tentative policy conclusion from the theoretical conclusions about education queues and job queues. It continues to make sense for policy in peripheral societies, such as Scotland and Wales, to invest in expanding access to secondary and higher education not only for the absolute benefits which education brings, but also to confer a competitive advantage, despite the conclusions that general expansion merely shifts inequality to higher levels of the system. Expansion of this kind can be of competitive value to young people from the education system of peripheral societies if they then gain an advantage in a job queue that extends across a wider territory. This advantage is contingent, because it depends on there being less expansion in the education queue of the core society, in this case England. Any advantage is also likely to be temporary, as the core society catches up.

Education across the Life Course

In the patterns of lifelong learning, Scotland was not strongly distinctive within Britain, despite its relatively higher attainment when people were in their late twenties. In all three countries, there was quite a lot of educational upgrading, and more of it among people born in 1970 – taking advantage of the expansion of higher education courses – than among those born in 1958. People in Scotland also shared in a common British tendency to do most upgrading in their late twenties or thirties. The main reason was probably related to occupational advancement, and certainly there were consistent associations of educational upgrading with upward social mobility. Most of that mobility had happened by the time that people were in their early forties, after which the instrumental value of their educational credentials diminished. If Scottish participation in adult education was lower than in England and Wales – as was suggested by our data – this would be consistent with previous research stretching far back in the twentieth century, in which the sheer strength of initial education in Scotland seemed to leave people feeling that further study, even of an informal kind, was unnecessary (Field, 2009, pp. 4, 12 and 15; Paterson, 2003, pp. 183–9).

The associations of education with upward social mobility do not prove that the link is causal. It is possible that people upgrade their qualifications after moving to a better job – perhaps because the opportunities to do educational courses there are better, or perhaps because the new context encourages them to strengthen their knowledge and skills. Nevertheless, what can be said is that upward mobility and upgrading of education are closely connected with each other, enhancing the sense that self-improvement is at least partly a meritocratic affair.

CHAPTER 10

Education, Social Attitudes and Scottish Governance

EDUCATION AND POLITICS

Two quite different kinds of debate are relevant to understanding the civic and political implications for Scotland of the massive expansion of education since the middle of the twentieth century which we have been considering so far. One debate is very old, certainly since the eighteenth-century Enlightenment, and in some respects since the first thinking about education and citizenship in ancient Greece: the main question is how education might contribute to strengthening civic values and democracy. The other debate is much more recent, and is a response to the rise of what has been called political populism, although it too has been around for a while, trying to understand how to prevent democracy being taken over by demagoguery. Because this populism has been associated with nationalism, and because the rise of political nationalism has been the dominant political development in Scotland since the 1960s, this second debate has provoked the question: what kind nationalism does Scotland have? Then these two debates have created a paradox because, historically, people with more education have tended to be much less willing to support Scottish independence, and yet independence support has grown at the same time as education has also grown.

Education and Democracy

The common conclusion of thinking about the connection between education and civic values is that education makes people more democratically responsible in the sense of taking part in civic groups and holding liberal and tolerant views that affirm the value of democracy (Bynner et al., 2003; Egerton, 2002; Emler and Frazer, 1999; Galston, 2001; Hall, 1999; Huang et al., 2009; Nie and Hillygus, 2001; Niemi and Junn, 1998; Paterson, 2014). The empirical evidence, however, suggests that matters are not straightforward. Campbell (2006) notes in his comprehensive review of relevant research that it is not sufficient to suppose that 'education has a universally positive effect on all forms of engagement' (p. 25). For example, while '[a]cross much of the industrialised world, education levels have been rising ... political engagement of all sorts has been falling.' (p. 26).

Three main points emerge from these academic debates, all with relevance to Scotland:

- The first is the importance of higher education. Campbell (2006) concludes from his questions that what matters is whether a course of study encourages independent thought. Thus the expansion of higher education may have been particularly likely to have made people more civic, insofar as higher education seeks to encourage this kind of critical thinking (Gutmann, 1987).
- The second point is that adult learning, even that undertaken when people are in their middle age, can lead to their being more engaged in civic activities (Bynner et al., 2003; Campbell, 2006). We noted the expansion of adult learning in Scotland in Chapter 9.
- The third point is that education might have more of an effect on attitudes than on participation (Nie et al., 1996). Much participation is like competition for a scarce resource (as in social mobility): there is not space for everyone to participate; therefore participation will be taken up only by those who have the most educational capital. Democratic attitudes, by contrast, are not competitive in this sense: in principle everyone could be enlightened.

So the first part of the empirical analysis here looks at the long-term implications for attitudes and for participation of the expansion of education which we have discussed in earlier chapters. As we explain shortly, our data for this purpose cover the period from 1979 to 2016, and so almost the full range of dates at which the respondents in our surveys of school leavers and of graduates entered into adult life. This allows us to consider the likely long-term effects of the educational changes which we have delineated in previous chapters.

Education and National Populism

That tradition of thinking about education and democracy is generally optimistic. In recent academic writing, the spirit has been more ambivalent, provoked by the rise of populism, a vague term which we discuss shortly, but which is usually taken to be epitomised internationally by the election of Donald Trump as US President in 2016, or by Brexit, the UK's decision, by a referendum in that same year, to leave the European Union. In this second debate, it is true, there is a persisting optimism that education might be a reply to populism insofar as it does have the potential to make people more liberally tolerant, to incline them to international cooperation over national sovereignty, and to make them wary of resentful types of nationalism. On the other hand, educated elites have been blamed for provoking nationalist rebellions against liberalism and globalisation. One theme of this chapter is that neither of these stories fully describes recent Scottish experience of nationalism.

One of the best-known pieces of evidence cited by the second, ambivalent story is a comment from the UK Conservative politician Michael Gove during the campaign which led to Brexit: 'people in this country have had enough of experts from organisations with acronyms' (Full Fact, 2016). Often misquoted as being an attack on expertise per se, this actually more subtle point succinctly encapsulates a rebellion against the power exercised by highly educated elites in powerful institutions. The same sentiment can be found in academic analysis that is canonical in politically left-wing educational research, notably in the tradition of thought deriving from Bourdieu and Passeron (1977, p. 123). Education, in this view, confers power through the habitus of the institutions where the highly educated work (a version of the idea of institutional habitus which we used in Chapter 7 to help understand the connection between high-status secondary schools and high-status universities). Modern elites form increasingly closed cultural groups because of merit selection, which has allegedly come to be a means by which advantage is reproduced rather than opened widely (Sandel, 2020, pp. 155–95; Wooldridge, 2021, pp. 306–28).

The disparate rebellions against this structure of power have been called 'national populism' by Eatwell and Goodwin (2018, pp. xxi–xxii). As well as Brexit and President Trump, there are electorally strong instances also in France, Germany, Hungary, Italy, Poland and Sweden. Eatwell and Goodwin point out (pp. 25–7) that education is 'one of the major fault lines that runs beneath national populism across the West', noting that, for example, in the 2016 EU referendum the 'educational divide' was greater than those by class, income or age.

Other writers have made similar points. Goodhart (2017, pp. 23–4) describes the opponents of Brexit as being typically a 'liberally-inclined graduate'. Curtice (2017) noted that 'support for Leave [in the 2016 referendum] and a hard Brexit is much higher amongst those with few, if any, educational qualifications than it is amongst university graduates'. Silver (2016) and Mounk (2018, p. 190) draw the same conclusions about the election of President Trump. Runciman (2018, p. 164) sums up this interpretation in a way that takes us back to the habitus of elites: 'the educated mistake their [own] tribalism for superior wisdom'.

Scottish nationalism might appear to offer a straightforward further instance of this story. Goodhart (2017, p. 53) draws the apparently obvious parallel with Brexit:

> Brexit was a movement to reclaim control/sovereignty from a supranational EU and the SNP [the main nationalist party] is a movement to reclaim control/sovereignty from a multinational United Kingdom.

Support for Scottish independence fits most authors' definitions of populism. For example, Mudde and Kaltwasser (2012, p. 8) define populism as 'a confrontation between "the people" and "the establishment"'. In the Scottish case, this contrast is between the people of Scotland and the UK political establishment in London. That is why it seems reasonable for Norris and Inglehart (2019, p. 486) to classify the SNP as a left-wing populist party.

Nevertheless, difficulties of classifying the Scottish case arise because the ideology of Scottish nationalism has generally been civic rather than ethnic (Jackson, 2020; McCrone, 1998). Moreover, because, as we have seen in earlier chapters, nearly all citizens of Scotland now have at least a decade of schooling (up to mid-secondary school), and a majority have more than that, it is inaccurate to describe the 'education divide' as setting the uneducated against the educated. With the intellectual resources provided by much more extensive education than their predecessors had, those who rebel against elites, it may be argued, are perfectly capable of making that choice on the basis of educated rationality. Curtice (2014) has repeatedly shown that the two most powerful influences on people's choice in the referendum on Scottish independence in 2014 were a combination of the affective and the rational: the power of one of these, national identity, may be thought to be consistent with the theories of national populism, but the influence of how people saw the economic prospects of an independent Scotland seemed the epitome of rational calculation.

This alternative view of the importance of rational evaluation of constitutional options has indeed been a strong current in Scottish nationalism, certainly in the long campaign for some kind of elected parliament when the case for devolution was made partly on the basis of liberal reform to the UK state (Paterson, 1998). Because devolution quickly became the settled consensus after 1999 (as we will see below), there did emerge a new political tension between the supporters of this new status quo – who were generally well-educated and well-connected – and the nationalist opposition that wanted to take the powers of the parliament further (McCrone, 2019; Paterson, 2009a). But the movement for Scottish independence, precisely because it had been on the left politically since the 1970s, has always had the capacity to attract to it the rebellious instincts of the young and educated (Jackson, 2020). The prominence of

EDUCATION, SOCIAL ATTITUDES AND SCOTTISH GOVERNANCE

young activists with university degrees was a widely noted feature of the campaigning for independence in the 2014 referendum (Crowther, 2018; Paterson, 2015d). Moreover, whereas men had previously shown higher levels of support for independence than women (McCrone and Paterson, 2002), there was some evidence that this sex difference may have weakened as independence support rose in the youngest cohorts.

This chapter investigates both of these debates – both the view of education's democratic potential that may be inferred from Enlightenment optimism, and the recent pessimism about the tendency of education to undermine democracy by creating a divide between people with a lot of education and those with minimal amounts. The conclusion supports neither position straightforwardly.

SURVEYS OF SOCIAL ATTITUDES

The data come from the Scottish Social Attitudes Surveys and the Scottish Election Surveys. These surveys are as important for understanding Scottish democracy as the school leavers' surveys are for understanding education; they are described in Chapter 2.

Sex was recorded dichotomously in all surveys. The other variables are as follows; they were asked in all 20 of the surveys unless specified otherwise:

Birth cohort: In all but the 1979 survey, this is derived from respondent's age at the time of the fieldwork; in 1979, it came from a question about year of birth. The cohorts are shown in Table 10.1 below: they are each a decade long (for example, 1957–66), except the oldest (1926 or earlier) and the youngest (1987–91). From the surveys where a relevant question was asked (2006–14), at least 90 per cent of respondents were born in the UK; we retain in the analysis people who were not born in the UK because they were mostly eligible to vote in the 2014 referendum.

One of the main interests in this chapter is the interactive effect of survey year and cohort: for example, in the surveys leading up to the 2014 referendum, did people born in the 1980s change their views about independence at a different rate from people born in the 1950s? Using multiple cross-sectional surveys to disentangle the effects of survey year and birth cohort has been shown by previous researchers to clarify educational change over time (Breen et al., 2009; Ganzeboom and Treiman, 1993). But there is a complication here because obviously not all birth cohorts appear in every survey year. In fact, only the first four cohorts appear in all the surveys. Respondents in the two cohorts from 1957 to 1976 appear in all but the 1979 survey, because, in that year, even the oldest person from these cohorts (aged 22) did not reach the threshold of age 25. The 1977–86 cohort appears in 2002–16, and the 1987–91 cohort only in 2012–16. In technical terms, in order to model statistically the interactive effect of year and cohort, it was necessary explicitly to exclude terms that corresponded to empty cells in the full year-by-cohort table. For example, there was no term representing the interaction of the 1957–66 cohort and the year 1979.

Education: This is the highest level of educational attainment at the survey date. For purposes of analysis, in order to have adequate sample sizes, the levels are grouped into three categories: higher education; secondary education (meaning at least a pass in the various mid-secondary courses which we have discussed in previous chapters); and levels lower than that. Cases with missing data on education are omitted from all the analysis (around 2 per cent of cases in every year except 1979, when it was 4 per cent).

National identity: This has been asked about in a variety of ways, but the only reasonably consistent version that allows 1979 to be included is what has been called 'forced choice national identity': respondents were asked to choose the identity that best described them, from the list: British, Scottish, Welsh, Northern Irish, Irish, European, and Other. In every year, at least 88 per cent of people chose either Scottish or British, and so we group this measure into these two categories and a category 'other'.

Support for Scottish Parliament or for independence: In all the surveys, a question was asked about the respondent's preferred constitutional arrangement. From 1997 to 2016, the offered categories were: independence outside the European Union, independence in the EU, devolution with taxation powers, devolution without taxation powers, and no elected parliament. The 1992 options were similar, but omitting the distinction of devolution with and without taxation. For all these years, support for independence is defined here to be choosing one of the first two options. In 1979, only one independence option was offered, along with a parliament responsible for most Scottish affairs, an assembly responsible for some affairs, and no elected assembly. Independence support in 1979 is defined to be that unique option. In all the years, support for any kind of parliament was defined to be all options but the last.

Evaluation of Scottish Parliament: In the surveys 1999–2013, 2015 and 2016, respondents were asked 'do you think having a Scottish Parliament is giving ordinary people more say in how Scotland is governed, less say or is it making no difference?' (with some minor variations of wording in particular years). We create a dichotomous variable combining 'less' and 'no difference'. Similar, they were asked 'do you think that having a Scottish Parliament is giving Scotland a stronger voice in the United Kingdom, a weaker voice, or is it making no difference?'. Again, our variable contrasts 'stronger' with the other two options.

Vote in 2016 referendum on the UK's membership of the European Union: In the 2016 survey (fieldwork for which took place after the referendum in June), respondents were asked how they had voted (remain or leave).

Economic expectations of independence: In 2013 and 2014 only, respondents were asked how independence would affect the Scottish economy, with a five-point response scale from 'a lot better' to 'a lot worse'. Because this variable has been shown to have been strongly associated with voting for or against independence in the 2014 referendum, it is included in analysis restricted to these two years to assess how it interacts with education.

Scale of views from liberal to conservative: In the surveys 2000–11 and 2014–16, this is built from the responses to six items:

People who break the law should be given stiffer sentences.
For some crimes the death penalty is the most appropriate sentence.
Schools should teach children to obey authority.
Young people today don't have enough respect for traditional British values.
Censorship of films and magazines is necessary to uphold moral standards.
The law should be obeyed, even if a particular law is wrong.

Each of these asked for replies on a five-point scale from 'strongly disagree' to 'strongly agree'. The replies were scored as consecutive integers, such that all the items contributing to a scale have positive correlations with each other, and such that low values corresponded to the liberal position, and then the overall scale for each respondent was calculated by taking the mean across the six items. We also look specifically at views on the item here relating to censorship.

Scale of views from left to right: In the surveys 2000, 2002 and 2004–16, this is built from the individual items:

Ordinary working people do not get their fair share of the nation's wealth.
There is one law for the rich and one for the poor.
Management will always try to get the better of employees if it gets the chance.
Government should redistribute income from the better off to those who are less well off.
Big business benefits owners at the expense of the workers.

The scoring and construction of the scale was the same as with the liberal-conservative scale, with low values corresponding to the left position.

Political interest: In the surveys 1997–2001 and 2003–16, respondents were asked how much interest they had in politics, on a five-point scale. A dichotomous variable was created contrasting 'a great deal' and 'quite a lot' with 'some', 'not very much' and 'none'.

Social trust: In the surveys 2000, 2004, 2006, 2009, 2013 and 2015, respondents were asked 'Generally speaking, would you say that most people can be trusted, or that you can't be too careful in dealing with people?' The 'trust' response is contrasted with 'can't be too careful' and other replies such as 'don't know'.

Political participation: In the surveys 2009, 2013, 2015 and 2016, respondents were asked if they had ever done any of the following. The scale was constructed as a simple count of how many were mentioned:

> contacted a member of the Scottish or UK parliaments;
> spoken to an influential person;
> contacted government department;
> contacted local council;
> contacted radio, TV or a newspaper;
> signed a petition;
> raised issue in an organisation already a member of;
> gone on a demonstration;
> formed a group of like-minded people;
> responded to a consultation document;
> attended an event as part of consultation;
> attended a public meeting;
> joined an existing organisation;
> taken an active part in a campaign;
> given money to a campaign or an organisation.

After the missing values on the education variable are omitted, there were around 1,300 people in each survey from 1999 to 2016, and 600–800 in each of the surveys of 1979–97; the total was 25,128.

EDUCATION AND DEMOCRATIC ATTITUDES

Social Engagement: Trust, Participation, and Interest in Politics

Over the whole series of surveys from 1979 to 2016, there was a large change in the distribution of educational attainment, consistent with the detailed analysis of Chapters 3 to 8. For example, the proportion with a higher education qualification rose from 9 per cent in 1979 to around 15 per cent at the turn of the century, 20 per cent a decade later, and 25 per cent in 2016. The proportion with education lower than mid-secondary fell from 53 per cent in 1979 to 28 per cent in 2016. These educational trends are even clearer when recorded by decade of birth. The proportion with a higher education qualification among the oldest cohorts is inflated by differential mortality (because people with high amounts of education tend to live longer). Nevertheless, even among surviving people in 2013–16, there was a very clear growth of education across the cohorts: higher education rose from 11 per cent to 53 per cent, and low or no formal attainment fell from 70 per cent to 16 per cent.

We introduce the investigation of the connection between educational expansion and democracy in Scotland by analysing associations with the general measure of social trust. Although this is available from only six of the surveys, they are spread across a 15-year period, with a combined sample size of 8,367, thus giving ample scope to investigate variation across birth cohorts as well as across survey years.

There was a gradient in trust across education categories in each of the survey years. The proportion who generally trust other people was around 60–70 per cent among people with higher education, which was mostly at least 10 percentage points greater than the proportion in the other two education categories. At each level of education, the proportion was slightly higher among men than among women, and there was a small rise between 2000 and 2004, but the education gradient is the main feature.

However, this is only the beginning of the story, because the proportion who were trusting varied across the birth cohorts. On average across all education levels and all of these six surveys, 57 per cent of men born in 1927–36 were generally trusting. This rose to a peak of 61 per cent in the 1937–46 cohort, and then fell steadily to 52 per cent in the 1977–86 cohort. Corresponding proportions for women were 51 per cent in the 1927–36 cohort, a peak of 54 per cent in the 1947–56 cohort, and 45 per cent in the 1977–86 cohort. At first sight, this is puzzling. Later cohorts have more education than earlier; more education is associated with more trust; and yet the later cohorts have less trust.

To resolve the paradox, we look simultaneously at both measures of time – birth cohort, and year of survey. Figure 10.1 shows that there are important differences by birth cohort. This graph extracts three cohorts to illustrate the main features: people born 1927–36, 1957–66 or 1977–86. The education gradient is evident in each cohort, but the significance of education for trust changes. Most notably, the lines for secondary education move down between the cohorts, from being similar to the higher education line to being close to the line for low or none. At the same time, the lines for higher education move up, and then down. So this joint analysis tends to confirm that the changes in trust were cohort effects which were strong enough to overcome the positive effects of rising levels of education. Putting that differently: as the average education level of the population rose, the effect of middling levels of education on trust declined.

The pattern for social participation is similar. This measure is available for only four years (2009, 2013, 2015 and 2016), but there was no evidence of any change over these years. So we combine the years to concentrate on the joint effect of education and birth cohort. The results are shown in Table 10.1.

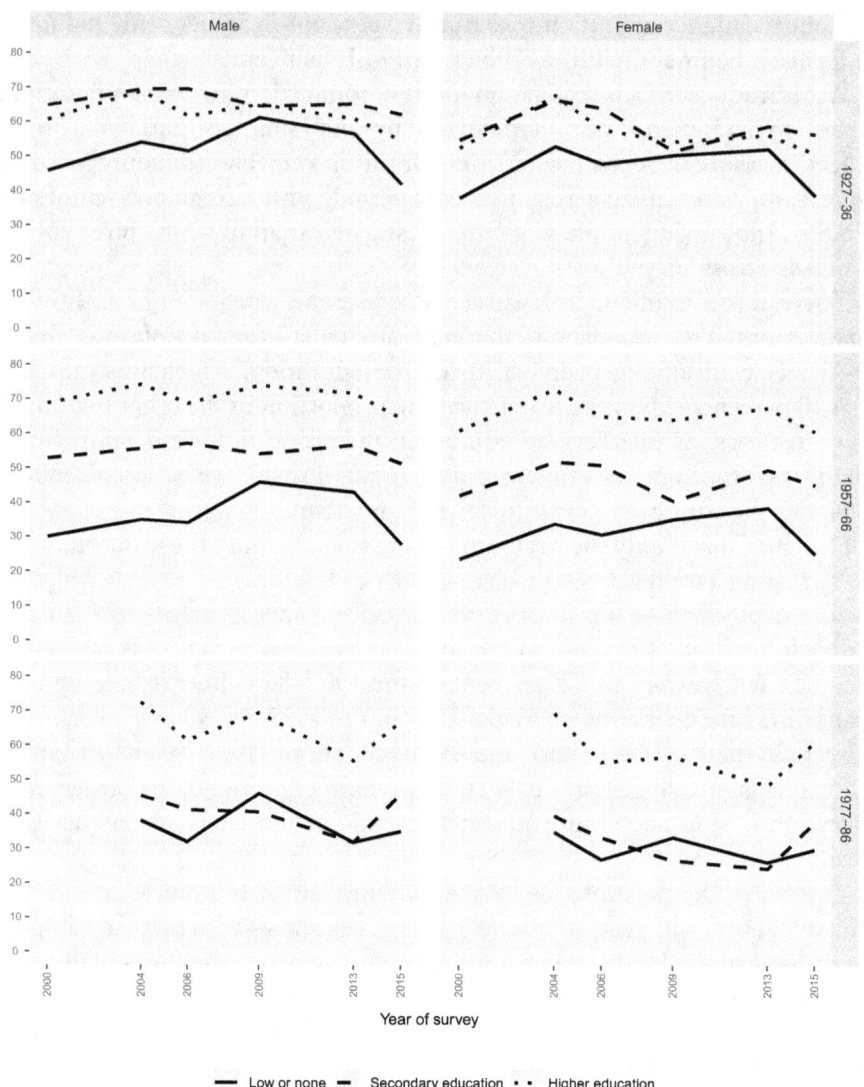

Figure 10.1 Percentage generally trusting of other people, by survey year (2000–15), sex and education: birth cohorts 1927–36, 1957–66 and 1977–86
Average standard error: 1927–36, 6.6; 1957–66, 4.7; 1977–86, 7.2.

Because the index of participation is essentially a count of the number of kinds of activity that respondents did, it is best thought of as a measure of how engaged in political networks the respondent was. The pattern is similar to that for social trust: there is a steep gradient across the education categories, in all the cohorts, such that people with more education tend to be more engaged. There is also similarity to trust in the change over time, in that, at each level of education, the index tends to be highest in middle cohorts (born 1947–76). Again, the values for secondary education move closer in the later cohorts to those for the lowest education category. So also do the values for the higher education category: for example, whereas in the middle cohorts the ratio of the index values for the highest and lowest education categories is around 3 (for both male and female), it is around 2.5 in the cohorts born after 1967. So we are led to conclude that expanding education did not lead to a consistently expanding engagement in political networks. Nevertheless, because the gradient in participation across education categories remained despite the reduction of participation across cohorts within each of them, the expanded education prevented the overall index from falling even further than it did. For example, suppose that the education distribution had remained as in the 1957–66 cohort, while the participation index within each education category had fallen as shown in the table. Then the average index for men, ignoring education, would have fallen from 2.4 in that cohort to 1.7 in the 1977–86 cohort,

Table 10.1 Scale of civic participation (2009–16), by sex, education and birth cohorts from pre-1926 to early 1990s

Birth cohort	Average, ignoring education	Highest education attained		
		Low or none	Secondary	Higher education
Male				
–1926	2.0	0.8	2.7	4.0
1927–36	1.2	0.8	1.7	1.9
1937–46	2.0	1.2	2.8	3.2
1947–56	2.3	1.2	2.0	3.6
1957–66	2.4	1.1	2.1	3.5
1967–76	2.3	1.3	1.8	3.2
1977–86	1.9	0.9	1.6	2.3
1987–91	1.8	0.7	1.1	2.7
Female				
–1926	0.7	0.6	0.8	1.8
1927–36	1.1	0.8	1.4	2.3
1937–46	1.7	1.1	2.0	3.0
1947–56	2.0	1.1	1.6	3.2
1957–66	2.2	1.1	1.6	3.6
1967–76	2.1	1.1	2.0	2.5
1977–86	1.6	1.2	1.5	1.7
1987–91	1.9	1.0	1.5	2.4

Notes:
Surveys in years 2009, 2013, 2015 and 2016.
Average standard error for column ignoring education: –1926, 0.33; 1927–87, 0.14; 1987–91, 0.33.
Average standard error for columns with education: –1926, 0.67; 1927–87, 0.26; 1987–91, 0.45.

lower than the 1.9 in the average column in the table. For women, the index would have been 1.5 compared to 1.6. Education expansion thus partly protected against the weakening of the association of education with participation.

Interest in politics grew slowly over the two decades after the Scottish Parliament was set up, from 25 per cent in 1999, through 33 per cent in 2007 to 43 per cent in 2016. But, again, the most striking feature is the education gradient. The group with higher education consistently had a higher percentage interested in politics than the other two education groups. But in each education category, interest was lower in younger cohorts than in older. For example, in the 1927–36 cohort, around 60–70 per cent of people with higher education were interested in politics in the decade leading up to the referendum in 2014. That was also true of men in the 1957–66 cohort, but for women the extent of interest was 40–50 per cent. In the 1977–86 cohort, the male percentage was mostly down to 40–50 per cent, and the female one to around 30 per cent. Although both of these rose by about 10 points after 2014, that still left the interest level among these younger women 20 points lower than in the oldest cohort at that time; for younger men, the gap was at least 10 points.

So for these three measures of social engagement – trust, participation and political interest – there are two consistent conclusions: there was always an education gradient, but also, at each level of education, there was a decline in engagement across the cohorts.

Political Ideology

At first sight, the story for ideology is similar to that for engagement. For the scale of views along the dimension from liberal to conservative, there was a consistently steep education gradient from 2000 to 2016, the most liberal being people with higher education. The patterns across birth cohorts and over time are shown in Table 10.2 and Figure 10.2. The graphs show that there was a gradient across the birth cohorts, with later cohorts being on average more liberal than earlier: this is shown in the first column of Table 10.2.

With engagement, we have seen that the cohort differences could be observed within each education category. This is not so consistently true of the liberal-conservative scale, especially at the two lower levels of education. For example, from Table 10.2, between the 1927–36 and 1977–86 cohorts, the male average in the secondary category was unchanged at 3.7, whereas the average change for men was from 3.9 to 3.5. For women, the secondary category was unchanged at 3.8, whereas the average fell from 3.9 to 3.6. The reason is essentially that the average is being mainly driven by the growth of higher education and by the generally more liberal views of graduates who were born after the mid-1950s. This may be seen from Figure 10.2. On the whole, the lines for the lowest and middle categories do not decline much, if at all, towards the end of

Table 10.2 Liberal-conservative scale (2000–16), by sex, education and birth cohorts from pre-1926 to early 1990s

Birth cohort	Average, ignoring education	Highest education attained		
		Low or none	Secondary	Higher education
Male				
–1926	3.9	4.0	4.0	3.5
1927–36	3.9	4.0	3.7	3.5
1937–46	3.8	4.0	3.7	3.5
1947–56	3.6	3.9	3.7	3.4
1957–66	3.6	3.8	3.7	3.4
1967–6	3.5	3.8	3.6	3.3
1977–86	3.5	3.6	3.7	3.3
1987–91	3.2	3.7	3.8	2.8
Female				
–1926	3.9	4.0	3.8	3.8
1927–36	3.9	3.9	3.8	3.7
1937–46	3.8	3.9	3.8	3.5
1947–56	3.6	3.9	3.7	3.3
1957–66	3.6	3.8	3.7	3.3
1967–76	3.6	3.8	3.7	3.4
1977–86	3.6	3.8	3.8	3.4
1987–91	3.5	3.6	3.7	3.3

Notes:
Low values = liberal.
Surveys in years 2000–16.
Average standard error for column ignoring education: –1926, 0.03; 1927–87, 0.02; 1987–91, 0.11.
Average standard error for columns with education: –1926, 0.07; 1927–87, 0.04; 1987–91, 0.15.

the period, whereas in each cohort the graduate lines move downwards in a firmly liberal direction.

Because there has been much public debate in recent years about freedom of speech and its relationship to education (Adekoya et al., 2020), it is worth looking specifically at the component of the liberal-authoritarian scale relating to censorship. It was recoded into a dichotomous variable contrasting, on the one hand, 'agreeing' or 'agreeing strongly' with censorship, with, on the other hand, 'disagreeing strongly', 'disagreeing', or not having a view. The same pattern in relation to education and birth cohort was found as in Table 10.2. In each cohort, the lowest support for censorship was among people with higher education, and the cohort with the lowest support was the youngest. So, for example, male graduates born in 1977–86 had 40 per cent support; men with minimal education in that cohort had 46 per cent support; men with minimal education in the 1927–36 cohort had 78 per cent support. The corresponding

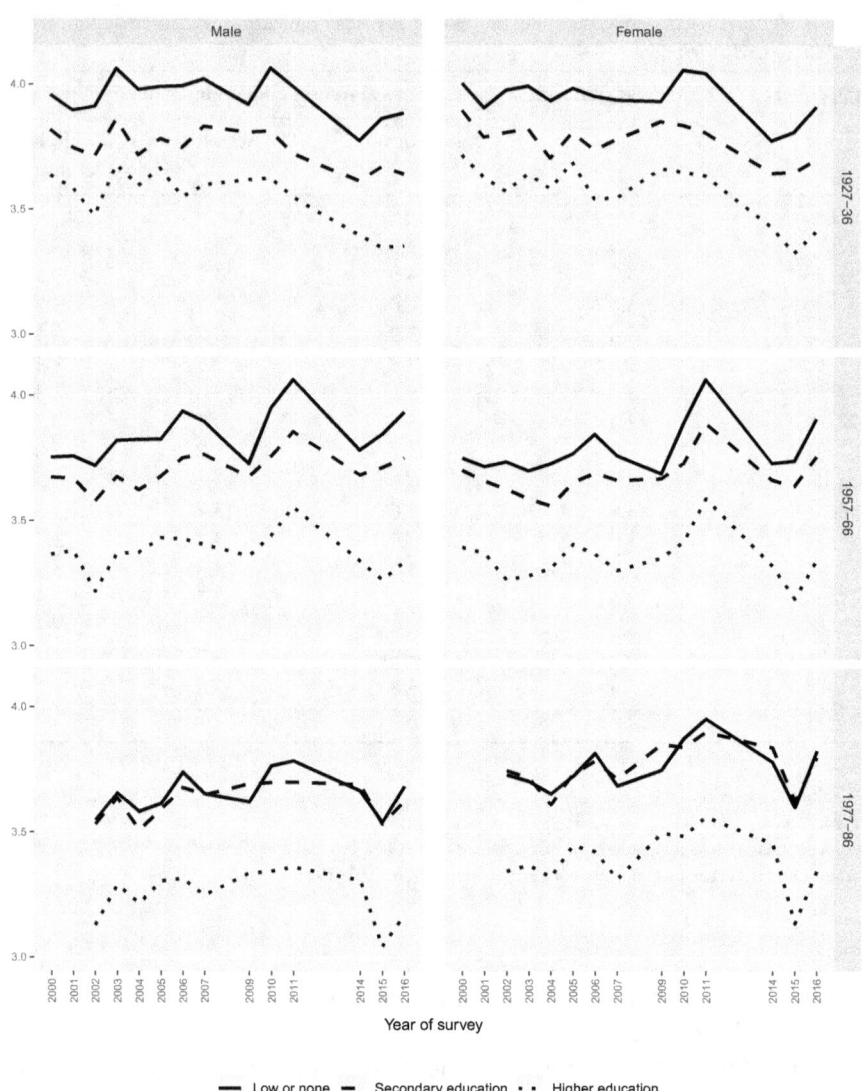

Figure 10.2 Position on liberal–conservative scale, by survey year (2000–16), sex and education: birth cohorts 1927–36, 1957–66 and 1977–86
Low values = liberal.
Average standard error: 1927–36, 0.076; 1957–66, 0.062; 1977–86, 0.094.

proportions among women were somewhat higher, but with the same gradient: 51 per cent, 59 per cent, 86 per cent.

In contrast to the more liberal average in the younger than in the older cohorts in Table 10.2, the patterns for the scale from left to right showed very little average variation across the cohorts. For both women and men, there was a clear education gradient in each cohort: people with higher education were, on average, to the right of people with less education. Taking the two ideological dimensions together, we can say, therefore, that the main point is that higher education graduates became more liberal after about 2011, whereas other education categories did not become more liberal. In contrast, there was no clear trajectory or cohort differences at any level of education on the scale that records attitudes to the market and to the state.

EDUCATION AND THE GOVERNANCE OF SCOTLAND

In many ways, therefore, the growth of education in Scotland over the second half of the twentieth century had the same kind of effect on civic attitudes and political engagement as has been found elsewhere. The newly expanded population of graduates was more liberal and more engaged than people without advanced education, even though that education gradient was less than it had been when higher education was rarer. But generic conclusions of this kind always interact with specific local conditions, because democracy is national, not global. In a Scotland where the constitutional question has dominated debate throughout the whole period of this educational expansion – since the 1960s – the main question is actually what impact all these educational and civic changes have had on views about how Scotland is governed. So we now turn to assessing the competing claims about nationalism that were outlined at the beginning of the chapter. Before we turn to this question, however, there is a final preliminary: how does education relate to views of the first-ever democratically elected Scottish Parliament that was set up in 1999?

Scottish Parliament

The proportion in favour of some kind of elected parliament had reached 80–90 per cent by 1997 in all categories defined by education, sex and birth cohort, and remained at over 90 per cent in most years after about 2006. Most of that emphatic shift towards consensus after the 1970s came in the higher education category, which had around 60 per cent support in the 1979 survey, and 65 per cent in 1992, before converging with the other education categories at 90 per cent in time for the 1997 UK general election. (It should be noted that only about one-third of graduates who, in principle, supported a parliament actually voted in favour of a Scottish Assembly in the 1979 referendum.) But even that shift is largely explained by birth cohort. Younger graduates were always more in favour of a parliament than older ones. For example, in 1992, fewer than 50 per cent of graduates born before 1936 supported a parliament, whereas the percentage among people born in 1947–56 was over 70 per cent.

Once the parliament had been set up, graduates generally had a more favourable view of its effectiveness than people in other categories of education. We consider here only the assessment of two aspects of its role in Scottish and UK democracy: whether it was perceived to be giving people more say in government, and whether it was giving Scotland a stronger voice in UK policy. (Analysis of views about the parliament's effect on policy may be found at the website What Scotland Thinks (2021).) Figure 10.3 shows the pattern on the latter question. After strong initial optimism immediately after the first parliament was elected in 1999, the average in each education category moved down from around 70 per cent to under one-half by the time of the second election in 2003. But after that there was a slow rise again, shared also by younger people who reached the voting age only at or after that election. Up to about 2013, moreover, the optimism was stronger among graduates than in the other education categories. After that, there was convergence among the education categories as graduates became somewhat more pessimistic again while the other education categories moved towards optimism.

The patterns for whether the Scottish Parliament was giving people more say in policy were similar to these. So we can say that, on the one hand, people in the education category that had shown greatest scepticism about a parliament before 1997 came to have the most positive evaluation of its democratic role a decade after it had been set up. That was true even of the oldest birth cohorts, for example those born in 1927–36 who were in their sixties and seventies at the time of the 1997 referendum, and thus in their seventies and eighties when they were showing the generally positive evaluation seen in the middle years of Figure 10.3.

It would thus be very misleading to say that attitudes to a parliament after the late 1990s was shaped by age, or even that it was mainly shaped by education. The main pattern was simply a nationwide shift in views. Nevertheless, that is not the whole story, as we will see when we return to looking at how these views about the democratic performance of the parliament related to views about independence at and after the 2014 referendum. Before we do that, however, we look at more basic demographic factors influencing support for independence: time, age, sex and education.

Independence

The surveys record the long-term growth in support for independence, which has been in two main phases. The first was during the long period of Conservative government in the 1980s and 1990s, when support rose from one in ten to one in three. There was then broad stability after the setting up of the Scottish Parliament in 1999, with brief spikes upwards when the SNP achieved an overall majority in the election of 2011, and also in 2004–5 in advance of

EDUCATION, SOCIAL ATTITUDES AND SCOTTISH GOVERNANCE 213

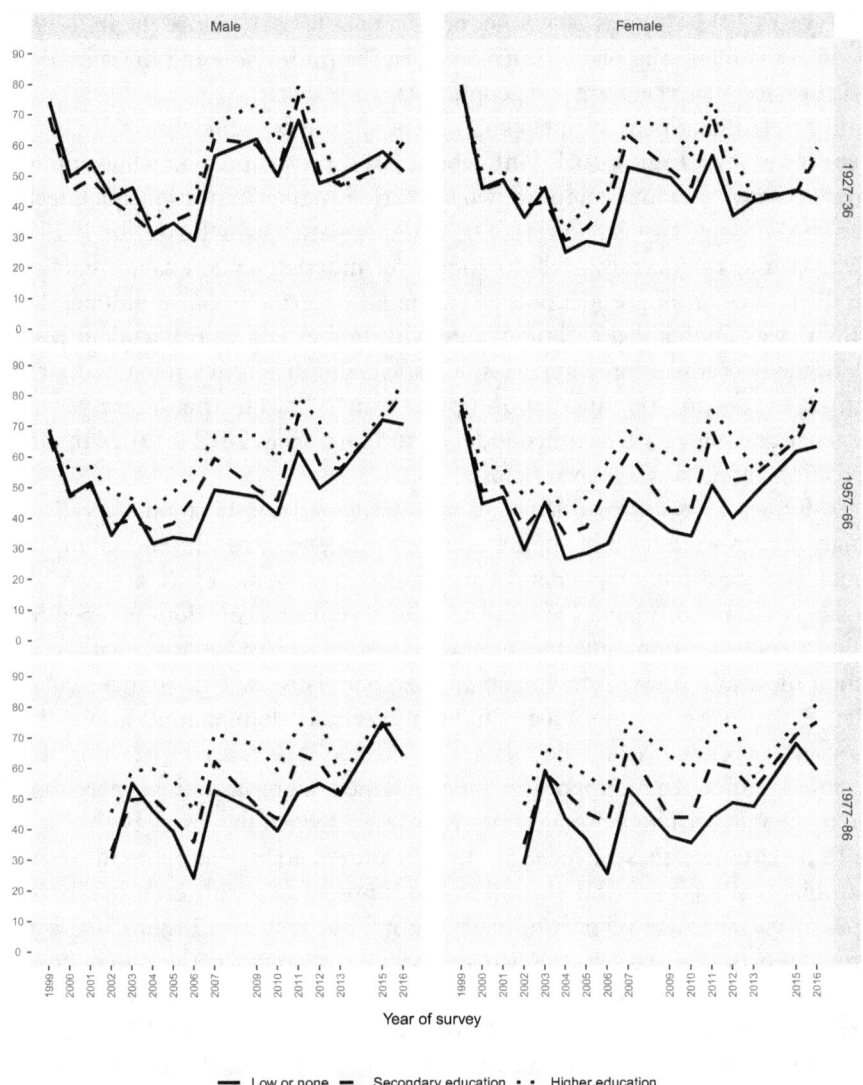

Figure 10.3 Percentage believing that Scottish Parliament gives Scotland a stronger voice in the UK, by survey year (2000–16), sex and education: birth cohorts 1927–36, 1957–66 and 1977–86
Average standard error: 1927–36, 6.1; 1957–66, 4.5; 1977–86, 7.5.

their narrow electoral victory in 2007. The second sustained rise was around and after the 2014 referendum, reaching well over 40 per cent. At any particular point in time, moreover, independence support has been higher among younger people than among older. We investigate this more thoroughly below, but, as an illustration, the independence support in the period around the referendum in

2014 (years 2013–16) was 20–25 per cent in people born before the mid-1940s, 35–45 per cent among people born between the mid-1940s and the mid-1970s, and close to 50 per cent among people born after that.

The relationship of support for independence to education has changed over the surveys: Figure 10.4. Until about 2011, the proportion who supported independence was lower among people with a higher education qualification than in the other two categories. The evidence is not conclusive for 1979 and 1992 because the overall level of support for independence was quite low, but the difference among education categories then grew because independence support was unchanged among people with higher education, while it rose in the other two education categories. This average difference remained similar until 2011, despite the fluctuation upwards in 2005, but then there was convergence at a high level of independence support: from 2012 to 2016, the three education categories were very close.

So Figure 10.4 seems to show an unprecedented combination after 2012 of a high and growing level of support for independence with the end of any association between that support and educational attainment. There are two broad possible explanations here. One is generational replacement. Both independence support and educational attainment have risen across birth cohorts. So if the association of education with independence support is weaker in younger cohorts, then, as they have come gradually to be numerically dominant, so also will that association decline over the population as a whole. The other explanation would be simpler: after 2012, support for independence might have risen more rapidly among people with higher education regardless of when they were born.

To disentangle these effects, we look at independence support in terms of year, birth cohort, sex and educational attainment. There were broadly three types of pattern with respect to birth cohort, illustrated in Figure 10.5 by the three cohorts that we have shown in previous graphs. In the oldest cohorts (represented here by 1927–36, but true also for the cohort born in 1926 or earlier), there was a rise in support for independence between 1979 and 1997 at all levels of education, but most sharply for people with low or no formal attainment. That pattern broadly persisted for the following decade, though fluctuating; then support declined by 2016, when the educational differences declined too. The pattern for these oldest cohorts at or around the referendum was thus barely different from the situation three decades earlier.

In contrast, in the graphs for all cohorts born from 1937 onward, there is a simple conclusion: there was a rise in support for independence at all levels of education. This rise is greater than any differences among cohorts in the association of independence with education. For people born between 1937 and the early 1970s – exemplified in Figure 10.5 by the 1957–66 cohort – the level of support in 2016 among those with higher education was at least as great as the support among people with low or no formal attainment in the 1990s:

EDUCATION, SOCIAL ATTITUDES AND SCOTTISH GOVERNANCE

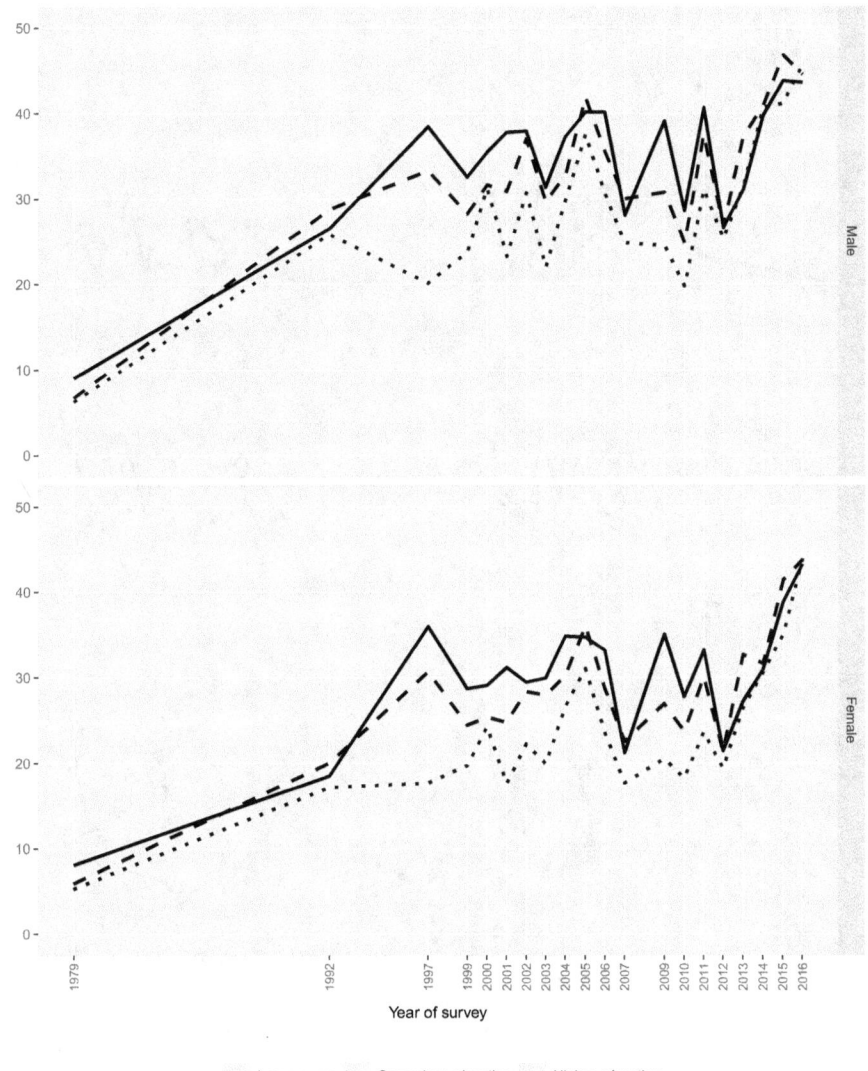

Figure 10.4 Percentage supporting independence, by survey year (1979–2016), sex and education
Average standard error: 3.1.

compare the dotted lines in 2016 with the solid lines in the 1990s. For the two youngest cohorts (represented here by 1977–86), these graduates had higher levels of independence support in 2016 than was found amongst those with low or no formal attainment as recently as 2011.

So the convergence of independence support among the education categories which is evident in Figure 10.5 is due to two distinct trends. One is

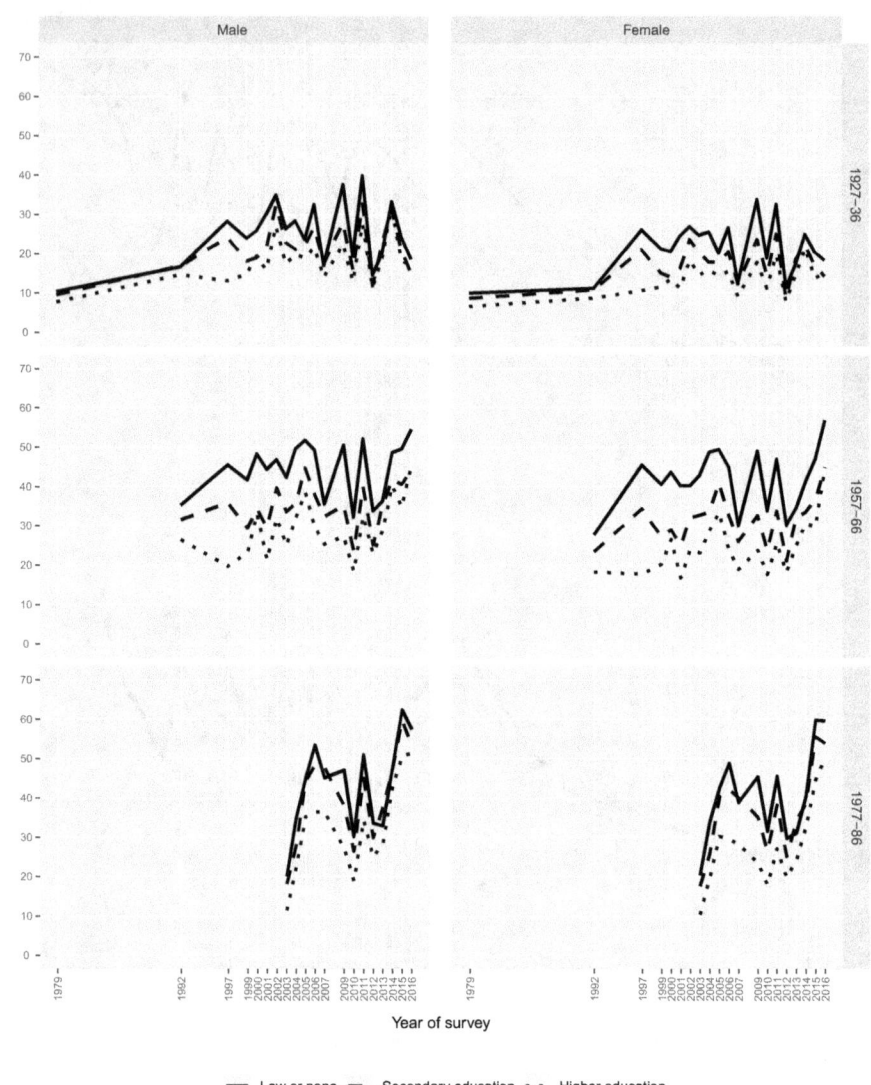

Figure 10.5 Percentage supporting independence, by survey year (1979–2016), sex, and education: birth cohorts 1927–36, 1957–66 and 1977–86
Average standard error: 1927–36, 4.7; 1957–66, 4.7; 1977–86, 6.8.

indeed convergence within the four older cohorts – downwards for the oldest cohorts (born up to 1936), and upwards for the wartime and first post-war cohorts (1937–56). But there was no such educational convergence for the four younger cohorts (born from 1957 onwards): all education categories showed a rise. Because many more people in these younger cohorts (especially the very youngest) had higher education, the overall effect during the period 2013–16 was to shift the higher education category in the population as a whole towards independence support.

The relationship of education to independence support was similar in different religious and ethnic groups. Most notably, the support among graduates rose in all these groups. For example, in the cohort 1977–86, and in the survey years 2013–16, the average independence support among female graduates who were Catholics was 39 per cent, almost exactly the same as the 37 per cent among female graduates as a whole. For male graduates, the corresponding proportions were 47 per cent and 41 per cent. All these graduate percentages had risen compared to previous years and older cohorts (as in Figure 10.5). This similarity of young Catholics' political views in recent years to people of a similar age in the population as a whole has been discussed more fully by Rosie (2014).

The sample sizes were too small to allow the detailed study of individual groups defined by ethnicity. For example, in the surveys 2011–16 combined, the total numbers of people of specific family origins were: Indian, 32; Pakistani or Bangladeshi, 48; Chinese, 20; African or Afro-Caribbean, 30. However, combining these four groups into a single 'minority' category (giving a more reliable basis of 130 respondents) allowed cohort differences to be calculated. The resulting patterns of independence support were, again, similar to the population as a whole. For example, in the 1977–86 cohort, the independence support among female graduates who were in the minority category was 32 per cent, while that in the non-minority category was 33 per cent. For men, the proportions were 37 per cent and 39 per cent. A distinctive educational feature of independence support in the minority category was that, across the cohorts, it was consistently as high among graduates as among those with minimal education; it was also higher than among people with at most secondary education. In the non-minority category, by contrast, graduates and minimally educated respondents converged only in the youngest cohorts (as for the population as a whole in Figure 10.5).

The combined effect of all these demographic trends was that the educational basis of independence support rose over time. As late as 2004, more than 40 per cent of independence supporters had low or no formal attainment and only a quarter had higher education. By 2014 and later, the position had reversed (respectively a quarter and over 40 per cent). The graduates in 2016 were very much younger, coming from the independence-supporting generation: 32 per cent had been born since 1977, and 59 per cent since 1967, in contrast to only 6 per cent and 32 per cent in 2004.

Independence and National Identity

A further clue to how this change in the educational basis of independence support came about is in the relationship of both of these variables to national identity. For people with a Scottish identity, independence support around the time of the referendum was very similar in the different education categories. For example, in that cohort in the years 2013–16, among women who called themselves Scottish, the difference of independence support between those with a higher education and those with low or no formal attainment was 7.9 points, less than the 12 points in Figure 10.5 (where identity is not controlled for). For men, the analogous differences were 3.2 and 10. For people with a British identity, by contrast, as well as independence support being generally at a lower level than among people with a Scottish identity, it was also lower among people with higher or secondary education than among people with low or no formal education. In women with a British identity, in the cohort 1977–8, independence support in the years 2012–16 was 18 points higher among those with low or no formal attainment than among those with higher education. The analogous gap for men was 14 points.

A partial explanation of these results for Scottish identity is that national identity is itself related to education. Consistently across the years, the proportion of people with a Scottish identity was somewhat lower among people whose attainment was higher; the educational gradient with respect to British identity was the reverse. But these education gradients did not change over time, and were never very strong (confirming a conclusion reached by Bechhofer and McCrone (2009)). The generally weak association of national identity with education has meant that having more graduates has not shifted identity away from Scottishness. One consequence of this is that a large part of the growth of support for independence is due to graduates who call themselves Scottish. Of all independence supporters in 2016, 32 per cent were graduates with a Scottish identity, and this was larger than any of the other groups defined by attainment and identity: 28 per cent were Scottish with secondary education, 23 per cent were Scottish with low or no formal attainment, and the remaining 17 per cent were from the other combinations of national identity and education. The percentage of independence supporters who were graduates with a Scottish identity was up from 23 per cent a decade earlier, 12 per cent in 1997 and a mere 7 per cent in 1979.

The previous research that was cited earlier found that, as well as national identity, the strongest predictor of voting for independence in the referendum was having a favourable view of an independent Scotland's economic prospects. However, this economic evaluation was only weakly related to education, probably because – as we noted earlier – even people in the lowest category of education here actually have a lot of education by historical standards. So the residual association with education after controlling for it was similar to that in Figure 10.5. As with national identity, then, the importance of education is less than people's beliefs.

In summary of the analysis of the demographic basis of independence support, we can conclude that there is no clear evidence that people with relatively low formal education were disproportionately likely to support independence in recent years as it has grown in popularity. In fact, that growth can be attributed in large part to graduates who identify as Scottish. Nor is the growth because of older cohorts, whether educated or not. In fact, some of the largest rise in support for independence was for people born in the 1950s and 1960s, the post-war cohorts. Younger cohorts had high levels of support from the time they reached voting age. Low-educated people in the cohort born before or around the war did show some increase in support in the 1990s, but this fell away when the campaigning for the 2014 referendum became salient, and graduates in these older cohorts always had low levels of support. Some of the association with education is explained by national identity, which may thus be thought of as one way in which education is translated into views about independence. There were more young graduates than ever before, and, although they were no more likely than their predecessors to choose a Scottish identity, they were more likely to combine that with support for independence. In short, if the movement for Scottish independence is a rebellion against elites, it is not based on the low-educated or the old.

Independence and Social Attitudes

The final analysis is then to bring together the role of education in the two aspects of Scottish politics that we have considered: democratic attitudes, and attitudes to independence. For this purpose, we have to restrict the analysis to the ten surveys where all the attitude variables are available: these are 2000, 2004, 2005, 2006, 2007, 2009, 2010, 2011, 2015, 2016. The measures of social trust and political participation were asked too infrequently to let the full analysis by year and cohort to be done, and so we consider only the two ideological scales, interest in politics, and the views about whether the Scottish Parliament was giving people more say, and was giving Scotland a stronger voice.

The pattern for the two ideological scales is similar. For people who were at the conservative end of the liberal–conservative scale, there was a clear gradient across education categories, the lowest support for independence being among people with higher education, even in the youngest cohort here. Among liberals, by contrast, the education gradient was much weaker, and for the youngest cohort may have vanished in the final year. A very similar pattern was evident for the left–right scale: graduates on the right had relatively low support for independence, whereas on the left there was little difference among the education categories. When both national identity and one of the ideological scales were in the statistical model, this tendency of beliefs to overcome the effects of education was even stronger. There was barely any education gradient among people who were liberal or on the left and whose national identity was Scottish, especially in the younger cohorts. For example, in 2015–16, the independence support among women who had liberal views and a Scottish identity, and who were born in the 1977–86 cohort, was 58 per cent with higher education, 59 per cent with secondary education, and 56 per cent with minimal education. For men of these same views and age, the proportions were 69 per cent, 69 per cent and 65 per cent. For all the other combinations of ideology with Scottish or British identity, graduates had lower support for independence than the other two groups.

We can then refine further the description of the main segments of support for independence which we noted above. If we dichotomise the liberal-authoritarian scale at its mean (over the whole series), and class as 'liberal' those whose views placed them below the mean, then we find that fully 24 per cent of all independence supporters in 2016 were liberal graduates with a Scottish identity. This was by far the largest segment of support in the categories defined by education, identity and whether classed as liberal in this sense. The next largest was 16 per cent who were liberal, Scottish and had completed secondary education. Each of the other groups had 12 per cent or less. Doing the same with the left-right scale gave similar results: 24 per cent were Scottish, left graduates, and 19 per cent were Scottish, on the left and had completed secondary education. The sense is then clear of a liberal and left leadership of the independence movement among people who are well-educated and have a Scottish identity.

The scale of political interest was related to views about independence, with higher support among those who were interested. As we have seen, that scale was related to education. But political interest did not modify the effects of education: the education gradient was the same at both high and low interest, graduates always having the lowest support for independence. Thus, unlike with the ideological scales, political interest did not override education.

Something the same was true of views on whether the Scottish Parliament was giving people more say in policy or giving Scotland a stronger voice in the UK: at each level of each of these variables, people with higher education showed the least support for independence. However, an interesting interaction emerged with views about the European Union. The fieldwork for the 2016 survey took place after that referendum result was known, and so the claim was already being made that a new argument in favour of independence was that Scotland had voted for the UK to remain in the EU, in contrast to the overall UK result. The details are summarised in Table 10.3, showing support for independence in 2016 according to how the respondent had voted in the EU referendum, education and views on whether the Scottish Parliament was giving Scotland a stronger voice in the UK. Sex is omitted from this table because, when restricting the analysis to just one survey, numbers in each cell become quite small, and because the patterns were similar for men and women. The size of each of these groups in the total population is also shown. (The pattern was similar for views about whether the parliament was giving people more say in policy, and so is not shown here.)

Table 10.3 Percentage supporting independence, by vote in EU referendum, views about effectiveness of Scottish Parliament, and education: 2016 only

View of Scottish Parliament*	Highest education attained		
	Low or none	Secondary	Higher education
Remain			
Not more voice	15	23	29
Percentage in group	5	4	6
More voice	48	51	47
Percentage in group	8	14	25
Leave			
Not more voice	29	27	34
Percentage in group	6	3	3
More voice	64	51	48
Percentage in group	7	10	7

Notes:
*Whether or not Scottish Parliament is giving Scotland a stronger voice in UK affairs.
The percentages in each group add to 100 across the whole table (except for rounding error).
Average standard error: 6.8.

The most striking feature of the table is that, at nearly all combinations of the other variables, independence support was higher among people who voted for the UK to leave the EU than among those who voted to remain. It is also notable that, at all combinations, independence support was higher among those who thought the Scottish Parliament was giving Scotland a stronger voice in the UK than among those who did not believe that. So merely believing that the Scottish Parliament was not powerful enough was not sufficient to create a majority for independence, despite the incapacity of the Scottish Parliament to act on the Scottish vote in the EU referendum. But the table shows two strategically important education gradients, only one of which could be said to be relevant to the SNP's claim that Scotland's vote for the UK to remain has become a new rationale for independence.

One group is highly educated remain voters who believed that the Scottish Parliament was not giving Scotland a stronger voice (last cell in the first row of the table). These graduates had higher support for independence than people who were in the other education categories and who had the same views of the EU and of the Scottish Parliament (29 per cent compared to 15 per cent in the lowest education category). We could describe this group – EU remainers who wanted to increase the parliament's powers – as a classic SNP target.

But there is actually an opposite education gradient that is more consistent with the story of national populism outside Scotland which was discussed above. This second group is people with minimal education who voted leave and who believed that the Scottish Parliament was giving Scotland a stronger voice (first cell in the final row of the table). This group had higher support for independence than people with more education who had the same views of the EU and of the Scottish Parliament (64 per cent compared to 48 per cent with higher education). It might reasonably be argued that this group of leave voters is a Scottish analogue of the core voters for Brexit in England: people with minimal education who believed strongly in the sovereignty of a national parliament. It is then also notable that this group has the strongest support for independence in the table.

That group is a segment of support for Scottish independence that is not usually represented in Scottish public debate. Perhaps the reason why it is ignored is that it is small (as seen in the 'percentage in group' values in Table 10.3): only 7 per cent of the electorate. But the first group is even smaller: only 6 per cent of the electorate. In fact, in this table, education has an impact on only a minority of people: either those remainers who thought the Scottish Parliament was not giving Scotland a voice (total in first row: 15 per cent), or those leavers who thought the opposite about the parliament (total in final row: 24 per cent of the total). The table is thus a further illustration of the point that education tends to have a weaker influence than current beliefs. (A fuller analysis of the relationship between attitudes to the EU and support for Scottish independence – but without attention to education – is provided by Curtice and Montagu (2020).)

CONCLUSIONS: EDUCATION AND SCOTTISH DEMOCRACY

Education is relevant to Scottish democracy in all the same kinds of ways as it strengthens democracy elsewhere. Even though educational expansion may have been associated with some weakening of the civic effects of education, they are still strong. Educated people still tend to be liberal, tolerant of diverse culture and forms of living, and interested in how society is governed. Despite the heated public debate in recent years about freedom of speech, the lowest support for censorship is among young people, especially young graduates. These findings are consistent with more general evidence that the more educated Scotland of the early twenty-first century is more pluralistic than it was in the past. Religious sectarianism has declined (Bruce, 2019; Bruce et al., 2004; Devine and Rosie, 2020). Views about the rights of women and of minority cultural groups have become more liberal (Bromley et al., 2006; Hussain and Miller, 2006; Kenny and Mackay, 2020; Macpherson and Bond, 2009). The Scottish Parliament, elected by proportional representation, has given a public platform to a wider range of political views than was ever represented from Scotland in the unreformed UK parliament. The debate at the time of the 2014 referendum on independence was heated and diverse, from all sides (Crowther, 2018; Jackson, 2020; Paterson, 2015d). In all these respects, Scotland has shared in a wider international current of thought in which education, everywhere, has played a central role.

At the same time, education has also had a civic role that is very specific to Scotland because of its association with the debate about independence. Support for independence has risen even in a population where there has been an increase in the size of educated groups which, historically, have had least support for independence. The analysis which we have discussed here has shown that, before the period around the 2014 referendum, there was a clear gradient of independence support across the educational categories, probably in fact widening in the first decade after the Scottish Parliament was established in 1999. But from 2012, there was unprecedented narrowing.

Part of the explanation is the differences among birth cohorts. The oldest cohorts – born before the Second World War – never had high support. It was not negligible among low attainers in these cohorts, but even that died away as the referendum approached, falling to no more than about one in five. These are the cohorts who experienced the British solidarity of the war mostly as adolescents or adults, and who, as voters and workers, contributed to creating the welfare state. This point about the war cohorts has been made by many previous writers, but what we can now see is that their growing opposition to independence in 2014 was, compared to earlier, especially a matter of the low attainers among them, who were by far their majority.

The other cohorts all showed a rise in support for independence around the referendum, or the maintenance of an already high level of support. Support in the wartime and post-war generation (born 1937–56) moved upwards, at all levels of education, as the referendum approached. The next cohorts, born 1957–76, showed high support even in the 1990s, and remained there, but with little change in the educational differences. These cohorts' first experience of politics was during the collapse of the post-war settlement in the 1970s and 1980s, and the growing alienation of the Scottish polity from the UK Conservative governments of Margaret Thatcher and John Major. But these cohorts were not young enough to experience mass higher education, and so some of the historical educational hierarchy of attitudes remained. Thus, by the referendum, although support for independence among higher education graduates in these cohorts had reached 40 per cent, that was still clearly less than among those with minimal education, where it was over 50 per cent. That educational pattern changed clearly in the youngest cohorts, who were born mainly in the 1980s, and who came to political maturity after the Scottish Parliament was established in 1999. The education gap was consistently smaller, and support among even those with higher education reached over 50 per cent.

The main summary point about independence support at different levels of education is then that the overall convergence around the time of the referendum was mainly due to generational replacement – to the electorate's gradually comprising more young people with more education who also were more likely than older cohorts to support independence. The only birth cohorts within which there was an upwards convergence among educational categories over time were those born in the third quarter of the twentieth century. There was also a convergence in people older than that, but it was downwards.

That was not the whole story, however, because the effect of national identity and ideological views outweighed education. Among people with a Scottish identity, there was almost no educational effect at the time of the referendum. Holding a Scottish identity was high in all educational categories, even as higher education expanded. So the demographic basis of independence support shifted to being predominantly graduates with a Scottish identity, who made up one-third of all independence supporters.

But even that point about identity is not enough, because there was also an intersection with the first debate about education's civic role. The kinds of civic attitudes which are shaped by education also mediated the relationship between education and attitudes to independence. In some respects this related to evaluating the parliament that was established in 1999. People with more education tended to a more positive assessment of the parliament's contribution to Scottish democracy than people with minimal education. Then that positive evaluation was translated into stronger support for independence (Table 10.3). In more profound ways, however, the mediation was through ideology. In Scotland as elsewhere, education has encouraged people to be more liberal. Being liberal has become associated with supporting independence; and so education has indirectly contributed to independence support in that way. In younger birth cohorts, education has also stopped being as strongly associated with being economically right wing as it was with people born in the middle of the twentieth century or earlier. Because the campaign for independence has had a socialist tone since the 1980s, this shift too has tended to produce a generation of liberal young graduates who support independence. Graduates with liberal views and who have a Scottish identity then form fully a quarter of the support for independence.

Summing this up, and returning to the paradox which we noted at the beginning of the chapter, we can say that, among people born since the 1960s, education became less strongly associated with views about independence than it had been in people born in the middle of the twentieth century. This was largely a matter of the views of liberal and left-wing graduates who express a Scottish identity. Graduates were, on average, more socially liberal over time (though not more left wing on the economy), and also more likely to call themselves Scottish.

We might then be tempted to conclude that one ultimate effect of the growth of higher education has been a growth in support for independence. But that would be as misleading as the claims that there is an education divide in relation to national populism. It might alternatively be concluded that graduates moved with the times in Scotland, participating in a more general social movement towards a more political interpretation of Scottishness and a firmer view of Scottish political autonomy. This alternative interpretation would be consistent with the extension of higher education to nearly half of the later-born cohorts, because it would not be surprising if an educational experience shared by half the population came to be associated with the current norms of identity and political belief, certainly to a far greater extent than when graduates were a small minority. The driving force is then not education but broad national change in social attitudes.

On the wider theories about national populism and attitudes to national sovereignty we can therefore say that the Scottish case warns us against too simple conclusions. The education gap even as recently as the first decade of the present century might originally have suggested that these theories were relevant, but the gap has diminished as independence support has grown. Moreover, support for independence among the young is far greater than among the old, at all levels of education, in stark contrast to the support for Brexit in England. At these very different levels of overall support, the education gap in 2014 was low among both the young (born in the last quarter of the twentieth century) and the old (born before the war). Only for people born in the third quarter of the century was the education gap quite stable (Figure 10.5), and so only for that specific generation does the theory of national populism have some persisting relevance, but, even there, this did not prevent graduates showing a steady rise in support from about 2010–12 onwards.

The Scottish case may thus show that general terms such as 'populism' are inadequate to explain attitudes to national sovereignty. In some countries, support for national sovereignty undoubtedly is associated with older people who have little formal education. But in Scotland the association has come to be almost the opposite, and allegiance to a national identity that has come to be felt to be in opposition to the existing state elites is common across all educational categories. The single word 'populism' does not capture this complexity.

CHAPTER 11

Conclusions

OPPORTUNITY AND IMPROVEMENT

Two kinds of conclusions may be drawn from the evidence reported in this book. One is about what happened, and the other is about the ways in which we can find out about what happened.

Education got measurably better. It is rare that something as unequivocal as that can be stated, but before we summarise any caveats it is important to remind ourselves just how much things have improved (Table 3.1). In the early 1950s, just one in ten school leavers had acquired any publicly recognised certificate; at the end of the century, this was 90 per cent, rising to 96 per cent in the second decade of the new century. Over the same period, the proportion who stayed in education after age 16 rose from 14 per cent to 88 per cent, the proportion successfully completing any course at senior-secondary level rose from one in ten to two-thirds, and the proportion reaching the threshold of university entry went from 6 per cent to 44 per cent. All these improvements then translated into steadily rising rates of entry to higher education.

The PISA studies early in the new century suggested that standards were not drastically falling, insofar as Scotland's performance was around the average for economically developed countries, though dropping from just above it to somewhat below (Table 4.5). Moreover, the social recognition conferred by official measures of attainment continued to translate into high-status occupations, though at a slowly declining rate: in Figure 9.5, the fall in the proportion of people with at least a full secondary education who entered professional or managerial careers from class origins lower than that is much more gentle than the rise in the proportion attaining that level of education in Figure 9.1. Education may be a positional good, as the economists put it, but pointing that out does not in itself show that expansion cannot outweigh positional advantage, if the employment and other opportunities that may be purchased with a good education are also expanding.

Much of this improvement was brought about because the whole school system became more meritocratic in the sense that it translated measured intelligence into measurable outcomes in a way that was decreasingly associated with pupils' sex or social class. Moreover, all of these changes were accompanied by a marked improvement in what it felt like to be at school (Chapter 5). Many more students enjoyed school, increasing proportions reported that their teachers supported them and gave them confidence, and they increasingly stayed on beyond age 16 in order to study subjects they found interesting.

These heartening messages are worth emphasising at the outset because so much academic discussion emphasises the opposite, usually paying scant regard to how students actually behaved and felt, or to how their education opened up opportunities that their grandparents or even their parents could only have dreamed of. Education has mainly not been about social control, or maintaining status distinctions, or inducting people into mind-numbing routines. It has increasingly not been any of these things, as we can notice only if we pay attention to what young people themselves have told us through surveys of the kind that we have used here.

Moreover, inequality fell. This, too, is controversial in the face of claims that it never falls, or only ever falls at any particular level when that level no longer leads to anything valuable. This is where a long time-series of survey data is crucial. Over short periods, inequality with respect to social class can seem intractable, often because the most advantaged social classes are the quickest to take advantage of any new opportunities that policy opens up. But the other classes catch up in the process that Raftery and Hout (1993) labelled maximally maintained inequality, but that the long perspective might lead us to prefer to call eventually reduced inequality. This long-term reduction of social-class disparities was true of attainment at school, staying on beyond age 16, satisfaction with school, and entry to higher education. In the same period, sex differences mostly reversed completely. The curriculum reforms that had their effects from the late 1980s onwards not only encouraged moderately attaining school leavers to find ways of entering higher education. They also helped low-attaining students to improve their prospects when they entered the labour market directly. These changes achieved all this not mainly by programmes of vocational education, but rather by expanding general education. The improvements belie the claim that what are sometimes called academic courses are not suitable for most students, a claim that started in academic sociology and has now spread to being a taken-for-granted assumption of public debate.

Nevertheless, because this process of expansion leading to both improvement and, eventually, to a reduction of inequality is never-ending, there is always some aspect of education that seems stuck at a less auspicious moment. All social groups showed increasing proportions able to take a broad curriculum in the middle years of secondary school (Figure 4.4), a point that is worth stressing first for its unprecedented cultural significance. Thus, by the second decade of the twenty-first century, a majority even of the lowest-status social classes was gaining access to at least the rudiments of the best that has been thought and said: Matthew Arnold, writing a century and a half earlier, would have found this basis of democracy astonishingly secure. Yet, despite this, the gap remained wide, because the proportion of the most advantaged groups with the same pattern of study was 80 per cent or greater, and the gap was not notably falling.

A similar sense of impatience might be engendered by the complex ways in which higher education expanded after the explosion of the early 1990s. The highest-status places were taken by the highest-status students, often from the highest-status schools that were independent of public management. At the same time, some of the reduction of inequality in the new century was because of downward pressure on the attainment of the most advantaged classes, not because of the emancipation of the least advantaged (Figures 4.5 and 4.6). That would have horrified the pioneers of education in the welfare state: 'socialists cannot ... afford to accept a lowering of the quality of higher education in the interests of social equality', as it was put around the time of our first survey by the highly influential socialist intellectual G.D.H. Cole (1952, p. 61).

In some respects, indeed, concentrating on the distribution of education is less important than its absolute level. This is not only because of what Arnold meant by 'the best': that is an absolute standard, speaking to the intrinsic character of anyone who attains it, and is not affected by how many have that opportunity. It is also, in peripheral societies such as Scotland, because credentials can be taken elsewhere. In Scotland from the 1960s onwards, the most disadvantaged were further behind the most advantaged than in England, but they were also ahead of the most disadvantaged in England, and so could compete in the labour market at rates corresponding to the relative value of secondary-school credentials or a university degree in the metropolitan core. It might be replied that educating young people for export is also the bane of peripheral societies, but the counter-argument to that, in turn, is that the relevant labour market operated increasingly across the whole of Britain, not only in the economic core around London. Economically, not spreading these opportunities geographically is not a sustainable position over the long term – inflationary pressures in the core eventually lead to a levelling-out of credentials as well as of criteria of employment – but, at any particular moment, it can be of very great benefit to young people leaving a high-performing education system such as Scotland's was in the second half of the twentieth century.

POLICY AND INSTITUTIONS

Yet, despite all the public arguments, much of this happened because deliberate policy merely facilitated social changes that were already under way. That is most true of sex differences. Scottish policy paid very little attention to differences in attainment between male and female students until far into the 1980s, and yet girls were pushing ahead from well before that. Something similar was probably true of social-class differences, even though explicit attention to these had been more common since at least the 1920s (McPherson, 1992; Paterson, 2018). Again, the long perspective helps. The ending of selection between the mid-1960s and the early 1980s almost certainly did directly reduce inequality of attainment within a broadly rising upward trend, but this was no more than a slight acceleration of a process that was already well underway.

In any case, policy in a plural society develops slowly, and has its impact hesitantly. Institutions matter, and each wave of policy interacts with preceding waves. The history of schools and universities makes a difference, but these legacies are not themselves unchanging. The history of schools was associated with school leavers' attainment, not always in predictable ways. It is true that in the new comprehensive system, the oldest schools at first had the highest attainment, but the policy of creating a common system did gradually increase the attainment in the schools that had been of much lower status before the reform. At the same time, though, that minority of formerly low-status schools which had insisted on teaching some academic courses for decades turned out to be among the most successful in the comprehensive era. They thus had a legacy of strong academic focus that had been sustained despite official discouragement from public authorities: they were pioneers when the establishment was still unshakeable in its faith in selection.

Perhaps the best way to characterise this influence of policy is as a long-term interaction between social change and institutions that themselves are the only really tangible way in which policy makers can shape the lives of pupils. The most visible instance of this in Scotland is in relation to the incorporation of Catholic schools into the public sector. This led to the slow convergence of attainment there with the attainment in other schools, leading to the gradual reaching by Catholics of equal social status. That policy too, though, was a partnership, because the founding moment – the 1918 Education Act – arose as a bargain between a Church that was willing to trust a secular (and still somewhat Protestant) state, and a state that saw the importance of educational opportunity in helping to forge a common, democratic citizenship. Above all, of course, Catholic parents and their children responded, behaving in the same way as other families in taking advantage of the increasingly meritocratic opportunities. Less formally, something similar probably explains the experience of minority ethnic groups at the end of the century. In a comprehensive system that was now infused with ideas of equal respect, they could achieve highly through the common system of certificated assessment.

Institutions mattered in many other ways. On the one hand, we saw this in what appeared to be the growing affinity between independent schools and higher education institutions as higher education expanded. That was certainly not a matter of public policy, but rather of an alignment between the preferences of relatively wealthy parents and astute schools that discovered how to use that wealth to turn themselves into agents of high attainment. This was thus an affinity found for highly advantaged students, and so it is perhaps a distinctive way in which long-established hierarchies of advantage are created afresh in an era of apparent democratisation, an instance of what Lucas called 'effectively maintained inequality'.

Nevertheless, policy can have an effect because it can modify what has been called institutional habitus, or, more colloquially, ethos. This was evident in the relation between the old secondary schools and the old universities. These old schools seemed to have an affinity to the oldest universities that gradually declined even while the independent-school affinity with these universities increased. The decline of these links, too, was not itself the deliberate intention of policy. It was a consequence of the slowly converging character of all the comprehensive schools, a homogeneity that certainly was deliberately intended. But it was intended only over a long period, stretching from the politicians and officials in the early 1960s who prepared for the end of selection to their successors in the 1990s, with barely any overlap in periods of office, far less in ideology and understanding of what education might be.

In fact, one abiding theme is that the ideology of governments is largely irrelevant. We like to think that comprehensive education was a programme of the political left, and that is usually how it is written about in the academic literature. The ending of selection had indeed become a centrepiece of socialist policy by the 1960s, although it had not been so when our survey series started with children entering secondary school in 1947 (Paterson, 2015a). But the policy was built upon a foundation that owes its origins to the social liberalism of the Liberal government which was elected in 1906, and which was the closest political source of the reforms that led to the secondary schools of the 1920s and 1930s. Comprehensive education depended on there being in place a system of secondary education for all, which itself, although depending on these liberal reforms, was in Scotland established by the cautious Conservative government of the mid-1930s. Then the following-through of the ending of selection happened mostly under the Conservative government of Margaret Thatcher. Indeed, the one piece of policy that seems definitely to have had quite an immediate effect – the breadth at mid-secondary level that became a strong requirement in the 1990s – came under perhaps the least decisive government in that whole half-century: John Major's Conservative government between

1992 and 1997. But that could not have been achieved without the new, potentially inclusive curricular context created under the Thatcher government, which in turn was made necessary by the decisive action of the 1960s Labour government. None of the political controversies of the 1980s – around parental choice, or alleged plans to privatise schooling – had any measurable impact on the experiences of students or on what they achieved, which continued on trajectories that had started long before and persisted long after.

This ideological complexity tends not to get a welcoming reception in Scotland, with its left-leaning self-perception. Even more awkward is the limited evidence on what happened to schools after the end of the century, but what we have suggests that the trajectory of improvement stalled, and perhaps reversed (Chapters 3 and 4). The improvement in basic access did continue. For example, the universal access to mid-secondary courses was maintained. There continued to be a steady increase in attainment at senior-secondary level, and inequality there also continued to fall. But the improvement slowed. There was no further increase in access to a broad liberal curriculum, and no further reduction of inequality in that respect, either.

Policy since the first decade of the new century has been controversial on these very grounds. The main change has been a new curriculum that was based on explicit hostility to the tradition of academic study and meritocratic selection that has been the main theme of Scottish policy since before the period we have been studying. The reform has been advocated on three grounds: that it would reduce the impact of academic courses on schooling, that it would encourage cross-curricular study, and that it would move attention away from formal assessment onto much wider types of learning. These claims cannot be evaluated, because there are no sources of relevant systematic evidence of the kind that we have been able to draw upon for the surveys used throughout the book. But we can tentatively note, using the 2016 survey data on people who were born in 2000, that the best that can be said for the new curriculum is that it has not overthrown the previous achievements. On those criteria where saturation at 90 per cent or more had not been attained by the end of the century, there has been no more progress. For example, there has been stability in access to breadth of study at senior-secondary level (Table 4.4), and barely any change of social inequality (Figure 4.5).

Our longer-term data also show that the problems which the reform was supposed to address were exaggerated. At the moment when the new Scottish Parliament took over responsibility for Scottish education, attainment was rising, inequality was falling, school was become more pleasant, and previous curricular reforms were helping people enter employment or post-school education. Social mobility had not stagnated except insofar as the number of high-status occupations had stopped rising, but there was nothing that education could do about that. The better-educated Scotland that all this had created was a society that had embraced political autonomy and where debates about independence were led by well-educated social groups on both sides of the argument. Educational expansion did not cause this political change, but it enabled the form that it has taken. The educational pessimism which this autonomy generated was too influenced by gloomy sociology, and inattentive to the history of its own society.

In short, the reforms of the second half of the twentieth century were always about both democracy and intellect. The democratic reach came partly from the country's history, but more strongly from the common international currents of the times. Participation was rising everywhere, and was extended everywhere to gradually higher age groups. Scotland was thoroughly typical in that respect in this period, even though it had been a pioneer of wide access to education in earlier centuries. Part of the story which the empirical analysis in this book has sought to tell is the gradual reform of educational institutions that had been inherited from a more selective past. That this was a gradual change, not a revolution, is well-captured in Alasdair MacIntyre's suggestion that some traditions embody 'continuities of conflict', here the conflict between selection and democracy (2007, p. 188). What had made these eventually transformed schools and universities distinctively Scottish was that they had never been merely about selection, but always in part places where democratic and selective interpretations of the country's traditions were contested. When George Davie regretted the loss of distinctiveness in his influential book of 1961, he forgot that the ideas of educational democracy were never more than part of the Scottish story, and never were exclusively Scottish; but he also failed to see that the tension between selection and democracy could itself be the best way of describing a tradition.

Nevertheless, Davie's philosophical analysis of the Scottish curricular tradition did capture something that was characteristic of the country's past. The religious legacies really did encourage respect for the intellect which then informed the development of secondary schooling very far into the period of radical expansion. The Standard Grade reforms of the 1980s and 1990s were the last, great flowering of that, an attempt to extend to everyone the generalist curriculum that had, even half a century earlier, been the property of a small, highly selected minority. One of the recurrent themes of this book has been the evolution of the social basis of this broad, academic curriculum. It then continued to give routes into worthwhile opportunities after leaving school, not only to university but also in direct access to the labour market. Beyond specialist study at university, a breadth of culture that had been acquired from school continued to be associated with entry to those professions that govern Scotland. Professional society is everywhere, as Perkin (1989) has pointed out, and in that sense Scotland is absolutely typical. But a generalist educational contribution to it has made professional society in Scotland also a distinctive development of the country's own recent history.

THE IMPORTANCE OF STATISTICAL EVIDENCE

That changing character of expertise brings us to our final point, which is the second kind of conclusion that we might draw from the evidence presented in this book. The series of surveys of school students came to an end, and with that came political ignorance.

The statistical data generated by carefully analysed and continually improving surveys have repeatedly provided, in the past, useful evidence about policy, through the contemporaneous analysis of the surveys which have been re-analysed here as a series. The series then allows the whole trajectory to be seen in the always clarifying light of hindsight. These surveys, long before Scotland had a national parliament, provided the stage on which a debate was had about Scotland's educational future. That was why there was widespread hope in the 1990s that a parliament would form a natural supporter of this kind of evidence (Paterson, 2000).

But nothing of the sort has come to pass. The regular surveys were discontinued. The one-off data point in 2016, valuable though it is, cannot be enough to monitor change, even when it will be supplemented in a few years' time by similar data from the excellent study called Growing Up in Scotland, which follows a cohort of people born in 2004–5 (Growing Up in Scotland website, 2022). As we have seen over and over again in this book, understanding policy and educational change requires many surveys, conducted over a very long period and sensitive in detail not only to policy but also to wider public debate.

After 2007, Scotland withdrew from most of the international comparative surveys, which in any case are never sufficiently sensitive to national particularities to allow the truly informative analysis of policy, institutions or cultural traditions. Of these international sources, only the triennial PISA study remains, and its finding that performance may be slowly declining is, as it were, suspended in mid-air, because the absence of data specific to Scottish policy precludes any close attention to explanations in terms of Scottish policy, practices or histories. The short PISA series (since the turn of the century), in other words, could never be used to carry out the kind of analysis which this book has offered, drawing, as we have been able to do, upon the far-seeing imagination of those social scientists who set our series in motion long ago. There is now no indigenous survey series with which to hold Scotland's new democracy to account in education. We can continue to track general social change, and education's place in it, through the Scottish parts of such high-quality surveys as the birth cohorts covering the whole of Britain or the UK, or the large UK Household Longitudinal Study. Some of the scope for doing that is shown in Chapter 9. We can study the influence of education on Scottish politics and civil society through the annual Scottish Social Attitudes Survey, as in Chapter 10, thus confirming in a different way the importance of regular surveys. But about education itself we are ignorant as never before since the 1920s.

This book has sought to show – even though only through examples – that the Scottish tradition of survey research in education has a scientific rigour and a social responsiveness that still holds the prospect of the kind of public account that Andrew McPherson and his colleagues at the Centre for Educational Sociology hoped for in the 1980s (Burnhill et al., 1987). The public scepticism that surveys can stimulate is at the heart of scientific method without which human reason is mere speculation. That was the original ideal, too, which inspired those autonomous civic organisations that set up the Scottish Council for Research in Education in the face of government indifference nearly a century ago, giving the institutional stage from which Godfrey Thomson could lead Scotland's pioneering development of educational surveys. So, if we are looking for a less pessimistic conclusion from the long series rather than from the period since its end, it might be found in its vindication of Thomson's belief in 1936 (Deary, Lawn et al., 2009, p. 58) that 'what is wanted is knowledge, classified, generalised, tested', in order 'to understand this changing world and to guide it aright'.

Further Information

The book draws upon some aspects of papers published in specialist journals. Details are (referring to items in the complete references section at the end of the book):

Chapter 3: Paterson (2020b, 2022d)
Chapter 4: Paterson (2020a)
Chapter 5: Paterson (2020c)
Chapter 6: Paterson (2022c)
Chapter 7: Paterson (2021b)
Chapter 8: Paterson (2022a, 2022g, 2022h)
Chapter 9: Paterson (2022b, 2022e, 2022f)
Chapter 10: Paterson (2021a)

These papers are available free from the Edinburgh University research repository at https://www.research.ed.ac.uk (by searching for the papers' titles as listed in the complete references section at the end of the book). I am grateful to the university for its payment of the fees that allowed open access. All of the chapters include further analysis that goes beyond what is described in these papers. Several aspects of the detailed presentation of results are different here from the papers, notably in the combinations of parental education and social class in the graphs and tables, as explained in Chapter 2. Here, for consistency, we have used the same combinations throughout the book, according to Tables 2.4 or 2.5 depending on the context, whereas the combinations used in several of the papers are different from this. The most notable difference is on science at secondary school, as described in Chapters 4 and 8 and also as discussed in Paterson (2022h). Because that paper deals with science at both school and higher education, for purposes of internal consistency its combinations of parental education and class were as in Table 2.5, whereas in Chapter 4 we use the combinations in Table 2.4. Thus what is meant by 'high-status social class' in that paper involves higher values of parental education than in Chapter 4. Overall, then, the papers are best thought of not as a replication of the results in the book, but rather as a guide to the technical statistical methods that have been used.

References

Adekoya, R., Kaufmann, E. and Simpson, T. (2020). *Academic Freedom in the UK*. London: Policy Exchange.
Anders, J. and Micklewright, J. (2015). 'Teenagers' expectations of applying to university: how do they change?' *Education Sciences*, 5(4), 281–305.
Anderson, R. D. (1983). *Education and Opportunity in Victorian Scotland*. Edinburgh: Edinburgh University Press.
Anderson, R. D. (1985). 'Education and society in modern Scotland: a comparative perspective'. *History of Education Quarterly*, 25(4), 459–81.
Archer, M. S. (1979). *The Social Origins of Educational Systems*. London: Sage.
Arum, R. and Shavit, Y. (1995). 'Secondary vocational education and the transition from school to work'. *Sociology of Education*, 68(3), 187–204.
Avvisati, F. (2020). 'The measure of socio-economic status in PISA: a review and some suggested improvements'. *Large-scale Assessments in Education*, 8(1), 1–37.
Ayalon, H. (2006). 'Nonhierarchical curriculum differentiation and inequality in achievement: a different story or more of the same?' *Teachers College Record*, 108, 1186–213.
Ball, S. (1990). *Politics and Policy Making in Education*. London: Routledge.
Barnett, R. A. (1987). 'The maintenance of quality in the public sector of UK higher education'. *Higher Education*, 16(3), 279–301.
Barone, C. (2009). 'A new look at schooling inequalities in Italy and their trends over time'. *Research in Social Stratification and Mobility*, 27(2), 92–109.
Barone, C. and Schizzerotto, A. (2011). 'Introduction: career mobility, education, and intergenerational reproduction in five European societies'. *European Societies*, 13(3), 331–45.
Bechhofer, F. and McCrone, D. (2009). 'Stating the obvious: ten truths about national identity'. *Scottish Affairs*, 67, 7–22.
Benavot, A. (1983). 'The rise and decline of vocational education'. *Sociology of Education*, 56(2), 63–76.
Bernstein, B. (2003). *Class, Codes and Control, Volume 4*, new edition. London: Routledge.
Boliver, V. (2013). 'How fair is access to more prestigious UK universities?' *British Journal of Sociology*, 64(2), 344–64.
Bolton, P. (2010). *Higher Education and Social Class*. Standard Note SN/SG/620. London: House of Commons Library.

Boscardin, C. K., Aguirre-Munoz, Z., Stoker, G., Kim, J., Kim, M. and Lee, J. (2005). 'Relationship between opportunity to learn and student performance on English and algebra assessments'. *Educational Assessment*, 10(4), 307–32.
Boudon, R. (1974). *Education, Opportunity and Social Inequality*. New York: Wiley.
Bourdieu, P. (1973). 'Cultural reproduction and social reproduction'. In R. Brown (ed.), *Knowledge, Education and Cultural Change*, 71–112. London: Tavistock.
Bourdieu, P. and Passeron, J.-C. (1977). *Reproduction in Education, Society and Culture*, tr. R. Nice. London: Sage.
Boyd, W. and Rawson, W. (1965). *The Story of the New Education*. London: Heinemann.
Breen, R. (1998). 'The persistence of class origin inequalities among school leavers in the Republic of Ireland, 1984–1993'. *British Journal of Sociology*, 49(2), 275–98.
Breen, R. (ed.) (2004). *Social Mobility in Europe*. Oxford: Oxford University Press.
Breen, R., Luijkx, R., Müller, W. and Pollak, R. (2009). 'Nonpersistent inequality in educational attainment: evidence from eight european countries'. *American Journal of Sociology*, 114(5), 1475–521.
Breen, R., Luijkx, R., Müller, W. and Pollak, R. (2010). 'Long-term trends in educational inequality in Europe: class inequalities and gender differences'. *European Sociological Review*, 26(1), 31–48.
Brehony, K. (2004). 'A new education for a new era: the contribution of the conferences of the New Education Fellowship to the disciplinary field of education 1921–1938'. *Paedagogica Historica*, 40(5–6), 733–55.
Brewer, R. I. (1986). 'A note on the changing status of the Registrar General's classification of occupations'. *British Journal of Sociology*, 37(1), 131–40.
Broadberry, S. N. (1994). 'Why was unemployment in postwar Britain so low?' *Bulletin of Economic Research*, 46(3), 241–61.
Bromley, C., Curtice, J. and Given, L. (2007). *Attitudes to Discrimination in Scotland: 2006: Scottish Social Attitudes Survey*. Edinburgh: Scottish Government Social Research.
Brown, A. and Webb, J. (1990). 'The higher education route to the labour market for mature students'. *British Journal of Education and Work*, 4(1), 5–21.
Brown, S. and Riddell, S. (eds) (1992). *Class, Race and Gender in Schools: A New Agenda for Policy and Practice in Scottish Education*. Edinburgh: Scottish Council for Research in Education.
Bruce, S. (2019). *Sectarianism in Scotland*. Edinburgh: Edinburgh University Press.
Bruce, S., Glendinning, T., Paterson, I. and Rosie, M. (2004). *Sectarianism in Scotland*. Edinburgh: Edinburgh University Press.
Buchmann, C., DiPrete, T. and McDaniel, A. (2008). 'Gender inequalities in education'. *Annual Review of Sociology*, 34(3), 319–37.
Bukodi, E. and Goldthorpe, J. H. (2013). 'Decomposing "social origins": the effects of parents' class, status, and education on the educational attainment of their children'. *European Sociological Review*, 29(5), 1024–39.
Bukodi, E. and Goldthorpe, J. H. (2016). 'Educational attainment – relative or absolute – as a mediator of intergenerational class mobility in Britain'. *Research in Social Stratification and Mobility*, 43 (March), 5–15.
Bukodi, E. and Goldthorpe, J. H. (2019). *Social Mobility and Education in Britain*. Cambridge: Cambridge University Press.
Bukodi, E., Goldthorpe, J. H., Waller, L. and Kuha, J. (2015). 'The mobility problem in Britain: new findings from the analysis of birth cohort data'. *British Journal of Sociology*, 66(1), 93–117.
Burnhill, P., McPherson, A., Raffe, D. and Tomes, N. (1987). 'Constructing a public account of an education system'. In G. Walford (ed.), *Doing Sociology of Education*, 207–29. Lewes: Falmer.

Buscha, F. and Sturgis, P. (2018). 'Declining social mobility? Evidence from five linked censuses in England and Wales 1971–2011'. *British Journal of Sociology*, 69(1), 154–82.

Bynner, J. (1999). 'New routes to employment: integration and exclusion'. In W. Heinz (ed.), *From Education to Work: Cross National Perspectives*, 65–86. Cambridge: Cambridge University Press.

Bynner, J. (2012). 'Policy reflections guided by longitudinal study, youth training, social exclusion, and more recently NEET'. *British Journal of Educational Studies*, 60(1), 39–52.

Bynner, J. and Parsons, S. (2001). 'Qualifications, basic skills and accelerating social exclusion'. *Journal of Education and Work*, 14(3), 279–91.

Bynner, J., Schuller, T. and Feinstein, L. (2003). 'Wider benefits of education: skills, higher education and civic engagement'. *Zeitschrift für Pädagogik*, 49(3), 341–61.

Bynner, J., Elias, P., McKnight, A., Pan, H. and Pierre, G. (2002). *Young People's Changing Routes to Independence*. York: Joseph Rowntree Foundation.

Cameron, E. (2010). *Impaled Upon a Thistle: Scotland since 1880*. Edinburgh: Edinburgh University Press.

Campbell, D. E. (2006). 'What is education's impact on civic and social engagement?' Symposium on Social Outcomes of Learning (23–24 March 2006). Copenhagen: Danish University of Education.

Campbell, J. and McLauchlan, R. (2020). *Haldane: the Forgotten Statesman who Shaped Modern Britain*. London: Hurst.

Caro, D. H. and Biecek, P. (2017). 'intsvy: an R package for analyzing international large-scale assessment data'. *Journal of Statistical Software*, 81(7), 1–44.

Cha, Y.-K. (1991). 'Effect of the global system on language instruction, 1850–1986'. *Sociology of Education*, 64(1), 19–32.

Champion, T. and Gordon, I. (2019). 'Linking spatial and social mobility: is London's "escalator" as strong as it was?' *Population, Space and Place*, 27(7), e2306.

Chisholm, L. (1999). 'From systems to networks: the reconstruction of youth transitions in Europe'. In W. Heinz (ed.), *From Education to Work: Cross National Perspectives*, 298–318. Cambridge: Cambridge University Press.

Chowdry, H., Crawford, C., Dearden, L., Goodman, A. and Vignoles, A. (2013). 'Widening participation in higher education: analysis using linked administrative data'. *Journal of the Royal Statistical Society Series A*, 176(2), 431–57.

Clemente, M., Durand, R. and Roulet, T. (2017). 'The recursive nature of institutional change: an Annales School perspective'. *Journal of Management Inquiry*, 26(1), 17–31.

Cole, G. D. H. (1952). 'Education and politics: a socialist view'. In J. A. Lauwerys and N. Hans (eds), *The Yearbook of Education*, 42–63. London: Institute of Education.

Committee on Higher Education (1963). *Higher Education: Report of the Committee Appointed by the Prime Minister under the Chairmanship of Lord Robbins: Appendix 1, The Demand for Places in Higher Education*. London: HMSO.

Consultative Committee on the Curriculum (1977). *The Structure of the Curriculum in the Third and Fourth Years of the Scottish Secondary School*. Edinburgh: Consultative Committee on the Curriculum.

Consultative Committee on the Curriculum (1986). *'More than Feelings of Concern': Guidance in Scottish Secondary Schools*. Edinburgh: Consultative Committee on the Curriculum.

Crawford, C., Duckworth, K., Vignoles, A. and Wyness, G. (2011). *Young People's Education and Labour Market Choices Aged 16/17 to 18/19*. London: Department for Education.

Crowther, J. (2018). 'The contradictions of populism: reasserting adult education for democracy'. *Andragoška Spoznanja*, 24(1), 19–34.

Croxford, L. (1994). 'Equal opportunities in the secondary school curriculum in Scotland'. *British Educational Research Journal*, 20(4), 371–91.

Croxford, L. (2015). 'Inequalities'. In D. Murphy, L. Croxford, C. Howieson and D. Raffe (eds), *Everyone's Future: Lessons from Fifty Years of Scottish Comprehensive Schooling*, 110–38. London: IoE Press.

Croxford, L. and Howieson, C. (2015). 'Young people's views of their experiences of comprehensive schooling'. In D. Murphy, L. Croxford, C. Howieson and D. Raffe (eds), *Everyone's Future: Lessons from Fifty Years of Scottish Comprehensive Schooling*, 32–68. London: IoE Press.

Croxford, L. and Paterson, L. (2006). 'Trends in social class segregation between schools in England, Wales and Scotland since 1984'. *Research Papers in Education*, 21(4), 381–406.

Croxford, L., Iannelli, C. and Shapira, M. (2007). *Documentation of the Youth Cohort Time-Series Datasets*. Study Number 5765. Colchester: UK Data Archive.

Curtice, J. (2014). 'Independence Referendum: a question of identity, economics or equality?' In A. Park, C. Bryson and J. Curtice (eds), *British Social Attitudes*, 1–19. London: NatCen Social Research.

Curtice, J. (2017). 'Why did Brexit not work for the Conservatives?' London: NatCen Social Research. http://www.natcen.ac.uk/blog/why-did-brexit-not-work-for-the-conservatives (downloaded 1 August 2021).

Curtice, J. and Montagu, I. (2020). 'Is Brexit fuelling support for independence?' Edinburgh: ScotCen Social Research. https://whatscotlandthinks.org/analysis/is-brexit-fuelling-support-for-independence/ (downloaded 26 July 2022).

Curtice, J., McCrone, D., Park, A. and Paterson, L. (eds) (2002). *New Scotland, New Society?* Edinburgh: Edinburgh University Press.

Davie, G. E. (1961). *The Democratic Intellect*. Edinburgh: Edinburgh University Press.

Davie, G. E. (1986). *The Crisis of the Democratic Intellect*. Edinburgh: Polygon.

Davie, G. E. (1990). 'The threat to Scottish education'. *Edinburgh Review*, 83, 35–7.

Davies, P., Telhaj, S., Hutton, D., Adnett, N. and Coe, R. (2008). 'Socioeconomic background, gender and subject choice in secondary schooling'. *Educational Research*, 50(3), 235–48.

de Graaf, N. D., de Graaf, P.M. and Kraaykamp, G. (2000). 'Parental cultural capital and educational attainment in the Netherlands: a refinement of the cultural capital perspective'. *Sociology of Education*, 73(2), 92–111.

Dearden, L., McGranahan, L. and Sianesi, B. (2004). *An In-Depth Analysis of the Returns to National Vocational Qualifications Obtained at Level 2*. London: Centre for the Economics of Education.

Deary, I. J., Lawn, M., Brett, C. E. and Bartholomew, D. J. (2009). '"Intelligence and Civilisation": A Ludwig Mond lecture delivered at the University of Manchester on 23rd October 1936 by Godfrey H. Thomson. A reprinting with background and commentary'. *Intelligence*, 37(1), 48–61.

Deary, I. J., Whalley, L. J. and Starr, J. M. (2009). *A Lifetime of Intelligence*. Washington, DC: American Psychological Association.

Devine, T. M. (1999). *The Scottish Nation*. Harmondsworth: Penguin.

Devine, T. M. and Rosie, M. (2020). 'The rise and fall of anti-Catholicism in Scotland'. In C. Gheeraert-Graffeuille and G. Vaughan (eds), *Anti-Catholicism in Britain and Ireland, 1600–2000*, 273–87. London: Palgrave Macmillan.

Dilnot, C. (2018). 'The relationship between A-level subject choice and league table score of university attended: the "facilitating", the "less suitable", and the counter-intuitive'. *Oxford Review of Education*, 44(1), 118–37.

DiMaggio, P. (1982). 'Cultural capital and school success: the impact of status culture participation on the grades of US high school students'. *American Sociological Review*, 47(2), 189–201.
Dobbie, F. and Jones, L. (2005). *24 in 2004 – Scotland's Young People: Findings from the Scottish School Leavers Survey: Technical Report*. Edinburgh: ScotCen.
Dolton, P. J., Makepeace, G. H. and Treble, J. G. (1994). 'The Youth Training Scheme and the school-to-work transition'. *Oxford Economic Papers*, 46(4), 629–57.
Donnelly, M. (2015). 'A new approach to researching school effects on higher education participation'. *British Journal of Sociology of Education*, 36(7), 1073–90.
Dronkers, J. (1993). 'Educational reform in the Netherlands: did it change the impact of parental occupation and education?' *Sociology of Education*, 66(4), 262–77.
Duffield, J., Allan, J., Turner, E. and Morris, B. (2000). 'Pupils' voices on achievement: an alternative to the standards agenda'. *Cambridge Journal of Education*, 30(2), 263–74.
Dumais, S. A. (2002). 'Cultural capital, gender, and school success: the role of habitus'. *Sociology of Education*, 75(1), 44–68.
Duta, A., An, B. and Iannelli, C. (2018). 'Social origins, academic strength of school curriculum and access to selective higher education institutions: evidence from Scotland and the USA'. *Higher Education*, 75(5), 769–84.
Eatwell, R. and Goodwin, M. (2018). *National Populism: the Revolt Against Liberal Democracy*. London: Pelican.
Education (Scotland) Act (1980). c. 44. https://www.legislation.gov.uk/ukpga/1980/44/contents.
Egerton, M. (2002). 'Higher education and civic engagement'. *British Journal of Sociology*, 53(4), 603–20.
Egerton, M. and Savage, M. (2000). 'Age stratification and class formation: a longitudinal study of the social mobility of young men and women, 1971–1991'. *Work, Employment and Society*, 14(1), 23–49.
Elias, P. and Gregory, M. (1994). *The Changing Structure of Occupations and Earnings in Great Britain, 1975–1990*. Research Series No. 27. London: Employment Department.
Elliott, C. D., Murray, D. J. and Pearson, L. S. (1978). *British Ability Scales*. London: National Foundation for Educational Research.
Emler, N. and Frazer, E. (1999). 'Politics: the education effect'. *Oxford Review of Education*, 25(1–2), 251–73.
Erikson, R. and Goldthorpe, J. H. (1992). *The Constant Flux: A Study of Class Mobility in Industrial Societies*. Oxford: Clarendon Press.
Espenshade, T. J., Hale, L. E. and Chung, C. Y. (2005). 'The frog pond revisited: high school academic context, class rank, and elite college admission'. *Sociology of Education*, 78(4), 269–93.
Eurydice (1997). *Measures Taken in the Member States of the European Union to Assist Young People who have Left the Education Eystem without Qualifications*. Brussels: Eurydice.
Favretto, I. (2000). '"Wilsonism" reconsidered: Labour party revisionism 1952–64'. *Contemporary British History*, 14(4), 54–80.
Field, J. (2009). 'Lifelong learning in Scotland: cohesion, equity and participation'. *Scottish Educational Review*, 41(2), 4–19.
Fielding, A. J. (1992). 'Migration and social mobility: south east England as an escalator region'. *Regional Studies*, 26(1), 1–15.
Findlay, A., Mason, C., Harrison, R., Houston, D. and McCollum, D. (2008). 'Getting off the escalator? A study of Scots out-migration from a global city region'. *Environment and Planning A*, 40(9), 2169–85.
Fitzpatrick, T. A. (1986). *Catholic Education in South-West Scotland before 1972*. Aberdeen: Aberdeen University Press.

Forbes, J. and Lingard, B. (2013). 'Elite school capitals and girls' schooling: understanding the (re) production of privilege through a habitus of "assuredness"'. In C. Maxwell and P. Aggleton (eds), *Privilege, Agency and Affect*, 50–68. London: Palgrave Macmillan.

Full Fact (2016). 'Has the public really had enough of experts?' https://fullfact.org/blog/2016/sep/has-public-really-had-enough-experts/ (Downloaded 28 July 2021).

Furlong, A. and Cartmel, F. (2007). *Young People and Social Change: New Perspectives*, second edition. Maidenhead: McGraw-Hill.

Gallie, D. (2000). 'The labour force'. In A. H. Halsey and J. Webb (eds), *Twentieth-Century British Social Trends*, 281–323. London: Macmillan.

Galston, W. A. (2001). 'Political knowledge, political engagement and civic education'. *Annual Review of Political Science*, 4(1), 217–34.

Gamoran, A. (1996). 'Curriculum standardisation and equality of opportunity in Scottish secondary education, 1984–1990'. *Sociology of Education*, 69(1), 1–21.

Gamoran, A., Porter, A. C., Smithson, J. and White, P. A. (1997). 'Upgrading high school mathematics instruction: improving learning opportunities for low-achieving, low-income youth'. *Educational Evaluation and Policy Analysis*, 19(4), 325–38.

Gangl, M., Müller, W. and Raffe, D. (2003). 'Conclusions: explaining cross-national differences in school-to-work transitions'. In W. Müller and M. Gangl (eds), *Transitions from Education to Work in Europe*, 277–305. Oxford: Oxford University Press.

Ganzeboom, H. B. G. and Treiman, D. J. (1993). 'Preliminary results on educational expansion and educational opportunity in comparative perspective'. In H. A. Becker and P. L. J. Hermkens (eds), *Solidarity of Generations*, 467–506. Amsterdam: Thesis Publishers.

Gayle, V., Berridge, D. and Davies, R. (2002). 'Young people's entry into higher education: quantifying influential factors'. *Oxford Review of Education*, 28(1), 5–20.

General Register Office (1960). *Classification of Occupations 1960*. London: HMSO.

Goisis, A., Özcan, B. and Myrskylä, M. (2017). 'Decline in the negative association between low birth weight and cognitive ability'. *Proceedings of the National Academy of Sciences*, 114(1), 84–8.

Goldthorpe, J. H. (2007), '"Cultural capital": some critical observations'. *Sociologica*, 1(2), 1–23.

Goldthorpe, J. H. (2014). 'The role of education in intergenerational social mobility: problems from empirical research in sociology and some theoretical pointers from economics'. *Rationality and Society*, 26(3), 265–89.

Goodhart, D. (2017). *The Road to Somewhere*. London: Hurst.

Gorard, S., Smith, E., May, H., Thomas, L., Adnett, N. and Slack, K. (2006). *Review of Widening Participation Research: Addressing the Barriers to Participation in Higher Education: A Report to HEFCE*. York: Department of Educational Studies.

Gow, L. and McPherson, A. F. (1980). *Tell Them From Me: Scottish School Leavers Write about School and Life Afterwards*. Aberdeen: Aberdeen University Press.

Gray, J., McPherson, A. and Raffe, D. (1983). *Reconstructions of Secondary Education: Theory, Myth and Practice since the War*. London: Routledge and Kegan Paul.

Grek, S. (2009). 'Governing by numbers: the PISA "effect" in Europe'. *Journal of Education Policy*, 24(1), 23–37.

Growing Up in Scotland website (2022). https://growingupinscotland.org.uk/about-gus/study-design-and-methodology/

Gugushvili, A., Bukodi, E. and Goldthrope, J. H. (2017). 'The direct effect of social origins on social mobility chances: "glass floors" and "glass ceilings" in Britain'. *European Sociological Review*, 33(2), 305–16.

Gutmann, A. (1987). *Democratic Education*. Princeton, NJ: Princeton University Press.

Hall, P. (1999). 'Social capital in Britain'. *British Journal of Politics*, 29(3), 417–61.

Halsey, A. H. and Trow, M. (1971). *The British Academics*. London: Faber.
Halsey, A. H., Heath, A. F. and Ridge, J. M. (1980). *Origins and Destinations*. Oxford: Clarendon.
Hannan, D., Hövels, B., van den Berg, S. and White, M. (1995). '"Early leavers" from education and training in Ireland, the Netherlands and the United Kingdom'. *European Journal of Education*, 30(3), 325–46.
Hargreaves, D. (1982). *The Challenge for the Comprehensive School*. London: Routledge and Kegan Paul.
Hartley, D. (1987). 'The convergence of learner - centred pedagogy in primary and further education in Scotland: 1965–1985'. *British Journal of Educational Studies*, 35(2), 115–28.
Hasluck, C. (1999). *Employers, Young people and the Unemployed: A Review of Research*. London: Employment Service.
Hawkes, D. and Plewis, I. (2006). 'Modelling non-response in the National Child Development Study'. *Journal of the Royal Statistical Society Series A*, 169(3), 479–91.
Heath, A. F. and Clifford, P. (1990). 'Class inequalities in education in the twentieth century'. *Journal of the Royal Statistical Society Series A*, 153(1), 1–16.
Hill, M. (2004). *The Public Policy Process*, fourth edition. London: Routledge.
Hirst, P. (1975). *Knowledge and the Curriculum*. London: Routledge and Kegan Paul.
Howieson, C. and Iannelli, C. (2008). 'The effects of low attainment on young people's outcomes at age 22–23 in Scotland'. *British Educational Research Journal*, 34(2), 269–90.
Howieson, C. and Semple, S. (2000). 'The evaluation of guidance: listening to pupils' views'. *British Journal of Guidance and Counselling*, 28(3), 373–87.
Howieson, C., Raffe, D., Spours, K. and Young, M. (1997). 'Unifying academic and vocational learning: the state of the debate in England and Scotland'. *Journal of Education and Work*, 10(1), 5–35.
Huang, J., van den Brink, H. M. and Groot, W. (2009). 'A meta-analysis of the effect of education on social capital'. *Economics of Education Review*, 28(4), 454–64.
Huang, Z., Feng, Z. and Dibben, C. (2016). *The Scottish Longitudinal Study 1936 Birth Cohort*. SLS Technical Working Paper 7. Edinburgh: Longitudinal Studies Centre Scotland.
Humes, W. (1986). *The Leadership Class in Scottish Education*. Edinburgh: John Donald.
Hussain, A. M. and Miller, W. L. (2006). *Multicultural Nationalism: Islamophobia, Anglophobia, and Devolution*. Oxford: Oxford University Press.
Iannelli, C. (2004). 'School variation in youth transitions in Ireland, Scotland and the Netherlands'. *Comparative Education*, 40(3), 401–25.
Iannelli, C. (2013). 'The role of the school curriculum in social mobility'. *British Journal of Sociology of Education*, 34(5–6), 907–28.
Iannelli, C. and Duta, A. (2018). 'Inequalities in school leavers' labour market outcomes: do school subject choices matter?' *Oxford Review of Education*, 44(1), 56–74.
Iannelli, C. and Paterson, L. (2006). 'Social mobility in Scotland since the middle of the twentieth century'. *Sociological Review*, 54(3), 520–45.
Iannelli, C., Gamoran, A. and Paterson, L. (2011). 'Expansion through diversion in Scottish higher education, 1987–2001'. *Oxford Review of Education*, 37(6), 717–41.
Iannelli, C., Smyth, E. and Klein, M. (2016). 'Curriculum differentiation and social inequality in higher education entry in Scotland and Ireland'. *British Educational Research Journal*, 42(4), 561–81.
Ichou, M. and Vallet, L.-A. (2011). 'Do all roads lead to inequality? Trends in French upper secondary school analysed with four longitudinal surveys'. *Oxford Review of Education*, 37(2), 167–94.
Jackson, B. (2020). *The Case for Scottish Independence*. Cambridge: Cambridge University Press.

Jones, I. (1988). 'An evaluation of YTS'. *Oxford Review of Economic Policy*, 4(3), 54–71.
Kamens, D. H., Meyer, J. W. and Benavot, A. (1996). 'Worldwide patterns in academic secondary education curricula'. *Comparative Education Review*, 40(2), 116–38.
Kelsall, R. K., Poole, A. and Kuhn, A. (1970). *Six Years After: First Report on a National Follow-up Survey of Ten Thousand Graduates of British Universities in 1960*. Sheffield: Higher Education Research Unit.
Kendrick, S. (1986). 'Occupational change in modern Scotland'. In D. McCrone (ed.), *Scottish Government Yearbook 1986*, 240–72. Edinburgh: Unit for the Study of Government in Scotland, University of Edinburgh.
Kenny, M. and Mackay, F. (2020). 'Women, gender, and politics in Scotland'. In M. Keating (ed.), *Oxford Handbook of Scottish Politics*. Oxford: Oxford University Press.
Kerckhoff, A. C., Fogelman, K. R., Crook, D. and Reeder, D. A. (1996). *Going Comprehensive in England and Wales*. London: Woburn.
Kirk, G. (1999). 'The passing of monotechnic teacher education in Scotland'. *Scottish Educational Review*, 31(2), 100–11.
Klein, M., Iannelli, C. and Smyth, E. (2016). 'School subject choices and social class differences in entry to higher education: comparing Scotland and Ireland'. In *Models of Secondary Education and Social Inequality – An International Comparison*, 233–48. Cheltenham: Edward Elgar Publishing.
Kuh, D., Pierce, M., Adams, J., Deanfield, J., Ekelund, U., Friberg, P., Ghosh, A. K., Harwood, N., Hughes, A., Macfarlane, P. W. and Mishra, G. (2011). 'Cohort profile: updating the cohort profile for the MRC National Survey of Health and Development: a new clinic-based data collection for ageing research'. *International Journal of Epidemiology*, 40(1), e1–e9.
Lawson, M. (1981). 'The new education fellowship: the formative years'. *Journal of Educational Administration and History*, 13(2), 24–28.
Lindbekk, T. (1998). 'The education backlash hypothesis: the Norwegian experience 1960–92'. *Acta Sociologica*, 41(2), 151–62.
Lloyd, J. M. (1979). *The Scottish School System and the Second World War: A Study in Central Policy and Administration*. PhD thesis. Stirling: Stirling University.
Lucas, S. R. (2001). 'Effectively maintained inequality: education transitions, track mobility, and social background effects'. *American Journal of Sociology*, 106(6), 1642–90.
Lumley, T. (2010). *Complex Surveys: A Guide to Analysis Using R*. New York: Wiley.
MacBeath, J. (2006). 'Finding a voice, finding self'. *Educational Review*, 58(2), 195–207.
McCrone, D. (1992). *Understanding Scotland*. London: Routledge.
McCrone, D. (1998). *The Sociology of Nationalism*. London: Routledge.
McCrone, D. (2019). 'Peeble them wi'stanes: twenty years of the Scottish Parliament'. *Scottish Affairs*, 28(2), 125–51.
McCrone, D. and Paterson, L (2002). 'The conundrum of Scottish independence'. *Scottish Affairs*, 40(1), 54–75.
Machin, S., McNally, S. and Wyness, G. (2013). 'Educational attainment across the UK nations: performance, inequality and evidence'. *Educational Research*, 55(2), 139–64.
MacIntyre, A. (2007). *After Virtue*, third edition. Notre Dame, IN: University of Notre Dame Press.
McPherson, A. (1992). 'Schooling'. In A. Dickson and J. H. Treble (eds), *People and Society in Scotland, Volume III, 1914–1990*, 80–107. Edinburgh: John Donald.
McPherson, A. and Neave, G. (1976). *The Scottish Sixth*. Slough: NFER.
McPherson, A. and Raab, C. D. (1988). *Governing Education*. Edinburgh: Edinburgh University Press.
Macpherson, J. (1958). *Eleven-Year-Olds Grow Up*. London: University of London Press.

McPherson, A. and Willms, J. D. (1986). 'Certification, class conflict, religion, and community: a socio-historical explanation of the effectiveness of contemporary schools'. In A. C. Kerckhoff (ed.), *Research in Sociology of Education and Socialization Volume 6*, 227–302. Greenwich, CT: JAI Press.

McPherson, A. and Willms, J. D. (1987). 'Equalisation and improvement: some effects of comprehensive reorganisation in Scotland'. *Sociology*, 21(4), 509–39.

Macpherson, S. and Bond, S. (2009). *Equality Issues in Scotland: A Review of Research, 2000–08*. Manchester: Equality and Human Rights Commission.

Main, B. G. M. and Shelly, M. (1988). 'Does it pay young people to go on YTS?' In D. Raffe (ed.), *Education and the Youth Labour Market*, 147–61. Lewes: Falmer.

Mancini, L. (2003). *Higher Education in the UK and the Market for Labour: Evidence from the Universities' Statistical Record*. PhD thesis. Warwick|: University of Warwick.

Mandler, P. (2020). *The Crisis of the Meritocracy: Britain's Transition to Mass Education since the Second World War*. Oxford: Oxford University Press.

Mangan, J., Hughes, A., Davie, P. and Slack, K. (2010). 'Fair access, achievement and geography: explaining the association between social class and students' choice of university'. *Studies in Higher Education*, 35(3), 335–50.

Marks, G. N. (2014). *Education, Social Background and Cognitive Ability*. Abingdon: Routledge.

Meyer, H.-D. (2006). 'The rise and decline of the common school as an institution: taking "myth and ceremony" seriously'. In H.-D. Meyer and B. Rowan, *The New Institutionalism in Education*, 51–66. New York: State University Press.

Meyer, J. W. and Rowan, B. (1977). 'Institutionalized organizations: formal structure as myth and ceremony'. *American Journal of Sociology*, 83(2), 340–63.

Moulton, V., Sullivan, A., Henderson, M. and Anders, J. (2018). 'Does what you study at age 14–16 matter for educational transitions post-16?' *Oxford Review of Education*, 44(1), 94–117.

Mounk, Y. (2018). *The People vs Democracy*. Cambridge, MA: Harvard University Press.

Mudde, C. and Kaltwasser, C. R. (2012). 'Populism and (liberal) democracy: a framework for analysis'. In C. Mudde and C. R. Kaltwasser (eds), *Populism in Europe and the Americas: Threat or Corrective for Democracy?*, 1–26. Cambridge: Cambridge University Press.

Müller, W. and Gangl, M. (eds) (2003). *Transitions from Education to Work in Europe*. Oxford: Oxford University Press.

Müller, W. and Karle, W. (1993). 'Social selection in educational systems in Europe'. *European Sociological Review*, 9(1), 1–23.

Müller, W. and Shavit, Y. (1998). 'The institutional embeddedness of the stratification process'. In Y. Shavit and W. Müller (eds), *From School to Work. A Comparative Study of Educational Qualifications and Occupational Destinations*, 1–48. Oxford: Clarendon Press.

Munn, P., Johnstone, M. and Sharp, S. (2004). *Discipline in Scottish Schools: A Comparative Survey over time of Teachers' and Headteachers' Perceptions*. Edinburgh: Scottish Executive.

Murphy, D., Croxford, L., Howieson, C. and Raffe, D. (eds) (2015). *Everyone's Future: Lessons from Fifty Years of Scottish Comprehensive Schooling*. London: IoE Press.

Nash, R. (1999). 'Bourdieu, "habitus", and educational research: is it all worth the candle?' *British Journal of Sociology of Education*, 20(2), 175–87.

Nathan, G. (1999). *A Review of Sample Attrition and Representativeness in Three Longitudinal Studies*. Methodology Series No. 13. London: Government Statistical Service.

National Records of Scotland (2022). *Education Records*. https://www.nrscotland.gov.uk/research/research-guides/research-guides-a-z/education-records

Neave, G. (1976). 'The development of Scottish education, 1958–1972'. *Comparative Education*, 12(2), 129–44.

Newton, P. E. (2021). 'Demythologising A level exam standards'. *Research Papers in Education*. doi: 10.1080/02671522.2020.1870543.

Nie, N. and Hillygus, D. S. (2001). 'Education and democratic citizenship'. In D. Ravitch and J. P. Vitteriti (eds), *Making Good Citizens*, 30–57. New Haven, CT: Yale University Press.

Nie, N. H., Junn, J. and Stehlik-Barry, K. (1996). *Education and Democratic Citizenship in America*. Chicago: University of Chicago Press.

Niemi, R. G. and Junn, J. (1998). *Civic Education: What Makes Students Learn*. New Haven, CT: Yale University Press.

Nikolai, R. (2019). 'After German reunification: the implementation of a two-tier school model in Berlin and Saxony'. *History of Education*, 48(3), 374–94.

Norris, P. and Inglehart, R. F. (2019). *Cultural Backlash: Trump, Brexit, and Authoritarian Populism*. Cambridge: Cambridge University Press.

Ocasio, W., Mauskapf, M. and Steele, C. W. (2016). 'History, society, and institutions: the role of collective memory in the emergence and evolution of societal logics'. *Academy of Management Review*, 41(4), 676–99.

OECD (2019). *PISA 2018 Assessment and Analytical Framework*. Paris: OECD Publishing. https://doi.org/10.1787/b25efab8-en

Office for National Statistics (2000). *Standard Occupational Classification 2000*. London: ONS.

Office for National Statistics (2004). *The National Statistics Socio-Economic Classification User Manual*. London: ONS.

Office of Population, Censuses and Surveys (1980). *Classification of Occupations 1980*. London: HMSO.

Office of Population, Censuses and Surveys (1990). *Classification of Occupations 1990*. London: HMSO.

Palardy, G. J. (2015). 'High school socioeconomic composition and college choice: multilevel mediation via organizational habitus, school practices, peer and staff attitudes'. *School Effectiveness and School Improvement*, 26(3), 329–53.

Paterson, L. (1996). 'Liberation or control: what are the Scottish educational traditions in the twentieth century?' In T. M. Devine and R. J. Finlay (eds), *Scotland in the Twentieth Century*, 233–49. Edinburgh: Edinburgh University Press.

Paterson, L. (ed.) (1998). *A Diverse Assembly: the Debate on a Scottish Parliament*. Edinburgh: Edinburgh University Press.

Paterson, L. (2000). *Education and the Scottish Parliament*. Edinburgh: Dunedin Academic Press.

Paterson, L. (2003). *Scottish Education in the Twentieth Century*. Edinburgh: Edinburgh University Press.

Paterson, L. (2004). 'The modernising of the democratic intellect: the role of English in Scottish secondary education, 1900–1939'. *Journal of Scottish Historical Studies*, 24(1), 45–79.

Paterson, L. (2009a). 'Civil society and the parliament'. In C. Jeffery and J. Mitchell (eds), *The Scottish Parliament 1999–2009: The First Decade*, 113–18. London: Hansard Society.

Paterson, L. (2009b). 'Civic values and the subject matter of educational courses'. *Oxford Review of Education*, 35(1), 81–98.

Paterson, L. (2011). 'The reinvention of Scottish liberal education: secondary schooling, 1900–1939'. *Scottish Historical Review*, 90(1), 96–130.

Paterson, L. (2014). 'Education, social attitudes and social participation among adults in Britain'. *Sociological Research Online*, 19(1). www.socresonline.org.uk/19/1/26.html

Paterson, L. (2015a). *Social Radicalism and Liberal Education*. Exeter: Imprint Academic.

Paterson, L. (2015b). 'Democracy or intellect? The Scottish educational dilemma of the twentieth century'. In R. D. Anderson, M. Freeman and L. Paterson (eds), *The Edinburgh History of Education in Scotland*, 226–45. Edinburgh: Edinburgh University Press.

Paterson, L. (2015c). 'George Davie and the democratic intellect'. In G. Graham (ed.), *Oxford History of Scottish Philosophy*, 236–69. Oxford: Oxford University Press.

Paterson, L. (2015d). 'Utopian pragmatism: Scotland's choice'. *Scottish Affairs*, 24(1), 22–46.

Paterson, L. (2018). 'The significance of the Education (Scotland) Act, 1918'. *Scottish Affairs*, 27(4), 401–24.

Paterson, L. (2020a). 'Curriculum and opportunity in Scottish secondary education: a half-century of expansion and inequality'. *Curriculum Journal*, 31(4), 722–44.

Paterson, L. (2020b). 'Social inequality in Catholic schools in Scotland in the second half of the twentieth century'. *British Journal of Sociology of Education*, 41(8), 1115–32.

Paterson, L. (2020c). 'The experience of school in Scotland, 1970s to 1990s'. *British Educational Research Journal*, 46(6), 1171–92.

Paterson, L. (2021a). 'Education and support for Scottish independence, 1979–2016'. *Journal of Education Policy*. doi: 10.1080/02680939.2021.2005148.

Paterson, L. (2021b). 'Higher education and school history in Scotland in the second half of the twentieth century'. *British Journal of Sociology of Education*, 42(7), 989–1007.

Paterson, L. (2021c). 'The relationship of the 1918 and 1872 Education (Scotland) Acts'. *Scottish Educational Review*, 53(2), 88–103.

Paterson, L. (2022a). 'Breadth of study at secondary school and the attainment and progression of university graduates in Scotland, 1960–2002'. *Higher Education*. doi.org/10.1007/s10734-022-00862-4.

Paterson, L. (2022b). 'Education and high-status occupations in the UK since the middle of the twentieth century'. *British Journal of Sociology of Education*, 43(3), 375–96.

Paterson, L. (2022c). 'School leavers and educational reform in Scotland in the second half of the twentieth century'. *Journal of Education and Work*, 35(1), 32–49.

Paterson, L. (2022d). 'Schools, policy and social change: Scottish secondary education in the second half of the twentieth century'. *Research Papers in Education*, 37(3), 344–69.

Paterson, L. (2022e). 'Social class and sex differences in absolute and relative educational attainment in England, Scotland and Wales since the middle of the twentieth century'. *Research Papers in Education*. doi: 10.1080/02671522.2022.2089213.

Paterson, L. (2022f). 'Social class and sex differences in higher education attainment among adults in Scotland since the 1960s'. *Longitudinal and Life Course Studies*, 13(1), 7–48.

Paterson, L. (2022g). 'Higher education expansion and the secondary school curriculum in Scotland in the second half of the twentieth century'. *Oxford Review of Education*, 48(5), 622–41, doi: 10.1080/03054985.2021.2002291.

Paterson, L. (2022h). 'Participation in science in secondary and higher education in Scotland in the second half of the twentieth century'. *Research Papers in Education*, 37(6), 1189–13, doi: 10.1080/02671522.2021.1931951.

Paterson, L. and Iannelli, C. (2006). 'Religion, social mobility and education in Scotland'. *British Journal of Sociology*, 57(3), 353–77.

Paterson, L. and Iannelli, C. (2007a). 'Social class and educational attainment: a comparative study of England, Wales and Scotland'. *Sociology of Education*, 80(4), 330–58.

Paterson, L. and Iannelli, C. (2007b). 'Patterns of absolute and relative social mobility: a comparative study of England, Wales and Scotland'. *Sociological Research Online*, 12. www.socresonline.org.uk/12/6/15.html/

Paterson, L. and Raffe, D. (1995). '"Staying on" in full time education in Scotland, 1985–1991'. *Oxford Review of Education*, 21(1), 3–23.

Paterson, L., Bechhofer, F. and McCrone, D. (2004). *Living in Scotland: Social and Economic Change since 1980*. Edinburgh: Edinburgh University Press.

Paterson, L., Pattie, A. and Deary, I. J. (2010). 'Post-school education and social class destinations in Scotland in the 1950s'. *Longitudinal and Life Course Studies*, 1(4), 371–93.

Payne, P. L. (1996). 'The economy'. In T. M. Devine and R. J. Finlay (eds), *Scotland in the Twentieth Century*, 13–45. Edinburgh: Edinburgh University Press.

Peden, G. (2012). 'A new Scotland? The economy'. In T. M. Devine and J. Wormald (eds), *Oxford Handbook of Modern Scottish History*. Oxford: Oxford University Press.

Perkin, H. (1989). *The Rise of Professional Society*. London: Routledge.

Pfeffer, F. T. (2008). 'Persistent inequality in educational attainment and its institutional context'. *European Sociological Review*, 24(5), 543–65.

Philip, H. (1992). *The Higher Tradition*. Dalkeith: Scottish Examination Board.

Pigeon, D. A. (1964). 'Tests used in the 1954 and 1957 surveys'. In J. W. B. Douglas (ed.), *The Home and the School*, 129–32. London: MacGibbon and Kee.

Pollock, G. J., Thorpe, W. G. and Freshwater, S. (1977). *Pupils' Attitude to School Rules and Punishments*. Edinburgh: Scottish Council for Research in Education.

Power, S. A. and Whitty, G. (2008). *Graduating and Gradations within the Middle Class: The Legacy of an Elite Higher Education*. Working Paper No. 118. Cardiff: Cardiff School of Social Sciences.

Purcell, K., Wilton, N. and Elias, P. (2006). *Scotland's Class of 99: the Early Career Paths of Graduates who Studied in Scottish Higher Education Institutions*. Warwick: Warwick Institute for Employment Research.

Purcell, K., Elias, P., Atfield, G., Behle, H., Ellison, R., Luchinskaya, D., Snape, J., Conaghan, L. and Tzanakou, C. (2012). *Futuretrack Stage 4: Transitions into Employment, Further Study and other Outcomes*. Warwick: Warwick Institute for Employment Research.

Pustjens, H., van de Gaer, E, van Damme, J. and Onghena, P. (2004). 'Effect of secondary schools on academic choices and on success in higher education'. *School Effectiveness and School Improvement*, 15(3–4), 281–311.

The R Project for Statistical Computing (2022). https://www.r-project.org/

Raffe, D. (1984a). 'School attainment and the labour market'. In D. Raffe (ed.), *Fourteen to Eighteen*, 174–93. Aberdeen: Aberdeen University Press.

Raffe, D. (1984b). 'Youth unemployment and the MSC: 1977–1983'. In D. McCrone (ed.), *Scottish Government Yearbook 1984*, 188–222. Edinburgh: Unit for the Study of Government in Scotland.

Raffe, D. (1985). 'The extendable ladder: Scotland's 16-plus Action Plan'. *Youth and Policy*, 12 (Spring), 27–33.

Raffe, D. (1987). 'The context of the Youth Training Scheme: an analysis of its strategy and development'. *British Journal of Education and Work*, 1(1), 1–31.

Raffe, D. (2009). 'The Action Plan, Scotland and the making of the modern educational world: the first quarter century'. *Scottish Educational Review*, 41(1), 22–35.

Raffe, D. and Courtenay, G. (1988). '16–18 on both sides of the border'. In D. Raffe (ed.), *Education and the Youth Labour Market*, 12–39. London: Falmer.

Raffe, D., Brannen, K., Croxford, L. and Martin, C. (1999). 'Comparing, England, Scotland, Wales and Northern Ireland: the case for "home internationals" in comparative research'. *Comparative Education*, 35(1), 9–25.

Raftery, A. E. and Hout, M. (1993). 'Maximally maintained inequality. expansion, reform, and opportunity in Irish education 1921–75.' *Sociology of Education*, 66(1), 41–62.

Reay, D., David, M. and Ball, S. (2001). 'Making a difference?: institutional habituses and higher education choice'. *Sociological Research Online*, 5. http://www.socresonline.org.uk/5/4/reay.html

Reay, D., David, M. and Ball, S. (2005). *Degrees of Choice*. London: Trentham.

Reeves, E. B. (2012). 'The effects of opportunity to learn, family socioeconomic status, and friends on the rural math achievement gap in high school'. *American Behavioral Scientist*, 56(7), 887–907.
Reynolds, D., Sullivan, M. and Murgatroyd, S. (1987). *The Comprehensive Experiment*. London: Falmer.
Roberts, K., Dench, S. and Richardson, D. (1986). 'Firms' uses of the Youth Training Scheme'. *Policy Studies*, 6(3), 37–53.
Rose, D., Pevalin, D. J. and O'Reilly, K. (2005). *The NS-SEC: Origins, Development and Use*. London: Office for National Statistics.
Rosie, M. (2014). 'Tall tales: understanding religion and Scottish independence'. *Scottish Affairs*, 23(3), 332–41.
Runciman, D. (2018). *How Democracy Ends*. London: Profile.
Sandel, M. (2020). *The Tyranny of Merit*. London: Allen Lane.
Schleicher, A. (2017). 'Seeing education through the prism of PISA'. *European Journal of Education*, 52(2), 124–30.
Schührer, S., Carbonaro, W. and Grodsky, E. (2016). 'Reproduction of inequality in educational attainment through curricular differentiation in secondary school – a case study of the USA'. In H.-P. Blossfeld, S. Buchholz, J. Skopek and M. Triventi (eds), *Models of Secondary Education and Social Inequality*, 248–67. Cheltenham: Edward Elgar Publishing.
Scotch Education Department (1908). *List of Day Schools Aided from Parliamentary Grant*, 507–630. Parliamentary Papers XXVIII.
Scotland, J. (1969). *The History of Scottish Education, Volume 2*. London: University of London Press.
Scottish Consultative Council on the Curriculum (1989). *Curriculum Design for the Secondary Stages*. Edinburgh: Scottish Consultative Council on the Curriculum.
Scottish Education Department (1946). *Primary Education: A Report of the Advisory Council on Education in Scotland*. Edinburgh: HMSO.
Scottish Education Department (1947). *Secondary Education: A Report of the Advisory Council on Education in Scotland*. Edinburgh: HMSO.
Scottish Education Department (1952). *English in Secondary Schools*. Edinburgh: HMSO.
Scottish Education Department (1965). *Primary Education in Scotland*. Edinburgh: HMSO.
Scottish Education Department (1971). *The Structure of Promoted Posts in Secondary Schools in Scotland*. Edinburgh: HMSO.
Scottish Education Department (1973). *Education in Scotland in 1972*. Edinburgh: SED.
Scottish Education Department (1977). *Assessment for All: Report of the Committee to Review Assessment in the Third and Fourth Years of Secondary Education in Scotland*. Edinburgh: HMSO.
Scottish Executive (2002). *Students in Higher Education in Scotland: 2000–1*. Edinburgh: Scottish Executive.
Scottish Government (2016). *Pupils in Scotland 2016: Supplementary Tables*. Edinburgh: Scottish Government.
Scottish Government (2017). *Summary Statistics for Attainment, Leaver Destinations and Healthy Living, No. 7: 2017 Edition*. Edinburgh: Scottish Government.
Scottish Office (1992). *Scottish Higher Education Statistics*. Statistical Bulletin Edn/J2/1992/18. Edinburgh: Scottish Office.
Scottish Qualifications Authority (2016). *Attainment Statistics (December) 2016*. Glasgow: SQA.
Seawright, J. and Gerring, J. (2008). 'Case selection techniques in case study research: a menu of qualitative and quantitative options'. *Political Research Quarterly*, 61(2), 294–308.

Shavit, Y. and Blossfeld, H.-P. (1993). *Persistent Inequality*. Boulder, CO: Westview.
Shavit, Y., Yaish, M. and Bar-haim, E. (2007). 'The persistence of persistent inequality'. http://citeseerx.ist.psu.edu/viewdoc/summary?doi=10.1.1.407.1245 (downloaded 28 May 2019).
Shelly, M. (1988). 'Has the bottom dropped out of the youth labour market?' In D. Raffe (ed.), *Education and the Youth Labour Market*, 100–16. Lewes: Falmer.
Shepherd, P. (2012). *1958 National Child Development Study User Guide: Measures of Ability At Ages 7 to 16*. London: Centre for Longitudinal Studies, University of London.
Schofer, E. and Meyer, J. W. (2005). 'The worldwide expansion of higher education in the twentieth century'. *American Sociological Review*, 70(6), 898–920.
ScotCen (2021). *Scottish Social Attitudes*. https://www.ssa.natcen.ac.uk/ (accessed 25 October 2022).
Shulruf, B., Hattie, J. and Tumen, S. (2008). 'Individual and school factors affecting students' participation and success in higher education'. *Higher Education*, 56(5), 613–32.
Silver, N. (2016). 'Education, not income, predicted who would vote for Trump'. http://fivethirtyeight.com/features/education-not-income-predicted-who-would-vote-for-trump/ (downloaded 28 July 2021).
Smith, E. and Gorard, S. (2002). *What Does PISA tell us about Equity in Education Systems?*. Occasional Paper Series, 54. Cardiff: Cardiff School of Social Sciences.
Smith, G. (2000). 'Schools'. In A. H. Halsey and J. Webb (eds), *Twentieth-Century British Social Trends*, 179–220. London: Macmillan.
Smith, J. and Naylor, R. (2005). 'Schooling effects on subsequent university performance: evidence for the UK university population'. *Economics of Education Review*, 24(5), 549–62.
Smith, J., McKnight, A. and Naylor, R. (2000). 'Graduate employability: policy and performance in higher education in the UK'. *Economic Journal*, 110(464), 382–411.
Smout, T. C. (1986). *A Century of the Scottish People, 1830–1950*. London: HarperCollins.
Smyth, E. (2005). 'Gender differentiation and early labour market integration across Europe'. *European Societies*, 7(3), 451–79.
Smyth, E. and Hannan, C. (2007). 'School processes and the transition to higher education'. *Oxford Review of Education*, 33(2), 175–94.
Solga, H. (2008). 'Lack of training: employment opportunities for low-skilled persons from a sociological and microeconomic perspective'. In K. Mayer (ed.), *Skill Formation: Interdisciplinary and Cross-National Perspectives*, 173–204. Cambridge: Cambridge University Press.
Stewart, J. (2006). 'Child guidance in interwar Scotland: international influences and domestic concerns'. *Bulletin of the History of Medicine*, 80(3), 513–39.
Sutton Trust (2011). *Degrees of Success: University Chances by Individual School*. London: Sutton Trust.
Taylor, C., C. Wright, R. Davies, G. Rees, C. Evans and S. Drinkwater. (2018). 'The effect of schools on school leavers' university participation'. *School Effectiveness and School Improvement*, 29(4), 590–613.
Thurow, L. C. (1976). *Generating Inequality*. London: Macmillan.
Tinklin, T. (2000). *High-attaining Female School Leavers*. Edinburgh: Scottish Executive.
Tinklin, T. (2003). 'Gender differences and high attainment'. *British Educational Research Journal*, 29(3), 307–25.
Tomlinson, J. (2021). 'Deindustrialisation and "Thatcherism": moral economy and unintended consequences'. *Contemporary British History*, 35(4), 620–42.
Treble, J. H. (1978). 'The development of Roman Catholic education in Scotland 1878–1978'. *Innes Review*, 29(2), 111–39.

Treble, J. H. (1980). 'The working of the 1918 Education Act in Glasgow archdiocese'. *Innes Review*, 31(1), 27–44.

Triventi, M., Panichella, M., Ballarino, G. and Barone, C. (2016). 'Education as a positional good: implications for social inequalities in educational attainment in Italy'. *Research in Social Stratification and Mobility*, 43 (March), 39–52.

Tymms, P. (1995). 'The long-term impact of schooling'. *Evaluation and Research in Education*, 9(2), 99–108.

Tymms, T. B. and Fitz-Gibbon, C. T. (1991). 'A comparison of examination boards: A levels'. *Oxford Review of Education*, 17(1), 17–32.

Universities Central Council on Admissions (1975). *Statistical Supplement to the Twelfth Report 1973–4*. Cheltenham: UCCA.

University of Essex, Institute for Social and Economic Research (2020). *Understanding Society: Waves 1–10, 2009–2019 and Harmonised BHPS: Waves 1–18, 1991–2009*. [Data collection.] 13th Edition. Study Number 6614. Colchester: UK Data Archive. http://doi.org/10.5255/UKDA-SN-6614-14 (downloaded 8 November 2021).

van de Werfhorst, H. G. (2002). 'A detailed examination of the role of education in intergenerational social-class mobility'. *Social Science Information*, 41(3), 407–38.

van de Werfhorst, H. G. and Kraaykamp, G. (2001). 'Four field-related educational resources and their impact on labor, consumption, and sociopolitical orientation'. *Sociology of Education*, 74(4), 296–317.

van de Werfhorst, H. G., Sullivan, A. and Cheung, S. Y. (2003). 'Social class, ability and choice of subject in secondary and tertiary education in Britain'. *British Educational Research Journal*, 29(1), 41–62.

van de Werfhorst, H. G., Tam, T., Shavit, Y. and Park, H. (2018). 'A positional model of intergenerational educational mobility: crucial tests based on 35 societies'. https://osf.io/2wk84/download

van Hek, M., Kraaykamp, G. and Wolbers, M. H. J. (2016). 'Comparing the gender gap in educational attainment: the impact of emancipatory contexts in 33 cohorts across 33 countries'. *Educational Research and Evaluation*, 22(5–6), 260–82.

Walford, G. (1987). 'How important is the independent sector in Scotland?' *Scottish Educational Review*, 19(2), 108–21.

Walford, G. (1988). 'The Scottish Assisted Places Scheme: a comparative study of the origins, nature and practice of the APSs in Scotland, England and Wales'. *Journal of Education Policy*, 3(2), 137–53.

Watts, A. G. and Kidd, J. M. (2000). 'Guidance in the United Kingdom: past, present and future'. *British Journal of Guidance and Counselling*, 28(4), 485–502.

What Scotland Thinks (2021). 'How would you vote in a Scottish independence referendum if held now?' Edinburgh: ScotCen Social Research. https://whatscotlandthinks.org/questions/how-would-you-vote-in-the-in-a-scottish-independence-referendum-if-held-now-ask/ (downloaded 28 July 2021).

Wilson, V., Hall, S., Hall, J., Davidson, J. and Schad, D. (2004). *Supporting Pupils: A Study of Guidance and Pupil Support in Scottish Schools*. Edinburgh: Scottish Executive.

Withrington, D. (1992). 'The Scottish universities: living traditions? Old problems renewed?' In L. Paterson and D. McCrone (eds), *Scottish Government Yearbook*, 131–41. Edinburgh: Unit for the Study of Government in Scotland.

Wolbers, M. H. J. (2003). 'Learning and working: double statuses in youth transitions'. In W. Müller and M. Gangl (eds), *Transitions from Education to Work in Europe*, 131–55. Oxford: Oxford University Press.

Wooldridge, A. (2021). *The Aristocracy of Talent*. London: Allen Lane.
Yorke, M. (2009). *Trends in Honours Degree Classifications, 1994–95 to 2006–07, for England, Wales and Northern Ireland*. York: Higher Education Academy. https://www.advance-he.ac.uk/ (downloaded 28 April 2021).
Young, M. (2007). *Bringing Knowledge Back In*. London: Routledge.

Index

Note: f indicates a figure, t indicates a table

Aberdeen University, 8
academic education, 60, 62, 64, 67, 70, 74, 86, 93, 100, 104, 117–18, 228, 230, 232–3
academic junior secondaries *see under* secondary schools
academic selection, xii, 30, 46–50, 58–9
adult education, 195; *see also* lifelong learning
adult learning, 187, 198; *see also* lifelong learning
Advisory Council on Scottish Education, 2
  and the curriculum, 5, 17
  report on primary education (1946), 8
  report on secondary education (1947), 2–3, 7, 8
aesthetic subjects, 6, 65, 81t, 152, 153t, 154, 155t
Anders, J., 129
apprenticeships, 12, 104, 106, 109, 122
Arnold, Matthew, xiv, 229
art *see* aesthetic subjects
arts graduates, 162, 163, 164t
Arum, R., 62
Ayalon, H., 148

Barone, C., 63
Bernstein, Basil, 62
Biecek, P., 32
Blossfeld, H.-P., 37
Boliver, V., 129
Boudon, Raymond, 62, 149, 156, 164, 165
Bourdieu, Pierre, 38, 62, 130–1, 132, 199
Boyd, William, 8
Breen, R., 20, 38
Brexit, 13, 198–9, 200, 202, 220–2, 225
British Household Panel Study, 22
British Social Attitudes Survey, 22
Bukodi, E., 38, 169–70, 174
Burnhill, P. et al., 18

Cambridge University, 128
Campbell, D. E., 198

Caro, D. H., 32
Catholic schools, 29, 31
  and educational attainment, 57t, 78–9, 84, 192–3, 230
  and integration, 2, 4
  and parental education, 56
Catholics: and Scottish independence, 217
censorship, 209–10, 222
Centre for Educational Sociology (CES), 16, 17–18, 24, 235
child-centred education, 8, 87
Chowdry, H. et al., 129
civic participation, 207t
Clemente, M. et al., 132
Clifford, P., 37–8
Cole, G. D. H., 229
colleges of education, 9, 87; *see also* training colleges
commercial subjects, 154
comprehensive schools
  and educational attainment, 124, 230
  effects of, 107–8, 125
  and guidance, 87–8
  and inequality, 47–9
  origins of, 3
  and reform, 4, 5, 31, 122–3, 125
  and social class, 52, 59–60, 62
  see also secondary schools
Conservative governments
  and comprehensive education, 231–2
  and educational inequality, 10
  and Scottish independence, 13, 212, 223
  and social development, 18–19
  and Youth Training Scheme (YTS), 106
corporal punishment, 88, 89, 94
Council for National Academic Awards, 173
Croxford, Linda, xv, 16, 66, 75
cultural mobility, 62–3; *see also* social class

curriculum *see under* secondary schools
Curtice, J., 199, 200

Davie, George, xiii, 10–11, 150, 233
Davies, P. et al., 63, 64
Deary, Ian J., xv, 16
democracy
　character of, 11
　and citizenship, 5
　'democratic intellect', 10–11
　and education, 61, 87, 197–8, 222–5
　and post-primary schooling, 3
　and Scottish independence, 13–14
　and selection, 233
　and social change, 2
devolution
　Scotland, 195, 200, 202; referendum (1979), 13, 211; referendum (1997), 13–14, 212 ; *see also* Scottish independence
　Wales, 172, 195
Dilnot, C., 148
DiMaggio, P., 62
Donnelly, M., 129, 130
Dumais, S. A., 64
Dundee University, 9
Duta, A., 107–8

Eatwell, R., 199
Edinburgh
　Heriot-Watt College, 9
　James Gillespie's School, 146
Edinburgh University, 8
Education Authorities, 5
Education (Scotland) Act (1872), 2
Education (Scotland) Act (1918), 2, 230
Education (Scotland) Act (1936), 4
educational attainment
　and civic participation, 206–8
　comparative studies of, 173–6; class attainment, 183–6, 192–3; educational attainment, 176–83; lifelong learning and social mobility, 187–91
　comprehensive schools, 124, 230
　England, 173, 174t, 175, 177t, 183t, 188t, 194, 229
　grant-aided schools, 100t
　independent schools, 55, 99–100, 127, 129, 130, 131, 138, 140, 144–5, 231
　and inequality, 40–6, 137–8, 173
　and political ideology, 208–11
　and religious denomination, 192–3; Catholic schools, 57t, 78–9, 84, 192–3, 230
　role of, 110–14
　and school history, 50–55, 77–9
　and Scottish independence, 13–14, 213f, 214–17
　and sex, 32, 42f, 45f, 47t, 50f, 53t, 54f, 55, 58, 76t, 77, 78f, 83t, 84f, 95, 97, 97t, 98–9, 110, 112–13, 114, 122, 162–3, 164t, 177, 179f, 180, 182f, 184–5, 186f, 187, 188t, 189, 192, 193, 230
　in social attitudes surveys, 202
　and social class, 42f, 45f, 47t, 48–9, 50f, 53t, 54f, 59–60, 75, 76t, 77, 78f, 83t, 84f, 95, 97–8, 99, 101–2, 110, 113–14, 122, 163, 164t, 175–86, 230
　and social trust, 205–6
　statistical measures of, 27–8, 111t
　Wales, 173, 174t, 175, 177t, 183t, 188t, 194
Elias, P., 26
elites
　and the curriculum, 61, 62, 64, 86, 104
　and nationalism, 199, 200, 219
　and populism, 14, 225
　and universities, 166
employment
　graduates and, 161–2, 163, 164t
　school leavers and, 12, 117t, 120–5, 161
　and sex, 12, 25, 26, 109–10, 115, 171
　and social change, 11–13
　and social class, 115–16, 117t, 124
　see also labour market; unemployment
England
　curriculum, 64
　education policy, 195
　educational attainment, 173, 174t, 175, 177t, 183t, 188t, 194, 229
　higher education entry, 129, 148
　labour market, 172
　school leaving assessment, 172–3
　vocational education, 108
　see also Cambridge University; London; Oxford University
English, 65, 67, 70, 72, 74, 77, 83
　and higher education entry, 129, 154
　Higher Grade in, 153t, 155t
　Standard Grade course, 31, 75
equal opportunities, 5, 103; *see also* inequality
Espenshade, T. J. et al., 129
ethnicity
　and attainment, 55–6
　and democracy, 222, 230–1
　and Scottish independence, 217
　statistical measures of, 27, 55
　see also race
European Union *see* Brexit

Forbes, J., 131
France
　baccalauréat, 62, 63–4
　curriculum, 62, 63
　higher education entry, 131
　inequality, 38
　surveys, 19–20
further education colleges, 9, 134t

Gamoran, A., xvi, 63, 66, 75, 85
Gayle, V. et al., 129
gender *see* sex
Germany
　inequality, 38
　secondary education, 107

Germany, East (former): institutional habitus, 132
Glasgow
  Royal College of Technology, 9, 21
  Scottish College of Commerce, 9
Glasgow University, 8
Goisis, A. et al., 28
Goldthorpe, J., 38, 86, 132, 169–70
Goodhart, D., 199, 200
Goodwin, M., 199
Gove, Michael, 199
graduates
  and employment, 161–2, 163, 164t
  surveys of, 21–2, 26
grant-aided schools, 64, 100t
Gray, J. et al., 65
Greek, 65
Gregory, M., 26
Gugushvili, A. et al., 38

Haldane, R. B., 10
Hannan, C., 129, 130
Heath, A. F., 37–8
higher education, 8–11, 127–46
  classification of, 132–3
  entry into, 129–32, 134t, 135f, 138, 140, 142, 144, 156–67
  expansion of, 9–10, 133–8, 165, 170–1, 198
  and inequality, 10–11, 147–8, 195, 229
  participation in, 8, 164–5
  sectors, 128
  see also universities
Higher Grade schools, 3–4
Highers *see under* secondary school certification
Hirst, Paul, 6
Hout, M., 38, 171, 228
Howieson, C., xv, 107

Iannelli, C., 107–8, 129, 148, 193
Ichou, M., 19, 63
independent schools, 3
  curriculum, 64, 77, 85–6
  and educational attainment, 55, 99–100, 127, 129, 130, 131, 138, 140, 144–5, 231
  and higher education, 129–30, 138–40
  income, 30–1
  and selection, 4
inequality
  comparative studies, 37–8
  and the curriculum, 62–4, 75, 148
  and educational attainment, 40–6, 137–8, 173
  and employment, 171
  and higher education entry, 157, 195, 229
  measurement of, 83
  modernisation theory of, 37–8
  and parental education, 38
  primary, 149
  reducing levels of, 59
  research, 24
  secondary, 149
  and sex, 38–9, 42–3, 48–9, 171

and social class, 38, 171, 228–9
Inglehart, R. F., 200
Ireland
  higher education entry, 129, 148
  inequality, 38
  surveys, 20
Italy
  cultural mobility, 62
  curriculum, 63
  inequality, 38, 63
  populism, 199

Johnston, Tom, 2
Jones, I., 123

Kaltwasser, C. R., 200
Kamens, D. H. et al., 62

Labour Force Survey, 26
Labour governments, 31, 106, 232
labour market
  collapse of, 88
  and competition, 170, 229
  labour-queue theory, 171–2, 194
  youth, 12, 37, 94, 104–8; *see also* school leavers
languages, 5, 6, 39, 62, 65–6, 67, 71, 73–4
  and higher education entry, 154
  Higher Grade in, 155t
  see also English; Greek; Latin
Latin, 62, 65
liberal education *see under* secondary schools: curriculum
lifelong learning, 171, 187–91, 195
Lingard, B., 131
London: employment opportunities, 12–13, 172, 229
Lucas, S. R., 63, 148, 167

McCrone, D., 1
MacIntyre, Alasdair, 233
McPherson, A., xii–xiii, xvi, 31, 59, 235
Major, John, 223, 231–2
Mancini, L., 26
Mangan, J. et al., 129
mathematics, 5, 6, 62, 63, 65, 67, 70, 72
  attainment in, 83t, 152
  Higher Grade in, 153t, 155t
Meyer, H.-D., 131–2
Meyer, J. W., 60, 131
Micklewright, J., 129
minimum wage, 106
Moulton, V. et al., 108
Mounk, Y., 199
Mudde, C., 200
music *see* aesthetic subjects

Nash, R., 130
NatCen Social Research, 22
national identity, 217–19
National Statistics Socio-Economic Classification (NSSEC), 23, 24, 58

nationalism *see* Scottish nationalism
Neave, G., 60
Netherlands
    higher education entry, 129
    inequality, 37, 38
    secondary education, 107
New Education Fellowship, 7–8, 87
New Zealand, 129
Nikolai, R., 132
Norris, P., 200

O grade *see under* secondary school certification
Ocasio, W. et al., 131, 132
omnibus schools, 3
Open University, 9, 190
Organisation for Economic Co-operation and Development, 21
Oxford University, 128

Palardy, G. J., 129, 130
parents
    education, 23, 24–6, 33, 34, 38, 47, 51f, 55, 56, 58, 175
    social class, 25, 33, 34t, 47, 51f
parish schools, 3
Passeron, J.-C., 199
Perkin, H., 233
physical education, 154
PISA *see* Programme for International Student Assessment
Poland, 38
policy
    effects of, 75–9
    and institutions, 230–3
political ideology, 208–11
populism
    and education, 198–201
    growth of, 14
    national, 13, 199, 225
    political, 197
post-school education
    and school history, 119–20
    and sex, 116f, 118, 119f
    and social class, 116f, 119f, 120
    see also lifelong learning; vocational education; youth training schemes
Power, S. A., 129–30
primary schools, 2
    and attainment, 28, 45–6
    child-centred, 87
    rights, 8
professional learning, 109, 134t
Programme for International Student Assessment (PISA), 21, 28, 32, 80, 82–3, 227, 234
Pustjens, H. et al., 129

race
    and rights, 8
    and vocational education, 108
    see also ethnicity

Raffe, D., xii, 124, 169
Raftery, A. E., 38, 171, 228
reading attainment, 83t
Reay, D. et al., 131
religion
    and democracy, 222
    and educational attainment, 192–3, 230
    statistical measures of, 27, 56, 57t
Rowan, B., 60, 131

school attainment *see* educational attainment
school history *see* secondary schools: classification of
school leavers
    and attainment, 40, 122, 227
    destinations of, 108–10, 111t, 112f, 116f
    and employment, 12, 120–5, 161; *see also* labour market: youth
    and higher education entry, 127–46
    and school reform, 103–4
    surveys of, 17–19
    training schemes for *see* youth training schemes
schools Inspectorate, 29
Schührer, S. et al., 148
science graduates, 162, 163, 164t
sciences, 5, 6, 8, 39, 62, 63, 65, 66, 67, 70–1, 72–3
    attainment in, 83t, 84f, 152, 161, 164t
    and higher education entry, 154, 157–8
    Higher Grade in, 153t, 155t
ScotCen Social Research, 16, 22
Scottish Council for Research in Education (SCRE), 15–16, 17, 235
Scottish/Scotch Education Department, 5, 17, 31
Scottish Election Surveys, 16, 22
Scottish Examination Board, 18, 29
Scottish Household Survey (2001), 193
Scottish independence
    and educational attainment, 13–14, 197, 213f, 214–17, 218–19, 221t, 222–5
    and ethnicity, 217
    and national identity, 217–19
    and populism, 200–1
    referendum on, 13–14, 200, 201, 203, 208, 212, 213–14, 218, 219, 222–4
    and sex, 201, 213f, 214–17, 218
    see also devolution
Scottish National Party (SNP), 13, 200, 212–13
Scottish nationalism, 197, 200
Scottish Parliament
    and Brexit, 220–2
    legislative responsibilities of, 13
    support for, 13–14, 202, 211–12, 213f, 222–3
Scottish Qualifications Authority, 18
secondary school certification, 4, 64–5
    Certificate of Secondary Education, 7, 107, 109
    Certificate of Sixth Year Studies, 7, 152
    Credit level, 6, 79
    General level, 6, 79
    Foundation level, 6, 79
    Group Certificate, 5

Higher Grade, 5, 27, 39t, 40, 43–4, 45f, 52, 53t, 54f, 66, 67, 69t, 70, 72, 73, 77, 81t, 110, 114, 133, 138, 139t, 143t, 144, 151, 152, 154, 155t, 158
Lower Grade, 5, 27
mid-secondary passes, 68t
National Certificate, 7, 27, 107, 109
National level, 79
Ordinary Grade, 27, 47t, 79, 85, 88
Standard Grade, 27, 31, 66, 75, 79, 85, 88, 120, 123, 125
and university entry, 149, 151
secondary schools, 2–8
academic junior, 30, 52, 54–5, 58, 60, 77
and attainment, 39–46, 127, 144
certification *see* secondary school certification
classification of, 29–30, 46–7
curriculum, 27, 39t, 40, 60–86; breadth in, 65, 66, 67, 70, 71–2, 75, 78, 79, 80f, 83, 86, 117–18, 156–67, 233; and employment, 99; extension of, 66–70; and higher education entry, 148–50; and inequality, 62–4, 148; Intermediate courses, 6–7, 24, 27, 65; liberal, 62–6, 232; reforms to, 79, 87, 104, 233; and sex, 39, 58, 64, 65–6, 70, 72, 73–4, 75, 162; and sex discrimination, 8; social basis of, 70–4; and social class, 62–3, 70, 71, 72; Standard Grade courses, 5–6, 7, 66; *see also* secondary school certification; vocational education
and higher education, 127–46, 158–60; institutional habitus, 127–8, 130–2, 144–6; socio-economic compostion, 129
junior, 4, 30, 31, 51, 52, 54–5, 56, 60, 77, 78f, 86, 121f, 142f
legislation, 2
reforms to, 103–4, 107, 114–20, 122–3, 165–6
senior, 4, 30, 40, 48–9, 56, 58, 59, 74, 145, 146, 149, 152–6, 174t, 176, 189, 191f, 227, 232
and social class, 51–2, 58
statistical analysis of, 31–5
structures, 2–5
student-centred, 7–8
vocational, 7
see also comprehensive schools
sex
and the curriculum, 64, 65–6, 70, 72, 73–4, 75, 80f, 162
and education, 3; post-school, 116f, 118, 119f
and educational attainment, 32, 42f, 45f, 47t, 50f, 53t, 54f, 55, 58, 76t, 77, 78f, 83t, 84f, 95, 97, 98–9, 110, 112–13, 114, 122, 162–3, 164t, 177, 179f, 180, 182f, 184–5, 186f, 187, 188t, 189, 192, 193, 230
and employment, 12, 25, 105, 109–10, 115, 117t
and higher education entry, 136f, 138, 140, 142 151, 156, 157–8, 159
and inequality, 38–9, 42–3, 48–9, 171
and intelligence, 45–6
and political ideology, 208–9, 210–11

and rights, 8
and Scottish independence, 201, 213f, 214–17, 218, 220
and social engagement, 205, 206f, 207–8
and surveys, 21, 201
and vocational education, 85, 108
as a statistical measure, 23
see also women
Shavit, Y., 37, 62
Shulruf, B. et al., 129
Silver, N., 199
Smith, Adam, 10
Smyth, E., 129, 130
social attitudes surveys, 16, 22–3, 201–4, 219–22
social class
and the curriculum, 62–3, 70, 71, 72, 80f
and educational attainment, 42f, 45f, 47t, 48–9, 50f, 53t, 54f, 59–60, 75, 76t, 77, 78f, 83t, 84f, 95, 97–8, 99, 101–2, 110, 113–14, 122, 163, 164t, 175–86, 230
and employment, 115–16, 117t, 124
and higher education entry, 129, 132, 134–5, 136f, 138, 142f, 143f, 144, 148, 151–2, 156–7, 159, 165, 167
and inequality, 38, 171, 228–9
measurement of, 23–7, 56, 58
of parents, 25, 33, 34t, 47, 51f
and political ideology, 208–9, 210–11
and post-school education, 116f, 119f, 120
and schools, 51–2
as a statistical measure, 23–7; Registrar General Social Class, 23, 24–6
and youth training schemes, 106
social engagement, 204–8
and birth cohort, 205, 206f
and sex, 205, 206f, 207–8
social mobility, 12–13, 232
and lifelong learning, 171, 187–91, 195
social subjects, 67, 70
attainment in, 164t
and higher education entry, 154
Higher Grade in, 153t, 155t
and sex, 162
Spark, Muriel: *The Prime of Miss Jean Brodie*, 146
Standard Grade *see under* secondary school certification
statistical measures, 23–31, 234–5
educational attainment, 27–8
ethnicity, 27, 55
intelligence, 28, 45–6
parental education, 23, 24–6
religion, 27, 56, 57t
schools, 28–31
sex, 23
social class, 23–7
see also surveys
staying on (in school beyond age 16), 39–40, 43, 46, 107
motives for, 88, 89–97, 99–101, 227–8
and school religious denomination, 57

Stirling University, 9
Strathclyde University, 9
students
  behaviour of, 90, 94, 96; truanting, 89, 91, 96, 98, 100
  guidance of, 87–8
  school experience of: and attainment, 95–6; changing, 87–8; improving, 91–5; measurement of, 89–91; school sector and, 99–100; sex and, 96–9; social class and, 96–9
  statistical analysis of, 31–5
  working, 108
surveys, 15–23
  birth cohort, 21
  critiques of, 18
  elections, 22
  graduates, 21–2, 26
  Growing Up in Scotland, 234
  international, 234
  school leavers, 17–19
  Scottish Household Survey (2001), 193
  school students, 16–20
  social attitudes: see social attitudes surveys
  see also Programme for International Student Assessment; statistical measures
Sutton Trust, 130
Sweden, 37–8

Taylor, C. et al., 129, 130
teachers
  students' attitudes to, 90, 93–4, 96, 100, 101, 228
  teacher-education institutions, 151
technical colleges, 8–9; see also further education colleges
technical subjects, 154
technocrats, 11
Thatcher, Margaret, 223, 231, 232
Thomson, Godfrey, xii, 235
training colleges, 104
truanting, 89, 91, 96, 98, 100
Trump, Donald, 198, 199
Tymms, P., 129

UK Data Archive, 16
UK Household Longitudinal Study, 16, 22, 26, 173–4, 192, 193
unemployment, 104–5, 124
  youth, 18, 62, 94, 104, 106, 110
UNESCO, 165

universities, 8
  curricula, 150
  degrees, 149, 161, 162–3, 173
  and 'democratic intellect', 10–11
  entry to, 134t, 136f, 137–8, 149, 150; and sex, 136f, 138, 140, 142, 143t; and social class, 142f, 143f, 144
  growth of, 9
  and participation, 164–5
  and school attainment, 151
  schools' affinity with, 127–9
  see also higher education; Open University
Universities' Statistical Record (USR), 21, 26
USA
  curriculum, 62, 63
  higher education entry, 129, 148
  inequality, 38
  institutional habitus, 131–2

Vallet, L.-A., 19–20, 63
van de Werfhorst, H. G. et al., 148
vocational education, 62, 63, 66, 67, 74, 76, 77, 85, 88, 104, 107–8, 124; see also youth training schemes
vocational subjects, 154

Wales
  education policy, 195
  educational attainment, 173, 174t, 175, 177t, 183t, 188t, 194
  educational autonomy, 172
  higher education entry, 129
  school leaving assessment, 172–3
Whitty, G., 129–30
Willms, J. D., xvi, 31, 59
Wolbers, M. H. J., 108
women
  and employment, 12, 25, 26, 171
  graduate survey of, 21
  and labour market, 104, 105, 106
  rights of, 222
  and training, 110
Wooldridge, A., 58

youth training schemes, 88, 94, 103, 105–6, 109, 122, 123
  Youth Opportunities Programme, 106
  Youth Training Scheme (YTS), 106
  see also apprenticeships

EU representative:
Easy Access System Europe
Mustamäe tee 50, 10621 Tallinn, Estonia
Gpsr.requests@easproject.com

www.ingramcontent.com/pod-product-compliance
Lightning Source LLC
Chambersburg PA
CBHW050212240426
43671CB00013B/2312